## ADVANCE PRAISE FOR *WHY DADS LEAVE*

"I have no doubt this book is a seminal work in the 21st century, helping shift our focus to assuring that the critical period of parent-child attachment is safeguarded for our highest human potential."

    Meg Jordan, PhD, RN, Chair, Integrative Health Studies
    Program, California Institute of Integral Studies

"Easy to read and guides us gently into insights and 'Aha' moments that can make a real difference in our lives and our relationships."

    Sue Johnson, PhD, author of *Hold Me Tight: Seven*
    *Conversations for a Lifetime of Love*

"For years, I was one of those 'men who leave.' How unfortunate that such a wisely conceived, exhaustively researched, and beautifully written book was not in my hands then. A profound, provocative, and passionate work. Bravo!"

    Emmett Miller, MD, author of *Deep Healing: The Essence*
    *of Mind-Body Medicine*

"The generations-long effects of Western parenting have been devastating to the health and wellbeing of all us, beginning from conception and birthing through infancy and childhood. Such dysfunction is evident in the basic ways we feel about ourselves, our partnership relationships as well as our relationships with our children, our friends, our world community: we lack the profound, joyful feelings of connection which include deep love, respect, caring and empathy.

    Through conditioning and self-preservation we have replaced our needs for connection with the very distant second best substitutes known as independence and self-sustainability. We are human animals and by nature meant to connect via love. Love in all but the most superficial ways have been conditioned out of us as an "educated" race.

    Callander's monumental effort in this book dissects not only the causes of our widespread cultural disconnection with self and others, but offers a magnificent myriad of tools for rediscovery, repair and long-term healing.

    I would love to see this book on every bookshelf, every nightstand, in every teen and adult's hand. There is real promise for a loving future here."

    Barb Lundgren, editor, *Rethinking Everything* Magazine

"Provocative and personal, *Why Dads Leave* is a major contribution to healing the family soul, individually and collectively."

    Sarah J. Buckley, MD, author of Gentle Birthing, Gentle Mothering

"I'm in awe at what you've accomplished and so grateful, because it pulls together numerous fields and diverse wisdom with a focus toward what makes humans and human societies thrive rather than be in a constant state of fear and defense, surviving, and coping."
    Suzanne Arms, author of *Immaculate Deception: Myth, Magic and Birth*

"Powerful, exquisite—hot, scary and exciting, this book revealed truths that I did not want to hear (I do believe I actually avoided it) yet I found myself drawn to as an oasis of the fresh possibility of love.
We are guided via Jack and Meryn's own journey and research into old, inner wounds; and then, in a flash, offered a 'how-to' path for not only addressing our own unmet needs but also nurturing truly healthy kids and community. This book is a bomb of balm waiting to explode all around the 'civilized' world. It is seminal work that must be read by every aspiring parent and those who love them."
    Bill Kauth, co-founder, ManKind Project, author of *We Need Each Other*

"If the new dad can see mothering from her perspective and vice versa they can better parent together, which is, of course, what baby wants, preventing a lot of breakdowns, suicide, child trauma and private and public expense (therapists, courts, hospitals, police)."
    —Paul Mason, LLB, BA(Hons), Australian family lawyer and former Commissioner for Children, State of Tasmania

"Being a parent is a profound growth experience. You will be challenged to confront your personal deficits and your life's unfinished business. This book gives parents and parents-to-be the tools they need to navigate the terrain of their own emotions--and to heal. It shows you how to support one another on this path instead of getting stuck in power struggles. I recommend it highly."
    Susan Campbell, PhD, author of *Getting Real: Ten Truth Skills to Live an Authentic Life*

"Ending the epidemic of disappearing dads will do more good in the world than curing cancer. Absent fathers have been implicated in such social problems as violence, child abuse, suicides, teen pregnancy, and war. I've been waiting for this book for a long time, perhaps all my life. Read it now! And buy more to give to your friends and family."
    Jed Diamond, PhD, author of *The Irritable Male Syndrome*

"To an infant, failed or impaired bonding feels like abandonment. As this infant grows into a man, the deep, but often hidden feelings of this early imprint leaves him unprepared for the mature intimacy parenting demands.

When the flirtatious playmate gets pregnant, her attention turns to the baby, leaving dad feeling abandoned once again, so he often leaves. *Why Dad's Leave*, explores why this happens and what couples can do to transform their intimacy, expanding it, rather than walking away."

Michael Mendizza, Touch the Future

"This is a must-read treatise on parenthood. The only problem I see is you have left very little for the rest of us to write!"

Patrick Houser, author of *Fathers-to-Be Handbook*

"Most songs are about getting your man. This book is about keeping your man—especially after a child comes along."

—Naomi Judd, Emmy Award–winning singer/songwriter

"This book has the potential to change history. It's the first truly healing approach I've seen for a long-neglected wound in so many people's lives. Callander and Travis not only show us what we need to know about why fathers disappear, but they also give us real how-to solutions."

—Gay Hendricks, PhD, author of *Conscious Loving*

"While childbirth had always been 'women's business,' the doctrine of fathers participating in birth suddenly emerged around 1970. Theoreticians supporting the doctrine claimed that this radically new behavior should create strong links within couples and a deep-rooted attachment between father and child. According to them, the incidence of separations, divorces, and disappearing dads would have dramatically decreased. They were obviously wrong. We must be grateful to Meryn and John to suggest the right questions at the right time."

Michel Odent, MD, author of *Birth Reborn*

"A desperately needed book that will make an enormous difference in people's lives. Hurrah for someone finally taking this perspective."

Robin Grille, author of *Heart-to-Heart Parenting*

"Provocative and powerful!"

David Isaacs, co-author of *The World Café*

"Addresses an issue that is epidemic in scale, largely unrecognized, and totally misunderstood. Childhood bonding, fatherly involvement and family cohesiveness are vitally important to the sustainability of this increasingly populated planet. Callander and Travis' groundbreaking work helps unravel this Gordian knot by explaining with great clarity why so many committed prospective fathers abandon their wives and children because of unresolved emotional issues that parenting raises. The first step toward solutions is recognition of a problem. *Why Dads Leave* offers a blueprint for raising consciousness and practical steps to help man and their families addressing this challenging issue."
—Kent W. Peterson, MD, Past Executive Director, American College of Preventive Medicine; Past President, American College of Occupational and Environmental Medicine

In my forty years as a marriage and family therapist, working with over 2500 students writing their autobiographies, and in my keynote speaking around the world, my experience resonates with this work. *Why Dads Leave* offers hope and a possibility for sustaining healthy families. The pursuit of wellness begins with the conception of a child, lasts a lifetime, and thrives in a supportive community. My deep gratitude for this incredible groundbreaking work.
—Elaine Sullivan, Board of Directors, National Wellness Institute

Meryn and Jack have shared their journey from partnership to parenthood in order to illuminate us and make our futures better. They not only lived through this common challenge, but named it, investigated it, and learned from it. Now they have created literature that will forever change families who embrace this knowledge. Society can only benefit from their long, hard endeavor. A simple thanks is all I have, but certainly not enough for this gift.
Barbara A. Hotelling, past president, Lamaze International and Doulas of North America (DONA).

**Growing list of additional endorsers:**
- John Breeding, PhD, author of *The Wildest Colts Make The Best Horses*
- Bob Collier, author of *Guiding Stars of the New Parenting Movement*, Vols. 1 & 2, parental-intelligence.com
- Richard Heinberg, author of *The Party's Over*
- Janel Mirendah, filmmaker: theothersideoftheglass.com
- Martin Rossman, MD, author of *The Worry Solution*
- Marilyn Schlitz, PhD, President, Institute of Noetic Sciences (IONS)
- Michael and Justine Willis Toms, New Dimensions Radio/Media
- Patrick Williams, EdD, Founder, Institute for Life Coach Training
- Ralph Wolff, PhD, President, Western Association of Schools and Colleges

**ALSO BY THE AUTHOR** (WITH COAUTHOR, JOHN W. TRAVIS, MD)
*Wellness for Helping Professionals*
*A Change of Heart: The Global Wellness Inventory*
Wellness Inventory Online

# Why Dads Leave

## Insights and Resources for When Partners Become Parents

Meryn G. Callander

Foreword by Gabor Maté, MD

Akasha Publications

**Disclaimer:** The information contained within this book is in no way intended as a substitute for counseling. Please do not attempt self-treatment of a problem without consulting a qualified practitioner. The author expressly disclaims any and all liability for any claims, damages, losses, judgments, expenses, costs, or injuries resulting from any advice offered. Nor does the inclusion of any resource group or company listed within this book constitute a guarantee of quality by the author.

Copyright © 2012 by Meryn G. Callander
All rights reserved. No part of this book may be reproduced in any form, except brief excerpts for the purpose of review, without written permission.

ISBN: 978-0-9625882-3-5

Cover design and layout: Siena Ariel Travis Callander
Cover photo: Dana Marek, tinytushphotography.com
Typesetting, book design, and layout: John W. Travis

Akasha Publications

PO Box 8422
Asheville, NC 28814

PO Box 496
Mullumbimby, New South Wales
Australia 2482

WhyDadsLeave.com

Library of Congress Control Number: 2011933542
Library of Congress Subject Headings:
Relationships
Marriage
Parenting
Fatherhood
Sex after birth
Attachment parenting
Divorce

# **Dedication**

To my daughter, Siena Tierra Ariel
And to you, the reader.

*May all beings be well,*
*May all beings be happy,*
*May all beings be at peace with themselves and their world.*

## Contents

Foreword ..................................................................................... xiii

Preface ........................................................................................ xv

### Part I: Why Dads Leave—An Overview 9

1: Introduction: Our Journey Through the
Dynamic of Disappearing Dads (DDD) ................................................ 1

2: Exploring The Dynamic of Disappearing Dads ............................... 17

3: Early Bonding, MPAS, and DDD: Making the Connections ........... 30

4: Early Childhood Experiences, Parenting Styles, and Adult Love ........ 37

5: Discovering Dad—And Staying Connected ..................................... 42

6: Ending the Dynamic of Disappearing Dads ..................................... 48

### Part II: Parenting—What the Books, Apps, and Websites Don't Tell Us

7: Why Dads Matter—A Lot ............................................................. 55

8: But Can They Do It? ..................................................................... 67

9: If They Can, Why Don't They? ..................................................... 75

10: A Society's FatherStory ................................................................ 90

11: Parenting: Are We Ready? ........................................................... 96

12: Pregnant Partners ....................................................................... 101

13: Pregnancy—Spotlight on Dad .................................................... 117

14: Preparing for the Birth of Your Baby .......................................... 124

15: After the Birth—Spotlight on Dad ............................................. 133

16: After the Birth—Growing Together or Growing Apart ............... 147

17: After the Birth: Spotlight on Dad ............................................... 165

18: Facing Our Own Unmet Childhood Needs and Self Love ........... 175

### Part III: Healing the Wounds—Rewiring for Connection

19: Addressing the Legacy of Unmet Needs ...................................... 188

20: Reflecting Back on Our Own Childhood .................................... 199

21: Healing Childhood Trauma—One Approach ............................. 219

22: Stories of Healing .................................................................. 226

23: Synopsis: *Do I Have to Give Up Me to Be Loved by You?* ................ 243

24: Synopsis: *The Unexpected Legacy of Divorce* ................................ 254

25: Synopsis: *Hold Me Tight: Conversations for a Lifetime of Love* ........ 262

26: Men's Secret Shame ............................................................... 275

27: Building a Friendship with Your Partner ..................................... 280

# Part IV: An Ounce of Prevention Is Worth 1.78 Tons of Cure

28: Attachment Parenting: An Ounce of Prevention ........................... 291

29: In the Absence of the Village .................................................... 305

30: Valuing the Art and Science of Parenting .................................... 312

Bibliography ............................................................................... 321

Resources .................................................................................. 323

Appendices ................................................................................ 324

About the Author ....................................................................... 325

Gratitude .................................................................................. 327

Index ....................................................................................... 329

Notes ....................................................................................... 332

# Foreword

What Meryn Callander and John Travis call the Dynamic of Disappearing Dads (DDD) is no exercise in empty syndrome mongering.

We are faced with the distressing fact that an increasing number of children are being diagnosed with an array of developmental disorders, from attention deficit disorder to oppositional defiant disorder, from autism spectrum disorder to anxiety and depression. According to recent statistics, nearly fifty per cent of American adolescents meet the diagnostic criteria for one or another mental health problem. The burgeoning numbers of troubled children, rising at almost exponential rates, cannot be explained by the narrowly biological perspective that still dominates medical thinking: that such conditions are genetically determined and reflect unfortunate aberrations of brain physiology.

Callander grounds her analysis in a bio-psycho-social view, according to which the biology—and most especially the neurobiology—of human beings is inseparable from the social and emotional environment in which they are conceived, develop, and live. This inextricable link between the bio-psychological functions of people is a lifelong process: malleable, thankfully, but deeply affected by early experience. The studies showing this lifelong interactive process, and especially the crucial influence of the early years, are hardly even controversial, albeit largely unknown to most mainstream health care professionals, such as physicians and psychologists.

The great child psychiatrist, D.W. Winnicott, pointed out that two things can go wrong in childhood that may adversely affect development: When things happen that shouldn't happen (e.g., trauma), and when things *do not happen that should happen*. The latter refers not to overt trauma, but to the stresses and distractions that keep many parents these days from offering their children the attuned, emotionally present interactions that optimal brain and personality development require. Many children are being negatively affected in this way, even if not formally traumatized.

In short, attachment—the bond between child and parent—is the crucial dynamic in human development. Most attachment work has focused on the mother-infant interaction, and properly so. In the first few months at least, that relationship provides the child with the world—and, in the final analysis—with the worldview that will shape his or her experience of life. But Callander rightly balances that by bringing the oft-forgotten figure of the father back into the picture.

Studies now point to the presence of the nurturing male parent as also important to healthy development—witness, for example, the fact that girls with absentee fathers tend to menstruate earlier, not to mention that they are also more likely to engage in precocious sexual behavior. In a society that tends to lay the duties of emotional nourishing almost exclusively onto the shoulders of women, we need hardly mention the crucial modeling that a nurturing father provides for male offspring. Dorothy Dinnerstein's book *The Mermaid and the Minotaur* argues persuasively that the absence of male nurturing, the making of nurturing an exclusively female domain, has a distorting effect on the development of both boys and girls.

Apart from the direct influence of the emotionally nurturing father on the infant, there is his essential role as the supporter of the mother, not just physically but—equally important—psychologically. Here, too, the studies are clear: women lacking such support are more likely to develop postpartum depression which, in turn, is a significant risk factor for developmental maladjustments such as ADHD. In all cases of postpartum depression I have seen as a physician, the woman lacked adequate emotional support, and this was often owing to the emotional withdrawal of the father because his own unconscious needs were being threatened by the presence of the infant.

Callander does not approach the issue of the disappearing dad as a moral crusade. She is no judge, but a compassionate investigator. Post-industrial society has torn asunder relationship ties, and has almost completely destroyed the historical attachment village—it really does take a village to raise a child— such a society exerts intolerable stresses on many couples and individuals. Without the multigenerational supportive context that previous eras took for granted, many men find themselves overburdened by the parenting task, especially if they themselves were denied the presence of an emotionally available father during their formative years.

As *Why Dad Leaves* points out, many men, "even if they remain in the home… are often emotionally absent—through depression, workaholism, violence and aggression, physical or emotional abuse or a retreat into addiction to substances, media, consumer goods, sports, food, or sex." This is the dynamic Alan Schore has called "proximal abandonment"—when the parents are physically present, but emotionally missing.

Beyond analysis—a science-based and balanced analysis, *Why Dads Leave* is also a call for action. It is no longer enough for health care providers, educators, social workers and policy makers to respond to the lamentable consequences of the dynamic of the disappearing dad. At all levels of social influence, the problem must be recognized and creative and humane solutions and preventive strategies must be created. Men do not need condemnation; they need help so that their children can be helped. *Why Dads Leave* will be a powerful support to anyone moved to take up that challenge. The "hidden epidemic" of fathers leaving their families needs to be stopped.

—Gabor Maté, MD, co-author, *Hold On To Your Kids,* Vancouver, British Columbia

# Preface

## Caution: The Great Divide Ahead

There is a great divide in that mountain range called parenting. Planning, conceiving and gestating the baby is like climbing up to a high mountain pass. Birth marks the couple's passage through the pass into a different watershed—new uncharted territory that, despite the best of maps, holds many surprises, some of them quite shocking. And once you're through the pass, there's no going back.

Believing an ounce of prevention is worth 1.78 tons* of cure, this book is written primarily for those on the pre-child side of the divide, hoping to alert them to some of the more challenging parts of the terrain. However, the likelihood is that it's mainly those who have already been through this rough territory that will really get the point of the book. Jack or I would probably not have picked up this book before our daughter Siena was born. We thought we knew what we were doing. Oh sure! It took us over five years to work out what happened to us, and then over a decade to refine it and set it in a larger social and cultural context. Now the question is how to reach those who can't imagine it happening to them—even more so, those who are completely oblivious to "the great divide"?

It may often be the about-to-be grandparents who recognize the terrain, or friends of soon-to-parents who at least have an inkling of the challenges ahead, or counselors who see couples floundering through this divide—who urge the uninitiated to read it, hopefully before they plunge into the divide.

From whence came this book? Having since the seventies, pursued a passion to reclaim the original definitions of wellness to include the mental, emotional, social, spiritual, and planetary dimensions of wellbeing, Jack's and my focus over the past two decades had been in the field of infant and child wellness. It is from this, and our own personal experiences in becoming parents, that we initially developed the hypothesis about why men leave, physically *or emotionally*, after the birth of a child.

Our premise and the supporting material in this book are drawn from our personal experience and observations, as well as that of friends and colleagues, and from written sources that touch on this dynamic, plus numerous leading voices in the fields of fathering, parenting, and couples' communication. The

---

* Ben Franklin had the right idea, but Jack thinks his ratio was seriously low. Ironically, the ratio of current spending on *fixing* problems vs. our spending on *preventing* problems is probably inversely proportional to this ratio.

intention here is not to present the final word on this phenomenon, but to initiate an inquiry into the Dynamic of Disappearing Dads (DDD).*

---

* This book focuses on our mammalian needs for physical and emotional connection. Minimal attention has been given to the significance of the spiritual/cosmic perspective, believing that once basic needs are met, individuals are better able to see the larger picture.

# PART I

# WHY DADS LEAVE

# AN OVERVIEW

# 1: Introduction: Our Journey Through the Dynamic of Disappearing Dads (DDD)

The initial hypothesis for *Why Dads Leave* emerged from one man's painful journey into fatherhood. It began with his first venture into this terrain over 40 years ago, which ended in divorce and his largely abandoning his then three-year-old daughter—and continued with the journey of the woman he married over 30 years ago, the mother of his second child, who struggled alongside him, and nearly lost him along the way. That man was my husband, and I am the mother of his second child.

> I spent most of my adolescence and early adulthood unconsciously looking for a substitute for the nurturing mother I never had. I thought getting married (along with becoming a doctor) would somehow fulfill me, and assumed the right "girl" would magically appear.
>
> I thought I found her my senior year in college and married her midway through my second year of medical school. Much to my surprise, marriage didn't suddenly make my life "all better," just more complicated. The feelings of emptiness and depression persisted, and she found marriage to a medical student along with working to support us, very stressful. After three years of marriage she said she had to have a baby or she would leave. I knew I wasn't ready to be a father, but didn't think that could change soon, so, reluctantly, I complied, because divorce wasn't an option in my family. We did a Lamaze course and found the only hospital in Baltimore that allowed fathers in the delivery room. In February of 1972, after a two-hour labor, I became a father for the first time.
>
> It was great at first, the excitement of this new being, but then reality hit—I was a lot lower on my wife's attention list. I became more and more depressed. Eventually we both got involved in intensive psychotherapy using Transactional Analysis and reparenting. Here I learned a lot about my childhood wounds, and that I actually had feelings and could express them, though with great difficulty. We began learning about the unconscious patterns we'd been playing out in our co-dependent marriage (I provided the thinking, she the feelings), but we seemed relatively powerless to change them. My experience with this work did, however, become the basis for my career in wellness and, later, my understanding of how failed connection is the primary impediment to wellbeing as an adult.
>
> Despite learning a great deal about my inner workings, I was depressed most of the first two years of our daughter's life. When she was two and a half, the pain became so great that I realized I had to leave in order to retain my own sanity.

> I was sometimes close to being suicidal. In order to start the wellness center I had been planning for two years, I had to return to California. This meant a 3,000-mile separation from my daughter who remained in Baltimore with her mother. So, in addition to having been emotionally absent for much of my daughter's life, I now physically abandoned her. Although I loved her to the extent I could open myself to anyone, I had never really developed a strong and healthy bond with her—clearly out of my own inexperience with bonding with a parent. At the time, I wasn't even aware we weren't bonded, i.e., that anything more was possible. —Jack

It was nearly 20 years after the birth of his first daughter, when Jack decided to venture again into this territory of fathering. This time, he thought he was ready. He'd come a long way, personally and professionally. Shortly after his first daughter's birth, he left the lucrative world of medicine to found the world's first wellness center in Mill Valley, California—at a time when the word "wellness" was unknown.

Jack recalls 1976 as one of the happiest years of his life. For the first time, at age 33, he was doing what he wanted to do professionally and wasn't beholden to someone else's agenda. He was in love with a tall blonde named Joy, and his career was starting to take off. The wellness center was getting national attention, and he traveled all over North America giving lectures and workshops. He was featured in conferences alongside such pioneers as Norm Shealy, Jerry Jampolsky, George Leonard, Will Schutz, Larry Dossey, and Norman Cousins.

> I bought a $1,200 Brioni suit and a '68 MGB sports car, but I also began to notice how empty I felt after receiving a burst of attention from a workshop or lecture. The attention I was getting was for what I had done, not who I was, and like a sugar rush, there was a crash afterward.

> The administrative responsibilities of the Center were taking a toll on me and deep inside me, something felt wrong.

> After two years of our living together, Joy realized she was unable to meet my desires for nurturing (here we go again). She fell in love with a musician and moved out—I felt abandoned like never before.

> Continuing to participate in a variety of "consciousness" programs ubiquitous in the 70s in California, I tried to learn to love myself and follow the tenets of self-responsibility that I was advocating, all the while struggling with my chronic depression.

> The following year, as our center was about to be featured (and favorably portrayed) on "60 Minutes" with Dan Rather, I realized that life in the fast lane was not for me. I longed to simplify.

*I met and fell in love with an Australian, Meryn Callander. My needs for attention were again met in the heights of romance. Meryn shared my dream of living more simply on the earth.* —Jack

We were married in a small ceremony, performed by Joy, and began a partnership—personal and professional—that spanned nearly a third of a century.

In 1980, we decided to move to the mountains of Costa Rica, Central America—a wonderful experience for both of us—but that's another story (see *Wellness for Helping Professionals*). We returned to rural northern California in 1983.

## The Roots of Wellness

Through my immersion in feminist spirituality, we began to notice how the patterns of dominator/victim (patriarchal/power-over) versus partnership (matrifocal/power-with) manifested in our own relationship as well as in the larger culture. We formed a network of helping professionals that addressed the need we had observed among colleagues for authentic partnership and connection. We were engaged in healing the estrangement—the disconnection from each other, the earth, the divine, and our own deep selves—that is normative in the Western world; and carrying the seeds of these experiences, as "culture-makers," into the world.*

In the early 90s, a member of our network introduced *The Continuum Concept*, by Jean Liedloff, as being relevant to our work. This book was to be more than that—it was to radically impact the way in which I perceived and tended she-who-was-to-become my daughter, and indeed, all children.

Liedloff, on an expedition in the rainforests of Venezuela, had encountered members of the Yequana tribe and found them to be the happiest people she had ever met. The children were remarkably content and cooperative. She wanted to know why.

After several extended visits to their village, she finally connected the temperament of the adults she'd met with the fact that their babies and small children were seldom out of arms, were breastfed on cue, were never left to cry, and their discomforts were quickly alleviated.

After seeing the shock on the faces of several Yequana mothers she brought to the US, when observing how we treat our infants, Liedloff surmised that the way we treat babies and children is a primary cause of the rampant unhappiness and alienation in Western civilization. We had spent decades exploring and facilitating many avenues of personal growth, only to discover that the roots of wellness are formed in the period from our conception through the early years of our childhood. Now we saw that the conditions that run counter to wellness—from

---

* It was at this time Jack and I co-authored *Wellness for Helping Professionals: Creating Compassionate Cultures*

chronic illness, depression, addiction, violence, materialism, to fundamentalism, and ecocide—are not just the "human condition," but a result of how children in our culture are raised. It was this discovery that fueled Jack's desire to become a father again. This time, he believed, fatherhood would be different—he knew what he could do to make it work.

In July of 1992, we conceived a child on our 40-acre homestead in the rolling hills of Mendocino County in Northern California. After a carefully tended pregnancy and beautifully orchestrated home water birth supported by a midwife, our beautiful (of course) daughter was born—Siena Ariel.

Days turned into weeks and weeks into months and, for Jack, the initial glow began to fade. Meanwhile, though exhausted, I was blossoming and simply loving being a mom and with that, redirecting much of the nurturing I had directed toward Jack to Siena.

Jack found himself spiraling down in despair and into the depression that was eventually to be the stimulus for discovering what we named Male Postpartum Abandonment Syndrome (MPAS)—and the resulting Dynamic of Disappearing Dads (DDD).

But it would be nearly a decade before he would actually be able to put a name to it. And another decade before we would begin to appreciate the strength of the currents that render many a Western man, in the process of becoming a father, as peripheral to his child's life as the mother is central.

## We Knew it All (Oh, Sure!)

We'd been there so many times—engaging in processes recovering from the unmet needs of our own childhoods, and learning to discover the gifts therein. And we'd facilitated many others through the same processes. We knew a crucial determinant of being a good parent is our ability to reflect on our own childhood and learn from it, so that we don't embody the same dysfunctional behaviors that our parents, albeit unwittingly, inflicted on us.

What we had not considered was how deeply these dysfunctional patterns, imprinted in the early years of life, are embedded in our brain's "wiring." Later, learning of discoveries in neurobiology and neuropsychology showing how early brain development is determined by an infant's experience with caregivers, we realized how greatly we had underestimated the role of the culturally condoned separation of mother and infant/child, in shaping how we approach life in general, and parenting in particular. More on this later.

## Meanwhile, Back to the Very Beginning

At 37, after reading *The Continuum Concept*, my biological alarm suddenly rang loud and clear—I wanted a baby.

While Jack had thought he could never reopen the painful experience of being a father again, *The Continuum Concept* had opened the doors to a whole new world of parenting and nurturing a well world. He was struck by the simplicity and insight of Liedloff's theory and how it explained so many of the issues he had encountered in counseling others in his professional wellness work, as well as the driving force of the unmet needs of his own childhood that he'd spend so many years trying to heal.

> *With these sudden revelations, I thought I might make up for my greatest failure in life—not being a "good" father. It was armed with these new insights, that I thought I could "get it right" this time. And so I made the decision to become a father a second time—this time not under the duress I had with my first marriage.*
>
> *Up until then I had lived a fairly pressured life of self-imposed deadlines using adrenalin to make myself accomplish things. I gave lip service to love and relationships as my highest values, but I was more deeply driven by the belief I needed to accomplish to earn my keep, always feeling like some unknown, but dreaded, thing was gaining on me if I didn't have something concrete to show myself at the end of each day. Now, I thought, I was gradually overcoming my depressions. Years of hard work on painful issues seemed to be paying off.* —Jack

Fascinated, I went on to find many other studies associating early childcare practices with later personality outcomes.* The theme was consistent: social interaction, initially with the mother, then within the family, forms the foundation from which the child will relate to the world. The infant/child who receives intermittent attention likely becomes a selfish, aggressive adult. The child who receives a great deal of attention, whose every need is promptly met, most likely becomes a gentle, cooperative adult.

I thrilled to the possibilities.

So inspired, I became a mother at 41 years of age. It surprises me, even today, that such an "everyday" event as "becoming mother" remains the most precious, profound—and at times heartbreaking—experience of my life.

As an adult, I had spent very little time in the presence of babies or the very young, and rarely held an infant in my arms. And so I had managed to imagine that, with our baby, life would continue pretty much as before. Why not? She would be with us, content in sling or backpack as we lived our lives pretty much as we always had, just as they did in the indigenous cultures I had read about.

In retrospect, it is difficult to imagine how I could have been so naïve. Along with a good dose of wishful thinking, I see my unrealistic expectations were, in part, the sad consequence of my lack of exposure to the very young.

---

* My all-time favorite, now out of print, was *Learning Nonaggression* by Ashley Montagu.

Little wonder, given the prevalence of the nuclear family and the ways in which we have thoroughly divorced so much of our lives from our children, who are tucked away behind the walls of "their" homes, daycare centers, or schools.

I now believe it is impossible—before a baby arrives—to appreciate the changes in lifestyle that will be demanded of us. And even more impossible to fathom, the changes that will occur *within* us as we become mother/father, and *between* us as we assume these roles.

Up until Siena's birth, Jack and I had been consumed by the excitement of being pregnant, preparing for the home birth, tending our new home and property, traveling and facilitating seminars, along with my working with a passion on a new book, *Dispelling the Myths: Conception through the Early Years*. We gave little thought to the needs of the postpartum period, beyond the thrilling purchase of a beautiful baby sling, a pile of cotton diapers and a few of the sweetest ever natural fiber (of course) baby outfits. And truly, in terms of what's required to meet a baby's material needs, when practicing attachment parenting, this proved to be enough. No need for cots, cribs, pacifiers, bottles, prams, formula, or teddy bears.

The morning of February 28, 1993, three days "early," I felt my water break. It hit me then: this was real! There is no turning back. I surrendered. It felt so precious. I was ready. Or so I thought.

At 9:29 PM Jack and I were two individuals, used to an unusually high level of independence and freedom from the schedules and demands of others. At 9:30 Siena slid down my birth canal and into the warm waters of the birthing pool, and I was transported to another planet, a whole new dimension of being (and doing). This new reality grew on me over the coming days. Everything was so different. Jack and I were parents together. I had been initiated into one of the most important roles I would ever play in my life. A role I suddenly found myself minimally prepared for—or supported in fulfilling.

## Caught Unawares: Growing Closer or Apart?

At the time of Siena's birth we had been together for 14 years. Thanks to our work in wellness, creating "safe spaces," encouraging personal disclosure, authenticity, partnership, "being real," etc., we knew each other inside out—more than most couples ever care, or dare, to know and understand. We had spent months reading and writing about "continuum practices," more widely known as attachment parenting. We had thought that we were prepared, but oh, how wrong we were!

After Siena's birth, we found ourselves floundering, exhausted, unprepared for the challenges we encountered, most especially those that impacted us as a couple, and with no framework to help us interpret them. Enthralled with the pregnancy and excitement of preparing for a homebirth, we somehow remained totally oblivious to the fact that the transition to parenthood is a time of rapid and profound change for a couple, presenting new stresses and tensions, and often bringing up new and distressing feelings about each other and the marriage. We did not know that while most couples approach parenthood imagining a new baby will bring them closer together, in reality, initially at least, a child tends to push them apart. Even if we *had* known of this, we'd have been sure it wouldn't happen to us.

While the challenges of this transition time may have been touched on in a few of the birthing books that I had devoured, it was never presented in an explicit way to catch my attention. Certainly there had been no mention that as many as 30% of men physically leave within a few years after a child is born.[1]

As for Jack, he hadn't read many of the books! After all, they were mostly written for women. And raising a child was, in a way, regarded as "women's business."

## MPAS Strikes Home

Brimming with "love" hormones from our truly "normal" birth, it appeared to Jack that I responded intuitively to Siena's every need. I rapidly became the "expert," at least in his eyes. Initially, I had taken comfort in the belief that Jack knew all about birthing and parenting. After all he was an MD, he had already fathered a child, and he had even delivered babies on an Apache reservation. His gradual withdrawal from the fathering role came as a shock to me. I had no idea of the depths of what he was struggling with.

> The birth had gone well. Meryn breezed through the final stage of labor, and I was in the pool with her to welcome Siena into the world. We had set up our bed in the dining room where the birthing pool was and a couple of hours after the birth, we were asleep with Siena nestled between us.
>
> The next day, as she lay contentedly on my bare chest, I felt my heart overflowing with love. I had no idea I could love anyone so much. At this time, I had no idea of the long repressed memories, the depth of pain and envy, that would be opened up from constantly being in the presence of someone who knew what her needs were, expressed those needs without qualification, and actually got the nurturing every infant needs and thrives on. I found myself plunged into ever-deeper layers of pain.
>
> Meryn became a superbly nurturing mother, instinctively meeting Siena's needs in just those myriad ways we had been advocating. And, as I should have anticipated, Siena's arrival supplanted much of the attention I'd been getting from Meryn, especially nurturance.
>
> While we provided her with a degree of physical and emotional nurturance unknown to most children in the West today, and she blossomed from it, our

> relationship became more and more strained. I went deeper into depressions, alternating with periods of hyperactivity trying to avoid feeling the pain, and to keep us afloat financially and make up for the downtime of my crashes. I knew it was unsustainable but was at a loss for how to be any other way. —Jack

It was only later that he could begin to articulate what had been happening for him—how his inner child felt abandoned and inadequate compared to the real child sharing a bed with him every night, sleeping and breastfeeding contentedly. His pain was further fueled by seeing how my similarly disconnected childhood was being healed through my biological connection with Siena. He was tormented by his inability to connect emotionally with either of us. Other than being the primary provider, maintainer of the homestead, and sometimes changer-of-diapers, he felt less and less useful as a father. He felt this despite the fact that he was, in my reality, a very involved and wonderfully caring and competent dad—except during his periods of withdrawal into neediness and depression.

> I tried to meet my own needs on a number of fronts: during the pregnancy I had converted our newly purchased small cabin, on 40 acres in the wilds of Mendocino County, into an open-ceiling home with a sleeping loft. Then during Siena's first year, I built a room for my office, a deck, and a greenhouse/solar atrium—all in my efforts to feel more creative, useful, and connected. I participated in men's groups, therapy, and time in nature—all to little avail. Our new friends, Bruce and Maggie, along with their son the same age as Siena, moved onto the land with us and built a cabin. Creating our own little community helped, but Bruce's long commute was a challenge and they eventually moved back to the coast. —Jack

Emotionally, he was slowly disappearing and throwing himself into work to minimize the pain.

> MPAS had struck home, but it would be years before I could name it. At this point all I can feel is a deep longing. I feel unloved, unlovable, disconnected, and superfluous. Meryn has the womb and the breasts—the physical connection with our child that no man can ever experience. —Jack

While Jack kept on adding rooms and renovating our little home in the hills, all I wanted was for him to rebuild and renovate his relationship—with me, and with our baby.

Our relationship has always been challenging as we have strived to live in partnership rather than power struggles, collaboration rather than competition, loving and learning rather than protecting and defending. Despite our many clearings and revelations, and a substantial degree of personal growth, we each carried a pretty typical layer of armoring, with many of our interactions charged with baggage from the past.

## Chapter 1: Our Journey Through the Dynamic of Disappearing Dads

Throughout the pregnancy and at the time of Siena's birth, our relationship felt positive and stable. I knew I was really fortunate in having a partner who supported me in these continuum practices, and there were many times we shared the joy of being parents. For the most part, except in his really down periods when it was so painful for him to be with either of us, he was there to share the caring for Siena, to take her into his own arms, diaper and delight her. Most important, I knew that he adored her, and that his intentions—like mine—were good.

While Siena brought great joy into our lives, and we were unwavering in our commitment to her wellbeing, her presence was inevitably a stress with respect to the allocation of time and priorities for attention. Jack had always had a greater need for attention from me than I from him. And now, all my nurturing energies were pouring onto Siena. The truth was, Siena was a delight to be with. He, on the other hand, had become more like a whiney, needy little child I didn't want to be around.

While I had always believed our marriage had been made in heaven, I had often wondered whether it could survive life on earth. This question now loomed larger than ever. By Siena's third year, Jack was depressed much of the time. Over our many years together, I had come to appreciate how debilitating his depressive periods were for him. I had seen him venture with such hope from one therapeutic approach to another attempting to counteract the basic S-SAD (see next chapter) he had carried since birth—all to no avail.

I had learned that the best I could do was to hold minimal expectations of him, "give him space" when he went under, knowing it would, in time, pass. I knew he dreaded these periods too, but it was so hard not to have expectations for him at this juncture in our lives. This, of course, made it even worse. I wanted a father for my child, a partner, a friend. Instead, it seemed I had not one, but two little children to care for. I felt his neediness as a constant drain on my energies. I struggled with the resentment I felt towards him. And the sadness I felt at the absence of his presence, as a father, that I had anticipated with so much pleasure.

In contrast, Siena's love for me was so pure, authentic, spontaneous, effervescent. She was so uncomplicated. And so why ever would I choose to be with him rather than with her? The more depressed and needy he became, the less I wanted to be with him. I would dread the times when he wanted to talk about how needy he was, how he wasn't getting what he wanted from our relationship. I had little patience for this litany, and so much more and better to do with my life: like hang out with Siena, the love of my life.

I was in love and I was loved—unconditionally. I bathed in this field of love. How could Jack ever compete? And if not, why would he want to stay?

I swung between feelings of sadness and anger that Jack had left emotionally. I felt alone, abandoned by him. If only I had understood what I understand now, I would have had more appreciation for the depths of his despair, and a deeper appreciation of the need to nurture our adult couple relationship—the foundation (or the ruins) on which the wellbeing of the family rests. But I did not know any of this at the time. And the very little literature that connected fathers with children described father absence. It was as if a father's presence did not factor into his child's health or happiness. As for MPAS, it hadn't yet been recognized.

> **MPAS in a Nutshell**
>
> A secure mother-infant bond, fundamental to all mammalian species, is the foundation on which all future relationships are built.
>
> Today we know from recent discoveries in neurobiology that—as many indigenous cultures have always known—a secure mother-infant bond depends on many factors: a natural (i.e., unmedicated, intervention-free) birth; breastfeeding; near-constant physical contact through carrying infants in-arms or wearing them in slings; shared sleeping arrangements; and the recognition that babies are social beings who thrive on loving connections. Today, these practices are known as "attachment parenting" or "connection parenting."
>
> Almost everyone in the Western world born since the 1930s has been subjected to modern practices that interfere with secure attachment—endured a high-tech rather than a high-touch birth; fed artificial baby food rather than breastmilk; placed in isolating and lifeless wheeled carriers, rather than on mother's—or dad's—body; left to "cry it out" rather than being lovingly responded to; left to sleep alone in cribs instead of co-sleeping in a family bed; if a boy, circumcised; and subjected to childrearing techniques built on coercion (like "Babywise" [sic] or Dr. Spock, for older generations) rather than connection.
>
> As a result, little boys grow up looking for the mommy they never connected with. If they're lucky, they find her, and marry her, and think everything's OK—until the first baby comes along.
>
> Suddenly the baby takes center stage, needing far more time and energy than a single human being can provide. The result is that the poorly connected father once again feels left out in the cold. He is vulnerable to adopting withdrawal and avoidance behaviors (through which he is unconsciously and unsuccessfully seeking connection) in order to cope with the anxiety that accompanies a brain with insecure infant attachment patterns.
>
> Meanwhile his partner may be simultaneously healing her own similar unmet needs, by being bathed in a cocktail of love hormones from her physical connection of carrying the baby in her womb and breastfeeding—which no man can ever experience. If she goes back to work in three months and puts their child in daycare, his pain of disconnection will not be as strongly restimulated and he will be less

susceptible to MPAS. But the stage is then set for their child to repeat the cycle of passing on this "normative abuse" to the next generation.

Ironically, the better the mother is able to nurture her child, the more likely the father will be to re-experience his childhood wounding because he sees even more of what he didn't get. MPAS is now in play, with neither partner understanding the origins, and both likely overwhelmed by the transition to parenthood. A common coping mechanism for him is to leave, either physically or emotionally.

While women are more likely to take the first step towards formal dissolution of the relationship, it is usually the man's earlier dissatisfaction—typically manifesting in emotional or physical absence—more than her own, which predicts her taking that step.[2]

## The FatherStory

Fatherhood, much more than motherhood, is a cultural construction. Its meaning is shaped by a culture that conditions a man into certain ways of behaving and perceiving himself. In this way fathers are made, not born.

In the West, our prevalent cultural story about fatherhood sees fathers as superfluous—either unnecessary or undesirable—or purely as provider or disciplinarian. This perspective is fueled by the belief that men don't have the biological programming to nurture their offspring. This belief lies behind the reluctance of many mothers to involve fathers in childcare, and behind an enormous range of social and economic policies and practices that not only fail to validate the father-child relationship, but frequently undermine it. Unwittingly beholden to some extent to this prevailing FatherStory, Jack saw himself, like his own father, as a mother's helper rather than a partner who could parent sensitively and competently, though differently. And I found myself at times wondering whether Siena and I would be better off without him. Unconsciously, Jack and I had begun to accept the myth of women's biological superiority as nurturer, and the irrelevance of a dad.

Yet, as we will see, anthropology, cross-cultural and cross-species research, and modern primatology, reveal a tremendous range of potentials for fathering. Variations do not appear in response to biological imperatives as much as to changing circumstances, a finding that invalidates the belief that fathering is rigid and gender-specific. An enormous discrepancy is emerging between cultural myth and the day-to-day reality of a father's ability and desire to nurture his offspring. Studies show men to be competent and sensitive to their children, and, given the opportunity, they seek to be with their children.

## Breaking the Cycle

Driven by the need to break the cycle of disconnection, and prevent passing on the same pattern to succeeding generations, we continued to learn about, and practice, attachment parenting. We arranged for Jean Liedloff to lead a daylong workshop as a kickoff for a local group of families practicing attachment parenting. We began to dialog with other professionals in the field, adding fuel to the abandonment hypothesis that had been brewing in the back of Jack's mind. In January 1998, he published "Why Men Leave: Confessions of a Bottlefed, Poorly Bonded, Thrice-Married, White Male Overachiever" in our 200-subscriber newsletter.

The next year we co-founded the Alliance for Transforming the Lives of Children (aTLC). In consultation with other international experts, the core group of the Alliance spent approximately 10,000 volunteer hours developing an evidence-based document outlining principles and actions that foster a child's optimal development—the *aTLC Blueprint* (Appendix E).

An expanded version of "Why Men Leave" was published in 2004 in both Australian and US parenting magazines (see Appendix A). The editor of one of the magazines reported that the article had the strongest reader response of any to date. We were surprised that our premise struck such a resonant chord with so many people, evident from the reader response and from Jack's speaking about it at several conferences. At the urging of a friend and colleague, Dean Edell, MD, we considered expanding the article into a book.

I began to review the literature to learn what, if anything, had been written about this subject. I searched for books written by and for men, and in the few I found, discovered a wealth of information I had not seen in all the many, many parenting books I had reviewed. Facts and figures about the multitude of ways fathers are relegated to the periphery of their child's life throughout pregnancy, birthing, and the early days and months. I was startled to learn, for example, a mother's relationship characteristics outweigh the father's relationship characteristics in predicting fathers' involvement with their children, and anywhere from 14–26% of fathers suffer from moderate or severe postpartum depression (Chapter 9).

I came across an older article by Michel Odent, MD, the French obstetrician who wrote *The Scientification of Love*, and head of the Primal Health Research Center in London, who made this connection between birth, men's "need to escape," and "covert depression" decades ago:

> [A]t a certain phase of my homebirth practice… it was too common… when visiting the family… to realize that health problems of the father are common during the days following birth…[it is] almost always a rather precise diagnosis, such as lumbago, kidney stones, generalized eczema, abdominal pain, or toothache.

*A woman gave birth at home on the French Riviera in the presence of her husband...[and] the day after the birth, the father disappeared and went back to Italy, his native country. Another man had his first schizophrenic attack at the age of 35, two days after the birth of his first baby. A woman told me that she divorced because her husband disappeared to play golf the day after the birth of their baby.*

*Obviously all these men felt the need to escape, one way or another. Modern physiology explains that, in adverse circumstances, there are two ways to protect our health: "fight or flight." These men had an urgent need to protect their health by escaping. What sort of disease were they preventing?*

Referring to Terrence Real's term "covert depression," a term coined in his studies of male depression, Odent concluded that we must introduce the concept of "male postnatal depression" and, more precisely, of "*covert* male postnatal depression." "Covert" because it is hidden from the men who suffer it, and also from those around them. Why? According to Real, "depression carries... a double stigma... of mental illness and also... 'feminine' emotionality. [Hence] men tend to express depression differently than women, usually 'masking' it by a great diversity of misleading symptoms."

While a couple of the books I found skirted the edges of MPAS, none directly connected postpartum depression, or men leaving, with the re-stimulation of unmet infancy needs. We believe this is the underlying factor that exacerbates all other issues in explaining MPAS—and DDD.

Why is this all-too-common event of men leaving—physically or emotionally—in what can only be considered epidemic proportions, not being directly addressed? This, alongside the intensity of our own experience of this MPAS, drove me to delve more deeply.

Perhaps the most difficult thing for many of us as we read this material, as we engage consciously in reviewing our own childhood and our own parenting, is confronting our feelings of regret, blame, and guilt. We do not like to think that what our parents did to us caused harm. We do not like to think that what we have done, or are doing, to our children is harming them. We are all doing the best we can, with the information and resources available to us. Neither guilt nor blame will serve us. We are all products of our time and culture, as were our parents and those who preceded them.

*Generational issues are with us always, but at few times are they more salient than when the generational cycle is about to begin again. A first child and grandchild bring the relationship between the parents and their parents into bold relief. When the relationships are going well, these close ties can be a great comfort for both generations.... For some couples, however, past and present relationships with parents can bring a great deal of pain. The birth of a baby* can force some parents and grandparents to grapple once more with issues they have not successfully resolved....

As we talk with friends, colleagues, and the parents [in our study], we can see how commonly we all make repeated overtures over the years to our parents and children to try to patch up earlier misunderstandings or rifts. One of our findings—something we did not know in our early years of family-making—is that all relationships across the generations have setbacks at times, but some of us are lucky enough to make some progress toward mending them.... [This is important because] new parents who do not see the connections between their struggles with their own parents and their distress as a couple are less likely to feel that they are on the same side when they tackle difficult issues in their life together.    —Carolyn Pape Cowan, PhD, and Philip Cowan, PhD
*When Partners Become Parents*

## Guilt Versus Regret

Pam Leo, in *Connection Parenting*, writes: "It is important to make the distinction between guilt and regret. Guilt is what we feel when we knew better and didn't act on what we knew. Regret is the sadness we feel when we learn something new that we wish we had known earlier. Making the distinction between guilt and regret is important as we embark on learning some different ways of parenting."

> *I was sexually abused by my dad as a child. Very few people understand what I am talking about when I tell this: I had a therapist years ago who said this to me "Try and re-live your memories not as the child you were, but as the adult you are now."*
>
> *She explained that when you do this, you do not "feel" as if you are being hurt again, instead you view it from a less emotional place, using an adult's perspective.*
>
> *WOW! As far as the sexual issues, this changed everything! I did nothing wrong, I was not to blame! This was just a sick man getting his kicks. What a relief.*
>
> *The other side of that knowledge was just as liberating, but harder....*
>
> *When I relived not having my dad in my life, it also hurt less. Two other thoughts battled as well. I was stronger than my father had been, I was more determined and aware, I was a good person! I also realized that I felt pity towards my father and his weaknesses that had kept him from knowing me. He was just a man who was not worth much to me. It was a double-edged sword for me because I then wondered why I wanted a worthless person's love so badly! I guess it is a never-ending cycle—and on it goes!* —Rebecca

Leo continues with, "Becoming better parents means we will always be learning. It also means we sometimes will be living in the gap between what we are learning and what we can do. The more we learn about healthier parenting, the more we will live in the 'gap.' As we strive to become more loving to our children, we must also strive to be more loving to ourselves."

Leo believes that it is never too late to strengthen our connection with our children. Every moment is a new opportunity to strengthen this bond.

**Key Points**
- As pioneers of the growing wellness movement, Meryn and Jack begin to understand how an insecure mother-infant bond is the primary impediment to wellbeing as an adult and discover that the roots of wellness are formed from our conception through the early years of our childhood.
- Meryn and Jack are introduced to the ideas of attachment, bonding and connection through Jean Liedloff's, *The Continuum Concept*. They now recognize dis-ease—from chronic illness, depression, addiction, violence, materialism, to ecocide—is not just the "human condition," but a result of how children in our culture are raised.
- It is the discovery of attachment parenting—and its promises of breaking generational cycles of disconnection and, instead, fostering a foundation for lifelong wellness—that led Meryn and Jack to a focus on infant wellness as well as fuel Jack's desire to become a father again.
- Fatherhood, much more than motherhood, is a cultural invention. Its meaning is shaped by a culture that conditions a man into certain ways of acting and perceiving himself. It may be said that fathers are made, not born. Anthropology, cross-cultural and cross-species research, and modern primatology, reveal a tremendous range of potentials for fathering.
- The intersection of their wellness expertise, parenting experiences, discoveries from neuroscience, S-SAD, Prescott, Odent, and Liedloff's insights form the foundational understanding of what will eventually be recognized as the Male Postpartum Abandonment Syndrome (MPAS)—and the Dynamic of Disappearing Dads (DDD)
- An enormous discrepancy is emerging between cultural myth and day-to-day reality of a father's ability and desire to nurture his offspring. Studies show men to be competent and sensitive to their children, and given the opportunity, they seek to be with them.
- We are all doing the best we can, with the information and resources available to us. Neither guilt nor blame will serve us. We are all products of our time and culture, as were our parents and those who preceded them.

# 2: Exploring The Dynamic of Disappearing Dads

*A generation ago, an American child could reasonably expect to grow up with his or her father; today, an American child could reasonably expect not to.*
—David Blankenhorn, *Fatherless America*

Most of us who were born in the United States after about 1940 were born in hospitals under bright lights and under the influence of drugs given to our mothers that may have rendered both mother and child semi-comatose during the birth, as well as for hours after the birth. We were physically removed from our mothers within minutes of being born and placed in the hospital nursery, isolated and alone, except for the cries of other inmates of that nursery. The next day the majority of male infants were strapped down on a board so that one of the most sensitive parts of the body, the foreskin, could be stripped loose from its attachment to the underlying glans (head of penis), and then cut off—circumcised—the majority with no anesthetic.*

*No one is aware of the deep implications and life-lasting effect [of circumcision]. The torture is experienced in a state of total helplessness, which makes it even more frightening and unbearable.*
—Frederick Leboyer, MD, *Birth Without Violence*

To this day, most infants are bottle-fed, left to sleep in a crib, left alone to "cry it out," and left in playpens or other containers like car seats or strollers, instead of being carried in-arms. While considered "normal," these practices, named "normative abuse" by Karen Walant,³ can severely compromise the infant-parent bond.

An infant's cry is designed for his (or her) survival—not to disturb us needlessly. A baby whose cries are not met does not become a "good baby" (though he may become a quiet baby); he becomes a discouraged baby, falling into a state called "learned helplessness." His world seems unpredictable, unreliable, and frightening. He learns he can't communicate or trust that his needs will be met—a belief he will likely carry throughout his life unless he seeks to resolve these unmet needs.

Today we know that the quality of our children's earliest years has a major impact on their entire lives. Their sense of security, resilience to stress, emotional balance, ability to make sense of life, *and to create meaningful*

---

* Babies feel pain more acutely than adults. Pain is serious. It is not something to be dismissed, ignored, or laughed at. It does not "toughen" little boys. In fact, baby boys who have been circumcised suffer from an abnormally lowered pain threshold and their heightened response to pain is consistent with post-traumatic stress disorder.

*interpersonal relationships* in the future is based on their experience of *connection and attachment to their primary caregivers.*

A very substantial body of evidence highlights the importance of early relationships in profoundly shaping the central nervous system. Infants' and children's health and wellbeing is dependent on their intrauterine experience and on the quality of the relationship with their primary caregivers during the first three to five years—the period when a child's brain develops most rapidly.

> The absence of a consistent, loving connection with a primary caregiver adversely affects the developing brain. Symptoms of insecure bonding include an inability to deal with stress and adversity, inability to form meaningful relationships with others, lack of self-control, antisocial attitudes and behaviors, learning difficulties, depression, susceptibility to chronic illness, aggression and violence.

The rapidly growing field of neurobiology, as well as Prescott's S-SAD theory (see box), explains why we are now seeing large numbers of adults with neuro-dissociative[*] brains. Generations of infants birthed through Western medical practices and raised with control-based, rather than connection-based parenting practices that compromise the infant-mother bond, grow up insecurely attached.

Attachment parenting practices support the biological and psychological needs that result in a securely bonded, neuro-integrative brain, which provides the foundation for adult wellness and ready access to experiences of joy, compassion, peace, and happiness.

> **Somato-Sensory Affectional Deprivation (S-SAD) Syndrome—Altering the Hardwiring and Software of the Developing Brain**[*]
>
> S-SAD is the process of impaired or failed mother-infant bonding that results from a deficiency in the infant's sensory stimulation via touch, body movement, smell and taste, and breastfeeding. Virtually all infant mammals are vulnerable to the emotional-behavioral disorders that are induced by this somato-sensory deprivation. The specific emotional-behavioral disorders that result, vary by species and have their influence throughout the lifespan of the individual.
>
> The principal emotional-behavioral disorders characteristic of most S-SAD-reared mammals include: depression; chronic-stimulus seeking (obsessive-compulsive) behaviors, (e.g., stereotypical rocking and thumb/penis sucking; self-mutilation; hyperactivity; and hyper-reactivity); tactile avoidance, impaired pain and pleasure perceptions; hypersensitivity

---

[*] A scientific term for "disconnected brain" coined by James W. Prescott, PhD.

to touch; impaired sexual pleasure and sexual functioning; alcohol/drug abuse, dependence, and addiction; and social alienation with anti-social behaviors that include violence, suicide, and homicide.

S-SAD induces a variety of neurobiological changes in the developing brain of S-SAD-reared mammals, particularly primates, which creates the above-described emotional-behavioral disorders. These brain-behavioral disorders occur primarily in the sub-cortical emotional-social-sexual part of the brain that unfolds early in development—not the neocortical rational/cognitive brain that results from later brain development.

Somatic (bodily) pleasure is the glue of affectional bonding. The failed development of the normal pleasure systems of the brain, through S-SAD, induces disordered pleasure-seeking behaviors, whether through misuse/abuse of the sensory systems or from biochemical drugs.

Primary treatment of S-SAD disorders must involve the reconstruction of the pleasure systems of the brain so that neuro-integrative pleasure and not neuro-dissociative pleasure becomes the reality. (Gender inequality, sexual violence, narcissism, sadomasochism, addictions and obsessive-compulsive pornography are examples of the consequences of the neuro-dissociative brain.) The neuro-dissociative brain, induced by S-SAD, mediates depression, addiction, and violence, whereas the neuro-integrative brain mediates joy, compassion, peace, and happiness. Integrated bodily pleasure is essential for the evolutionary development of love in Homo sapiens, which has been displaced by a disembodied platonic/divine love that drives human alienation, depression, and violence.

\* *James W. Prescott, PhD, former Health Scientist Administrator, National Institute of Child Health & Human Development, NIH, www.violence.de*

Biologically, the male is the more fragile gender of our species: many more male than female fetuses die *in utero*. Developmentally, males lag years behind females until well into adulthood (some may argue that they never catch up), and on average, die at a significantly earlier age.

Boys, rather than getting the additional nurturing needed to compensate for being the more fragile sex, especially as they move beyond infancy, receive far less nurturing than girls *and* less permission to express their feelings and emotions. Note the common expressions: "Don't make a sissy out of him," and "Big boys don't cry." Thus the pattern is set for the massive repression of males' needs and feelings that is common to most men raised in English-speaking cultures, and is in turn a primary factor in the Dynamic of Disappearing Dads (DDD).

Most of these poorly bonded and emotionally repressed boys grow into men who unconsciously seek someone to provide them with the nurturing they were denied as infants and children. When they find her and marry her, they may manage pretty well for a while—until a child comes along. Suddenly, virtually all her nurturing energies are directed towards her newborn. Many men interpret—consciously or unconsciously—the withdrawal of their partner's attention as abandonment or rejection.

> *Emotional starvation is a reality. Feeling emotionally deserted, rejected, or abandoned sparks physical and emotional pain and panic.*
> —Sue Johnson, PhD, *Hold Me Tight*

Concurrent with the withdrawal of his partner's attention at the time of the child's birth is the father's sudden and intense exposure to an infant who has not yet been fully "trained" in the denial of her own needs—and so expresses them without reservation.

Witnessing his child suckling at the breast, being lovingly held in arms, and receiving the attention and nurturance he craves, can be devastating to a new father. It will often stir up suppressed implicit memories of the denied needs of his infancy and plunge him into deep pain. MPAS has hit.

> *So much pain cropping up and me wanting to avoid writing this… why did I leave? Emotional illiteracy, inability to directly ask for what I needed, weak personal boundaries (difficulty saying no), resentment in seeing my baby's needs being wholeheartedly expressed and then met by my lover. And underneath that anger was a well of sadness that I couldn't handle.* —Andy

A relevant issue that is rarely addressed is the adult's need for physical connection and how that need gets confused with sexual contact. Compounding this dynamic is that in most modern, non-Latin or non-French Western cultures, physical contact between males, other than handshakes or contact sports, is still largely taboo in public. Because most of us begin life with an enormous deficit of physical contact, this results in compensatory behaviors that attempt to fill the void left by this unmet early need, e.g., addictions to food, drugs, sex, and work (see "Oral Needs" Chapter 17).

> *One of the things that nurtured me the most was lying in bed at night in Maya's arms, usually watching TV and having my head, chest, or tummy stroked. We spent an hour several nights a week, doing this before going to sleep. In the mornings, I would hold her in a similar way, or we would lay together "heart-to-heart" as we called it, before getting out of bed. Unlike the common male stereotype of always thinking about sex and wanting more what I mainly wanted was nurturing attention from a mother figure, though I was only dimly aware of it at the time. I would sometimes think something must be wrong with me for not being more sexually interested. Being held and stroked was the lifeline that kept me going, though I didn't fully get how important this need was until I lost it.* —Tim

It is helpful if we can differentiate between the old longings and present-time physical and emotional connection needed by an adult. As long as we remain unaware that the intense neediness or longing for connection is not only a present-time need, but also a deep longing for contact and connection that wasn't fully met when our developing brain needed it, we can become trapped by those longings. Regardless of how much sexual contact a man may be able to "score," sexual attention will never be able to supply the unmet infancy needs—there can never be "enough."

> **Implicit Memory**
>
> It's important to recognize that many past traumatic events are recorded as *implicit* memories.* These differ from the familiar *explicit* memories that we're conscious of, and can describe in words. Implicit memories may surface as uncomfortable bodily sensations and emotions rather than anything we recognize as a "memory." Our left brain then makes up a reason that we are feeling the way we are feeling (because that's what left brains do) but that reason probably has nothing to do with what we are *actually* feeling.

*Brain image studies show rejection and exclusion trigger the same circuits in the same part of the brain (anterior cingulate) as physical pain. Indeed, this part of the brain turns on anytime we are emotionally separated from those who are close to us. "Hurt feelings" really do hurt!* —Sue Johnson, PhD, *Hold Me Tight*

The re-stimulation of the father's unmet needs and the rejection or abandonment he experienced as an infant may leave him feeling resentful, even hostile towards his wife and possibly toward his child. At the same time he is expected to assume the entirely new and mature role of "father." Not only have most men not had their infantile nurturing needs met, most men have no experience of a nurturing father to draw on. It can be so hard to give what we have not known or received ourselves. Faced with the exceedingly difficult task of trying to become a father—most often in the absence of a healthy role model or support system—a man may well feel guilty, and ashamed of himself for feeling this way.

---

* Implicit memory is a type of memory in which previous experiences aid in the performance of a task without conscious awareness of these previous experiences. In daily life, people rely on implicit memory in the form of procedural memory, the type of memory that allows people to remember how to tie their shoes or ride a bicycle without consciously thinking. Implicit memory operates through a different mental process from explicit memory.

> *[Fatherhood] is a terrifying beginning.... He wants mother and child to feel his protective strength, not his quivering insecurity. And often, that is what the new mother wants from him, too.* —Will Glennon, *Fathering: Strengthening Connection with Your Children*

Asking for help is perceived as a weakness.

> *If only we had the freedom not to have it all figured out, not to know everything before we started, if we were able to ask for help, to say "I don't know what to do..." or "I'm having a really hard time with this." What a difference it would have made.* —Chris Maple, PhD

Many men sense the need to be different from the fathers they grew up with, who were strong, unemotional, and absent (physically or emotionally). Many men today want to *be there* for their child but are uncertain how to go about *doing* that. Unfamiliar with and unsupported in the task of nurturing, they are bombarded with conflicting messages as to *how* to go about being a good father. Deeply embedded in our cultural heritage that they be protectors and providers, men are considered failures if they fail to provide for their family, yet providing for them brings them under criticism for leaving the family alone. It can feel like an impossible situation. Feeling scared and superfluous, he is likely to withdraw, conceding the role of nurturer to his partner.

As a means of compensation and/or to defend himself against the perceived rejection and suppress the primal pain that was temporarily alleviated by his finding a nurturing source, he may reject his family.

> *You ask me why I left? Such a painful question—it has put me in a funk for the last three weeks. A 41-year-old male, unable to function, feeling shame for not replying to your request sooner.*
>
> *Five years ago, I agreed—after a great deal of resistance—to adopt a little boy. I wanted to adopt an older child to avoid the trying infant times.*
>
> *As we went through the adoption process, I experienced waves of intense sadness—punctuated by crying in front of my then 8- and 11-year-old daughters. At one point, I left my family on the downtown mall, overcome with emotion, confused, feeling small, weak and helpless. I was depressed.*
>
> *I wanted touch, sex from K. I wanted to play with her breasts, to suck them, to touch her nipples and trace her areolas. She refused me often. Our touch was limited to sex about once a week, which sometimes stretched out to every 10-11 days. She had forbidden my touching her breasts from the time of my first daughter's birth. By the time my son came, it had been ten years. I curled up in a ball—fetal-like.*

> *I felt like I had to leave. I was drinking a six-pack a day. I told the girls and K. that I needed to take care of myself—that I couldn't do it in the current situation. I don't know if it's needing more time in the cave, or withdrawal, or self-preservation, or inability to deal with the pain/sadness that was/is welling up from my body.* —Andy

As Jack and I found from the variety of responses to the original magazine article, DDD can take many forms and may occur on a variety of levels:

1. While a father may pretend all is well (remember men are well-schooled in the repression of feelings) he may leave emotionally, pick fights, retreat into depression, dull the pain through the abuse of any number of substances, disappear into work or projects, or embark on an affair.

   > *Initially supportive, my husband had been withdrawing more and more since the birth of our son. When our son was eight months, my husband told me that he was completely unhappy, had been unhappy throughout our six years of marriage (I don't see how this was possible), and didn't know if he wanted to stay married. He told me that while he always thought he wanted a family, now that he has one, he doesn't think he wants it.*
   >
   > *I am at a complete loss—I don't want to lose my husband, but he won't let me in past the "brick wall" he's built around himself.* —Linda

2. When or if men's defense mechanisms fail to adequately suppress their pain, as they are apt to do because the real need is not addressed, many believe that their very sanity or survival is dependent on *departing* from the scene.

   > *After a little over a year of being married, I became pregnant. Elated, I could not think of anything more romantic than having my husband's baby. I gave birth to a high-needs child who cried constantly and required my full attention. One morning my husband woke, sat up in bed, and told me he was not in love with me anymore. He dressed and walked out the door. Now, six months later, I'm still so devastated I can hardly function. I can hardly believe that he could walk away from his son and me without any sign of remorse or giving me the opportunity to change.* —Amy

3. A third level of leaving is through *suicide or fatal "accidents."* Or perhaps, doing it "with honor," by signing up for a likely death in a war.

## Females: A Biological Advantage

Most women similarly experienced insecure bonding as infants and are often searching, in a partner/husband, for the nurturing father/mother they never had.

Women, especially before they have children, may also exhibit this pattern of seeking physical connection through sex to supply unmet infancy needs, however, as mentioned earlier, they have more of an opportunity to heal those unmet needs through their biological relationship with their children.

> *This was my way of coping in my 20s—promiscuity, without an interest in forming deeper bonds, and I was even conscious that it was related to unmet infancy needs as well as unmet needs for healthy, caring connection, physically and emotionally, with a stable loving family, during my teen years. At the time, I actually thought that my behavior was a healthy solution to what I had experienced.* —Barbara

Women have a strong biological advantage supporting them in forging a secure bond with their offspring initially, sharing the same physical/emotional space by carrying another being in their womb.

Mother Nature has designed the female body to support the mother-baby unit through the birth and bonding processes. The gestating mother is intimately and exquisitely connected with her baby for a full nine months. During labor, if mother—and by association, infant—has not been given drugs to block pain or speed the process, they are primed to continue this symbiotic connection.

A surge of bonding hormones moves the laboring mother into an altered state of consciousness, softening the labor pains and easing the baby's passage. Throughout the perinatal period, hormones, primarily oxytocin, are released in both mother and baby preparing them to "fall in love"—to bond with each other. When mother and baby have not experienced a natural birth, this does not mean that they will not be able to attach and bond, but that the process may take more effort than otherwise.

Over the ensuing weeks and months, if they are able to successfully resist the cultural parenting practices that encourage the separation of mother and infant and are able to forge a secure bond, mothers can heal much of their own unbondedness.

Having always loved time alone, I had wondered how I would manage with a baby. While in the newness and exhaustion of the early weeks there were times I longed for this, it was only a short time until I simply wanted to be with Siena, to snuggle with her, carry her, respond to her. These mothering instincts soon outweighed any feelings I may have had to get time to myself. I later recognized this as what Liedloff wrote of as "the ancient instinct" taking over. Not that I never felt the need for time alone, but I found, to a surprising and delightful degree, that nurturing Siena nurtured me—physically, emotionally, and spiritually.

> *Once a mother begins to serve her baby's continuum (and thus her own as a mother), the culturally confused instinct in her will reassert itself and reconnect her natural motives. She will not want to put her baby down… the ancient instinct will soon take over; for the continuum is a powerful force and never ceases to try and reinstate itself. The sense of rightness felt by the mother when she is behaving in accordance with nature will do far more to reestablish the continuum in her than anything this book may have conveyed to her as theory.* —Jean Liedloff, *The Continuum Concept*

Fathers, too, experience increasing oxytocin levels that coincide with mothers', but these are nowhere near the levels that flood their partners. So while fathering can also offer men an opportunity to heal, this opening tends to be easier for the mother, in that the biological advantage she holds is further reinforced by eons of cultural conditioning and social mores.

Ironically, the greater the connection of the mother to the child, *the more it may restimulate the father's primal pain*, trigger his defenses, and increase the likelihood of his rejecting, and ultimately leaving, his family.

> *One of the reasons he wanted to be with me and marry me was the fact that I was so knowledgeable and good with children... that I would be a great mother. Ironic that my good mothering is one of the main reasons that he is abandoning his family.* —Mandy

---

### Identifying MPAS

Most couples go through a number of predictable and challenging passages during their life together. An informed awareness of these peak periods,* prior to their emergence, and support during them, can ensure a better outcome for both parents and children.

The transition to parenthood is one of these challenging passages, and this is what this book is about—the factors that arise and may lead to a couple separating in the early years after the birth of a child. Many couples separate later, and at that stage many other factors have come into play, such that a father's postpartum abandonment (MPAS) issues are not resolved, compensatory behaviors instituted by both partners may further serve to distance them from each other.†

---

As Western adults, men and women, mostly unconsciously, seek partners to fulfill their unresolved needs for bonding experiences that would allow their capacity for wellness and wholeness to unfold. When couples become parents, it is possible for men and women to be blindsided by their unmet bonding needs which can manifest in myriad ways.

---

\* These include a change of occupation, a health crisis, a death of either partner's parent, a child's leaving home, a mid- and late-life crisis, as well as the birth of a child.

† To claim years after the birth of a child that a marriage is coming apart because of MPAS, may indicate an absence of accountability—an unwillingness to take responsibility for inquiring into and attending to other issues that have arisen over the passage of time, and have contributed to the dissatisfaction that is current within the relationship. Even so, MPAS reflects a deeper cultural mass disconnection and failure to bond that can become self perpetuating and last a lifetime unless healed.

## The Severity of the DDD Epidemic

While nearly half of all marriages in the US end in divorce, an estimated 30% of fathers in the US physically leave home within the few years of their first child's birth.[1]

While it's clear that the phenomenon is rampant, it appears that there are no *actual statistics* revealing the exact numbers of fathers who physically leave home within the three years of their first child's birth. And of course a much larger percentage leave emotionally, which can often be detected by careful observation.

According to the 2009 U.S. Census Bureau, over 24 million children live apart from their biological fathers. This is 1 out of every 3 (33%) children in America. In 1960, only 11% of children lived in father-absent homes.

In 1960, only 11% of children in the U.S. lived apart from their fathers. By 2010, that share had risen to 27%. According to a new Pew Research Center analysis of the National Survey of Family Growth (NSFG), more than one-in-four fathers with children 18 or younger now live apart from their children—with 11% living apart from some of their children and 16% living apart from all of their children.[1]

Almost all fathers who live with their children take an active role in their day-to-day lives through activities such as sharing meals, helping with homework, and playing. One-in-five absent fathers say they visit their children more than once a week, but an even greater share (27%) say they have not seen their children at all in the past year.[4]

## The Costs to Society

Most major indicators of children's wellbeing show that children are in trouble. Despite unprecedented medical and technological advances, children of all races, backgrounds, and socioeconomic classes are evidencing escalating rates of learning and behavioral disorders, drug abuse, chronic illness, depression, violence, and suicide. For example, there has been a massive increase in child suicide rates in the past generation to where suicide is now the third most common cause of death for youth. The US National Institute of Mental Health estimates that for every suicide there are ten attempts.

Depression may be one of the largest public health problems in our culture. Addiction, violence, and a host of other mental and physical problems begin as symptoms of failed parent-child bonding (compounded by other stressful factors of modern life—from overexposure to media to environmental toxins and a lack of connection to the natural world). The children of these circumstances grow up to join the large numbers of couples separating after the birth of a child.

Nearly 80% of the children who end up in our juvenile justice system live in homes without a father. The majority of our adult prison population grew up without fathers. The societal costs of insecure bonding include allocations of tax monies to law enforcement, incarceration, and an overburdened medical and welfare system. A high percentage of those using these services are from single-parent families.

Yet only about a third of American children will reach age 18 living with both biological parents.[5]

The Federal Government spent at least $99.8 billion providing assistance to father-absent homes in 2006. This is a conservative estimate; it does not include federal benefit programs for communities, indirect costs to poor outcomes of children from father-absent homes, and long-term costs in reduced tax income from low-earning single parent families.

## A Problem *About* the Problem

> *I was stirred and troubled by [your article "Why Men Leave"]. I realized, looking into my own soul... that my wound is much greater than I usually realize! It's a powerful service that you do in opening it up, even though it's hard to look at. Your article also explains the interrelationships between all those "leaving" behaviors, which at first blush seem like very different problems.* —Danson

A huge component of the problem of men leaving their families—physically *or* emotionally—is that *it isn't even recognized* as an epidemic. Nor is an identifiable cause considered. Instead, this epidemic of men leaving is accepted as "the way it is," a belief that is compounded by the fact that most men don't talk about their feelings. Indeed, many men are not even *aware* of their feelings.

> *It was nearing midnight in April of 1972. Our two-month-old daughter is sleeping in the nursery in the cherry cradle I built for her from plans out of the* Ladies' Home Journal *(if only I had known what I know now about the importance of children sleeping with their parents, we would not have "abandoned" her to sleep alone). In the next room her mother and I are in bed having an argument—she shouting angrily at me and me saying nothing, looking very martyred and wondering what the neighbors will think.*
>
> *The subject of her anger is my lack of emotional expression. I feel hurt inside, but am speechless when I try to express any of my feelings. I experience a growing pressure inside and sense of unreality, and suddenly sit up, yell*

*something, ram my head into the plasterboard at the head of the bed (I happen to be a Capricorn—the Goat—but the symbolism eluded me at that point).*

*Stunned, I look at the smashed hole conforming to the size of my head, mentally expressing gratitude that I missed the studs in the wall—or it would have really hurt—and collapse, sobbing. She put on her overcoat and ran to the next-door neighbor, a former campus minister, who returns alone to our apartment. Through my tears I told him I don't know what's come over me since our daughter's birth. My depressions are getting worse and my wife is spending so much time nurturing my daughter that she hardly has any time for me. David suggested I talk with our mutual friend, Ann, who knows several pastoral counselors.*

*This event marked a major milestone in my personal and professional development, as I began one-to-one counseling the next week and discovered a wholly different world of feelings and my own responsibility to deal with them effectively. The implications for my own health and for others were profound, yet nowhere in my previous medical training had I learned to be open to the concept of self-expression and self-responsibility.* —Jack (from *Wellness Workbook*)

Another "problem about the problem" is that even if and when men are able to talk about their feelings of rejection, loss and abandonment, they will, in all likelihood, just be told to "get used to it," "grow up," "be a man."

Unfortunately, this is neither an informed, compassionate, nor helpful interpretation of what is happening.

### Key Points
- While modern birth—from the long list of medical interventions, drugs, and forceps to the isolation and separation of the infant and mother, to circumcision of males—is considered "normal," these practices, named "normative abuse" by Karen Walant, can severely compromise the infant-parent bond.
- Today, a substantial body of evidence highlights the importance of early relationships in profoundly shaping the central nervous system. Infants' and children's health and wellbeing is dependent on their intrauterine experience and on the quality of the relationship with their primary caregivers during the first three to five years—the period when a child's brain develops most rapidly.
- Biologically, the male is the more fragile gender of our species. Boys receive far less nurturing than girls and less permission to express their feelings and emotions. Thus the pattern is set for the massive repression of males' needs and feelings that is common to most men

- raised in English-speaking cultures, and is in turn is a primary factor in Male Postpartum Abandonment Syndrome (MPAS) and the Dynamic of Disappearing Dads (DDD).
- Most of these poorly bonded and emotionally repressed boys grow into men who unconsciously seek someone to provide them with the nurturing they were denied as infants and children. When they find her and marry her, they may manage pretty well until a child comes along. Then, when the new mother's primary focus becomes diverted to the baby, many men experience this withdrawal of their partner's attention as abandonment or rejection.
- DDD can take many forms and may occur on a variety of levels: While a father may pretend all is well, he may leave emotionally. When or if men's defense mechanisms fail to adequately suppress their pain, many believe that their very sanity or survival is dependent on departing from the scene. A third level of leaving is through suicide or fatal "accidents," or by signing up for a likely death in a war.
- Women have a strong biological advantage supporting them in forging a secure bond with their offspring. Over the ensuing weeks and months, if they are able to successfully resist the cultural parenting practices that encourage the separation of mother and infant and are able to forge a secure bond, mothers can heal much of their own unbondedness.
- A huge component of the problem of men leaving their families—physically or emotionally—is that it isn't even recognized as an epidemic. Nor is an identifiable cause considered. Instead, this epidemic of men leaving is accepted as "the way it is," a belief that is compounded by the fact that most men don't talk about their feelings. Indeed many men are not even *aware* of their feelings. Even if and when men are able to talk about their feelings of rejection, loss and abandonment, they will, in all likelihood, just be told to "get used to it," "grow up," or "be a man." Unfortunately, this is neither an informed, compassionate, nor helpful response.
- Statistics illustrating the severity of DDD and its cost to society are revealed in this chapter.

# 3: EARLY BONDING, MPAS, AND DDD: MAKING THE CONNECTIONS

> *[A] secure psycho-physiological body-connection between mother and infant is the first foundation of love upon which all other love relationships are built. The human primate is the only mammal that separates the newborn and mother, and denies the newborn succor from the mother's breast. This separation violates the most universal of all evolutionary principles.*
> —James W. Prescott, PhD, Former Health Scientist Administrator, National Institute of Child Health and Human Development, NIH

> *To interfere with or destroy this intimacy is to risk interrupting a vital psychological process that may reduce the woman's confidence in herself as a mother and interfere with the flow of communication between her and her baby.*
> —Marshall Klaus et al, *Mothering the Mother*

Throughout our life, our wellbeing is dependent on the connections we establish. The first bond we form is *in utero*, with the mother. Mother and newborn are biologically programmed to connect physically and emotionally with each other. Babies have amazing abilities right after birth to interest their mothers in taking care of them.* Little wonder given that our species' wellbeing is dependent on this bond.† Joseph Chilton Pearce, in *Magical Child*, claims that the quality of the bond secured between mother and infant lays the foundation for all subsequent bonds—initially with our father, then with the family, the larger community, nature, and the earth.

## Our Earliest Beginnings—the Development of Trust

English psychoanalyst Sir John Bowlby formulated attachment theory in the 1940s. At the time, conventional wisdom held that "coddling" created clingy, overdependent children who grew into immature adults. Bowlby's theory was strongly resisted by adherents to the prevailing psychoanalytic theories.

Aided by his collaboration with American researcher, Mary Ainsworth, PhD, in the 1950s and 60s, his attachment theory eventually became recognized. It began to revolutionize the treatment of children with severe attachment disorders, and later influenced childcare practices. Today it is widely acknowledged that children have an absolute requirement for ongoing

---

\* Postnatal maternal depression may well be in large part the result of their nocturnal separation at a time when the two are hormonally programmed to be together.

† Sarah Blaffer Hrdy, in *Mothers and Others,* found that while children can develop satisfactorily provided they have a secure attachment with at least one intimate caregiver, the optimum for infants and young children is three secure attachments.

physical and emotional closeness that we ignore only at great cost. In the late 70s, Bowlby's work spawned a second revolution—the attachment parenting movement.

Attachment parenting usually begins with pregnancy. Even while in the womb, babies are sensitive, conscious beings.[6] Their experiences during the transition from womb to world, and in the early days and months, have a powerful and lasting impact on their developing brain and personality.

Babies instinctively employ many attachment-promoting behaviors—from coos and smiles, to clinging movements, eye contact, and other body signals—to draw a parent or caregiver to them. All babies feel most secure when in close proximity to a caring person. Being left alone, most especially to cry alone, is a terrifying experience for all babies. The attachment, or bond, between baby and caregiver grows as the caregiver nurtures on cue to the infant's signals—with breastmilk, singing or cooing, holding and rocking.

When an infant learns that a particular caregiver provides her with a safe, predictable, and comfortable world, trust—one of the primary developmental tasks of the pre-verbal years--emerges. This secure attachment then provides a solid base from which the child feels free to explore the larger social and physical world. Lack of positive caregiving in the early years leads to *later* social consequences, since the type of attachment (secure or insecure) that forms between child and caregiver is the model for all *later* relationships.

A child's early interactions with caregivers create his expectations of how he will be treated throughout his life, coloring his perceptions and interpretations of all events. Babies who receive responsive and consistent care develop the sense that their world is essentially satisfying and the people around them are responsive and caring. Those who learn they cannot trust anyone may feel that adults are replaceable, love is uncertain, and human attachment is a dangerous proposition. They will likely become adults that experience the world as an unpredictable, unreliable, and untrustworthy place, and be left with trauma that is difficult to heal. Any therapeutic experience is initially based on trust—and poorly bonded children have not learned to trust.

> *My father's authoritarianism and physical violence (AKA "discipline") is definitely the catalyst for my lack of true connection with him. My mother was rather emotionally distant.... [This and] my being raised by a sitter from early infancy (starting around six weeks), all contribute to my lack of connection to myself as well as my perception of lowered self-worth.*
>
> *[So] I lack the willingness to stay connected to friends and family. As a result, I really don't have any close friends. Other than my blood relatives, there's no one in my life who's known me before 1994 (I was born in '65).* —Tom

### Basic Premises of Meeting Children's Needs*

- The greatest emotional need of every child is to bond securely to at least one other human being.
- Our most important task as parents is to secure and maintain a healthy, strong parent-child bond.
- Maintaining connection is the key to loving, effective parenting and to our children's optimal human development.
- Parents are always doing the best they can with the information, resources, and support they have at any given moment.
- The level of cooperation parents get from their children is usually equal to the level of connection children feel with their parents.
- What children want and need most is to be with us and to do what we do.
- Children want to be with us to maintain connection.
- Children want to do what we do because we are their models.
- All behaviors are need-driven. We do what we do to get our needs met.
- When children's needs are met and nothing is hurting them, they are delightful. When children are not being delightful, their behavior is telling us about something they need.
- At times, children are not able to identify or communicate with words what they need or what hurts. Children communicate by acting out their needs and hurts through their behavior (thus acting-out behavior).
- We can't teach children to behave better by making them feel worse. Children behave better when they feel better.
- We can learn to decode children's behavior and respond to their needs, instead of react to their behaviors.
- It takes the same amount of time and attention to meet children's needs as it does to deal with the behaviors caused by their unmet needs.
- The only conflict that exists between parents and children is between the strategies that we use to get our needs met.
- Whether we are unconsciously raising our children the way our parents raised us or we are consciously trying to do the exact opposite, the way we parent is influenced by the way we were parented.
- Parenting never used to be and was never intended by nature to be a one or two person job. Families work best when everyone's needs are met. It does take a village to meet the needs of children and parents.

> - We will never become perfect parents who raise perfect children, but we can learn how to make it better for our children, for us, and for our world.
> - It is never too late to create a stronger connection with our children.
>
> \* From *Connection Parenting*, Pam Leo, reprinted with permission.

## Who, Me? Disconnected?

While most men—and women—living in the "developed" nations today never securely bonded with their mothers, most of them *are not even aware that they have not bonded*, and are even less aware of the significance of its absence. And as a culture, we *don't even notice* how disconnected we are from each other.

> *Some years ago, I gave a guest lecture, "Why Men Leave," at a colleague's holistic studies course at San Francisco State University. In the months after my lecture, she observed an interesting phenomenon among the non-American-born students, mainly Asian and Hispanic, who we surmised had experienced a more normal level of connection with their mothers and families. In class papers, they would mention they had always noticed something odd about the American-born students, but they didn't realize what it was until my explanation of primal disconnection.* —Jack

This points out a deep dark shadow in our culture that is too painful for most to acknowledge, let alone explore—the pain of disconnection. It is a disconnection so deep and subtle that few people have any clue about what they're missing.

This becomes obvious when we look at those cultures where the bond is still intact, such as Bali, indigenous cultures of Latin America, and some rural Mediterranean cultures that have not been as influenced by Western ways. Yes, we may notice how much more some Italian or Latino families laugh, play, and touch each other, but few of us appreciate how that observation, when contrasted with the northern European/American cultures' relative reserve, reveals the vastly different degree of bonding and connection that occurs between these different cultures. And the irony of it is that most of those cultures that retain these elements of connectedness yearn to have some of the affluent advantages of a highly technological affluent society. Our culture, too, idealizes the very isolation that is destroying us: the bigger the house, the more status it holds—and the more closed off and distanced the residents are from each other.

> *I had a strong emotional response to your article, which pinpoints a major dilemma for people in our culture. It's hard to fix something that seems so broken. As I write I can still feel myself trying to find solutions, to smooth over the raw and frightening truth of how hard and deeply hurt we are by loss of*

> bonding and contact. How very difficult it is to change that hard wiring, and how profoundly we are all affected by the type of loss you describe.... —Debby

Today most of us take our disconnected, unbonded condition for granted. We may even be proud of it—calling it rugged individualism, the backbone of the American way of life. The experience of connection has deteriorated so gradually over several generations that we're like the proverbial frog in the pot that is slowly brought to a boil—oblivious to the rising temperature until it is too late.

> My husband and I are one month away from divorce. I gave birth at home and breastfed my children.... Every time I gave birth, my husband happened to lose his job—for over a year. He was born by C-section, following a stillbirth. He was circumcised, bottle-fed, left to cry-it-out, and he has some seriously repressed deep anger issues that are related to why he keeps creating unemployment crises for himself and his family. When he was in college he put a saying above his desk that read, "Make every word a knife." I am completely aware of the deeper issues at play. I've read about 150 books on birth and parenting, starting when I was 17 and first awakened into the understanding that my parents were doing it wrong (like most others their age).
>
> My husband thinks there's nothing wrong with him—that I'm the one with all the healing to do. I've worked for nearly five years on my own healing (following the homebirth that transformed me from the inside out and enabled me to experience a total awareness of my deep connection to the divine and everything else that exists). But he refuses. Perhaps the truth is just too painful for him to face. —Sandy

Can it be that our society so highly values autonomy and independence because the vast majority of us never received communal-quality nurturing when we were raised, and so never learned, nor even experienced, the value of deep and authentic connection? It's convenient, given our cultural setup, to view independence as a social value; but as Suzanne Arms, author of *Immaculate Deception II* posits, that may only be because we're actually afraid to be close to each other, our neighbors, the world at large, and by extension the whole universe.

> Statistics reveal that we are creating so many violent children so rapidly that we will never be able to treat or rehabilitate them all. And the alarming statistics of infanticide, delinquency, and criminality are just the tip of the iceberg.
>
> Underneath the water are the invisible scars on each child's soul, subtle changes that will, depending on the presence or absence of certain protective factors, lead to a life assailed by anxiety, depression, failed relationships, addiction, or suicide. To solve the problems passed from one generation to the next, we must revolutionize the culture of childrearing itself.
>
> —Thomas Verny, MD, *Pre-parenting: Nurturing Your Baby from Conception*

As becomes evident in the following chapters, this revolution in childrearing requires not only understanding the attachment needs of infants and children, it also requires:
- parents being supported in meeting children's attachment needs,
- understanding the application of attachment theory to parenting styles,
- understanding of the application of attachment theory to adult love.

*We will never become perfect parents who raise perfect children, but we can learn how to make it better for our children, for us, and for our world.*
—Pam Leo, *Connection Parenting*

## Key Points

- Joseph Chilton Pearce, in *Magical Child*, believes that the quality of the bond secured between mother and infant lays the foundation for all subsequent bonds—initially with our father, then with the family, the community, nature, and the earth. Sarah Blaffer Hrdy, in *Mothers and Others*, found that while children can develop satisfactorily, provided they have a secure attachment with at least one intimate caregiver, the optimum for infants and young children is at least three secure attachments.
- Attachment theory was formulated by English psychoanalyst Sir John Bowlby in the 1940s. At the time, conventional wisdom held that "coddling" created clingy, over dependent children who grew into immature adults. Bowlby's theory was strongly resisted by adherents to the prevailing psychoanalytic theories.
- In collaboration with American researcher, Mary Ainsworth, PhD, in the 1950s and 60s, Bowlby's attachment theory gained recognition.
- In the late 70s, Bowlby's work spawned a second revolution—the attachment parenting movement. Today, it is recognized that children have an absolute need for ongoing physical and emotional connection that we ignore only at great cost.
- Today most of us take our disconnected, unbonded condition for granted. We may even be proud of it—calling it rugged individualism, the backbone of the American way of life.
- The cost to society of disconnection is revealed by Thomas Verny, MD: "Statistics reveal that we are creating so many violent children so rapidly that we will never be able to treat or rehabilitate them all. And the alarming statistics of infanticide, delinquency, and criminality are just the tip of the iceberg. Underneath the water are the invisible scars on each child's soul, subtle changes that will, depending on the presence or absence of certain protective factors, lead to a life assailed by anxiety, depression, failed relationships, addiction, or suicide. To solve problems passed from one generation to the next, we must revolutionize the culture of child rearing itself."
- This revolution in child rearing requires not only understanding the attachment needs of infants and children, but also parents being supported in meeting children's and parents' attachment needs, understanding the application of attachment theory to parenting styles, understanding the application of attachment theory to adult love.
- "The Basic Premises of Meeting Children's Needs" concludes the chapter.

# 4: Early Childhood Experiences, Parenting Styles, and Adult Love

## How Attachment Patterns Shape Parenting Styles

It was some years after the naming of MPAS that I discovered *Becoming Attached: First Relationships and How They Shape Our Capacity to Love* by Robert Karen, PhD. I was surprised, given the amount of literature I had reviewed, that none had made mention of this important contribution. Here, I learned that John Bowlby himself had spoken about the feelings of resentment, even hatred, that may arise in a parent after the birth of a child, and are usually *associated with feelings residual from their own infancy and childhood.* He saw that these negative feelings existed to some degree in almost every parent, and were not necessarily harmful.

> [T]he important question from Bowlby's point of view, was, "Could I tolerate such feelings in myself or were they so threatening that I would have to banish them? For it's in the banishment that the feelings would become treacherous."
> —Robert Karen, PhD, *Becoming Attached*

Bowlby emphasized the importance of not simply *blaming* the mother or father for being overanxious or rejecting, but rather looking to the unconscious origin of their attitudes and behavior—in other words, their own attachment history.

While as early as the 1950s Bowlby spoke of the need to address not only the attachment needs of infants and children, but also the psychological forces driving the parents that keep them from being able to connect—securely attach—to their children, it was decades before attachment research began to direct attention to adults' attachment needs and histories.

Parents often pore over books, watch television programs on parenting, and endlessly consult with others to learn how their baby is likely to behave at each new stage of development, what she is to eat, even what her emotional needs are, etc.

> [A]s useful as this is, none of it will help potentially anxious parents do the one thing they most need to do—gain a deeper understanding of their own motivations, conflicts, and inner needs. In the self-help literature directed at parents, virtually no attention is paid to the emotional upheavals that the parent is likely to face—the disturbing return of long-banished feelings, the sense of being driven to behave in ways that one would rather not think about, the haunting sensation of being inhabited by the ghost of one's own mother or father as one tries to relate to the child....

> *If there is one thing, then, that the anxious parent in each of us is truly guilty of—and that our culture colludes in—it is not necessarily a lack of love, but a failure to look at and to know ourselves.*
> —Robert Karen, PhD, *Becoming Attached*

This research generated a whole new arena for psychotherapists centering on how the attachment history of parents influenced their parenting; and the discovery that the key was not as much their early attachment experiences as it was how, as adults, they reflected on these experiences.

> *I struggled with very different feelings after the birth of my second child than my first, and I was also a second child. I do believe I was reliving feelings related to my own unmet infancy needs, and I was able to acknowledge them as such.* —Barbara

## Our Adult Need for Emotional Connection

Bowlby believed that the tie to the parent gradually weakens as a child gets older and that the dependence on a secure base is slowly shifted to other figures, eventually resting fully on the adult's mate. Secure attachment in adulthood affects not only the quality of a person's parenting, but also the quality of their entire emotional life.

> *Evidence is accumulating that human beings of all ages are happiest and able to deploy their talents to best advantage when they are confident that, standing behind them, there are one or more trusted persons who will come to their aid should difficulties arise.* —John Bowlby, 1970 lecture: "Self Reliance and Some Conditions That Promote It"

Bowlby died in 1990. The third revolution sparked by his work—the application of attachment theory to adult love, came after his death. Bowlby himself had maintained that adults have the same need as children for attachment, and that this need is the force that shapes adult relationships. Not surprisingly, given how radically his assertion diverged from conventional social and psychological beliefs that adult maturity equated with independence and self-sufficiency, his ideas were again trivialized, ridiculed, and dismissed by the mainstream psychiatric community. While psychologists used words such as undifferentiated, codependent, and symbiotic to describe people who don't live up to these ideals, Bowlby talked about "effective dependency" and how being able, from "cradle to grave," to turn to others for emotional support is a sign and source of strength.

> *Bowlby argued that self-reliance and healthy, or mutual, dependence are inexorably linked. A good balance of the two allows us to both give spontaneously to others and ask for help from appropriate others and to do so*

> *directly, without hints or manipulations. If a person has a difficult time with dependency, if he is either unable to ask for support or does it in demanding and aggressive ways, Bowlby saw this as suggestive of his lack of confidence that true support would ever be forthcoming. Typically they were dissatisfied with what they received and in the end, not adept at giving themselves.*
> —Robert Karen, PhD, *Becoming Attached*

Research documenting adult attachment needs expanded significantly after social psychologists, Cindy Shaver and Phillip Hazen, began asking couples about their love relationships to see if they exhibited similar responses and patterns to those of mothers and children.[7] And as Bowlby had predicted, adults spoke of their:

- need for emotional closeness with their lover,
- desire for assurance that their lover would respond when they were upset,
- distress when they felt separate and distant from their loved one,
- feelings of confidence about exploring the world when they knew that their lover "had their back."

When couples felt secure with their lover they could reach out and connect easily; when insecure they either became anxious, angry and controlling, or avoided contact and stayed distant. This is just what Bowlby and Ainsworth had found with mothers and children.

Shaver and Hazen's work set off an avalanche of research, and today hundreds of studies validate Bowlby's predictions about adult attachment. The overall conclusion is that a sense of secure connection between romantic partners is key in a positive loving relationship, and a huge source of strength for the individuals in those relationships. Of course our ability to create and sustain these relationships is, in good part, dependent on our level of attachment, or the repair work we have done.

> *Implicit in all this is that one builds on the other, that having an internalized secure base, a strong sense of having been loved and of having confidence in one's essential ability to love and be loved, enables one to both enjoy solitude and to confidently seek nourishment when one needs it.*
> —Robert Karen, PhD, *Becoming Attached*

We did not know of Bowlby's early insights or of these subsequent studies at the time we formulated the Dynamic of Disappearing Dads. Somehow, despite their relevance and significance to couples embarking on parenthood, the studies have not found their way into the parenting guidebooks. Yet these very themes are so evident in MPAS.

> *The drive to emotionally attach—to find someone to whom we can turn and say "Hold me tight"—is wired into our genes and our bodies and doesn't disappear when we grow beyond childhood.... We need emotional attachments with a few irreplaceable others to be physically and mentally healthy—to survive.*
> —Sue Johnson, PhD, *Hold Me Tight*

These findings both validate and help us to better understand the importance of a healthy couple relationship prior to conceiving; of nurturing the adult couple relationship throughout the transition period; recognizing the new father's need for reassurance and connection, most especially when a baby arrives and the father is likely to perceive his primary love relationship as threatened. It is neither fair nor helpful to minimize a father's needs, nor shame him as a "needy, greedy child."

Recent discoveries in neurobiology and neuropsychology dispel any illusions we may harbor as to our being doomed to repeat the sins or suffering of our fathers—or mothers. Fostering safe, loving connections with others, and integrating these experiences, literally "rewires" our brains, and with this we begin to experience a new world. And research has shown again and again that a key quality of adults who have an inner sense of trust and security with others is not that they have always had happy relationships with caregivers in the past, but that they have been able to reflect on those experiences and make sense of them. Forming a new family, we have a rich opportunity to grow and to heal—together.

**Key Points**
- As early as the 1950s, John Bowlby spoke about the feelings of resentment a parent may experience after the birth of a child.
- Bowlby emphasized the importance of not simply *blaming* the parent for being overanxious or rejecting, but rather looking to the unconscious origin of their attitudes and behavior—their own attachment history. What was crucial was not so much their early attachment experiences but how, as adults, they reflected on these experiences.
- The third revolution sparked by Bowlby's work—the application of attachment theory to adult love, came after his death. He believed adults have the same need as children for attachment and that this need is the force shaping adult relationships.
- Contrary to conventional social and psychological beliefs, Bowlby argued that self-reliance and healthy dependence are inexorably linked. Secure attachment in adulthood to one's mate, affects not only the quality of a person's parenting, but of their entire emotional life.
- Today hundreds of studies validate Bowlby's predictions about adult attachment: a secure connection between romantic partners is key in a positive loving relationship, and a huge source of strength for the individuals in those relationships.
- These findings emphasize the importance of 1) a healthy couple relationship prior to conceiving; 2) nurturing the adult couple relationship throughout the transition period; 3) recognizing the new father's need for reassurance and connection when a baby arrives, and 4) the father being likely to perceive his primary love relationship as threatened.
- Neurobiology reveals that safe, loving connections with others literally "rewires" our brains. Forming a new family, we have a rich opportunity to grow and to heal—together.

# 5: Discovering Dad—And Staying Connected

A couple of decades ago, the very little literature that connected fathers with children, was about father *absence*. It was as if a father's presence did not factor into a child's health or happiness. Even in scientific studies of children's development, father's presence rarely figured into the equation. While these studies showed us that father absence is a deeply painful reality that profoundly impacts the wellbeing of the 20 million children within the US growing up without a father, they told nothing of the impact of father *presence*.

Today, father is factoring more prominently in research studies, and the findings are fascinating— children yearn deeply, and from a very young age, for their dads. They are born with a drive to find and connect to the father; and father's instincts—when allowed—prompt them to respond appropriately. While the ways in which the father relates to and cares for his offspring differs in style to that of the mother, it seems father and mother have equal, if slightly different, parenting abilities. There is no evidence that, given equal experience and support, parents of one gender necessarily excel as caregivers over the other. Mother and father contribute in *unique* and *complementary* ways to their children's wellbeing, and children thrive when they experience these different styles throughout all developmental stages.

Paralleling these findings is the evidence that men want to be involved with their children in ways their own dads weren't. *And*, parents' sharing in the physical and emotional care of their infants and children, as well as in the responsibilities and decision-making, is now a major expectation among newly marrying couples. In the US, in 1981, when researchers asked newly marrying couples to rank-order values they hoped to instill into their marriages, "sharing responsibilities, decision-making, and physical and emotional care of infants and young children" was rated 11 out of 15. In 1997, when the same question was asked, it was prioritized second.[8]

Parenting is easier for partners. Married parents report more global happiness and less depression than single parents, in contrast to a recent spate of films, books and magazine stories about the joys of conceiving and rearing a baby alone. Cohabiting couples fall in between. Married parents experience more meaning in their lives than their childless peers, and a substantial minority of married parents are "very happy" in their marriages. A substantial minority of husbands (35 percent) and wives (37 percent) do not experience parenthood as an obstacle to marital happiness.[9] Married men and women are markedly more likely to report that they find life meaningful compared with their childless peers. The fact that the transition to parenthood places unique strains on couples' relationships is rarely talked about or addressed.[10] Some studies have shown mothers' satisfaction declining most sharply during the first year[11] and fathers' satisfaction in the second year[12] while others have reported more congruent declines.[13]

These findings give further weight to the tremendous importance of seeking to understand how children and mothers and fathers can stay connected, most especially in the time it matters most to the healthy development of their children. As they get older, the value of this connection extends beyond their immediate family to their community and our world.

## Why It's Harder for Today's Parents

While research confirms the profound formative impact of *in utero* and early childhood experiences in shaping the adults we will become, conception through age three is the time of greatest stress and isolation for most parents and children. The strong parent-child bond developed naturally when children were born at home, breastfed, and spent their early years within the network of support offered through extended family or community.

The nuclear family is a relatively recent aberration of the extended family, and reached the height of its idealization in the 1950s, with television shows like *Father Knows Best*, and *Leave it to Beaver*. The 1970s saw the beginnings of what was steadily becoming the *nuclear family disaster*, further devolving for many into the *single parent trap*, as divorce became more acceptable and the numbers of couples separating. Interestingly, these adults would be the first full generation to have endured medical model birthing and early mother-infant separation practices. The isolation and alienation that emerged concurrent with the dissolution of the village structure and extended families, has had immense consequences for all of us.*

> *We are building a culture of separateness that is at odds with our biology.*
> —Sue Johnson, PhD, *Hold Me Tight*

Within the nuclear family, not only are parents supposed to be the sole caregivers for their children, they are supposed to be "everything" to each other. Working longer hours, commuting more miles, many couples today live in a "community of two," and seek from their partners the emotional connection and sense of belonging that earlier generations got from the immediate presence of an extended family and community. Compounding this is not only the promise of romantic love propagated by the media, but a culture that promotes competition and control at the expense of community and connection.

---

* The nuclear family itself was largely unknown until shortly after the War Between the States, which created a mass migration of rural people into the relative anonymity of the cities, leaving behind most of their family and village networks. The nuclear family was seen as the norm by the 1950s after another mass migration to cities during and following WWII.

Tensions inevitably run high and both can too readily perceive the other as "the enemy" rather than recognize that the other, like themselves, has been flung into a venture for which they are ill prepared and unsupported. This is even more true for those who find themselves raising a child alone. Single parents are expected to be "everything" to their child: the child in turn, and to the detriment to both, is often "everything" to the parent.

> ### Children Living in Single Parent Families
> Recent demographic data show that an increasing proportion of children are living in single-parent families and at an increasingly young age.
>
> Thirty years ago, almost 25 percent of children were either born to a single mother or had experienced their parents' separation before the age of twenty. Half of the parents of this group had separated after the child reached the age of ten.
>
> Children who were born ten years later (1971–1973) experienced their parents' separation at an even younger age. By age fifteen, 25 percent of these children had already experienced life in a single-parent family. Three times out of four, the child had experienced this before the age of ten.
>
> Children who were born after 1983 experienced their parents' separation even earlier. By age ten, one child out of four born in 1983-1984 had experienced life in a single-parent family and nearly 23 percent of children in the younger cohorts (those born in 1987–1988) experienced the same by the age of six.[14]

Essentially, whether as a couple or single parent, parents are expected, and are attempting to do, what it takes a village to do—in the absence of the village.

When Siena was 16 months old, our new friends from Mendocino—Maggie, Bruce, and Julian (who was a couple of weeks older then Siena), joined us on our land. Similarly committed to "continuum parenting," together we explored the ups and downs of the theory and practice. I didn't appreciate at the time just how important a lifeline our little "community" was.

Almost every afternoon Maggie and I would put the children—now out of arms and gleefully toddling about—into the jogging strollers and go for a long walk. This time provided an invaluable venue for release as we shared our struggles—and revelations—in our efforts to "continuum parent." While with the men we shared endless, very wonderful discussions about the challenges of implementing these practices in the absence of the "village," Maggie and I on our walks talked of the "absence" of our men; well-intended though we knew they were. We shared our resentment and disappointment of their neediness for us and their inability to "be there" for us and our babies in the way we wanted and needed. Today we recognize that, had we been more able to see and appreciate what our partners were facing—the efforts they were making—it could have been very different. Oh, if we had had the fuller picture that we have now.

Prior to becoming a mother, Maggie had thrived in her role as a community worker. Now, while wanting to give herself heart and soul to mothering, she struggled in the absence of an outlet for these energies. Bruce left early each morning for the long trek to work in Mendocino. Unlike Maggie, I had a partner at home all day, a mother to support us, and an outlet through which I could feel "productive" and creative—the book I was writing. I had it made. And, it still seemed so hard, left me so sad. So much of my attention was focused on the absence of my mate who I so wanted to *be with* me—even when I didn't act like it.

## And On Top of This!

- There is no longer a single, universally accepted set of roles for mother and father. Not too long ago, couples embarking on parenthood knew what to expect of each other: he would be the breadwinner, she the nurturer and homemaker. Today's expectations are that men and women share responsibilities.
- And once the baby arrives, couples find themselves fighting about issues earlier generations of parents never considered… who diapers the baby, who does the dishes and laundry, who goes to work and who stays at home… not to mention, who gets mom's attention, baby or dad?
- Families face mounting economic pressures to cover the mortgage, car payments, or a new baby pack. Struggles over how to pay the next bill are as much a part of the transition as 3 AM feedings.
- Society no longer honors the altruistic attitudes that are the essence of everyday parenting. Parents get little public acknowledgement, support, or gratitude for their selflessness and devotion. It is difficult to sacrifice—or to value—yourself as a parent when society's overriding goals focus on devotion to self, not others.

Not only have we lost the needed context for successfully meeting a child's needs, we also have a world of unprecedented pace and complexity, media that too frequently trivialize and undermine parenting, economic disincentives for parents, and parent/child social, economic and political practices and policies that work against the development of a secure parent-child bond.

Atop this mountain of stresses on parents, most parents are themselves products of insecure experiences, and that insecure attachment is passed on from one generation to the next unless intervention occurs. Insecure attachment doesn't only make for "needy" dads, it also makes for men who have difficulty with forming intimate relationships.

> *Even though we are programmed by millions of years of evolution to relentlessly seek out belonging and intimate connections, we persist in defining healthy people as those who do not need others. This is especially dangerous at a time when our sense of community is daily being eroded by an endless preoccupation with getting more done in less time and filling our lives with more and more goods.* —Sue Johnson, PhD, *Hold Me Tight*

Little wonder divorce rates continue to escalate and children are exhibiting an unprecedented range of behavioral and emotional problems. All is far from well in the family and subsequently in our communities.

> *While in time we will see a new kind of family—one in which responsibilities are allocated according to talent, desire, and need rather than black and white notions of masculinity or femininity—today, new parents are entering parenthood not knowing what to expect of each other.* —Carolyn Pape Cowan, PhD, and Philip Cowan, PhD, *When Partners Become Parents*

As we will see in later chapters, regardless of the shape these families may take, an important factor in their wellbeing will be aspects of the much romanticized "village," where parenting is seen not simply as the responsibility of the parents, but as a wider community responsibility.

> *In our culture of privacy, social isolation, and dislocation, the concept of group or "tribal" childcare is difficult to embrace. Parenting becomes a burden, rather than a joy, when we are bereft of community. Responsibility for children's wellbeing is as societal and communal as it is parental.*
> —Robin Grille, *Parenting for a Peaceful World*

## Key Points

- While studies have long shown the disturbing impact of father *absence*, it's only more recently that studies have focused on the impact of father *presence*, and the findings are fascinating.
- Children are born with a drive to connect to their fathers, and very young children yearn deeply for them.
- There is no evidence that given equal experience and support, parents of either gender necessarily excel as caregivers.
- Mother and father contribute in unique and complimentary ways to their children's wellbeing.
- Men today want to be involved with their children in ways their own dads weren't.
- Sharing the physical and emotional care of their infants and young children is now a major expectation among newly marrying couples.
- The fact that the transition to parenthood places strong and unique strains on a couple's relationship is rarely addressed, yet can be critical in their growing together—or apart.
- While research confirms the profound formative impact of the early years of life, conception through age three is the time of greatest stress and isolation for most parents.
- Within the nuclear family, parents are sole caregivers for their child and supposed to be "everything" to each other. Tensions inevitably run high.
- There is no longer a single, universally accepted set of roles for mother and father; families face mounting economic pressures; society no longer honors the altruistic attitudes that are the essence of everyday parenting; and social, economic and political policies work do not support the parent-child connection.
- Atop these stresses, most parents are themselves products of insecure experiences, and in the absence of intervention, this insecure attachment is passed from one generation to the next, so compounding their difficulties in forming healthy intimate relationships.
- In time we may see the emergence of a new kind of family, one where responsibilities are allocated according to talent, desire, and need—but regardless of the shape these new families may take, a crucial factor in their sustainability will be the recognition that responsibility for children is social and communal as well as parental.

# 6: Ending the Dynamic of Disappearing Dads

*The emotional state of caregivers is the real cradle in which the new baby is held.*
—John Gottman, PhD

Studies indicate that a decline in relationship satisfaction post-birth is not inevitable: 18–33% of couples report an improved relationship[15] and this can even be the case where couples experience enormous challenges, such as giving birth to a child with disabilities.[16] Couples who feel they have "pulled through" a difficult time together may ultimately experience enhanced relationship satisfaction.[17] The salience of "teamwork" to a couple's relationship satisfaction may be increasing: 70% of new mothers currently turn to their partner for emotional support, compared with only 47% in the 1960s.[18]

At this point in time, most couples are unaware that they are likely to find their relationship becoming very much more difficult once the baby arrives. Alerting couples to the challenges they may face, as well as to the fact that there is much they can do prior to the birth to minimize the stresses, can reduce the risk of future unhappiness and separation.

Steps toward ending the Dynamic of Disappearing Dads include:

1. **Becoming aware of the forces underlying DDD.** Before an identifiable cause of DDD can even be acknowledged, we have to recognize that men leaving—physically or emotionally—cannot simply be accepted as "the way it is." A barrier to dispelling this rampant belief is that most men won't talk about their feelings—a core ingredient in DDD.

2. **Realizing that is not just a personal phenomenon.** DDD is created and perpetuated by the dominant culture that values rugged individualism and the denial of feelings and needs. Taking it out of the sphere of personal shortcomings reduces the guilt and blame that usually accompanies DDD.

*When I read the article "Why Men Leave" I almost fell over. I look all around me at the impact of what you call normative abuse. I recognize it in myself. Having a better understanding of my experience growing up, it is easier to move forward. Most people will cringe at this writing. I still catch myself getting angry, but you have shown me what I had experienced, but did not see. When I was younger, I used to rely on women, drugs, and alcohol to fill the void of not being able to connect. My wife is supportive, but it is easier to be with her and my son now that I have a better idea what sets me off.* —Jason

3. **Recognizing the risk to the relationship.** Any one who *is* considering conceiving a child, or currently caring for a child, needs to realize that this phenomenon may be putting their relationship personally at risk. This requires finding the courage to acknowledge and counter the "it can't happen to us" syndrome.

> *The belief that all mothers automatically love their babies, or that all fathers can let go of past hurts to nurture their offspring, is naïve. Without exception, we are all descendants of generations of neurotic parents. This is not a criticism but a fact. The scars on our psyches tend to interfere with our natural capacity to love and respect both ourselves and others.*
> —Thomas Verny, MD, *Pre-parenting*

**4. Reviewing our own birth and early childhood.** It is important, ideally prior to conceiving a child, to identify any unresolved unmet needs or trauma that may be restimulated or triggered with the birth of a child, and seek help to resolve these issues.

**5. Embracing the relevance of attachment theory to:**

- adult love,
- parenting styles,
- and the ultimate preventative, connecting more securely with our children, and sustaining this connection as they move toward adulthood.

> *Adults' needs—as well as children's—for emotional connection are absolute.*
> —Sue Johnson, PhD, *Hold Me Tight*

> *Your article "Why Men Leave" provided me with such clarity and knowledge, yet I don't know what to do with it. This is not solely about reconciliation; it's about caring, helping someone I love to heal a lifetime of anger. My husband described all the feelings you did in the article from really not wanting children to trying to manage personal rage by self-medicating with marijuana. He is also a recovering alcoholic. He refuses to talk to anyone except his brothers and father, all of whom are in the same situation. He is the sixth of nine children, son of a non-participating, alcoholic father.*
>
> *We have been apart nine months and will soon be legally divorced. We have talked off and on and have exchanged books. A month ago I gave him Carolyn Myss' Anatomy of the Spirit and Men's Secret Wars. Both books denoted the subject of your article but did not go into detail. I was raised in pretty much the same circumstances as my husband, but overcame so much by becoming a mother and raising four well nurtured, breastfed babies into secure adults.*
>
> *Needless to say, it was hard to watch and was even harder to be shut out when we were living together. If I knew nine months ago what I understand now, I believe we would still be together. Life is just so short, isn't it?* —Colleen

It is only when we acknowledge a problem that we can begin to seek its resolution. Only as more men become aware of their own unmet needs and the re-stimulation of these unmet needs that comes with seeing their own children's needs being met, will we see the end of this widespread denial.

Men will then be better able to comprehend, appreciate, communicate, and cope with their issues instead of denying, hiding, inflicting them on others, or medicating them—and their female partners and others will be better able to understand and support them.

> *Denial. It's more than a river in Egypt, and I think I'm seeing a lot of it amongst friends and acquaintances. Some men who have contributed to this book have shared that they found it extremely painful to write their stories. Others I had to interview and write up because it was too painful for them to write themselves.*
>
> *A puzzling number of men I know, who have either left their wives, are visibly in a lot of pain, or are talking about leaving, don't seem to "get" that they are experiencing DDD. I'm guessing that some may actually get it, and simply not want to think about it further, let alone contribute a piece about it for the book. But many people, mostly women, immediately get it and are excited to find an explanation for the pain they've been experiencing or seen others experience.* —Jack

What was previously perceived as selfishness will now be reframed and recognized as restimulated unmet childhood needs for *connection*. Similarly, couples will learn to recognize arguments and upsets as expressions of a legitimate, innate unmet need for connection. Reframing them in this way will engender compassionate connection, rather than judgment.

> *The quality of our love relationships is also a big factor in how mentally and emotionally healthy we are. Hundreds of studies show positive, loving connections with others protect us from stress and help us cope better with life's challenges and traumas. Simply holding the hand of a loving partner can affect us profoundly, literally calming jittery neurons in the brain.* —Sue Johnson, PhD, *Hold Me Tight*

6. **Engaging the support and embrace of community.** By creating cooperative parenting groups, extended families of choice, and caring intergenerational communities, we can find support to parent, and thus, experience more of the nurturing we need. As psychologist Robin Grille underscores in *Parenting for a Peaceful World*, our relationships—with partner or child—do not exist in a vacuum. Our ability to form healthy and meaningful relationships with others is deeply influenced by the parenting we received as children. Parents, to give their best—to their partner and offspring—require the support and embrace of community.

## Where Next?

In the following chapters, we look more deeply at the issues raised for many couples—and most especially for men—from the time of conception through the first months and years of becoming a parent.

> *This article has been very well timed to answer some questions in our house. I feel that I am enjoying a wonderful bond with my 5-month-old son, Elijah, but that his father is finding it more difficult than either of us expected. I am sure that when he reads this he will recognize himself in many of the assertions, and hopefully this self-awareness will make it easier for him to become closer with his son.* —Sally

> *Your article brought tears to my eyes. I will send it to my ex-partner, my eldest son's father. You have told his story here. Many men, women, and children will benefit. I really love getting people into conversation around it. It's such an important issue. One thing I am starting to do more in my antenatal talks is to urge people to look into their own attachment histories so they become more aware of what they are bringing into their parenting.* —Hilary

I outline many of the steps that parents can take to help them grow together, rather than apart, through the early years of parenting. These include assessing preparedness to parent, *prior* to conception; developing an awareness of the unmet needs of their own childhood; seeking peer support or counseling in healing any unresolved trauma; involving fathers as key players in pregnancy and birth; welcoming their diverse but equally significant roles in parenting; preparing for the postnatal period well prior to the birth of a baby; and recognizing that adults crave and thrive on connection just as infants and children do.

> *It is important to help new parents to develop a strong parenting alliance (and sharing care of infants and young children is likely to help with this), since even relationships that are happy and appear stable at the time of the birth, can be seriously and quite quickly eroded when partners hold different ideas about parenting.* —Carolyn Pape Cowan, PhD, and Philip Cowan, PhD
> *When Partners Become Parents*

Much of our wounding began in disconnection. It can be healed through reconnection: reaching out, sharing our feelings rather than denying, medicating our pain, or inflicting it on others. We will heal as we shape new stories, casting ourselves as the creators rather than victims, and consciously and compassionately reaching out to connect with others.

In particular, I focus here on the multiple generations of un-bonded men, who fail to bond with their offspring, and leave in one form or another—the men who experience MPAS—and DDD.

**Key Points**
- Studies indicate that a decline in relationship satisfaction post-birth is not inevitable, and that the salience of teamwork leads to a couple's relationship satisfaction increasing.
- Most couples are unaware of the challenges they inevitably encounter by becoming parents. Information and preparation prior to the birth can minimize the stresses and reduce the risk of dads' leaving—physically or emotionally.
- It is only when we acknowledge a problem that we can begin to seek its resolution. Steps toward ending the dynamic of disappearing dads include:
  - An awareness of the underlying forces of DDD—and recognizing men's leaving cannot simply be accepted as "the way it is."
  - Realizing DDD is not just a personal phenomenon, but created and perpetuated by the dominant culture.
  - Recognizing that the birth of a child almost inevitably put a couple's relationship at risk—countering the "it can't happen to us" syndrome.
  - Reviewing our own birth and childhood so as to identify unresolved issues that may be restimulated.
  - Embracing the significance of attachment theory to adult love, parenting styles, and connecting more securely with our children—the ultimate preventative.
  - Social, communal, economic, and political policies and practices supporting parents in experiencing the joys of parenting.

# PART II

# PARENTING

# WHAT THE BOOKS, APPS, AND WEBSITES DON'T TELL US

## 7: Why Dads Matter—A Lot

A cross-cultural anthropological study[19] of six non-industrial cultures found that the most violent tribes were those in which the father was least associated with the family, and had minimal to no involvement in childrearing. Closer to home, a mountain of studies show what the absence of a dad can mean for a child. While statistics can never reveal the real-life pain and distress that lies behind the statistics, they reveal a lot about the impact of father absence.

### In the Absence of a Father…

- Fatherless children are more prone to depression than children with a father, and twice as likely to be school dropouts.
- They do less well and are more violent when in school.
- Violent schoolboys are *eleven times* more likely to be living without a father.
- Surveys repeatedly show children living apart from their fathers are far more likely than others to:
    - be expelled or suspended from school,
    - display emotional or behavioral problems, and
    - evidence difficulties in getting along with peers.

These boys will also abuse more drugs, be more criminally active, and try (and succeed at) suicide more often. They are at high risk for becoming teen parents.

Girls who grow up without fathers are at much greater risk for:

- early sexual activity,
- adolescent childbearing,
- divorce,
- being sexually abused,
- lack of sexual confidence and orgasmic satisfaction.

These girls struggle with issues of security and trust that well-fathered girls have successfully resolved. Girls for whom basic acceptance and love are primary motivating forces have little interest or emotional energy to invest in school or work-related activities unless they are exceptionally bright and talented.

### Caution: These *Are,* after All, Just Statistics

Child development depends on many things—from a child's genetic endowment to the health, wealth, education, confidence, and competence of their caregivers, to the availability of extended family and community support, and the environment they inhabit.

Kyle Pruett, MD, in *Fatherneed*, reminds us that it is important to recognize that, aside from the statistics, many single women succeed in raising wonderful children. A single mother, with the support of caring, competent men in her life and community, can provide her child with opportunities for ongoing and meaningful interactions with men. In so doing, she can come a good way toward meeting her son's hunger to understand and practice what it means to be a man.

Adrienne Burgess, researcher and consultant to the Fatherhood Project in the UK, reports that there is no evidence that children from lone-parent families do worse than children from highly conflicted (but intact) marriages. In fact, one study showed that the single most important indicator of maladjustment in children is their parents' active hostility to each other. Parental conflict is very destructive. And, it is possible for fathers who do not live with their children to have meaningful relationships with them.

Pruett cites a study showing that even the level of a child's attachment to a partnered mother had little impact on the child's wellbeing as they entered adulthood, unless it was associated with a good parental relationship. The study concluded that a poor father-son relationship was worse than no relationship at all, because it interfered with a child's capacity to form other, healthier connections, while also hindering the mother's ability to nurture well.

However, as Burgess notes, lone parents tend to be poor and may find it difficult to provide adequate child supervision. If they re-partner (most will) they may have even less time to offer their children, or may bring someone into the family whose presence is harmful. Child abuse rates are much higher in lone-parent households (whether headed by mom or dad) than in two-parent families.

The fact remains, raising a boy without an involved father in the home raises the statistical probability that he will, for example, become violent, just as a girl raised without an involved dad will more likely become pregnant as a teenager. While individual lone parents can do a good job if they are sufficiently supported and emotionally healthy, they are generally the exception rather than the rule. We look more closely at the exceptions forming as "collected families" in a later chapter, but the primary focus of this book is supporting the growing numbers of couples who want to share equally in parenting their children. For the children of these couples, fathers are part of the "two-parent advantage," which shows children from two-parent families doing better than children in lone parent households.

## Why Dads Are Good for Kids

As noted earlier, until quite recently the very little literature that connected fathers with children was about father *absence*, and told nothing of the impact of father *presence*.

Over more recent decades, the impact of father *presence* has begun to figure more prominently in studies, and indeed, as Pruett reveals, the findings are fascinating. Research shows that children yearn deeply for their dads. They are born with a drive to find and connect to the father, and the father's instincts—when allowed—prompt them to respond appropriately to their child. While much is made of the role of hormones in promoting bonding between mother and infant, higher levels of prolactin also appear in new fathers, and may correlate with men being more nurturing.

From the first moments after birth, children are equipped to find father and distinguish him from mother, even before they have 20/20 vision. At six weeks they can distinguish the difference between father's and mother's voice. At eight weeks they are able to anticipate complex differences in mother and father caretaking and handling styles. Infants approached by mother slowed and regulated their heart and respiratory rates, relaxed their shoulders, lowered their eyelids (Ahh, Mom!). Approached by father, infants' heart and respiratory rates quicken, shoulders hunch up, eyes widen and brighten (Dad's here, party time!).

## Involved Fathering

Pruett defines *involved* fathering as "male behavior beyond insemination that promotes the wellbeing and healthy development of your child and family in active ways." Associated behaviors may include a father:
- feeling and behaving responsibly toward your child,
- being emotionally engaged, being physically accessible,
- providing material support to sustain the child's needs, and
- exerting influence in childcare decisions.

On a day-to-day level, it encompasses everything from changing diapers to bathing, snuggling with, feeding, rough-housing, going to the beach, helping with homework, going to the school play.

> *I started being an involved dad before my wife became pregnant. I was part of planning when we wanted to conceive, and I did lots of reading and educating myself about decisions we needed to make about the birth, breastfeeding, vaccinations, co-sleeping, and carrying our baby. Then I could make educated choices about what was best for myself, my wife, and our children. I don't assume that anyone, including my wife and our doctors, knows what is best for us.*

*Being an involved dad is giving me a lifetime of fulfillment versus a lifetime of regrets and is the single greatest experience of my life. I know I'm laying the foundation for our two children to be happy adults and giving them the tools I feel they'll need in life. The more time and love I put into it the more joy and fulfillment I get back.* —Orion

## How Much Is Enough?

Research confirms that what matters most is the *quality* of what father and child do together, which may be doing nothing at all. The father's attitude toward, and behavioral sensitivity to, the care of his child has a more positive influence on the child's socio-emotional development than the total amount of time spent in interaction with the child. It is the closeness the child feels towards the father, not just his physical presence, that's most predictably associated with positive life outcomes for the child both now and in the future.

However, there seems to be a certain minimum requirement in terms of quantity which, if not met, affects quality. Generally, quality of interaction will be better when you *know* someone well. Sensitivity to the child seems to be the key, and it may be that a minimum level of involvement is not so hard to reach. Burgess reports a study of Israeli dads of 9-month-old babies, who had spent 45 minutes each day actively engaged with their infants, and understood them as well as the mothers, i.e., when playing with their infants, they offered the appropriate responses.

## Kids Thrive with an Involved Dad

A father's active involvement promotes:
- the child's emotional, physical, and intellectual development, and social competencies,
- adaptive and problem-solving competencies,
- strengthened cognitive abilities,
- increased capacity for attachment—involved fathering fosters secure attachment,
- less stereotyping in the choice of friends and in overall social and behavioral expectations of peers,
- less impulsivity and more self-control, particularly in unfamiliar social situations,
- a greater degree of internal locus of control—a clearer and more trusting sense of how the world works in relationship to their ability to affect change around them,
- more empathy with others,
- greater pro-social and positive moral behavior.

These positive effects show up *even more strongly* when complemented by the mother's support of her partner's active contribution to her child's emotional, social, and intellectual life.

Even the way a newborn enters the world can be positively affected by the father's presence. Positive involvement of father matters *from birth*. Babies "so blessed" in the first four weeks perform better than their peers on their first birthdays.

Pruett notes that children who feel close to their fathers are:

- twice as likely to go to college as those who do not,
- twice as likely to find stable employment after high school,
- seventy-five percent less likely to have a teen birth,
- eighty percent less likely to spend time in jail, and
- half as likely to experience multiple depression symptoms.

## A Unique and Essential Role for Fathers?

Despite the research noted above and the assertion of many psychiatrists, psychologists, and popular contemporary culture that the presence of a strong male father-figure is vital to a child's development, and that a boy needs a dad if he is to become a happy, well-functioning adult, the reality is not that clear-cut. Some qualifications are in order.

Burgess draws our attention to the fact that many of the studies simply compare fatherless families with families where a dad is present. Some of the differences between the two may be the result of social factors—fatherless families tend to be poorer and subject to a variety of associated stresses—rather than the direct influence of the presence or absence of a dad. A substantial body of research indicates that it is not the absence of the father, but the *isolation of the mother*, that predisposes children to difficulties in social adaptation. And that the key to preventing social problems with peers and authority figures is in having at *least* one other adult in the home sphere, which serves as a positive influence on the child and provides help for the single parent.

> *In our case, the presence of a supportive community helped when my sons' father was no longer present in the home. In the small town where they were raised, the community knew their father and knew that they had a father. When we moved to a larger city, and they had almost no contact with their dad, I felt that the energetic feeling of the greater community was that they were kids without a dad, without a history of a dad, and that we were an isolated family of three. This was especially difficult when they were teens. It was then and in that atmosphere that I most felt the lack of their father.* —Barbara

Some research casts doubt on a unique and essential role for fathers. Burgess notes "father absence" studies, done over five decades, showing the vast majority of boys without fathers develop quite normally in terms of sex-role identity and performance, and there is no evidence that without a father's presence, mother and infant fail to "separate."

Peggy Drexler, PhD, in *Raising Boys Without Men: How Maverick Moms are Creating the Next Generation of Exceptional Men*, concludes that it is the quality of parenting, not the gender of parents, that counts. What makes strong and resilient young men is the love, respect, and understanding of their parents—regardless of gender. What boys (and girls) need, is a loving, growth-encouraging parent—mother or father—who enables a boy to develop to his full potential, respecting and supporting his individuality, manliness, courage, and developing conscience.*

Drexler believes that boys with secure attachments to their female caregivers are no more at risk of "father hunger" than boys in the general population whose dads are minimally involved in their lives.

Many scientists would now agree that boys are hard-wired from birth to be boys. A boy developing a healthy masculinity and morality is a naturally occurring process that can be cultivated without a live-in dad. Role models can be teachers, family friends, coaches, or neighbors—even movie stars.

Patrick Houser, in *Fathers-to-Be Handbook*, identifies the many "bonus dads" in our culture—the uncles, ministers, Scout leaders, teachers, coaches, grandfathers, step-dads, charity workers, etc.—who are non-biological fathers, yet "do fathering" for our children. Naming and acknowledging them supports the process—and expands it.

> *The message emanating from this is that there is no free ride for fatherhood, no magical role for fathers just because they are fathers or because they are men. It is what each man gives on a personal level that makes him a key player in his child's development.* —Adrienne Burgess, *Fatherhood Reclaimed*

When discussing the importance of the father's role it must be acknowledged that some fathers can be destructive and a boy may be better off without him. Adults and kids in happy marriages get a host of benefits, but this is not so in bad marriages. While many boys contend with a largely absent dad—a typical American dad spends on average a mere 11 minutes a day with his children—others contend with a destructive dad. How much time they spend together, and how they interact, is all-important.

---

* Did boys from lesbian-led families feel they were missing out on not having a dad? Well, yes and no. These boys had a heightened fascination with sports and sports heroes. The study does not deny there is a very powerful pull for boys to identify with their dads—some more than others. These boys were curious about their friends' dads, but when asked to speculate what it would be like to have a dad in the house, most thought a dad would be "strict" with them—that they wouldn't have as much opportunity to be who they are and choose what they do with a dad.

Even if it is true that there is not a unique and essential role for fathers, the sheer volume of evidence seems to indicate a range of very positive benefits for children who enjoy close, stable, loving relationships with a father; and there are certainly correlations between father-absence and a range of personality problems. All the more reason for those many couples becoming parents to be aware of the factors that may draw them together, or set them apart, after the birth of a child.

## Predictors of Involved Fathering

Three primary indicators of involved fathering are:
1. **A man's experience of the fathering he himself received.** Pruett reports this to be one of the strongest *predictors of engaged and responsible fathering*. From this context, two very different paradigms emerge:
   - The modeling paradigm: the father emulates the strengths of the fathering he remembers himself receiving. Happy memories of being fathered by an involved and nurturing dad encourage men to identify with and model these qualities in fathering their own children.
   - The reworking paradigm: the sons of passive, non-nurturing, withdrawn, and even abusive fathers extend themselves to compensate for their own father's failings. While probably less commonly found among men who are positively fathering their children, it is important to recognize that this paradigm can also promote responsible fathering.

*My first child was born at home. I was the midwife. My wife's mother's presence at the birth, and for some weeks thereafter, added tensions for many reasons. I felt left out of the bond between them. They even spoke in German, a language I could not understand. Also, I felt left out of the bond between the nursing mom and baby. Within a few months, a flirtation developed between another woman and me. I got caught up in it, unconscious of anything beyond the passionate, obsessive attraction I felt. The affair was brief. I ended it after about a week, having become overwhelmed with remorse and empathic feelings for my baby son and young wife. I had been abandoned by my father before I was even born—he left my mother for another woman—and now I imagined how terrible it would be for them, practically and emotionally, to be abandoned by me at such a vulnerable time. Painfully, my wife and I reconciled. I wondered whether my straying into that brief affair during my first child's first year had unconsciously been a compulsive repetition of what my father had done. As a dad, I was determined to be there for my kids. I wanted to be a devoted dad, not a disappearing one.* —Mick

We can expect to see more of this as fathers—and mothers—become more aware of the value of reviewing and repairing any unresolved issues from their own attachment history and childhood experiences. We look at this more closely in Chapter 17 and 18.

2. **A man's satisfaction in his relationship with his partner.** Fathers' involvement in infant care is strongly correlated with their relationship satisfaction: the more involved the fathers are, the more satisfied they are.[20]

    Men in an unsatisfying relationship are more likely to withdraw from their wife and children, with or without divorce, than men in a satisfying marriage. The happier a couple are together, the more time fathers tend to spend with their children. Marital satisfaction itself is, then, both source and consequence of paternal involvement.

3. **His partner's attitudes and expectations about fathering.**

    *A father's involvement with his children, especially his young children, when it matters most, is powerfully contingent on the mother's attitudes towards, and expectations of, support from him.* —Kyle Pruett, MD, *Fatherneed*

We look at this third factor more closely in the next chapter.

## Involved Dads Are Good for Moms, Too

The father's involvement has significant indirect effects for the entire family system. When the mother feels supported by the father, she is more patient, flexible, emotionally responsive, and available to their children. High levels of father involvement are strongly linked with both mothers' and fathers' satisfaction with their relationship and with family life.[21] A couple's more equitable sharing of earning and caring roles is associated with lower rates of separation and divorce.[22] And a clear correlation has been shown between involved fathering and the happiness and stability of parents' marriage in midlife.

An additional benefit of involved fathering is the example it sets in demonstrating both men and women can nurture well. It shows young boys that being an involved father is something to aspire to when they themselves become fathers, and shows young girls they can expect their future husband to be involved fathers as well.

---

### The Ultimate Aphrodisiac

There is one plea commonly heard from wives, but rarely heard from husbands. "I wish he were more involved with the children."...

If your children are the most important elements in your life, you are going to feel most sensitive about their care and most hurt if your husband seems to be neglecting them.... "Loving me means loving my children," she feels. A man, therefore, who does not actively father, will inevitably trigger his wife's resentment. —Aaron Hass, *The Gift of Fatherhood*

## *And,* the Icing on the Cake—Good Fathering Makes Great Men

The core of what fathering does for a man, for his heart, for his soul, for his engagement with life, for his *manhood,* cannot be fully put into words. Here is a summary of findings about how fathering changes a man, gleaned largely from Pruett and also from Armin Brott in *Father for Life*:

- **Greater emotional resilience:** dealing with the joys and frustrations of parenting makes many men more patient, understanding and empathetic. They become more aware of their own strengths and weaknesses; more tolerant of others, more flexible; and more able to feel and express their emotions.
- **Confidence and pride:** a close relationship with his child helps build not only the child's confidence and self-esteem, but also the father's, as he feels pride in his child's accomplishments and his role in helping his child achieve them.
- **Self-esteem:** men who take a more active role in childcare and running the household, tend to feel better about themselves and about their family relationships than men less involved in family activities.
- **More effective parenting:** fathers who are warm and firm with their child feel they are doing a good job, and that they have a good relationship with their child. That, in turn, leads them to want to get even more involved.
- **More love:** usually, fathers with very high levels of involvement and responsibility, develop stronger-than-average attachments with their young children.
- **Enhanced meaning and direction in life:** many men find themselves restructuring priorities, placing family and children first, slowing down, engaging less in risky behaviors, and being more concerned about making the world a better place.
- **Enhanced career success and community participation:** high involvement may have a positive effect on work productivity and career success, and citizenship in later years, as it catalyzes men to achieve higher goals in the workplace, and to become involved in broader caregiving roles as workplace managers or mentors, or as civic and community leaders.
- **More affection and lovemaking:** a man's loving and active involvement with his child is a turn-on for many women. Father's involvement makes mother happy. Mother's happiness and gratitude may well be expressed with more affectionate touch and lovemaking.
- **Playfulness:** dads have not only an excuse, but a good reason to play as a little kid again.

- **Healing childhood traumas:** memories of a man's own childhood—the happy and the sad—inevitably surface as he fathers his own child. These allow him to both re-experience the pleasures of childhood, and also to heal the unmet needs of his early years through his own compassionate presence to the wounded child that may be restimulated in him (see Chapter 20).
- **Better physical health:** involved fathers evidence less substance abuse, and are less subject than other men to physical illness, hospital admissions, and suffer fewer accidents and premature death. The men with the least worries about their relationship with their children also had the fewest health problems. Those with the most troubled relationships with their children had the most health problems.
- **Better mental health:** high levels of involvement may promote mental health. Conversely, low levels of paternal involvement can lead to depression.
- **More respectful:** involved fathering may contribute significantly to socializing any innate tendencies toward aggression and violent behavior. There is a significant correlation between lack of active involvement in childcare and eventual child abuse.* Fathers who feel involved in their child's life are less likely to default on child support.
- **Community phase:** as dads become more comfortable juggling roles as husband, father, son, and provider, dads enter what Bruce Lipton calls the "community phase" of fathering. At this point, "Parenting brings new levels of insight and social commitment that contribute in positive ways to the overall evolution of the culture."
- **A happier midlife:** fathers' involvement in routine everyday childcare, including play/school contact throughout a child's life, accounts for 21% of the variance in fathers' marital happiness at midlife.[23]
- **A happier family:** in addition to these benefits that accrue directly to dad, are the many benefits that accrue to his baby, and to his relationship with his partner, and to her happiness—and so, the circle returns, to you.

*The act of caring for babies renders fathers/men more nurturing and is correlated with raised levels of hormones associated with tolerance/trust*

---

* Furthermore, according to Pruett, while we know that stepfathers tend to abuse children at higher rates than do biological fathers, when comparing stepfathers who were involved in the nurturing and physical care of their stepdaughter during the first three years and biological fathers likewise involved, a man's involvement in the physical care of a child prior to three years of age reduces the probability that he will exploit that physical intimacy later.

*(oxytocin), sensitivity to infants (cortisol) and brooding/lactation/bonding (prolactin). Among males, physiological changes can occur with 15 minutes of holding a baby; and the more experienced a male is as a caregiver, the more pronounced are the changes.*

*This may in part explain findings that fathers' involvement in infant care is positively correlated with their satisfaction with family life and adjustment to fatherhood. In Norway, promoting men's early involvement with infants and children is being seen as a potential tool for reducing domestic and other violence.* —Fatherhood Institute

## The Ups and Downs of Fathering

*Being an involved dad takes time and places demands on whatever freedoms you previously held dear. It can mean sacrificing, or at least putting on hold for a time, fulfillment of cherished goals or dreams. Financially, children can cost a lot these days, so there's less money for you yourself to play with. Much of the physical and emotional intimacy you shared with your partner before parenthood will be, for a good period, a thing of the past. Depleted energy levels are pretty much inevitable, in the early days it's about sleep deprivation, later the physical exhaustion of chasing a baby around, and then the mental drain of answering "Why? Daddy." Quite simply, whatever time and energy you put into being a dad is time and energy you don't have for something else. But as most every involved dad will say, "But man… it is worth it!"*

—Armin Brott, *Father for Life*

So, you see, involved fathering is not only great for our children, and good for the man himself, it is good for his partner, good for his community, and good for the planet—involved fathering is an all-around winner for everyone.

## Key Points

- A cross-cultural anthropological study of six non-industrial cultures found that the most violent tribes were those in which the father was least associated with the family, and had minimal to little involvement in childrearing.
- Children living apart from their dads are more prone to emotional and behavioral problems, depression, drugs, criminal activity, violence, and becoming teen parents.
- While individual lone parents can do a good job if they are sufficiently supported and emotionally healthy, these are generally the exception rather than the rule.
- Children are born with a drive to find and connect to their father, and father's instincts—when allowed—prompts them to respond appropriately to their child. Higher levels of prolactin—a bonding hormone—appear in new dads as well as moms.
- A father's active involvement promotes a child's emotional, physical and intellectual development, and social competencies. These positive effects are further enhanced by a mother's support of her partner's active contribution to their child's life.
- Primary predictors of involved fathering are a man's experience of the fathering he himself received; his satisfaction in his relationship with his partner; and his partner's attitudes and expectations about fathering.
- High levels of father involvement are strongly linked with both mothers' and fathers' satisfaction with their relationship and with family life.
- Good fathering makes great men. Fathering promotes a range of positive qualities including emotional resilience, self-esteem, career success and community involvement, affection and lovemaking, physical and mental health.
- In Norway, promoting men's early involvement with infants and children is seen as a potential tool for reducing violence.
- Involved fathering is an all-round win for everyone.

## 8: But Can They Do It?

Western culture assumes that a woman intuitively knows how to mother—that the ability and desire to nurture a child is the chief province of women. And it does appear that mother is equipped to be the most essential figure in the baby's world. We are, after all, mammalian, and in every species it is the mother who has the breasts to nourish her baby, and in some cases a pouch to keep the two intimately connected, night and day. In the human realm, mother has been the unborn baby's world for nine full months, and when the baby *is* born, it is mother that Nature has so exquisitely primed with a "hormonal cocktail."

Delivered at birth, this enables her to attune and respond to the baby's every need, to produce the milk to nourish the baby both physically and physiologically, and for the two to fall deeply in love.

This is not to say that dad isn't important, but in the earliest period, primarily his role is a complementary one, that of supporter and protector of his partner and child.

> *My husband was vital in helping our baby calm down when colicky at night in the early months. He often did this better than I did. However, we both were committed to preserving the mother-child breastfeeding relationship and I am grateful for that.* —Barbara

A large body of research indicates that while mother is seen as nurturer and father as playmate and/or disciplinarian, there is no evidence that *given equal experience and support*, parents of either gender necessarily excel as caregivers. It appears that father and mother have equal, if slightly different abilities (the most notable being lactation), to nurture a child; and that many of the perceived differences are situational and/or cultural, rather than innate or gender-driven.*

When the natural bonding of mother and child is allowed to unfold without interference—unfortunately not a common occurrence in the West—the hormones secreted not only prepare her to be the prominent caregiver in the early days and months, but also continue to flow through the early years, giving a significant advantage to the lactating mother in connecting with her child. However, fathers too, come equipped with the desire and ability to

---

* It's interesting to note that these studies have been conducted on populations of women who did not give birth naturally and many of whom may not have breastfed their babies, so this assertion may not be an authentic representation of how women are actually "wired." Regardless, as we will see, many of the perceived differences are situational and cultural.

connect deeply with their children in ways that are often discounted and unsupported in Western culture:*

- Both evidence a similar physiological capacity to differentiate their newborn from others in the nursery. Blindfolded, both are equally able to recognize their baby by the shape of their little hands.
- Both are similarly predisposed emotionally to nurture their children in most ordinary circumstances, although men are rarely prepared or supported by their own families or by society to do so.
- Given the chance to interact *independently* with their newborns, new fathers are as deft (or clumsy) as new mothers.
- Both evidence the same biological sensitivity—changes in heart rate, respiratory rate, or skin temperature—to infants in distress.
- Both are equally able to interpret their child's behavioral cues indicating hunger, gastric distress, and fatigue, *and* equally able to respond appropriately.
- While it was earlier thought that fathers were less warm toward their children than mothers, in private they may behave as affectionately as mothers.
- Both are equally anxious when leaving their baby in someone else's care.
- Both share the desire to feel emotionally connected to their children throughout life, although they may express this desire in different ways.
- Single parenting is similar for both, i.e., the concerns of single fathers are remarkably similar to those of single mothers.

In all studies of parenting potential in the West, only one clear difference emerges with respect to physical response: women's pupils tend to dilate when they look at little babies, whether or not they are themselves mothers. Men's pupils don't, until they are fathers, and then they do. Of course the question emerges: How much is this biology? And how much is this due to interest in babies being actively fostered in young girls, but suppressed in boys?

When recordings of crying babies were played to boys and girls, ages 8 and 14 years, their social responses—whether they smiled or frowned—were different, with girls on the whole showing greater concern. However their *concealed* responses—heart rates, blood pressure, etc.—showed no differences. Both were equally disturbed. Interesting.

---

* Drawn from both Pruett and Burgess.

## Moving Beyond Physiological Responses into Styles of Interaction:

- Fathers and mothers approach their infants in different ways. Mother-care tends be more rhythmic and repetitive, father-care less predictable and more playful. Mothers tend to pick up infants usually to care for them in the same way, time after time, bending over them, and usually speaking softly. Fathers pick up the infant to *do* something with them, and pick them up in generally unpredictable ways. They may surprise the child by picking them up without warning or approaching them head first instead of feet first.
- With respect to play style, fathers are more "jokey" with their children, and engage more often and vigorously in "rough-and-tumble." While mother's body has been extensively used by the child, sometimes to the point of exhaustion, especially if breastfeeding, father appreciates the physical interaction. Indeed, the toy most used by dads tends to be their own bodies. Many experience use of their body-as-jungle-gym as some compensation for the absence of the intense—and for mother often exhausting—physical connection she experiences with her offspring.

    *Siena loved to climb on me like a jungle gym—I called myself her Jungle Jack. I'd lie on my back with my legs up and she'd climb all over me. A variant was "Airplane" where she was hoisted up with her belly resting on both of my feet, arms out as wings.* —Jack

- Fathers of young children are slightly less likely than mothers to engage in more intellectual play (puzzles, construction toys), and more likely to choose activity toys such as balls or vehicles, or watch TV with them. Mothers play less with their children, spend more of their time on their physical care, and emphasize instruction and self-control. Fathers are more likely to encourage their children to tolerate frustration and master tasks on their own before offering help, where mothers tend to step in and help fussing children earlier. Fathers, as compared to mothers, spend less of their time in play that is simply for entertainment or distraction and more in activities that encourage exploration.
- Fathers' tendency to introduce children to the world around them is evidenced, too, in the way they carry a child face forward, while mothers tend to carry the child facing inward or over their shoulder. Interestingly, 80% of the time, *both* hold the child on their left side, next to the heart.

- Fathers tend to discipline less with shame and disappointment and more with real life consequences. While we tend to think of dads as the disciplinarians, in most cases it seems that they simply aren't home enough. Mothers tend to not only hit their children more often but also to give more orders and hand out more threats and punishments. This is likely due to the fact they are home more with the children, i.e., it appears to be situation-driven rather than gender-driven.

## Parenting Mandates: Social or Biological?

While it appears that there are some differences in the styles of interaction between mother/child and father/child, evidence points to these differences being situational and gender driven by socially constructed roles, rather than by biologically driven mandates. It will be interesting to see if these differences become less tied to gender as a new generation of children, socialized according to different gender role models, become parents.

Performance of caregiving tasks seems more modifiable and more linked to role than gender—a ready example being the studies finding fathers are more likely to wipe their toddlers' faces in playgrounds or sports centers where they feel they're in charge, than in restaurants, which they may see as female territory. Studies revealing a discrepancy between the public and private face and experience of fathering have been duplicated in many countries, where fathers who are seen to find it difficult to interact and play freely with their children in public without embarrassment, interact more when unaware they are being observed.

## Dads as Primary Caregivers

Both Pruett and Burgess look at the growing number of "primary caregiver dads " who afford us a window into the social versus biological influences on parenting styles . These dads are their children's main caregivers, spending a minimum of 25 hours per week in *sole charge* of their children. They come from all walks of life, and find themselves in this role for a variety of reasons. While they take a more relaxed attitude than their children's mothers to housework, tidy clothes, and clean faces, these dads are almost indistinguishable from mothers in the way they relate to their children—they exhibit as much patience, sensitivity, baby talk, and public kissing of their young children as women who are primary parents. After a time, these dads cease to favor outdoor over indoor activities and, though they still initiate rough-and-tumble-style play, they also begin to initiate other kinds of more intellectual play and stimulation.

Here, it is apparent that *differences arise not through the amount of time fathers spend with their children, but the time they spend alone with them* and the degree of responsibility they hold for their daily routine. Again, the indicators are that many of the so-called "gender differences" may be situational in origin.

It seems that having the father serve as a primary nurturing figure during the early years while the mother works outside the home but stays very close, affords children a foundation of trust and comfort with present and future male and female relationships. What especially characterizes these children as preteens is the closeness of their friendships with opposite-sex peers. Their relationships with peers of both genders are very satisfying for them. The gender of the friend, while significant, appears to be less important than the overall quality of the friendship. Wives of these dads appreciate them and feel their love and respect for their husband deepen. They are happy they are showing their children that they too, will have options for parenting their own children that extend beyond the prevailing stereotypical roles.

> *Traditionally the roles of male and female were very different. Male and female were socialized from childhood to be separate and distinct from each other. Today there is very good reason to want to socialize men to feel deeply, and to be able to express their feelings, right from infancy, and to receive love and nurturing when they do. We need to raise boys who become men—who can transcend the Mars archetype of the protector-warrior, partly because the shadow-side of the protector-warrior is the abusive husband, abusive father, and the man who looks forward to going to war.*
>
> *We can no longer afford to rear boys into men who perpetrate violence or disappear from their families. We need men who are both strong and supportive, and able to feel their vulnerability, and allow themselves to reach out in need and be comforted. We need this, just as we must have women who feel empowered to state what they want and need, and to get those needs met, as well as women who allow themselves to be vulnerable and need others, especially men.*
>
> —Suzanne Arms

The trend of fathers as primary caregivers is likely to continue to rise:
- The gender pay-gap has all but disappeared in low-income households where automatically designating the father as breadwinner no longer makes obvious economic sense.[24]
- 44% of women now earn as much, or more than, their partners—a percentage that is climbing sharply[25] and is likely to continue to increase.
- Young girls/women now outstrip boys/men not only in school graduation participation and results, but also in further education/training.[26]

Throughout industrialized countries, fathers' involvement in family work (both housework and childcare) is increasing; and the gap between mothers' and fathers' contributions has narrowed.[27] In 1965, married fathers with children under age 18 living in their household spent an average of 2.6 hours per week caring for those children. Fathers' time spent caring for their children rose gradually over the next two decades—to 2.7 hours per week in 1975 and 3 hours per week in 1985. From 1985 to 2000, the amount of time that married fathers spent with their children more than doubled—to 6.5 hours in 2000.

> Alongside this trend toward more time spent with children is a trend toward more children living apart from their fathers. When it comes to spending time with a child, being in the same home makes a huge difference. More than nine-in-ten fathers who live with their children at least part of the time report that they shared a meal with their child or talked with their child about the child's day almost daily over the past several weeks. Nearly two-thirds (63%) say they helped their child with homework or checked on their homework at least several times a week, and 54% say they took their child to or from activities several times a week or more. By comparison, relatively few fathers who live apart from their children report taking part in these activities.

In both the UK and the US, fathers in two-parent families carry out an average of a quarter of the family's childcare related activities during the week, and one-third at weekends, with higher absolute and relative levels (one-third) where both parents work fulltime.[28] In the US, 1 in 3 working class couples stagger their shift work to be available to care for their children.[29] In a 2010 study, fathers remain the sole or main earners in almost 3 out of 5 two-parent households containing a 5-year-old; a substantial number of fathers are now full- or part-time "home dads."[30]

## Fashioning a New Role for Dads

At this point in time, the involved father who serves as primary caregiver for his children during the day usually faces a great deal of "matronizing" behavior. While the intention may be to be supportive, the message is clear: "You're only a man, so you don't know how to do that properly. I'll do it for you."

*When I was at the unschooling conference last September, there was a session organized for dads to share their problems and concerns. I had absolutely nothing to contribute. I didn't say a word the entire hour and a half. That was because all their problems and concerns were problems and concerns I don't have, or haven't had for a very long time (mainly because I haven't had a "real job" since 1998 and have spent 20 of my 25 years of parenthood as a stay-at-home dad).*

*All my problems and concerns are something else—masculinity issues, I suppose I could call them, rather than fatherhood issues. On the first day of the conference, one of the co-organizers asked me if I would mind her baby son while she took care of some urgent business because he'd apparently taken a liking to me. So I was standing there having a conversation with this baby in my arms, as I do, and the other co-organizer came over and said something like, "I hope you won't be offended if I use this word, but my friend and I couldn't help but notice how maternal you are." And I chuckled and said something like, "Oh, okay. No, I'm not offended." That evening, instead of going to the bush dance, I went over to the local Surf Life Saving Club* [every Australian coastal town has one] *and had a couple of beers and watched the footy on TV!* —Bob

Whether seeking to serve as primary caregiver or as an involved father equally sharing the parenting role with his partner, these men are challenging society's view of male and female roles—not an easy ride. Even the existence of the choice itself appears as new and radical to most. A decade or two ago, it simply wasn't on the agenda. Now, for a small but increasing number of couples, it emerges as a matter for consideration on philosophical, emotional and practical grounds.

Involved fathers—and their partners—are challenged to both fashion a paternal role different from that of their fathers, and also to prepare their children for flexible adult roles that are not blindly gender-driven.

## Yes, They *Can* Do It

Nurturance refers to a range of feelings and skills that can and must be learned and practiced. Some women seem to be "born mothers," but many more learn how to care for their children just as they learn the depth and limits of maternal feelings—on the job. Men's capacity for emotional involvement with children, and their ability to care for them in practical ways, may come naturally or may need to be developed. Until recently, parent education has been synonymous with mother education. Programs are needed for not only men, but for boys, providing them with skills and experiences that will later facilitate their development of nurturing parenting roles.

As will become evident, given the tremendous obstacles to a father's involvement, it often takes concerted effort on part of both mom and dad to "make room for daddy." When men override their doubts about their competence in this family domain, and women overcome their ambivalence about sharing the role of expert regarding their child, fathers are able to be centrally involved in their children's lives.

**Key Points**
- Western culture assumes that a woman intuitively knows how to mother, and that the ability and desire to nurture a child is the chief province of women.
- There is no evidence that given equal experience and support, parents of either gender necessarily excel as caregivers. Both have equal, if slightly different, abilities to nurture a child (the notable exception being lactation); and many of the perceived differences are situational and cultural, rather than innate or gender-driven.
- Fathers come equipped with the desire and ability to connect deeply with their children in ways that are often discounted and unsupported.
- A growing number of primary caregiver dads affords a window into the social versus biological influences. They exhibit as much patience, sensitivity, baby talk, and kissing of their young children as women who are primary caregivers.
- Throughout industrialized countries, fathers' involvement in both housework and childcare is increasing.
- Involved fathers—and their partners—are challenged to both fashion a paternal role different from that of their fathers, and to prepare their children for adult roles that are not blindly gender-driven.
- When men override the doubts about their competence, and women overcome their ambivalence about sharing the role of expert with their partner, fathers are able to be centrally involved in their children's lives.

# 9: IF THEY CAN, WHY DON'T THEY?

## Gatekeeping

> *Of course what makes a man a father is a mother, and what women think and feel about the men with whom they create children strongly shapes fathering opportunities.* —Kyle Pruett, MD, *Fatherneed*

Gatekeeping, the vigilant and often covert and unconscious control by a mother of her partner's access to "her" children, is a very potent, very real, yet rarely mentioned phenomenon. While a growing majority of men want to be more involved in the care of their children, mothers often unwittingly discourage their partners' involvement.

In over a decade of reviewing parenting material and research with The Alliance for Transforming the Lives of Children (aTLC.org—see Appendix F), I hadn't even heard the term "gatekeeping." Why? And, if only I had! Did I do it? Did Jack sense it? Would it have made a difference if I had known about it? I was startled to learn that a mother's attitudes shape her partner's fathering competence and incompetence much more than his attitude shapes her competence in mothering; how a woman thinks and feels about the father of her child strongly shapes his fathering opportunities.

Adrienne Burgess refers to many studies confirming that a mother's characteristics outweigh the father's characteristics in predicting a father's involvement with his child. Researchers observing couples in the weeks following their babies' births found themselves "amazed" at how little time fathers allowed themselves for uncertainty, and how quickly mothers stepped in if father or baby looked uneasy. Burgess observes that while at times it may appear that mothers are keener for fathers to be involved than are the fathers themselves, father's self-confidence and skills can be a factor here. When fathers are assumed to be busy or not interested (or even when they themselves, believe they are busy or not interested), they are often feeling uncomfortable, or at a loss, and afraid of being seen as incompetent.

> *It is important to understand this, because through training, explanation, gradation, and familiarization you can set up situations where the idiot factor is reduced.* —Richard Fletcher, men's health researcher, as quoted in Burgess.

Some men, recognizing their wives' need to feel in control, actually hold back when they would have loved to be more involved in caring for the baby. But, for the most part, when fathers withdraw, it often is because they feel incompetent. And the more that fathers withdraw, and the more mothers pick up the slack, the more incompetent fathers feel… and the whole sad cycle is set into motion.

> ...while a new father is expected to share in the trials and tribulations of becoming a parent he is, at the same time, instructed to remain an outsider, and this to a far greater extent than is dictated by the realities of pregnancy and birth. —Adrienne Burgess, *Fatherhood Reclaimed*

## Male Postpartum Depression

I was surprised to learn that while 5-25% (due to different methodologies) of mothers suffer from moderate or severe postpartum depression after a child's birth, so do fathers. Internationally, the average rate for new dads is 8%. In the US, it's estimated to be 14%. However, during the 3-6 month period postpartum, the rate increases to 26%. Another study has shown that risk doubles when the mother has postpartum depression, jumping to 50%.[31]

More incapacitating than the "baby blues" implies, postpartum depression is a severe sadness or emptiness, withdrawal from family and friends, a strong sense of failure, and even includes thoughts of suicide. These emotions can begin two or three weeks after birth and can last up to a year or longer if untreated.

Several causal factors of male postpartum depression have been identified. New dads may be:
- feeling burdened at the prospect of caring for a child,
- feeling entrapped with the financial responsibility they may now carry alone,
- suffering withdrawal from being tended to in their marital relationship.

In other words, they are missing, and feeling abandoned by, their wives.

And indeed, there may be plenty for a new dad to feel rejected, abandoned, or on the most apparent level, jealous about:
- the attention his partner is getting as the new mom,
- the intimacy of his partner's close relationship with the baby,
- the time she gets with her baby that consumes her ability to give him attention and affection,
- having full access to her breasts, especially if they're too tender for him to touch, or she is too exhausted to want him near them.

Here we have the precursors to MPAS, re-stimulating the new father's early abandonment experience and exacerbating the suppressed, ever-present terror of further abandonment.

Being depressed, men are even less likely to engage with their child, and may withdraw further, setting in motion a downward cycle that can be very difficult to stop. While women often show signs of frank sadness when they are depressed, men are more likely to be irritable, aggressive, and sometimes hostile when depressed. And when dads appear this way, most women will then, to a greater or lesser extent—as I did—turn their focus even further from their partner and more and more towards their child. Others will, initially at least, become more and more aggressive in their demands that he support or "be with" her and their baby. Either way, dad is likely crawling or running more and more deeply into MPAS and DDD. And so the cycle builds, the behavior of each exacerbating that of their partner, and pushing the two further and further apart—when what each of them *wants and longs for,* is connection with the other. Their own early unmet needs are driving these misguided attempts to connect.

The fact that depressed fathers are less likely to interact with their infants is of real concern, as this interaction is essential to their forming a healthy connection with their offspring, and an important factor in a child's cognitive and emotional development. Even babies know an unhappy father from a happy one. Even 11-month-olds are less likely to look to father for help in novel learning situations when father is in a distressed marriage. Besides not feeling able to interact with his baby, a depressed dad is unable to be supportive of the mother and mother is likely feeling less and less supportive of him—feeling sad or mad that she has "another baby" to take care of.

Failure to understand what MPAS is and why it happens is part of the problem—as illustrated by a friend's recent comment, when asked if she recognized the phenomenon in her relationship, "all men are adolescents, but he came through it" (though depression is still an issue with both parents).

While some researchers argue paternal depression is due to the father's feeling displaced—a "greedy child"—others have begun to challenge this. Again, what is not factored into the "greedy/needy" diagnosis, is the attachment perspective that recognizes that our need, as adults as well as children, for connection is legitimate and absolute.

In many cases, depression may be the result of low levels of paternal involvement of his being disabled as an involved parent, with the most depressed fathers having wives who are "over-involved" with their baby. A wealth of attachment themes are wrung open when a dad is disabled by his partner: feeling unimportant or not valued; experiencing separateness in terms of life and death; feeling excluded and alone; feeling abandoned at a time of need or being unable to depend on a partner; longing for emotional connection and feeling anger at a partner's lack of responsiveness....

## But, Why...?

While at times pregnant women receive negative, unasked for attention from people who assume that they won't know what to do as a mother, for the most part, from pregnancy onward, the new mother gains in status and attention from family, friends, and community—even from strangers. Reveling in this new state of power and purpose which, despite the tremendous strides of the women's movement, remains beyond the dominant experience of most women today, she may not want—at least unconsciously—to share it with anyone else. And then, if and when she does allow her partner in, it's frequently with a weight of directives on "how" to "do it."

While it is true that some women discourage fathers' involvement in the care of their child because of the deeply ingrained belief that men just can't "do it" or can't "do it as well" as they can, there is perhaps a deeper current running beneath this territoriality.

The symbiotic nature of the mother-child union exudes an innocence, wholeness, beauty, and completion that has been the inspiration of mystics, poets and artists throughout time, such that to conceive of any other—most especially a male—intruding into this domain is to verge on violation of this "holy union."

This is perhaps better understood when we recognize motherhood as being the sole domain within which women have held, at least in Western culture, unquestioned rights, power, and authority, the one arena in which they have reigned supreme. Little wonder that many women are loath to share the territory.

> *There are many ways to leave. I found myself throwing myself into my work, becoming a semi-workaholic. I got to be boss at my office, while my wife was boss at our home. It wasn't satisfying, but at least I had some sense of control over one place in my life.* —Ken

Pruett observes that at the same time men are struggling with what it means to father, indeed, *how* to father, women are struggling with how to relate to the man who created this child with them, as both their child's father and as their husband/partner: What to expect of him, what is reasonable he expect of her, and indeed how much to allow—even more so encourage—*him* in joining her in what has hitherto been *women's* domain?

## When the Gate Is Open:

The partners of involved dads are repeatedly shown to be less intrusive and controlling than those of traditional, or less involved, fathers. And, the more flexible and welcoming the gatekeeper, the better a dad the dad will be. While a mother's negative feelings may be conveyed through a tightness in her facial expression and armoring of her body towards her partner, as much as by her discouraging, devaluing, or ridiculing his approach to *her* child, a mother conveys positive feelings and expectations through the tone and pitch of her voice, and the softness of her body and face—a reaching towards rather than away from. Men who felt supported by their wives in finding their own way of doing things were not depressed, and soon developed a strong connection with their infants. And not surprisingly, when mothers respect their partner's fathering, fathers are more responsive, encouraging, and communicative with their offspring, and children thrive.

> *Secure connection to a loved one is empowering. When we feel safely connected to others we understand ourselves better and like ourselves more. We are more curious and more open to new information—curiosity comes out of a sense of safety; rigidity out of being vigilant to threats.*
> —Sue Johnson, PhD, *Hold Me Tight*

Researchers have found depression in some fathers lifts when they gain skills and confidence, and feel themselves capable of caring for their infants. Higher levels of engagement—ideally from the very beginning—between father and child, may actually counter any tendencies to depression, especially in those dads with a past history of depression.

Pruett identifies two key factors that encourage a mother to support and facilitate a father's connection and involvement with their child:

1. Her own fathering. A mother's childhood experience of her own father is a potent factor in shaping her expectations, hopes, and fears about her partner as a father to their child. From pregnancy onward, this influences the way she encourages or discourages her partner's connecting with their child, and so also the access of the child to the father. Mothers who felt rejected by their own father want to heal their father-wound by encouraging the fathering of their own children.
2. Her relationship with her partner. A mother's satisfaction with her relationship with her partner is a major factor in determining how involved the father will be with his children. Mothers who are happy in their marriage are shown to be more supportive of their partner's involvement.

## Staking Their Claim

Even when the gate is open, many fathers find it difficult to "stake their claim." While women have been socialized throughout their life in the art and science of nurturing, not only have most men been actively discouraged from developing their nurturing abilities, the nurturing male remains fuel for ridicule and engenders suspicions about gender identity in many corners of male society. This is all the more reason for women not only to open the gate, but open their hearts and hold out their hands to welcome their partner in.

Only a generation or two ago, being a good father was synonymous with being a good provider and protector. Good dads "brought home the bacon," mowed the lawn, washed the car, and could be called on to discipline the children. Today's "good father' is still expected, in most relationships, to be the breadwinner, and *also* to be a real presence, physically and emotionally, in his family. It's what many new dads want; and what their partners say they want of them. But it can be a tough call for even the most well-meaning and motivated. Not only do dads have no training in things like being nurturing and "emotionally available," they carry a lifetime of being socialized—as were their dads and their dads before them—to associate masculinity with independence and goal-orientation, and to perceive asking for help as a sign of weakness. After all, a guy is meant to know what to *do*.

During the first year, most new dads—being unprepared—feel scared, frightened, even terrified. It is frightening to find yourself feeling helpless, frustrated, tense, and even angry when the baby won't stop crying; you are exhausted from lack of sleep, unable to think straight and deprived of any quality time alone with your partner. Fears can range from not being able to live up to your own expectations, or not being able to protect your child from harm, or from war, disease, and environmental destruction, to fears of simply not being "ready" to assume the role of father, and of repeating mistakes made by your own father. On top of all this, as we saw above, there may be plenty of reasons that dad is feeling jealous—and afraid of being abandoned by his partner.

Many a well-intended and even highly committed father will find himself facing a rapidly closing, or even locked gate, after the birth of his child. Sadly, many of these men will begin to lose touch with their earlier high hopes and ideals of fathering their child with their partners, and of happy homes and families. As a man feels himself to be incompetent, invisible, superfluous, he distances himself from home and from involvement with his child, and seeks redemption in the world of work and career—or at the bar or in bed with another woman. Many a new dad will still believe in the ideals of commitment, involvement, and power sharing, but the practicalities are just too difficult. In this sad situation, there is no winner.

## Juggling Work and Involved Fathering

Many women today *expect* fathers to be more involved as parents and to care for the children. And many men want this, too. Most men and women today think that childcare should be shared, and that it's best when father is involved from the very beginning. And many dads are saying they find being a father more satisfying than their job. A challenge most new dads face is how to provide for a growing family while being a nurturing, involved dad. Work and involved fathering often seem to be incompatible.

Men who are committed to either traditional or involved fathering, at least have clear priorities with respect to home and work, but a growing number of men want a foot in both camps. They want to be meaningfully involved in the daily life of their child, and they want the rewards of employment. And many of mothers want this of their partners, too. Balancing the two is difficult:

- Their commitment to family may be resented by others who see it as a criticism of their own choices,
- Rising levels of unemployment mean increasing pressures to conform and perform well,
- Success at work is typically dependent on being:
    o decisive,
    o having clear goals,
    o working with deadlines,
    o performing specific tasks in a specified way and time.

These qualities and attitudes conflict with being a nurturing father, and the transition from one set of qualities to another can be difficult. While men may want or sense they need to behave differently at home, now that they are a dad, many have no idea what they need to do differently, and don't have the interpersonal skills to negotiate family relationships, especially in times of stress.

*Transitions from work to home were challenging. Many times I phoned home saying I was leaving to drive home for dinner, only to actually depart 30-45 minutes later. Usually, I arrived home to find a dinner of cold leftovers, an angry wife, and a disappointed family who had already eaten. This was my level of unconscious resistance and passive aggression, keeping me from the very intimacy and closeness that I craved.* —Ken

Many new dads fear that if they discuss their fears with their partner, she will not understand and will think he doesn't love her or the baby. While few men feel able to talk about their fears, admitting they exist—even to themselves—is a big step forward. Another will be sharing these fears with someone else—and some will find it initially easier to share with other dads, or perhaps a counselor. What's important is to recognize the fear, and share it with a trusted and empathetic other.

Before becoming fathers, men may not be conscious of the different personal qualities typically required at home and at work. Men who are most miserable at work are most likely to report bad relationships with their children. Work stresses inevitably affect father-child relationships. Returning home from a stressful day at work, fathers may ignore their children, behave coldly towards them, and be prone to outbursts of anger or impatience. While some fathers find immersing themselves in their child's world a welcome way of unwinding after a day at work, they are the exception. Limited time, exhaustion from a long day at work, arriving home to an exhausted new mom… it's hard to unwind, relax, and play.

*The temptation is always to try to direct the child's play: "Look, build up these two towers of bricks and then we can make a bridge so that Teddy can walk from this*

*one to that one. No, don't knock it down. No..." The trap so many men fall into, even when aware of it, is never being able to give up their control and surrender themselves to the child.* —Richard Seel, The Uncertain Father

Competency of—and joy in—fathering, as with mothering, is learned through the day-to-day heart-and-hands-on care of a child. But this level of care is rare for a dad, and virtually impossible for a working dad—as most dads are. Burgess notes that fathers typically spend almost no time alone with their (awake) babies, while stay-at-home mothers may be alone with them for more than 60 hours a week. While the temperamental fit between father and child will influence the level of competency he experiences in relating, even more important may be the amount of time father and child have together, especially in the absence of the mother, and wherein he is able to develop his own style of interaction.

> *Clearly some fathers are not interested in becoming an involved dad, but the dynamics are complex, rarely articulated, and mothers often hold very real power. When men successfully combine work and family with high levels of competence in both areas, their partners are frequently the catalyst.*
> —Adrienne Burgess, Fatherhood Reclaimed

It is interesting to note that while 74% of fathers reported that spending time with the family or finding time for key relationships is their *biggest concern* in daily life, so did 64% of mothers.[32]

Combining fatherhood with employment is not necessarily a losing game. After becoming fathers, many men find themselves developing new abilities to juggle conflicting demands, make decisions, and communicate quickly and clearly both at home and work. Some described themselves as more aware of their personal relationships on the job and more able to use some of their managerial skills in resolving family problems.

However at this point in time, while some fathers are finding that developing good relationships with their children is part of career success, and that the skills they learn at home are useful to them at work, most men see their professional and family lives as separate and conflicting. This may be because women draw social status from both work and family, while men's status is drawn almost exclusively from work and income.

## Dad in the Workplace

While men and women today are saying their families are more important than their careers, few social and economic policies reflect these priorities. Yet it makes *good business* sense. For example:

The men who are most miserable at work are most likely to report bad relationships with their children. This has enormous implications for cost-effectiveness in business. An American study of 300 dual career couples found the *only* consistent predictor of men's bad physical health to be whether they had concerns about their relationships with their children. Note the ripple effect: a sample of US employees revealed that about half thought that other people's childcare problems disrupted their work.

More involved fathers are happier with themselves, show fewer symptoms of ill health, and have wives who report greater satisfaction with their marriage. Clearly, there is real value in families being supported in negotiating more balanced marital, parenting, and work arrangements.

## Family-Friendly Employment Policies

Many companies favor family-friendly employment as long as family-friendly means mother-friendly. Family-friendly policies need to be reframed with men in mind.

American fathers who attended in-depth parent education programs before their babies' births, and had come to feel responsible for what was happening at home even if their wives, on maternity leave, did most of the baby care, seemed better able to leave their distress *at* work.

Each of the 34 countries in the Organization for Economic Co-operation and Development (OECD), except the US, offers paid parental leave (Australia's plan was instituted in 2010). In most European countries, except the UK, legislation is increasingly allowing couples more choice in how they share parenting and work responsibilities—actively promoting caring by fathers.* Leave uptake by fathers has increased dramatically in some countries; with resulting benefits to the quality of family relationships, including couple-stability. Until similar support is offered to parents in the US, this poses a real obstacle to dads parenting as partners.

Paternity leave may be as valuable to employer as to employee. As men get involved in pregnancy, birth, and the early weeks after birth, it takes them longer to regain the level-headedness to work efficiently and effectively. A period of leave—minimally two weeks and better six weeks or more—may be in everyone's best interest.

---

* In Sweden, parents get twelve months parental benefits, divided between them as they wish, although only one parent can be on leave at a time. They receive: two months' prenatal maternity leave and ten days paternity leave; 90% of gross income for the first nine months' parental leave, and a basic flat rate for the last three months. Some parents take leave consecutively, so infants are cared for full time. Uptake for fathers runs at 50%. Fathers who stay at home alone with their children for a minimum of three months develop independent relationships with them and remain highly involved after returning to work. Other couples take their leave mostly part-time and use it to subsidize shorter hours working while their children are small.

More flexible work schedules can enable some men and women to share more of the child-care responsibilities, although this is not a possibility for those many families needing two incomes just to survive.

## Gender Inequalities in the Workplace

On the most obvious and immediate level, as underscored by the Fatherhood Institute, the system as it stands is highly gendered, directing men and women into starkly divided breadwinning and child-caring roles right from the beginning of their experience as parents.

It is assumed that the mother will be the main caregiver for a baby right through to his or her first birthday. This is at odds with a growing body of evidence indicating the growing desire of both men and women to share the physical and emotional care of their children. Studies show, for instance:

- Under 50% of men (and fewer than 33% of women) believe the provider role to be the man's;
- Men are disadvantaged in that the division of infant care sets a pattern which may well endure through many years of parenting, with fathers who are more involved at the outset tending to remain so right through to adolescence.

More men are looking to balancing work and family, working flexible hours, cutting down on overtime, and refusing promotions; but most experience seniority systems as insensitive to the needs of young families and feel they suffer from negative evaluations by colleagues when dads take time for family responsibilities.

*In Norway the introduction of reserved parental leave for fathers has resulted in a dramatic increase in the numbers of fathers taking time off to care for children....*

*Norway's gender-equality experiment... for challenging the gender-stereotypes, which are reproduced through adults' gender-segmented working lives is meeting with remarkable success, with male workers now very visible in Norwegian nurseries. This, together with greater involvement by fathers at home, is mounting a profound challenge to children's "lived experience" of care by women as the norm. In the UK, by contrast, where only 2 males under 25 are currently working in state-funded nurseries, even children who experience substantial levels of care from their own fathers step into a world of women once they enter professional childcare. This reinforces, possibly more than words ever can, that childcare is women's business—and women's alone.* —Fatherhood Institute

It is important to note that women's career prospects suffer too, from a system which structurally inclines them towards prolonged absence from the workplace. Equality of opportunity for women depends on the expanding role of men in family work—and doing so makes good economic sense.

Hope is on the horizon with new opportunities for mixing home and work with work practices that are changing due to computerization and information technology. Meanwhile, despite their desires and intentions, many men end up working more hours after the birth. Many feel they can't win either way. If they don't put in the hours at work, they're not providing for their family. If they do, they're in trouble because they're not home to help. Many of these dads will give up and leave—emotionally, if not physically.

Strategies from the Fatherhood Institute that enable fathers to increase their involvement at home within the current paradigm of mainly full-time working include:*

- Fathers being encouraged to use existing family-friendly provisions in their workplaces.
- Fathers who work beyond the standard working hours for their occupation reducing their work hours, yet still working full time.
- Fathers reducing their leisure time further to care for their children, while still working full time.
- Support and strategies to help fathers optimize the quality of the time spent with their children, including developing appropriate parenting skills.
- Contract, self-employed, under-employed, or casually employed fathers being encouraged to take greater opportunities to design their work hours around childcare.
- Unemployed/low paid fathers being encouraged to focus time and attention on their children, both for their own sake, and so that mothers are freer to take up employment.

## Lessons in "Of Little Importance"

Gatekeeping is not simply the domain of the mother. Even William Sears, MD, who coined the term attachment parenting and has made a very significant contribution to the adoption by many new parents of attachment parenting theory and practice, states in *Becoming a Father: How to Nurture and Enjoy Your Family*, that "many mothers are justified in their unwillingness to let fathers care for the baby, because these fathers have not demonstrated that they are capable of comforting the baby."

As we will see more clearly in the following chapters, even before the baby's birth, dad may be treated as a nuisance or novelty in the prenatal clinic and birth education classes. He is typically at the bottom of the ladder in the labor room and often sent home after witnessing the birth of his baby. Most childcare facilities exude equally potent forms of gatekeeping, being highly

---

* Fatherhood Institute Research Summary: *Fathers, Mothers, Work and Family* 19 January, 2011

mother-centered. Most are staffed by females, with magazines, posters, classes, and notices sent to the home being geared to the needs and interests of the mother, and almost to the exclusion of the father.

> *In our considerable experience, few of the mainstream relationship or parenting support interventions currently delivered in the UK across the transition to parenthood (and in most other settings) are really thoughtful about, or effective in, engaging men.* —Fatherhood Institute

Other cultural factors that discourage competent fathering include glass ceilings for fathers of young children seeking flextime and paternity leave; bureaucracies involved with children's health care that don't include a place for fathers' names on their routine forms; and the media's all-too-frequent portrayal of fathers as incompetents.

Much of the father-child relationship depends on the value accorded their relationship by the local and wider community. In the absence of this, it is extremely difficult for men to see themselves as being of value to their children, and therefore, difficult to be there for the kids.

> *Because they don't believe their presence and attention there to be of the highest importance, or, let it be said, of much importance at all.*
> —Adrienne Burgess, *Fatherhood Reclaimed*

## Affirming Fathering

Pruett offers a list of ways and means by which men can begin to deconstruct the image of father being of little importance.[33]

### *In yourself:*

- Embrace the irreplaceable value of fatherhood in your life as a man.
- Think long, hard, and often about what you want to give your children besides your money.
- Acknowledge fatherhood as one of the longest, most creative, and rewarding adventures of your inner life.
- Leave room for failure and forgiveness in yourself (and of course, others). There is no perfect father—yours wasn't and neither are you.
- Responsibly communicate to abusive or neglecting fathers your concerns about their kids and them.
- Look hard at your father's presence in you. He's there. Understand what you are doing with your father's parenting style in the realizing of your own child—modeling, overcoming, repairing, emulating—or a quilt of all these.
- Ask yourself, "How do I want the mother of my child to think and feel about me as a father?"

- Talk every day with someone outside your family, especially other men, about your fathering. It's called witnessing.
- Examine your own prejudices regarding men's and women's types of work.

## *With your children:*
- Your affection is the irreplaceable communication of your child's unique value to you.
- Listen to your child's view of the world, and *share* the last word occasionally.
- Your skills and passions outside work are a fascination to your kids. Share these with them. You are as unique as they are.
- Discipline means to teach, not punish. So forget intimidation and threats, both physical and emotional. They teach your child to fear and avoid, not respect and emulate, you.
- When with your child, be actively attentive and emotionally present. Quality time is a myth. Your children are raised in ordinary time, and being there—being with your kids—gives you the authority you need to do a good job. Fathering takes more than weekends.
- Live the values and habits you'd be thrilled to see in your children. They remember better than you.
- Time alone together is critical at all ages—read when they're little, drive when they're older.
- Know your kids' world, their friends, their doctor. Meet their teachers early and often, and speak up to resist sidelining yourself. Volunteer in the classroom; you'll learn volumes.

## *With your children's mother:*
- Parenting is an equal partnership emotionally, if not always mathematically, within and outside marriage.
- Engage in discussions with your children's mother about shared authority and power between men and women.
- Ask yourself, "How can my relationship with their mother be a positive resource in my kids' lives?" Start always with what you respect.
- Keep up on your parenting skills together. Share articles or books discussing appropriate expectations for your children at relevant ages.
- When married, carefully maintain your relationship with your kids' mother: date her, snuggle with her, and ritualize times to be together. A short talk is better than no talk when you're exhausted.

## In your work:

- Discourage negative stereotypes of fathers wherever you find them—at the water cooler, in meetings, in policy statements, etc.
- Support family leave for men and women, pitch in to cover, confront the naysayers.
- Bring your children to work. Show them your space. Introduce them to your colleagues. Talk to them about what you do.
- Invite your children to know this side of your world outside home. Ask them what they see and think. Seek their advice occasionally for some eye-opening wisdom.

And now, onto the bigger picture, a society's FatherStory, the shared understanding of what it mean for a man to be a father.

# Key Points

- While a growing number of men want to be more involved in the care of their children, mothers often unwittingly discourage their partner's involvement.
- While 15–25% of mothers suffer from moderate to severe postpartum depression after a child's birth, dads experience it similarly.
- A significant causal factor is their suffering a withdrawal from being tended to in their marital relationship. Depressed, they are likely to themselves withdraw and/or be irritable and aggressive. Women are likely to respond by turning their focus even further from their partner and even more to their child.
- Researchers who argue that paternal depression is due to the father's feeling displaced—a "greedy child"—have not factored in the attachment perspective that recognizes that our need, as adults as well as children, for emotional connection is legitimate and absolute.
- While men are struggling with what it means to be a father, women are struggling with what to expect of him, what is reasonable that he expect of her, and how much to allow—and encourage—him in joining her in what has previously been women's exclusive domain.
- Fathers who feel supported by their wives in finding their own way of caring for the child are less prone to depression and soon develop a strong connection with their infant.
- During the first year, most new dads will feel scared, frightened, helpless, exhausted. In addition, they may feel jealous, and afraid of being abandoned by their wife.
- The challenge for most new dads is finding the demands of employment and fathering to be separate and conflicting roles, and attempting to balance the two.
- While men and women say their families are more important than their careers, few social and economic policies reflect this. And most dads soon learn they are "of little importance"—treated as nuisance or novelty in the prenatal clinic and at birth education classes, at bottom of the ladder in the labor room, and sent home after witnessing the birth. Most childcare facilities are highly mother centered.
- Accorded little real value by their community, it is difficult for new fathers to value themselves and so, to be there for their children.
- Most men and women today think that childcare should be shared, and that it's best when dad is involved from the very beginning.

# 10: A Society's FatherStory

*Fatherhood, much more than motherhood, is a cultural invention. Its meaning for the individual man shaped less by biology than by a cultural script or story that guides and at times pressures him into certain ways of acting and of understanding himself as a man.* —David Blankenhorn, *Fatherless America*

Underlying the gatekeeping by mother, by father (the internalized negative images of man as father), by helping professionals and other well-meaning parties, as well as by most current economic and social policies, is a society's FatherStory—the shared understanding of what it means for a man to have a child. A society's FatherStory is a primary indicator of the number of children who will grow up with—and without—a father. As evident in the preceding chapter, our society's prevailing story of fatherhood sees fatherhood as a distinctive social role for men as superfluous—unnecessary, even undesirable.

In many corners, controversy continues to rage over the true nature of the functions and capacities of men to father and women to mother:

*On one side stands a mother, armed with womb and breasts: symbols and expressions of her nurturing capabilities. Opposite her stands a father, wombless and breastless, designated the provider through deficiency not abundance, his paternal identity formed not from what he possesses but from what he lacks, it is not only women for whom biology has been perceived as destiny. Men are caught in the same trap.* —Adrienne Burgess, *Fatherhood Reclaimed*

Burgess underscores the key to maternal dominance as being sourced in the biological facts that bond mother and infant together: the infant is carried in the womb of the mother, and nourished by the milk from her breast. Yet it is the male sea horses that give birth and the male Emperor Penguins that devotedly protect the eggs of their offspring. These are but the tip of the iceberg of parenting behaviors that challenge the belief that mothering and fathering behaviors are biologically determined and relatively fixed—mothers nurture, fathers provide.

Burgess then draws our attention to an alternative paradigm. Just as feminists challenged conventional thinking through uncovering mythological and anthropological evidence of very different notions of woman, fatherhood imagery is now under scrutiny. In Western culture the two images—father and ruler—have become so strongly fused that it can be difficult to separate the two, to imagine a father who is not also a "ruler." The discovery of new archetypes of a nurturing earth father challenges this prevailing archetype of man as patriarch—which literally means "father and ruler." Some appear with erect penises, said to symbolize not dominance, but fertility. Bacchus changed his flesh into corn and his blood into wine each year, to feed humankind. Some earth fathers can also give birth. In Australian aboriginal myth, Karora, buried in the earth, produces bandicoots from his navel and human souls from his armpits. Similar tales appear in Scandinavian and Chinese mythology. Societies that retain earth fathers in their mythologies tend to see nurturing behavior by men towards children as normal and natural.

Burgess writes, of Western culture, "in the virtual absence of any connections between men and nature or nurture, such images can be so alien as to seem aberrant." However, the fact is that anthropological, cross-cultural and cross species research, as well as modern primatology, reveals a tremendous range of potentials for fathering behavior, and a tremendous diversity of father-child relationships.

## Insights from Primatology and Anthropology

Burgess draws attention to modern primatology that reveals fathering behaviors among nonhuman primates to be both immensely varied and far from fixed. They vary more in response to changing circumstances than to biological imperatives. Only one in ten mammalian species have males that provide any form of direct infant care in the wild—many more do so in captivity. The key to maternal dominance appears to rest on the biological fact that the young are initially and exclusively nourished by their mother's milk. In half the species of non-human primates (apes and monkeys), males are regularly found providing direct care to infants. While mom is primary caregiver in most animal species, examples of dad as primary caregiver are found in animals such as the wolf and stickleback, and even in primates such as marmoset and gibbon. Many creatures of the natural world—butterflies, turtles, spiders—provide no parental care. Others—such as over 90% of bird species—share parenting care equally. In some species, the male remains the primary (or sole) caregiver until the young are grown.

Best fathering awards go to species like owls and titi monkeys, tamarins, and marmosets. Males assist at births, pre-masticate food for newborns, and carry them day and night, only handing them to their mothers for feeding. Can these "new dads" be sure they're the fathers? Only sometimes.

But it doesn't even end there. Male chimps, baboons, and macaques have been found to adopt orphans in the wild, and even as aggressive a primate as the rhesus male, when reared in a nuclear family environment in a laboratory, interacts playfully with his infant.

This brings into question any tendency to consider human fathering as naturally rigid and gender-specific, and human fathers as biologically programmed to be uninvolved with their young, or with the young of other males. Moving from primatology to anthropological data affords a fascinating insight into the way social and cultural variables influence a father's involvement with his children. In cultures such as the Arapesh of Papua New Guinea, fathers take an active and joint role with mother during pregnancy, as well as in caring for the infant after birth. !Kung San fathers, representative of the earliest hunter, gatherer societies, are affectionate and indulgent, often holding and fondling their infants, though the mother provides most of the routine care. Fathers from Lesu villages in Melanesia, gardeners, living in monogamous nuclear families, spend hours playing with their infants. An analysis of social organization in different cultures suggests males have closer relationships with infants when families are monogamous, when both parents live together in isolated nuclear families, when women contribute to subsistence by working, and when men are not required to be warriors.

## Can It Be True That Our Society Has Vested Interests in Separating Men and Babies?

Burgess quotes sociologist Margaret Mead's observations that carry us ever more deeply into the myriad forces separating men from their babies:

No developing society that needs men to leave home and do their thing for society ever allows young men to handle or touch their newborns, for they know somewhere that if they did, the new fathers would become so "hooked" that they would never go out and do their thing properly.

Burgess elaborates, proposing that emotionally and physically distancing men from infants so that they will be cut off from their most tender feelings, ultimately, prepares them to kill and be killed in times of war. She goes on to suggest that if it is then true, then it is only when violence is seen as antisocial, and it is unlikely that large numbers of young men will ever again be called upon to fight for "their country," that a review of father role is deemed possible.

Although a cross-cultural review of fathering behaviors reveals individual men (or groups of men) can be as intimately involved in infant care as any woman, the overwhelming picture is one of less involvement by males than females, particularly during infancy and the early years. Still, the question holds true: what's biological, what's environmental?

> *Mexico has an odd combination of machismo and a FatherStory that involves men being tender with babies; there are lots of models for this within the culture, and my sons grew up there with a love of babies.* —Barbara

## Back to Contemporary Western Society

Within contemporary Western society, the evidence of similarities between the psychological experiences of pregnancy for mothers and fathers is striking (see Chapter 8). As we will see, an estimated 60% of men experience physical signs of pregnancy remarkably like those associated with pregnant women. With some 90% of fathers now present at birth, their description of feelings after witnessing the birth—extreme elation, relief the baby is healthy, pride and increased self-esteem, closeness when baby opened her eyes—are almost identical to those of a mother. Estimates of mothers suffering from moderate to severe postpartum depression range from 12-20%, but if these numbers are subject to the same extreme under-reporting of "regular" depression, then the number is much higher. Similarly, the estimates of 10–15% of fathers' postpartum depression are low.

Both evidence similar behaviors when interacting with their newborn. Early contact with the newborn affects the father-infant attachment just as it does the mother-infant attachment. And from early infancy, fathers are capable of sensitive and skilled social interactions with their child, and a like capacity to form secure attachments.

## A New Story of Fatherhood

Burgess underscores the fact that some fathers from all eras have been intimately involved in their children's upbringing, and deeply attached to them. The nature and degree of father-child interaction has shown, and continues to show, considerable variation, across both time and place, but also between individuals and even within families where father (like mother), may be close to one child and distant from another.

What is emerging is an enormous discrepancy between cultural myth and expectations concerning a father's capacity to nurture, and the day-to-day reality. Research is showing human males to be competent with, and sensitive to, children, and given the opening, they seek to be with them.

> *If men are asked what fathers are for, they may respond with traditional ideas such as providing, protecting, advising. But if they are asked to outline their own value to their own children, such functions, if mentioned at all, will appear towards the bottom of the list. Instead, these dads will prioritize intimacy, tenderness.* —Adrienne Burgess, *Fatherhood Reclaimed*

Most men and women today think that childcare should be shared, and that it's best when father is involved from the very beginning. A growing body of evidence indicates that both parents are more satisfied when roles are more equally shared—and less satisfied when they are not. And many dads are saying they find being a father more satisfying than their job.

> *There is a growing realization that it is not only women who lose from gendered role-division. While masculinity is primarily defined through paid work, men suffer, too, in terms of the quality of their relationships with their children and their marginalisation from the daily activities of family life, which can translate into marginalisation from society. The equality of opportunity for women in the workforce depends on expanding the role of men in family work.*
> —Fatherhood Institute (quoting Connell)

A prominent challenge to women will be to give up their dominance over their children and acknowledge their partners as equal partners in parenting, while finding the obligation to be breadwinners imposed on them as it currently is on men. Can they do it? Do they want to? Doubtless, some will, some won't, and there will be even more shades of grey between the two.

> *I must admit that I enjoyed being the primary caregiver, the one who was "allowed" to stay home with young children and not be the primary breadwinner. I looked for a man who would be OK with me having this role; it was hard to find someone in our culture who would appreciate or accept me taking that role. I never completely gave up wage earning; I was an integral part of our family jewelry business, but I loved having the primary role of nurturer and leaving what I considered the more pressured role of ultimately being responsible for most of the wage earning to my husband. So this suggestion in the above paragraph stirred up some fear and loss in me.* —Barbara

Prevailing images of fatherhood need to be challenged and re-envisioned, men's parenting potential needs to be recognized and treated with respect, and the reality of father's private longings and lives made more visible. An informed awareness of both mothers and fathers of their own and each other's significance to the wellbeing of their children; and of the imperative of recognizing the importance of attachment—of not only parent-child but also adult-adult—to wellbeing, are vital elements in the sustenance of a new FatherStory.

New cultural stories of fatherhood that shape our understanding of fatherhood as a fulfilling and vital social role, are critical to turning the tide of men leaving. As expanded on in Chapter 30, backing these stories with social, economic, and legal policies and practices supporting fathers in maintaining a close alliance with their child's mother, and a responsible and active involvement in the life of their child, is the other side of the coin that will give currency to optimal connections between not only parent and child, but parent with parent, each parent with child, and the trinity of mother and father and child.

> *It is only a few decades since women were widely believed to be sexually passionless, intellectually weak, and emotionally flimsy by nature.... Bearing this in mind, perhaps it is not unreasonable to suggest that, before too long we will discard the beliefs... that men are by nature less sensitive to their children and less deeply attached to them. Or that men should defer to women in parenting... on grounds of their biological fitness for the task.* —Adrienne Burgess, *Fatherhood Reclaimed*

## Key Points

- A society's FatherStory—the shared understanding of what it means for a man to have a child—is a primary indicator of the number of children who will grow up with, and without, a father.
- Our society's Fatherstory sees fatherhood as a distinctive social role for men, as superfluous—unnecessary, even as undesirable.
- Anthropological, cross-cultural, and cross-species research, as well as modern primatology, reveals a tremendous range of potentials for fathering behavior, and a tremendous diversity of father-child relationships.
- Social and cultural variables greatly influence a father's involvement with his children.
- An enormous discrepancy is emerging between cultural myth and expectations concerning fathers' capacities to nurture, and day-to-day reality.
- Fathers are proving to be competent with, and sensitive to, children.
- New cultural stories of fatherhood that shape our understanding of fatherhood as a fulfilling and vital social role, are critical to turning the tide of men leaving.
- Elements vital to the sustenance of a new Fatherstory include: respect of men's parenting potential, an informed awareness of both moms and dads of their own *and* the others significance to the wellbeing of their children, and the imperative of recognizing the importance of connection—parent-child and adult-adult. All need to be backed by both a supportive community and social, economic, and legal policies and practices.

# 11: PARENTING: ARE WE READY?

*When I was a resident in preventive medicine, my first wife decided it was time to have a baby. We'd been married almost five years and I was finally earning enough to support us, but I wasn't ready to be a father, and I knew it. In fact, I had never even seriously thought about it, as obvious as that trajectory would have been.*

*She said it had to be now or she'd leave, but in 1971, divorce in my family was not an option, so I gave in and shortly she was pregnant.* —Jack

Contrary to popular pronouncements, contrary to all that you might want to believe, you cannot have it all. You cannot keep a full-time job, work out regularly at the gym, entertain your friends, re-experience the pre-pregnancy delights of sexual play with your partner, and parent your child. Choices must be made. The birth of a baby will change your life, forever. You simply cannot expect to live the way you did before, after you have had a baby. Jack and I learned this the hard way!

Most couples enter parenting with virtually no idea, and even less experience, of what it means to parent a child: how it will impact them, their partner, their relationship, the life they bring into this world. It is crucial for prospective parents to consider whether they are reading to assume the roles and responsibilities required of them, in order to fully meet the needs of an infant and child. This necessitates an appreciation of the skills and resources—mental, physical and emotional—needed. Taking the time to talk with others, read, learn about, and discuss together the sensitivities and developmental needs of a baby and child, the changes in lifestyle and priorities parenting demands, your abilities to allow a child to develop as an individual rather than according to your expectations, and the level of physical and emotional support available from family and community. Another crucial factor to consider is your own childhood history, what unmet needs or unresolved issues might be restimulated with the birth of a child (see Chapters 15 &18).

*Even the best prospective parents can fall short if they choose to have a baby for the wrong reason—to please others, to compensate for a loss in the wrong relationship, or during a troublesome period of life. Emotionally volatile, unpredictable, and depressed high-risk men and women must resolve their own problems before they can hope to nurture another life.*

—Thomas Verny, MD, *Preparenting*

*Although I haven't yet experienced the challenges of fatherhood, I've certainly spent a lot of time thinking, feeling, and reflecting about my experiences as a child, and I can certainly relate to the experience of "wounds" created by insufficient attachment, despite my having being raised in a stable (albeit nuclear) family unit with a loving mother. The years of psychotherapy, NLP, hypnosis, meditation, and Tai Chi may have taken the edge off these wounds to the point that they might not be too sensitive to the upheavals of having a baby, but again I guess I'll find out soon enough.*

—Ben, two months before the birth of his first child.

An email a few months later:

*We're three weeks into the thick of it, and so far so good. Our little boy James., aka "Tigger," was born at home in a birth pool.*

*So far he's proven to be a remarkably relaxed little character, fond of his sleep, feeding well, and putting on weight. Giselle and I are doing great as well. I haven't had any MPAS feelings so far, but I'm glad to have recently learned about the concept.*

*On reflection, I think there are probably a couple of reasons for this. First, we're pretty much sharing all the parenting work (except breastfeeding, obviously). I burp and change Tigger, sing him songs and tell him stories, and some nights I take him away to the spare room to sleep with me when G. is really tired. Sharing the parenting is really essential for us because we don't have much by way of family or a community support network, as we only moved down here a few years ago.*

*I suspect that the other reason I'm not experiencing MPAS is that I have spent quite a bit of time over the last several years reworking my own attachment issues. The motivation for me dealing with these issues were breakdowns and deep depressions that were triggered by other life circumstances, but might well have turned into DDD if I had had children earlier in life.*

*It's hard to know for sure of course, I guess all I can say at this stage is "so far so good."* —Ben

Perhaps the most important factor in considering readiness to parent, is the quality of a couple's existing relationship.

Studies *consistently* point to the *quality of a marriage* being the best predictor of:
- both mothers' and fathers' adjustments to parenthood,
- the father's level of involvement as father and husband, and later,
- their satisfaction with the marriage.

*While our early days together were passionate, my partner, age 42, announced at the start that she wanted a baby soon and would give me one ovulation to make up my mind. Needless to say, that didn't work out, so we did IVF for a year. During this time we began slowly drifting from each other. The all-loving-and-understanding-mother-replacement that I wanted in a partner,*

> which I actually knew on a conscious level I wanted, never eventuated. Her previous traumatic divorce had left her untrusting and independent, while I wanted to share a life together. But I was blinded by hope.
>
> After our son's birth, the focus of our lives conveniently turned to him—rather than each other. Sex no longer interested her and our relationship has continued to deteriorate. Her refusal to marry me, or to let me co-own "her" home, plus frequent harsh criticism and emotional abuse has replaced our once more-loving relationship.
>
> So now, with our son age three, we are planning a separation where I will live upstairs and she downstairs, sharing the care of our son.
>
> Rather than falling in love, I always thought that, "love is action." I just have to choose her. And choose her again, and again, and again. At each trial and tribulation. And that was how I could love and be with her. And I now believe that I can still choose her—but not necessarily stay physically with her. —Hank

Unfortunately, Hank and his partner learned the hard way that the quality of a marriage, prior to parenting, is the best predictor of later success and satisfaction. They have since separated.

## Partners in Parenting

As a clinical psychologist trained by John Gray, PhD (*Men Are from Mars, Women Are from Venus*), Mitzi Gold, PhD, sees many couples that are striving for partnership, "a relationship of equals co-creating and participating together." Gold has identified what she terms "The Five C's"—"connectors" to assure a successful and harmonious relationship: **Communication, Commitment, Compassion, Caring, and Change.**

How do these all work together? Gold counsels that each person in the relationship needs to develop the skills to be able to **communicate** truthfully, openly, honestly, and completely. **Commit** to each other to be the best you can be individually and as a couple. Develop a **compassionate** attitude and **caring** behavior toward yourself and each other. Accept **change** and embrace your process of continued growth as an individual and as a couple.

Gold offers an example of a couple whose commitment to partnership and preparation prior to conceiving clearly paid dividends:

> A couple came in after four years of marriage, unsure if they could stay together. He wanted to please his wife but felt frequently criticized. She complained about his habits of coming home and crashing on the couch and being unreliable with his home chores.
>
> By practicing communication skills in sessions, they began to hear and respond to each other in new ways. He began to develop his "voice" and was able to

*respond to her and share his own issues with the relationship. It took courage to listen to each other as negative feelings were openly shared.*

*As time went by, she wanted to get pregnant. He was able to say strongly that he did not want her to become pregnant until he believed that their relationship was stable and that he could trust that their relationship would remain a priority. He did not want to lose his connection with her. She was upset that he was now taking charge; however, she also wanted to strengthen their relationship.*

*They took time to share and challenge each other with the issues confronting them. Eventually, they both agreed they were ready for a child. He was able to express his love for her during her pregnancy and she was able to accept it. They talked about their childhood experiences, and what kind of parents they wanted to be. He rubbed her feet when she felt uncomfortable during the later stages of pregnancy. She let him rest when he came home tired from work. They began to function as the team that they had been talking about in their sessions.*

*He became even more helpful during her pregnancy since he could see how tired she would become, or that she needed help with meals and couldn't do as much as usual. She changed jobs and they managed their finances so she was able to take an additional three months off work.*

*After their baby was born they realized they needed each other even more than before. She discovered that she didn't know much about being a mom and there was a lot to know. He felt confident stepping into this area since they were more on equal footing with their first child. They shared and discussed their responsibilities and how they could be good parents while maintaining their special marital relationship. When issues arose with their new baby, they read together and researched solutions.*

*She was enjoying her time off, but also aware that she would soon return to work. Fortunately, her parents were thrilled to step in and take over the childcare during the daytime. They realized how fortunate they are to have adoring grandparents take care of their child. Her parents are also on board with their parenting philosophy, so there is stability and consistency with the baby care. They make it through challenging times and see this time as their adventures together.*

Couples willing to do the tough work to heal their hearts or develop new skills will learn to evolve and flow with the many situations confronting them. When couples are able to stay connected by knowing that they have a partner, this builds confidence. From this experience of being valuable members in a relationship, it extends to our families and our communities.

**Key Points**
- Most couples enter parenting with virtually no idea of how it will impact them. The birth of a baby will changes their lives—forever.
- It is vitally important that prospective parents consider whether they are ready to assume the roles and responsibilities required in caring for an infant and child. This requires an informed awareness of:
  - the developmental needs of an infant/child,
  - the changes in lifestyle and priorities required to meet an infant/child's needs,
  - how it might impact their relationship,
  - the level of support available from family and community,
  - their own childhood history and how it may impact their parenting.
- The quality of a couple's existing relationship is the single most important factor to access in considering readiness to parent. This is the primary predictor of a couple's adjustment to parenthood and satisfaction with their marriage after baby.
- The five Cs are important elements in a successful partnership: Communication, Commitment, Compassion, Caring, and Change.

## 12: Pregnant Partners

> *Until recently, a father's emotions were disregarded. Our latest studies show that this view is dangerously wrong. How a man feels about his wife and unborn child is one of the single most important factors in determining the success of a pregnancy.* —Thomas Verny, MD, *The Secret Life of the Unborn Child*

While there is a mountain of resources supporting expectant mothers, information and support for men during pregnancy and the perinatal period is notable primarily for its absence. This is especially concerning, as early involvement in pregnancy is highly significant to a father's bonding with his child, and fathers who are involved are more likely to be around for the long haul. Furthermore, information and support for dads is important because during pregnancy, they contribute directly to the mother's emotional state, and thereby to the child's, and their future relationship as a family. It is a well-established fact that parents have an enormous influence on the mental and physical attributes of their children, and that this influence begins before birth.

> *The father's relationship with the mother during this period is second in importance only to her relationship with the prenate. The way the father relates to the mother, the emotional support and nurturance he gives her, directly impacts her feelings of wellbeing and therefore the wellbeing of the unborn child. His rage or tenderness, anger or joy, touch both mother and the unborn. Together, mother and father can focus intentions on creating a sense of calm throughout the pregnancy.* —Thomas Verny, MD, *Preparenting*

Mothers have an easier, happier, and healthier pregnancy if father is involved and supportive. The more involved father is from the very beginning, the more seriously his partner will take him, the more confident she will be in his fathering, and the more supportive of the father's relationship with their child she will be. Then, too, men who receive their partner's emotional support during pregnancy have better physical and emotional health, and are better able to maintain good relationships with their partners through the bumpy periods, than are men who don't have their partner's emotional support. The more supportive partners are of each other, the better the couple's relationship.

How a mother and father care for themselves and each other during the pregnancy deeply touches their unborn. This means it is important that a couple address the emotional, relational, and spiritual dimensions as well as the physical and intellectual aspects of pregnancy.

> *Many of us think of conception and prenatal care as optimizing the physical health of the child and mother. We rarely consider the father's health, the psychological health of the parents and their relationship, and the whole health—body, mind, and soul—of the unborn child.*
> —Carista Luminare-Rosen, *Parenting Begins Before Conception*

## Feelings of Exclusion

During pregnancy and birth, men, too, have legitimate needs, and meeting these enables a man to be more fully present with his partner and baby.

Richard Seel, in *The Uncertain Father,* underscores pregnancy as a very physical and visible experience for a woman, with many months drawing attention to the fact that she is becoming a mother. Visibly she is undergoing a major life transition and everybody—even strangers—fusses over her. The fact that her partner is in the process of becoming a father is invisible to the world, except through *her* presence. For him, this transition to fatherhood is primarily an internal experience. In all likelihood, he will navigate through most of this experience alone and with difficulty, especially given a man's tendency to be ill at ease with feelings, with not being in control, and with not "having the answers." Compounding these difficulties are the expectations coming at him from all directions to "be strong" for his partner. The more pronounced the physical signs of her pregnancy, the more alienated he may become, and the more inadequate, superfluous, and disconnected he may feel.

> *Perhaps most difficult of all, is the knowing, deep down inside, that this is something he can never experience himself.*
> —Richard Seel, *The Uncertain Father*

Feelings of exclusion are frequently reinforced by the way he is treated at prenatal visits—at best as a novelty, perhaps a nuisance, at worst, as an irrelevance. When he is directly addressed, it's usually in terms of how he can support his partner. Pregnant dads receive little, if any, recognition or acknowledgement of their specific concerns, needs, and emotional stresses. If people notice a man is having a difficult time, they tend to joke rather than empathize.

Lack of recognition of a father's emotional involvement in a pregnancy is of special concern. Counseling and educating fathers at this stage can improve the quality of the father-child attachment, father involvement, mother-child involvement, and breastfeeding rates. A skilled birth worker talking with an expectant father can tell a lot about what will likely happen in the family after the birth—whether the man will have trouble bonding with his baby or is at risk of postnatal depression, or whether his partner will manage to breastfeed, to become very involved with her baby, or become depressed.

With respect to couple-relationships, paying attention to fathers' satisfaction in the postnatal period may be particularly important, given that the first year after the birth is the peak time for parental separation, fathers' satisfaction is more likely than mothers' to decline during this time, and men's dissatisfaction is more predictive than women's of the relationship ending.[34]

## So What Is a Dad's Role in Pregnancy?

Fathers have traditionally borne the role of protecting and providing for their families. Traditionally, protecting has meant against danger from wild animals or intruders. Today, it may mean protection from obnoxious neighbors and financial worries. And the form and setting of providing has, as noted by Patrick Houser, now morphed from "forest and field" to "factory and office."

The importance of having someone to rely on is illustrated by the behavior of women who cope successfully with the immense demands of pregnancy and early mothering. Robert Karen noted that those who fared best were able to ask for help from appropriate people and to do so directly, without hints or manipulations. They had relationships with their husbands whose support they happily sought, and they themselves had the capacity to give spontaneously to others, including their babies.

When a midwife introduced Houser to the concept that he, too, was "pregnant," it clicked:

> *From that moment on I adopted the stance that I was also having this baby... it allowed me to more easily engage with Kathryn's pregnancy and our child, and to begin fathering.... Kathryn was carrying our baby and I was carrying our family... by caring for her I was also caring for our child, I was no longer a bystander, baggage holder, or just the sperm donor. I was embracing my new family at an early stage.* —Patrick Houser, *Fathers-to-Be Handbook*

Houser suggests that a modern interpretation of "to protect and provide for" could include the environment of the pregnancy and birth. This means being informed of his partner's needs and doing his best to ensure a calm and nurturing womb time and birth environment. This role takes on special significance in the event of a medicalized birth because of the alien environment of bright lights, noise, uncomfortable furnishings, plus the profusion of extraneous, multi-tasking people focused on technical concerns, and often the additional stressors of cascading interventions. However as we will see, dads, too, need support at their child's birth.

## A New Understanding of the Unborn Child

While many people believe that the human fetus is a blank slate lacking true sensation, emotional affect, or the ability to feel pain, pregnant women through the ages have known what science today has proven to be true: a mother's unborn child hears her voice, and senses her love. The unborn can see, hear, and feel.

Thomas Verny, MD, *Preparenting: Nurturing Your Child from Conception*, underscores recent discoveries in neuroscience that have brought a new understanding of fetal development: from the moment of conception, the "wiring" of a child's brain is strongly influenced by her environment. While the brain is sensitive to experiences throughout life, experience during the critical periods of prenatal and early postnatal life play a primary role in determining the architecture of the brain, and the extent of adult capacities. Our brains, and consequently our personalities, emerge from a complex interplay between the genes we are born with and the experiences we have.

In his classic, *The Secret Life of the Unborn Child*, Verny first brought attention to the fact that everything the pregnant mother feels and thinks is communicated to her unborn child through the neurohormones that circulate within her, just as surely as the effects of alcohol and nicotine. From the moment of conception, experience in the womb shapes the brain and lays the foundations for personality, emotional temperament, and the powers of higher thought.

> *While the realization that genetics is not destiny and that environment is paramount to development places new responsibilities on parents, it also engenders new opportunities.*
> —Thomas Verny, MD, *Preparenting: Nurturing Your Baby from Conception*

Verny hastens to assure us that there are no one-to-one correlations in human psychology. Because the baby is the product of an unhappy or even abusive marriage, or of an unhappy, even depressed mother, this does not necessarily mean the child will become a depressed, disordered adult. But the womb is the child's first world. How he experiences it—as loving or hostile—creates personality and character predispositions. The womb shapes his expectations. If the environment in the womb is hostile, the child will move into the world with fear and suspicion. It will take a great deal of love to heal this. On the other hand, maternal feelings centered on joy and love bathe the growing brain in "feel good" endorphins and neurohormones such as oxytocin, and promote a lifelong sense of wellbeing. If optimism is engraved on his mind, it will take a great deal of adversity later to erase it.\*

Expectant dads can find creative ways to connect with their unborn child. Like many dads before him, Jack reached out to connect emotionally and

---

\* In the UK, the Family Nurse Partnership has approached couple conflict via the impact on the unborn child, explaining the possible effects of maternal stress on the baby's developing brain, and combining this with relationship skills training—resulting in one couple commenting "we don't fight any more because we know what it does to the baby."

spiritually with his baby *in utero*: singing songs, pressing his mouth up against Meryn's belly and blowing raspberries (which he then did on Siena's tummy the following year). Laughing! Massaging her pregnant belly. Decorating her pregnant belly with body paints. Expressions of love between father and mother nourish baby as well as parents.

> *Fathers who are well prepared for their children's birth by being closely involved during pregnancy soon discover that while the male experience of pregnancy is necessarily different from that of the female, it need neither be second-hand nor second-class. For there exists a sense in which both fathers and mothers are outside looking in, and are building a relationship with a fantasy baby, before its birth.* —Adrienne Burgess, *Fatherhood Reclaimed*

## Onto the Roller Coaster

Not only the physical, but also the emotional challenges of pregnancy inevitably impact a couple's relationship. Even those who are thrilled at the prospect of becoming parents may at times find themselves caught in a whirlpool of doubts and fears: will our baby be healthy? Will I be a good parent? How will we manage with the loss of a job—the income and social support? How will I cope with diaper changing or sleep deprivation? For both parents, there are anxieties about labor itself: how will I cope with pain? The loss of control? The alien hospital environment? And memories of their own birth and childhood may be surfacing—both the highs and the lows—around the edges of consciousness or rumbling just below.

While dad may experience mom as totally preoccupied with the unborn child, unpredictable and irrational, she may see him as unsympathetic and unavailable. She may not appreciate the depths of the emotions that he, too, may be experiencing. He may fear that sharing his worries with her will not only stress her, but also expose his own vulnerability at a time when he is expected to be strong for his partner.

It is important to remember that there are two people having the baby, and that the man also goes through a transitional period of stress when deep emotions may be stirred and his behavior may be hard to understand.

Dad may be feeling excluded, obsolete, and resentful, guilty for feeling that way, and apt to withdraw rather than engage in his role as father and lover, protector and supporter, of his partner and their unborn child. Anxiety can also provide the impetus to examine options, plan ahead, and prepare emotionally and practically for the reality of birth, and then the astonishing reality of a new baby.

Despite—and even because of—the challenges, pregnancy can be a time of profound connectedness for many couples. Clearly, neither partner holds all the cards as to the success of this period. Developing empathy and respect for each other's feelings and emotional states and needs, a couple can grow together rather than apart. This requires that partners share their feelings, talk and listen, love and learn, laugh and forgive; and that both take care *not* to assume they know what the other needs, wants, or is feeling.

> *Alert:* If communications aren't flowing—if either partner feels unheard, misunderstood, or unsupported—find a friend, mentor, coach, or counselor who can help you. It is hard to imagine how much more difficult it can be to communicate after a baby arrives, and having the tools to communicate with the intention to connect and understand, rather than to protect and defend, will be key to a couple's successfully transiting this period together (see Chapter 23).

*Learning how to nurture the bonds of love is an urgent task. Loving connection provides the dependable web of intimacy that allows us to cope with life and to live life well.* —Sue Johnson, PhD, *Hold Me Tight*

## Partnering in Pregnancy

It bears repeating: the quality of a couple's relationship is shown to be the primary factor in their successfully navigating the transition to parenthood. Giving attention during pregnancy to developing and refining partnership skills will go a long way toward a couple's ability to sustain a loving and supportive relationship in which mom, dad, and baby can flourish, after baby is born.

Below, Connie Allen, author of *Joyous Child, Joyous Parent,* shares three *principles of partnership.* While these apply in all relationships, whether it is with your partner, your child, your parents, or a good friend, here she focuses these principles on the adult couple relationship.

### *1. Focus on yourself first.*

There is only one person whose behavior you can change and that is you. It is tempting and easy to direct your attention toward your partner, to blame her for whatever inadequacies you believe you see.

This path of trying to get your partner to change damages your connection with your partner and may ultimately destroy the beauty and good things you share. Plus, trying to get another person to change is futile and results in your feeling frustrated and powerless.

When you focus on yourself, you put your attention and energy in a direction that allows you to make changes in your own attitudes, perceptions, and actions—where you have the power to change. Then you are in a position to create the relationship you want.

Being more self-aware and conscious of the choices you make is a full-time job, leaving you with little time or desire to worry about what your partner is doing. You may also develop a greater appreciation of your partner's good heart and desire to be a good parent with you.

Focus on being the best partner and parent you can be. This alone will make a profound difference for you, your partner, and your relationship with one another.

## 2. Support your partner in being who he is, not who you want him to be.

The key to getting and enjoying the very best from your partner is to want him to be who he truly is. He needs to be able to hear his own inner voice, and only then can he truly hear and respond fully to what you say.

Your partner wants to do well in life and to be a good parent and partner with you. He often doesn't know how to do that. All of us have things to learn in life, places where we need to become more aware and to grow. By trusting in and seeing the goodness in your partner, you call forth the best from him, in a powerful, life-changing way, enhancing life for you and your partner.

## 3. Nurture your emotional connection with your partner.

Your emotional connection, the intangible, unseen feelings between each other, forms the foundation of everything that you share with your partner. If you are critical or blaming, these behaviors negatively impact everything you share together and make it difficult to work together in harmonious partnership. You struggle to find solutions to your life challenges, and you create arguments, misunderstandings, and hurt feelings, which tend to perpetuate into more feelings of criticism, mistrust, and emotional unavailability.

When you consciously choose to nurture feelings of appreciation, trust, and openness between you, you create and share moments of play, laughter, and fun. You focus on the concerns and challenges themselves, rather than judging each other, and build a strong emotional foundation that creates more wonderful feelings that bring you closer together.

# A Weekly Commitment to Connect

A good relationship between pregnant women and their partners leads to easier pregnancies and a healthier baby at birth. A couple's agreeing to a time that will work for both to sit down and spend at least 30 minutes together each week, creates an opening for sharing feelings about each other, the upcoming birth, the responsibilities of parenting and *appreciations*. A commitment to keep this date, even if either or both feels they have nothing to say, is important. Given an opening, there will always be something to share. This is an invaluable practice to develop now and to continue after the baby comes.

> **Co-Active Parenting™ Connection Exercise**[*]
>
> Partners sit face-to-face. Choose who shares first. The first partner speaks honestly without judging self while the other partner listens without judgment. Give time and space for answering the questions. Breathe to stay relaxed. When complete, switch roles.
>
> *Questions asked by partner:*
> 1. What is a concern, thought, or behavior you have that puts you in survival mode?
> 2. How is this concern affecting your life right now—your relationships, your work, your health?
> 3. When you think about this, what emotions do you feel and where do you feel them in your body?
> 4. Have you had this feeling before? Describe your experience in as much detail as you can remember. (If needed, remind your partner to breathe.)
> 5. What would you rather be experiencing and feeling?
> 6. What small step could you take, or what thought could you change, that will bring you a greater sense of calm and ease?
> 7. How can I best support you in taking this step?
>
> [*] *Kim Griffith, The Wellness Way, Dallas, Texas, wellnesswayworks.com.*

> **Ground rules for dialogue:**[*]
> - Tell the truth
> - Speak from the heart
> - Share your feelings
> - Really listen to what your partner is saying
> - Be supportive • Do not interrupt
> - Do not try to make your partner feel guilty for what he is saying, and avoid feelings of guilt within yourself
> - Forgive yourself and your partner • Look into your partner's eyes while sharing thoughts and feelings
> - Take responsibility for your own feelings.
>
> [*] From Thomas Verny, MD, *The Secret Life of the Unborn Child*

## Basic Style of Expectant Dads

Sharing their hopes and expectations for the father's involvement during the pregnancy enables a couple to minimize unrealistic expectations and conflicts and to be aware of adjustments that might need to be made. Katharyn Antle May, PhD, has found that expectant fathers have one of three basic styles:[35]

- The **observer-father** maintains a certain emotional distance and sees himself largely as bystander;
- The **expressive-father** is emotionally very involved and sees himself as full partner;
- The **instrumental-father** sees himself as manager of the pregnancy and feels the need to plan every medical appointment, meal, and trip to the yoga class.

Many a dad, like Jack, will not fit neatly into only one category.

## About Those Prenatal Classes

As already noted, most prenatal classes are led and attended by women and not designed to include or to be relevant to the father. Most regard the father's role as "supportive" to the mother during pregnancy and the birth process.* Most are held during the daytime, making it difficult for fathers to attend. And sitting with a group of women talking about babies will be a rather daunting proposition for most men.

A 2009 review of prenatal education found it delivered almost no benefits.[36] A key problem may be the lack of focus on the couple and their relationship in all but a tiny percentage of these programs. This is of real concern, as couple-focused education impacts positively on relationship quality, satisfaction, and stability over a considerable period;[37] also because the perinatal period is a "teachable moment," especially for first-time fathers who are actively interested in engaging with professionals and learning about pregnancy, birth, parenting— and the likely changes in their relationship.[38] While even brief programs show positive outcomes,[39] the results of more intensive programs, covering areas including friendship and intimacy, constructive conflict management, the couple relationship post-birth, and father involvement, have very substantial results.†

---

* An English health visiting service upped fathers' attendance at registration meetings from 20% to 70% simply by re-addressing the invitation letter from "Dear Parents" to "Dear Mum and Dad," and expressing the wish to meet both parents.
† Among the more substantial and successful perinatal interventions are the Cowan & Cowan 24-session group workshops.
  Gottman et al. (endnote 11) report very positive outcomes from a two-day intensive couple-focused prenatal workshop during which the issues addressed include: friendship and intimacy, constructive conflict management, couple relationship post-birth, and father involvement.
  In a later development of this program, a 24-session Cowan-style support group was added to the two-day intensive workshop: early indications from the three-year follow up of this model produced excellent results. The same Gottman team has also been

While prenatal classes may not prevent arguments in the middle of the night as to who is going to change the baby's diaper, the better classes can help couples prepare for the realities of the birth and postpartum period. And it can be reassuring finding others who share like concerns and anxieties. While not separating mothers and fathers enables both to hear about the experiences of their partners, dividing into male and female groups for part of the time allows men and women to share concerns and ask questions they would not feel comfortable expressing before the whole class. We can expect—and need to demand—more hospital and maternity centers to offer childbirth education courses to both expectant parents.

## Talking About Being Prepared

Breastfeeding offers both physiological and psychological benefits to both mother and baby, and is unqualifiedly the optimal form of infant nutrition; however because it tends to foster the notion of an exclusive mother-infant relationship, it may leave dad feeling not only excluded, jealous, and resentful, but ultimately unsupportive of the breastfeeding and the couple relationship.[40]

When dads are informed about the realities of breastfeeding, including the issues that surface for a couple, they can be better prepared and able to improve his, and consequently the mother's, satisfaction with breastfeeding, duration of breastfeeding, and the transition of both parents to parenthood. Time alone talking with expectant, new, and experienced fathers can allow a dad to more openly share his concerns. Talking with a breastfeeding mother, birth educator, midwife, or obstetrician can also offer the support that is needed both prior to and in the early days, weeks, even months of parenting.

## Contemplating the Parent We Want to Be

A crucial determinant of being a good parent is our ability to reflect back on our own childhood and learn from it, so we don't repeat the same mistakes our parents made.

Pregnancy is a poignant time to explore the unresolved themes of our own birth and childhood. Emotions and memories of how we were parented in our early years may surface and call us to think more deeply about our relationship with our own parents. Was our mother, or our father, the kind of mom or dad we want to be?

Consciously contemplating what we hope to pass on to our children, and what we hope to leave behind from our own childhood experiences, is of tremendous importance. Without this, we will find ourselves reacting to our

---

piloting a pre/postnatal curriculum for lower income families called "Loving Couples, Loving Children."

children out of our own childhood trauma, and embodying the same dysfunctional behaviors that our parents—albeit unwittingly—inflicted on us. For example, parents who were abused as children tend to abuse their own children unless they reflect on and learn from their own experiences of abuse, acknowledge what happened, recall the pain of it, and find a means of dealing with stress without taking it out on their children.

In Part 3, we look at how—with compassion, informed awareness, and intention—we *can* become the parent that we want to be.

## Parenting Your Inner Child

Capacchione and Bardsley, *Creating a Joyful Birth Experience: Developing a Partnership with Your Unborn Child for Healthy Pregnancy, Labor, and Early Parenting*, have discovered in their clinical work, a phenomenon that they call the "Inner Child Sibling Rivalry Syndrome." This occurs when the inner child of the parent competes with the new baby for attention. The authors have found that when the expectant mother doesn't care for her own emotional and physical needs, her inner child (see Chapter 20) may feel abandoned, and attempt to get her attention through physical discomfort or emotional upset.

While Capacchione and Bardsley write of this phenomenon as the experience of the woman, it's clearly alive in the expectant or new father as well as the mother. It is vitally important for fathers, as well as mothers, to nurture themselves throughout the stages of parenting from conception on. Parenting your own inner child, tending to his or her feelings and needs throughout pregnancy and the years of parenting, enables you to be fully present and to better partner your partner and parent your child.

## New Ways of Loving

Many couples find that sex in the early months of pregnancy is better than ever. Some feel a desire for greater closeness. Others revel in the freedom from birth control. Others experience a drop in sexual activity.

A lack of intercourse is best viewed, not as the end of an intimate or physical relationship, but rather an opportunity to explore new ways of loving. When partners share their feelings and tell each other what feels good to them, they can practice sensual ways to please each other short of intercourse—snuggling, hugging, touching, and bathing together (yes, you need a big tub).

> *It was an incredibly sexy period. I mean, we both felt really great about ourselves and about our lives; and part of my involvement with the baby took a fairly sort of sexual turn. I would massage Kate and Kate's tummy with baby oil and it was really nice.* —"Stuart" in Richard Seel, *The Uncertain Father*

These new expressions of intimacy can enhance a sense of caring partnership as they expand their love to embrace their newborn.

> *Adult love also involves sexuality and caretaking. Attachment is the scaffold on which these are built. Sexuality is best when there is a safe connection, and you are able to stay close to your partner emotionally. Caretaking and support come naturally when we feel close and connected. Secure partners are more sensitive to each other's needs for care. In a romantic relationship, secure attachment, sexuality, and supportiveness all come together. Partners create a positive loop of closeness, responsiveness, caring, and desire.*
>
> —Sue Johnson, PhD, *Hold Me Tight*

## Readying for Life After Birth

Pregnant couples are usually so focused on the anxieties and excitement of pregnancy and birthing that they give little or no thought to how they will manage after the birth. Ideally, parents will have contemplated and prepared for the emotional and mental considerations and responsibilities of becoming parents, and the lifestyle changes that they will be faced with, *before* becoming pregnant; but if not, now is the time to consider the needs of the postpartum period. Ideally, this will include a home-based postpartum support network—best arranged prenatally. Rather than looking to each other to meet all of your needs, clarify the support you can draw from other resources—people, programs, places—to support you independently and/or together. It will be vitally important that you do not think you can "go this alone" as a couple.

---

### Kinds of Intimacy

Howard and Charlotte Clinebell[41] distinguished at least twelve different types of intimacy that can apply to relationships:

- Sexual intimacy (erotic or orgasmic closeness).
- Emotional intimacy (being tuned to each other's wavelength).
- Intellectual intimacy (closeness in the world of ideas).
- Aesthetic intimacy (sharing experiences of beauty).
- Creative intimacy (sharing in acts of creating together).
- Recreational intimacy (relating in experiences of fun and play).
- Work intimacy (the closeness of sharing common tasks).
- Crisis intimacy (closeness in coping with problems and pain).
- Conflict intimacy (facing/struggling with differences).
- Commitment intimacy (mutuality derived from common self-investment).
- Spiritual intimacy (the we-ness in sharing ultimate concerns)
- Communication intimacy (the source of all types of true intimacy).

## Getting Real

Talking with new parents, experienced parents, and other expectant couples can help an expectant couple prepare for the realities of the early days and weeks, and alert then to resources and services that can be accessed from friends and community.

Dad and Mom: Learn and talk about the needs of the newborn for consistency of care, skin-to-skin contact, holding and carrying, breastfeeding (see Chapter 28). Share what you are each learning, observe how others are parenting their young ones, and how you feel about it—and how your child might feel about it!

It's important to consider the source of any advice you get about the "realities of life with baby."

> *I found a real danger of getting negative advice from family, strangers, etc., who are based in the fear culture and wanted to convince me that I wouldn't have enough milk, that sleeping with my children will damage them and exhaust me, that I need to have regular "breaks" from small babies and that frequent nursing would make me a slave to my child.* —Barbara

> *Thank you for strengthening my determination to meet the needs of my two small boys in a sensitive and loving and nurturing way in the face of all the advice from my liberated friends who work and bottle feed. I rarely leave my boys, aged one and three. My elder son is choosing to attend a small school that he loves, several mornings a week, and is developing into an extremely happy, secure, and confident child. He doesn't have confidence in that he throws himself into situations or relationships, he has a confidence that is a deep, quiet inner confidence that is almost like a glow coming from him that lights up my world and the lives of everyone he meets.*

> *It is hard though, meeting the emotional and physical needs of my two small children. Sometimes I think that one or other of them isn't having their needs met as I would like but your story has strengthened my resolve to not let either of them feel less nurtured just because they have a sibling, but like to think that the benefits they get from having each other negates having a little less of me. I like to think that my older son has received so much love that he has plenty to pass on to his brother who is madly in love with his big brother.* —Vanessa

As individuals, and as a couple, prospective parents do well to consider what they can most readily let go of during the early days and months when it is so important to be there for their baby: lengthy dinner preparations, frequent restaurant dining, daily workouts at the gym, a tidy house, entertaining friends. Work-related and cherished personal interests may need revising, and personal, financial, and career goals and commitments renegotiated.

> *The most productive attitude is to understand that, at least for a while, your former productivity may be just a memory.*
> —Carista Luminare-Rosen, *Parenting Begins Before Conception*

Dad: Be aware that your partner is not going to be able to do nearly as much as she had been doing. What are you willing to take on? Can you get help? How much are you going to share the baby care? Do you want to consider sharing the childcare and provider roles equally? Ask about paternity leave and family leave. Talk about how it might be possible to take time off, together, when the baby arrives.

## Babymoon Time

With the arrival of a new baby, both mom *and* dad experience intense hormonal changes. A quiet, unpressured time following the birth, often called a babymoon,* affords mother and father a sensitive and sacred space that allows them to deeply connect—physically, emotionally, and spiritually with their newborn. It is the strength of this connection that makes it possible for parents to make the sacrifices needed to care optimally for their newborn, who is totally dependent on them.

> *We should give thanks to our children for bringing us back to our hearts so irresistibly, for helping us be more human.*
> —Robin Grille, *Heart-to-Heart Parenting*

You may find yourselves feeling especially sensitive and wide-open emotionally. You may be feeling vulnerable, teary, elated, or tender, protective, tense, or uncertain. You may be aware of a softening—an opening of the heart.

> *It is precisely this emotional aliveness that helps you to be protective and helps you to tune in and connect to your baby.... It is a time to give in to the power of irrational and senseless love. We do a great injustice to parents—and worse to their baby—if we interfere with or judge this beautiful and natural process*
> —Robin Grille, *Heart-to-Heart Parenting*

This sensitivity can be such a magnificent gift, but it can be something of a shock if you are caught unaware. A period free of obligations and pressures from the outside world affords a very precious and beautiful time for both mom and dad, together, to get to know and enjoy their newborn baby.

---

* The word has recently been redefined/co-opted by the hotel/spa industry, to refer to a vacation taken *before* the baby arrives—a good idea, but not at the expense of foregoing the bonding period after the baby arrives, which is best fostered by minimizing competing activities for a short period.

## And, So Vital: Caring for the Couple Relationship

The adult relationship between mother and father is the foundation on which the happiness and wellbeing of the growing family is built. Recognizing, planning for, and exploring ways to nurture the adult couple relationship is an essential element in a successful transition to parenthood, and for the wellbeing of mother and father as a couple, as individuals, and as parents to their child.

> *When we feel generally secure, that is we are comfortable with closeness and confident about depending on loved ones, we are better at seeking support and better at giving it....* —Sue Johnson, PhD, *Hold Me Tight*

All three relationships will inevitably suffer if couples do not give high priority to the need for quality time for meaningful communication, caring physical contact, intimate moments together, and socializing as a couple. This will be much more challenging to do after the baby comes along, so beginning to weave a web of caring and connecting now, is vitally important.

---

### Weaving a Web of Connection[*]

*I believe that we personally imprint our world through our children. What we model for them in our relationships is one way we can take what we were given and pass on something better.*

*When all is said and done, we have to ask ourselves: what legacy are we leaving?*

Put your family relationship first:
- Create an environment of "we are in this together."
- During pregnancy, both mom and dad talk and read to your unborn child.
- Explore fears and beliefs about parenthood with each other.
- Participate in pregnancy classes together and create a birth plan.
- Create a mission statement and have all family members participate.
- Learn to see through each other's eyes and validate each other's feelings.
- Use authentic positive language.
- Accept and hold each other in their highest light, let go of labels.
- Be reflective; learn to observe quietly without jumping to conclusions.
- Spend quality time together as a family: reading together, sharing family dinners, playing games, volunteering, creating family traditions, exploring nature, sparking conversations, sharing ideas and helping each other.

[*] *Kim Griffith, The Wellness Way, Dallas, Texas, wellnesswayworks.com.*

**Key Points**
- It is important to address the emotional and relational, as well as the physical and intellectual, aspects of pregnancy.
- While the woman is visibly in a major life transition, the father's transition is primarily internal. Typically he is left to navigate it alone, with little acknowledgement of his specific concerns and emotional stresses.
- Counseling and education for pregnant dads can be vital, especially given that the first year after birth is a peak time for parental separation; fathers satisfaction is more likely than mothers' to decline at this time; and men's dissatisfaction is more predictive than women's of the relationship ending.
- Men may adopt unconscious strategies to help them identify with their baby. Pregnant dads "couvade" symptoms—or sympathetic pregnancy--are remarkably like those of pregnant women, from morning sickness and weight gain, to abdominal pains.
- Experiences within the womb shape the brain and lay the foundations for character predispositions. Dads can find creative ways to connect with their baby *in utero*. Expressions of love between a couple nourish the baby as well as parents.
- Emotional, as well as physical changes, impact a couple's relationship. Memories of their own birth and childhood may be surfacing, calling for attention.
- A couple's developing empathy and respect for each others' feelings and needs, and communicating with the intent to love and to learn, rather that protect and defend, is key. Make spacious time to talk—ideally daily—at least weekly!
- Breastfeeding, optimal for baby and mother, can leave dad feeling excluded. Education prior to birth, can improve fathers' support.
- Sex may increase, stay the same, or decrease—any and all is normal. Lack of intercourse can be an opportunity to explore new ways of intimacy and loving.
- Talking with other parents and pregnant couples helps prepare couples for realities of life after birth.
- With the arrival of the baby, both mom and dad experience intense hormonal and emotional changes. Time free of pressures from the outside world affords precious time to deeply connect and bond as a new family.

# 13: Pregnancy—Spotlight on Dad

## Initiation to Sexism

Richard Seel notes that becoming a father will be most men's first experience of sexism—that is, prejudice against them simply on grounds of their sex. As noted earlier, he may be ignored in the prenatal clinic, and matronized in the prenatal class. He may be considered irrelevant in the labor room, and an inconvenience in the hospital. After the excitement and intensity of being at his child's birth, most fathers go home to sleep alone. Most accept this without question, as normal.

While a growing number of dads are appearing at prenatal classes and clinics with their partners, and some educators and obstetricians are genuine in their efforts to include them, they are still the exception. The fact remains that in the West, little acknowledgement is given to pregnancy as a time of tremendous change and uncertainty for many men. This is not true of all cultures.

Many societies practice rituals to help prospective parents get used to the idea of having a child, and become involved with the unborn. For example, on the Andaman Islands in the Indian Ocean, the unborn child is given a name early in the pregnancy. From that time onward, until some weeks after the baby is born, no one is allowed to call the expectant mother and father by their own names. Instead they must be called by their relationship to the child: "mother of so-and-so" or "father of so-and-so." They are also both required to abstain from eating certain foods. In this way the father's identification with the pregnancy is continually and publicly acknowledged.

In the West, a father's meaningful identification with the pregnancy remains a novel idea. Seel suggests that, in the absence of acknowledgment or support, many men adopt various other unconscious strategies to help them identify with the baby.

## The French Connection

"Couvade," (from French: *couver* "to brood, or hatch") is a term adopted by anthropologists to refer to various customs performed by men when their partners are giving birth. In all cultures that practice it, the man stops his social activities in a ritualistic way, e.g., he goes to bed so that other people care for him, and offer him their congratulations. Various forms of couvade have been practiced by many diverse cultures around the world.

The phenomenon of couvade, with local variations, has been known from ancient times and far flung places: from various African tribes, and the Scythians of the Black Sea to mountain tribes of Miau-tse described by Marco

Polo. Couvade is still found in places as widespread as Siberia, South America, Africa and Malaysia.

Couvade *syndrome* is a medical term drawn from the same French word. In this context it describes a wide range of changes that a father can experience during pregnancy and shortly after birth. The most dramatic couvade symptoms are physical, and many are remarkably like those of pregnant women. While they may be quite bizarre and extreme, the more common and less severe symptoms range from morning sickness, weight gain and backache, to severe abdominal pains. Some expectant fathers may experience strong changes in the sensation of taste, and develop broken sleep patterns. Studies have estimated that as many as 60% of men experience some physical signs of pregnancy, which usually appear about the third month, decrease for a few months, then recur a month or two before the baby is born. The symptoms almost always disappear at the birth. Fathers who are closely involved in the pregnancy do not usually experience these symptoms.

Seel proposes that while stress is commonly cited as a reason for these symptoms, it doesn't acknowledge the depth of the emotions these men are experiencing. It may be that couvade symptoms are a perfectly understandable phenomenon, given the prevailing social circumstances in the West. He suggests that in the absence of public ritual, exhibiting couvade syndrome—or sympathetic pregnancy—may be a man's only recourse to visibly assert his paternity. It may be nature's way of allowing a man to show his partner how committed he is.

Another explanation posits couvade as a man's instinct, when his loved one is suffering, to take her pain away, to make it his instead of hers, especially if he has the feeling—no matter how irrational—of having "gotten her pregnant," and thus being responsible for her pain. Or perhaps it is a man's jealousy, and his symptoms are an unconscious attention-getting strategy to shift at least some of the focus of the pregnancy to him. Armin Brott, in *Father for Life*, notes that couvade syndrome is also common among couples who are adopting.

Equally interesting is the discovery that an expectant dad's hormones change along with his partner's. The two hormones identified are prolactin, which primes the mother's breasts to lactate, and cortisol, which appears to be associated with parent-child bonding. While it had been thought that these hormonal changes were triggered by the developing fetus, that can't be the case with expectant dads' levels of prolactin and cortisol paralleling their partners'. The levels for moms are much more intense, but the patterns are similar. Hormone levels—for both mother and dad—return to normal not long after the baby is born if the mother is not nursing.

While some men will evidence physical symptoms, others will be drawn to alter their lifestyle, or reflect on their goals and priorities. Some may be overwhelmed by financial responsibilities, especially if they are now the sole income earner. Others feel burdened by a growing sense of responsibility to perform well and keep their job, especially in an unstable economy. Some show a new interest in babies, especially if they have friends with young children. Still others engage in "nesting" activity, suddenly taking an interest in the home, attending to unfinished jobs or areas needing attention.

### Jack's Couvade

*On the morning Meryn's labor began, we awoke at 6 AM with her first contractions. Labor began three days earlier than predicted and I had been sure, for a first-time birth, it would be later.*

*I had just finished painting the wallboards, and plaster dust was still everywhere from my having torn out the ceilings to open up where I had raised the roof and installed windows. The dust was ground into the subflooring and tracked onto everything, making the house very un-home-like. I was desperate to at least get the carpet padding down to cover the old, grimy plywood subfloor we'd tolerated for months.*

*It was only a couple of hours' work, so I set about it immediately, wanting the space for my daughter to be clean, if not aesthetic. Meryn got very upset that I did this, wanting me to "be" with her in a way I barely understood, but my discomfort with our still unfinished nest drove me to finish putting down the carpet padding later that morning.*

The father may believe these nesting tasks are the first opportunity he has to do something for the baby rather than for his pregnant mate.

## Real Men *Do* Have Feelings

*My husband and I married in 1997. He is quite a bit younger than I, but he pursued me aggressively and I finally gave in because he seemed so nice. He was the most romantic man I had ever known. After a little over a year of being married, I became pregnant—my first, his second. I was never so elated and could not think of anything more romantic than having his baby. We had a boy, and he was a difficult child until about the age of four. He cried constantly and required my full attention. I was getting a little bitter because I missed the cuddling my husband and I used to do.*

*Our child had to sleep with us in order for me to get any sleep. Anyway, my son has come a long way and is the joy of my life. On April 2, 2005, my husband woke up, sat down, and told me he was not in love with me anymore and walked out the door. This is now October, and I am still so devastated I can hardly function. I blame myself and wish he had talked to me so that I could make things right for him. I can hardly believe that he could walk away from his son and me without any sign of remorse or giving me the opportunity to change. He went right into the arms of another older woman, with grown children. By the way, my husband's mother left their home when he was 12, never to return. He never spoke of any pain regarding this, as I tried to get him to talk about it. He just didn't talk about it or act like he felt anything about it. Anyway, that is my story. I just cannot imagine him turning away my love, as it is so deep for him.* —Amy

Sharing feelings assumes a level of self-awareness that most men have never been schooled in. While the men's movement has never garnered the momentum of the women's movement, more and more men *are* becoming aware that they have feelings, and that there is value in acknowledging and sharing these feelings. Still, this sharing of feelings can be a tough chore for a dad, at any time, and perhaps especially during a time like pregnancy when he is encountering so many new emotions at the same time and he is also expected to "be strong" for his partner.

*Traditionally, men have focused on communicating ideas, while women share feelings. This often leads to parallel conversations where both feel dissatisfied, misunderstood, and confused. Typically, learning the skill of listening is the key for a man to change the relationship with his partner. Most men haven't learned how helpful and insightful listening can be. Sometimes they don't want to listen because they believe they will be the target of criticism or negativity, they often think they have to defend themselves rather than support their partner in sharing her feelings. It can take courage to participate in an honest conversation without taking what is said personally and then reacting.*
—Mitzi Gold, Director, Mars & Venus Counseling Center of Hawaii

Talking with other dads can offer men a safe, supportive, and encouraging route into this domain, allowing them to share concerns and ask questions they would not otherwise be comfortable articulating. Despite the stereotype of men's emotional illiteracy, many men are truly relieved to hear from other fathers, and this experience deepens their willingness and ability to trust and be honest about what they are thinking and feeling.

*Sharing stories, acknowledging they are having a deep personal experience, and just being heard can sometimes make the difference to today's fathers-to-be. It is all about freeing the father, in the* man.
—Patrick Houser, *Fathers-to-Be Handbook*

Houser invites men to take some time to consider the following questions:
- As a father-to-be, what are you experiencing during this time?
- What kind of support do you need, right now?
- What information or experience would help you to be more relaxed and present in your role?

- Do you need a confidant or mentor?
- How can you get support for yourself?
- What will allow you to engage more fully at this time and in the best way possible, for you?

## Like a Good Scout, Be Prepared

The more a man can learn about what his partner is going through, how their baby is developing, and what he himself is going through—emotionally, psychologically and physically—the better he will be able to "protect and provide for" rather than be a spectator or sidekick through the pregnancy and birth of his offspring. The more he is around at prenatal appointments, the more seriously the doctor and staff will take him, and in all probability the more involved they'll let him be. The more he knows about what to expect, the more prepared he can be and the less likely he is to worry.

So Dad, show up at your midwife or obstetrician appointments with your partner. Participate in childbirth classes that address your needs and concerns as well as those of your partner. If one is not to be found, you will need to do your own research. A small but steadily growing number of books are written by dads for dads. These are the books you need to read, not just the ones by your partner's bedside. And/or check out the websites that are addressing you, the father (see Resources). Make a birth plan with your partner. Well-prepared dads are less likely to exclude themselves, or be excluded, after the birth of their baby.

And, keep talking. How you feel in the first trimester may well be hugely different from how you feel in the second and third—and certainly how you feel after your baby is born.

## Men, Let's Talk About It: Sex During Pregnancy

Most men find that pregnancy changes their attitudes toward sex.

*Some men are fascinated by this demonstration of their fertility; others fear changes that may be ahead.* —Richard Seel, *The Uncertain Father*

Masters and Johnson found that 31 out of the 79 expectant fathers interviewed gradually ceased sexual activity as the pregnancy progressed.[42] Many men are afraid of hurting the baby or their partner, or causing a miscarriage, or bringing "bad luck" on the pregnancy. Some men are turned on by their partner's changing figure, others are turned off. Some think there is no sense in having sex now that they are pregnant, others are simply too exhausted. While the first two trimesters may be a time of increased or decreased sexual activity, by the third trimester, engaging in intercourse becomes "but a distant memory."

Although there are many reasons a man may avoid intercourse during pregnancy, there is no physical reason to do so unless it causes his partner discomfort or vaginal bleeding. Seel suggests that, regardless, a decline in sexual activity is not a "problem" to be cured, nor a sign of inadequacy or failure, but a common, normal male reaction to pregnancy.

He proposes that a man's lowered sex interest may be in part a result of couvade syndrome. Abstaining from sex, the man marks the period of pregnancy as being special. This may reflect his coming to terms with his partner's new role of mother. Some men start to behave in babyish ways, wanting to be mothered by their partners. Some may find it difficult to face up to the responsibility of fatherhood, or may be "rehearsing" for the more tender role they sense will be required when the baby arrives. However, Dads please note, treating your partner like a mother figure is not conducive to lovemaking.

*There may be other, even more fundamental, reasons for men to feel wary of sex during pregnancy. Women's fertility has been held in awe since the dawn of time—men have tried to control it, mimic it, and deny it. But still it remains—the one power that we can never have. It is not surprising that some men are a little reticent in the presence of pregnancy. For it is during pregnancy that the power of fertility is most obviously displayed; that the physical differences between men and women are most openly shown. She changes, swells, matures; he stays the same, pedestrian, unable to match her. The wonder is not that so many men feel diffident about intercourse during pregnancy, but rather that so many are able to use the experience to develop a new closeness.*
—Richard Seel, *The Uncertain Father*

*My wife went totally off any sort of sex during the pregnancy, almost as if the act of procreation sort of made any further attempts unnecessary. But I felt no sort of deep frustration or anything. It was sufficient just that we were together. And we had sensual relationships, beautiful times, just sort of massaging her tummy and feeling the baby moving and just going to sleep with my arms sort of round, holding the baby as well.*
—"Andrew" in Richard Seel, *The Uncertain Father*

## Key Points

- Little acknowledgement is given to pregnancy as a time of tremendous change and uncertainty for many men.
- Couvade syndrome refers to a range of symptoms a father can experience during pregnancy and shortly after birth. Many are very similar to those of pregnant women—from morning sickness to abdominal pain.
- Becoming a father will be most men's first experience of sexism. He may be ignored or matronized, and considered an irrelevance or inconvenience in the prenatal clinic, in the labor room, and in the hospital. After the birth of his child, most go home to sleep alone.
- An expectant dad's levels of prolactin and cortisol, while not as intense, parallel that of their partner's.
- Sharing feelings can be especially tough for men. Talking with other trusted men can help them to deepen their own ability to communicate their thoughts and feelings.
- The more a man learns about pregnancy and his baby, the more he is able to "protect and provide for" rather than be spectator through pregnancy and birth.
- Most men find that pregnancy changes their attitudes towards sex. Some men are turned on, others off. A decline in interest is a normal male reaction, not a sign of inadequacy or failure.
- Men will do well need to consider the kind of support or information that would help them to be more relaxed and able to engage more fully.
- Well-prepared dads are less likely to exclude themselves, or be excluded, after the birth of the baby.

# 14: Preparing for the Birth of Your Baby

## The Birthing Process

Giving birth to her fourth baby, unassisted at home, Australian family physician Sarah Buckley, MD, discovered just how very simple—even ecstatic—the process of birth can be, if we can avoid disturbing it. She found that essentially we need the same conditions for both making love and giving birth: to feel private, safe, and unobserved. Anything that disturbs the laboring woman's sense of safety and privacy disrupts this process.

> *Yet the conditions we provide for birthing women are almost diametrically opposed to these; no wonder giving birth is so difficult for most women today.*
> —Sarah Buckley, MD, *Gentle Birth, Gentle Mothering*

Suzanne Arms observes that Western culture has built an entire system of care—obstetrics—around the belief a woman is not able to successfully birth on her own, and that the female body is not designed to cope with the pain of birth. The modern attitude of asserting control over, and attempting to "manage," a birth is not only the antithesis of trust in a woman's body and the normalcy of childbirth, but renders impossible the experience of childbirth at its best:

> *…an exuberant experience of enormous courage, effort, and incredible pleasure. We are losing the kind of childbirth experience that empowers us, makes us feel better about ourselves as women, helps us grow and develop as mothers, and is important in the attachment process with our babies.*
> —Diana Korte & Roberta Scaer, *A Good Birth, A Safe Birth*

Medicalizing childbirth and removing it from the home separates it from the family. Our culture has made birth, like death, a fearful ordeal that can be dealt with only by trained experts. While most doctors think that what they are doing is best, right, and safe for the majority of women and babies, Korte and Scaer point to an avalanche of studies showing that there is no scientific justification for most standard hospital procedures, and much of the evidence favors no, or at least cautious, intervention. Routine hospital practices initiate a vicious cycle, disturbing the natural process of birthing and increasing the likelihood of complications and the need for increasingly complex interventions and pain-relieving drugs. Some of the techniques used are painful or uncomfortable at best, and performed by people who are strangers to the woman herself.

"Managed" or "disturbed births" have come to be what women expect when they have a baby and perhaps, Buckley observes, how in a "strange circularity," it works. In this model, women are almost certain to need the interventions modern medicine employs, and to come away grateful to be saved, no matter how difficult or traumatic their experience.

> ### Drugs, Drugs, Drugs...
> Suzanne Arms observes that the history of twentieth century birth practices could be told in terms of drugs: drugs to stop excessive bleeding, to reduce or numb the body to pain, to treat mothers and babies for infectious diseases, to start labor, to stop it, or speed it up. Whether given in pregnancy or birth, whatever is given the mother is also given the baby via the placenta that binds them together. A baby's system is not mature enough to metabolize and throw off drugs like an adult body can. Drugs reach the baby in higher dosages and settle in the liver and brain. It is often weeks or months before all traces of a drug passes out of a baby's system. Long-term studies show the dramatic increase in all kinds of learning disabilities associated with both complicated delivery and the use of drugs in pregnancy and birth.

Painkillers given the mother pass through to the baby. Artificially dulling the sensations of labor alters both mother and baby physiologically, alters the way they relate to each other, and alters the way in which the baby perceives its new world. For example, Arms highlights the oft-ignored fact that the baby has an active part to play in its journey down the birth canal, and in positioning itself to be born. The baby's whole body is massaged in this process and its entire nervous system stimulated in preparation for breathing and taking in the sensory information it will encounter on emerging into the world. For the mother, the physical sensations of labor create a shift of consciousness, and hormones flood the body, softening the labor pains. Labor releases a set of hormones in both mother and baby, preparing them to fall in love and to bond with each other.

Drugs interfere with, or destroy, nature's exquisitely composed orchestration of a natural birth. The issue is not whether or not we should stop all drugs, but that we need to be extremely cautious in their use, using them only when every other alternative has been exhausted. No drug given to a woman who is carrying a baby inside her can be considered safe for her baby, no matter what the reason for its use. After birth, the same principle should follow for women who breastfeed.

While in rare cases, small amounts of a drug can be worth the risk, the most effective and safest support for a birthing woman is the continuous presence and reassurance of another person. For the most part, drugs are simply used to replace human caring and support. They make it possible for administrators to staff maternity units so that nurses can care for several patients at a time, and for physicians to continue with their office hours or nighttime sleep while their patients labor elsewhere. The rate of drug-induced labors increases dramatically on Fridays.

This is not to suggest a total disregard for medical expertise and technology. It is, rather, a call to support women in trusting their bodies, and their abilities to make informed decisions. It advocates medical technology be reserved for cases in which it is required (high-risk pregnancies that can be detected through prenatal care), and unforeseen complications (the latter occur in 5–10% of prepared homebirths).

## Birthing, Naturally

*Undisturbed birth represents the smoothest hormonal orchestration of the birth process, and therefore the easiest transition possible—physiologically and hormonally. Psychologically, and emotionally, from pregnancy and birth to new motherhood and lactation, for each woman… her baby's safety is also enhanced, not only during labor and delivery, but also in the critical transition from womb to world.* —Sarah Buckley, MD, *Gentle Birth, Gentle Mothering*

Women's bodies are designed, and have evolved over millions of years, to give birth naturally. A woman who has given birth naturally will experience an immense sense of personal accomplishment and satisfaction, giving her the confidence that she can care for her baby. This confidence is reinforced by a cocktail of hormones that peak most dramatically after birth, suffusing the brains of both mother and newborn—catalyzing profound neurological changes that serve to engage a mutually fulfilling mother-infant bond. Medical interventions interfere with this exquisitely orchestrated release of hormones, both during and immediately after the birth.

In the absence of drugs, the newborn baby will be alert and display the full range of early breastfeeding and attachment behaviors. Mother will be alert and able to hold her baby. And, the early days after the birth will not be compromised by the need to recover from drugs or other interventions.

After a natural birth, the umbilical cord connecting mother and baby is left intact until it has ceased pulsing, and preferably until after the placenta is expelled. This allows the last few ounces of blood to be squeezed into the baby.* The newborn remains in close contact with the mother, and is helped to latch on to her breast within an hour of birth. For the first hour or so after birth, the baby will be highly alert, and primed to connect with her parents. The early

---

* While largely ignored, many medically-birthed newborns are actually anemic from premature clamping of the cord, which may well account for unnecessary admissions to neonatal intensive care.

minutes, hours and days are her first experience of life outside the womb, and will remain imprinted on her for the remainder of her life.

*After one big contraction, our midwife, Betty, said, "Jack, get in the pool, Meryn's having a baby!" This was a sudden surprise. She had skipped "transition," the stage of back-to-back contractions. She apparently just surrendered her body to the Mother.*

*I quickly got in behind her and could feel Siena's head bulging. The next push brought it out, and I quickly felt around trying to find Meryn's perineum to support with my fingers so it wouldn't tear when Siena's shoulder passed by (we were avoiding an episiotomy, and it worked). In the process of feeling for where Meryn ended and Siena started, I stuck a finger up Siena's nose! Then I knew she was really there. One more push and she was out, but still under the water, still using her cord for oxygen. Then Betty lifted her up into Meryn's arms. No tears and no tears!*

*Siena opened her eyes and looked directly into Meryn's eyes. Then she shifted her gaze to me, over Meryn's left shoulder. After a bit she started looking around at the ceiling and apparently started to think about breathing (her cord was still pulsating so there was no rush). A few coughs and sputters, and she started the first of the 600 million breaths that she will probably take in her life.* —Jack

Babies remember their birth experiences. Reactions to any trauma are stored in the body and memory, and can be accessed months or many years later. This is well documented by psychologist David Chamberlain in *Babies Remember Birth*, and psychiatrist Thomas Verny in *The Secret Life of the Unborn Child*. The feelings and consciousness of babies both *in utero* and at birth have an impact on our entire life experience.

*Remember this: Birth is a process that nature has successfully refined through tens of thousands of years. Knowledge of how to give birth without interventions lies deep within each woman.... All that most women need in order to do this is the belief that birth works and will work for them. But this is no small thing to hold on to. We are in the midst of an era of high-tech, managed childbirth. Women must reclaim childbirth themselves, for themselves. In the process I believe we will reclaim an important part of womanhood and do a great service to our children.* —Suzanne Arms, *Immaculate Deception II*

## Birthing: Home or Hospital?

While a minority of women choose to give birth at home, a home birth is safer than a hospital birth for most birthing mothers and their babies. Birthing centers adjacent to hospitals and one-on-one midwifery care are the choice for a growing number of couples, and usually the best option to a homebirth.

Studies of birth center deliveries show the superiority of fewer interventions. Studies of homebirths with prenatal care and a skilled birth attendant, show a mortality rate as good or better than hospital births, and a much better record in terms of complications and damage to the baby. Note that these statistics do not attempt to measure the emotional, spiritual, and transforming qualities of the birth, which are as important to women as the act of giving birth.

> *The United States trails far behind other countries that have neither our technological resources nor our numbers of sub-specialist physicians in perinatal and neonatal care.... Despite all the resources we have thrown at intensive care, we have slipped continually in the past decade in the number of healthy babies born in this country. We've gone from ninth to twenty-first place [ed. Note: more recent figures show the US has dropped to #33 or #46, depending on the source]. We have one of the highest rates of infant mortality in the developed world, and we continue to slide... despite the fact that we boast the most sophisticated medical care in the world.* —Suzanne Arms, *Immaculate Deception II*

Parents-to-be, most especially if you are giving birth at a hospital, be sure to have a birth plan that both fosters a supportive environment, and supports you in asserting yourself in the face of any unexpected interventions. Insuring beforehand that all those who are to be present at the birth are in alignment with your wishes, and have confidence in the birthing woman's ability to give birth naturally, will give you the best possible start to a healthy birth and postnatal experience. As Sarah Buckley assures us, "undisturbed" does not mean unsupported. It means having people with us whom we have chosen as familiar and loving companions who are confident in our birthing abilities and will intervene as little and gently as possible. Consider how you can make the birth environment as calm, familiar, and nurturing as possible. If it's in a hospital setting, plan to bring some favorite items from home. When possible, give birth in a birthing center or hospital that allows dads to stay overnight.

Whether giving birth at home or in a hospital, a midwife who sees you both through the pregnancy and birth can make a tremendous difference to your experience. As can a doula, a woman who helps with the birth and early postpartum. She stays with the mother throughout the labor and birth, supporting her in whatever way is necessary.

> *It's crucially important that anyone birthing in a hospital today find someone to be with them in the role of doula—nurturer, physical support, advocate and protector of what they want for their baby's birth. Nurses, no matter how wonderful, simply cannot be counted upon to be there when needed. That's the nature of hospital nursing today. And even a fine, caring physician—or midwife, for that matter—has hospital policies to deal with, and time schedules, and simply cannot do what a good doula can do.*

*While there are never any guarantees, having a doula whom you have prepared to be your and your partner's support and advocate, can be the difference between having a totally uncomplicated labor and birth and healthy baby and mom, and a disastrous, complicated birth ending in a so-called "emergency cesarean" and a baby spending days in intensive care, separated from its mother and father! And that difference can spell the difference between a happy postpartum period where the couple are well bonded to their child, and a divorce, or an emotionally absent father who is just a physical presence and paycheck in the home.* —Suzanne Arms, personal communication

At the birth, a doula can reduce a dad's anxiety by keeping him informed of what is happening. She can free dad up to be the loving care person for his partner, and also take the pressure off him to "be there" should he need time out from the emotional intensity of the experience.

*You will be in a very strong supporting role and you need support as well.*
—Patrick Houser, *Fathers-to-Be Handbook*

For dad, male support—not necessarily in the birthing room but nearby, even on call by phone, can provide a break from the intensity, or offer reassurance when needed.

*A doula can provide the interface with hospital staff to ensure the birthing couple has as little interruption as possible during the birth, as well as explaining medical procedures in layperson's language. She provides "hands-on" support when needed; however, for me the role of the doula is also to be fully present and aware of the birthing couple's wishes.*

*At a recent hospital birth, the father had expressed his desire to "catch" the baby himself in their birth plan. When the time came, I ensured the midwife (who had just come on duty after a change of shift) was aware of this request. The midwife agreed and the mother birthed in a powerful standing position with the father receiving his child into his own hands—a magical moment!*
—Anna Watts, *celebrationofbirth.com*

## If the Birth Does Not Go as Planned

Suzanne Arms offers parents this guidance as to what to do, when a birth does not go as planned.

- The simplest ways to help a baby heal from any trauma it may experience, is breastfeeding, spending lots of time in-arms and skin-to-skin, talking with your baby honestly about the conception, in-womb life, birth, and early days and weeks after birth. Babies understand without the language of words. Lots of playful time together, too! And co-sleeping, keeping the baby within three feet of your body, whether or not you put the baby in bed with you. That's the distance from the baby's heart to yours that keeps the baby's heart in sync with yours. And it can prevent sudden infant death.

- Interventions that are very helpful include baby massage and/or gentle manipulation, and other forms of body healing (such as Reiki), and homeopathic remedies.
- Resolve not to feel guilty for what you may have allowed or couldn't prevent, or didn't even know about. Guilt is not helpful. However, grieving and allowing feelings of anger or frustration are appropriate and can help you heal.

Be sure that you get support to help you process your own emotions, with love.

## Reviewing Your Own Birth:

Parents to be, if either of you know or suspect that you carry unresolved trauma or issues from any difficulties in your own birth or childhood, and/or if you carry negative experiences or beliefs with respect to pregnancy or birthing—whether it be infertility, difficult pregnancies, miscarriages, abortions or infant deaths, or if you have been raped or emotionally or physically abused, it is important to clear the painful memories that may be lingering in your mind, feelings, even the cells of your body. Often, there has been no counseling or emotional support for processing this pain at the time. The pain needs to be acknowledged and expressed in a way that can clear these past traumas in a safe and healing environment.

This means, in preparing for the birth of your child, it can be very helpful to learn about the circumstance of your birth *and* the experiences and attitudes and emotions that your mother had regarding their conception, her pregnancy, and her life after birth, caring for you. If you not able to talk with your mother about your birth, remember that your body has recorded all of these things, even though you likely don't have any conscious memory of them. Writing with your non-dominant hand immediately on waking, even if you can hardly read your handwriting, is one way to access your unconscious. Journaling processes such as those in *Creating a Joyful Birth Experience* by Lucia Capacchione, PhD, and Sandra Beardsley, RN, can be very helpful. Talking about your own birth experience, perhaps with your doula or a counselor, may help uncover and release emotional trauma.

> *Andrew didn't know why, but he just didn't feel like attending the birth. Julie asked me to be their doula, saying "he just isn't emotionally there for me." When I met with them both, I discovered Andrew had been adopted himself at birth (well, after a 10-day wait in the hospital for things to be finalized with his adoptive mother).*

*I worked with Andrew, talking about his feelings when he reconnected with his own birth mother as an adult; dispelling some misconceptions about birth and encouraging his participation in the birth in whatever way he felt comfortable.*

*He went on to fully be fully present for Julie—supporting her from behind as she birthed their 12lb, 12oz daughter naturally. Bonding immediately with the baby, he is becoming a loving and caring father. The healing he received from working through his fears and being present at the birth is enormous, I am sure nurturing his new baby is healing the lack of nurturing he received as a newborn, too.*

—Anna Watts, *celebrationofbirth.com*

Rebirthing, bodywork, and energetic or spiritual healing can release trauma on a cellular level. It is important to seek professional guidance or counseling if you suspect this kind of work is advisable. If you suspect it is, it probably is.

Suzanne Arms reminds us that not everyone experiences shock and emotional or physical pain and a feeling of helplessness as trauma. Some of us are more innately resilient than others: we come into the world with a higher tolerance for unpleasant experiences. So trauma is not a simple equation. However, it is well worth finding out as much as possible about our birth and our mother's experiences carrying and bringing us into the world. We may be surprised to find out that we are more resilient than we thought, given the experiences we had, and our mother had, at the start of our life. If we find our lives perpetually or repeatedly made difficult and unhappy by patterns we just cannot seem to shake off, then it's worth looking into the possibility of early trauma. As Arms emphasizes, the good news is how much healing is possible.

We look more closely at this in Part III.

**Key Points**
- If either partner knows or suspects unresolved trauma or issues from their own birth or childhood—or any negative beliefs or experiences in respect to infertility, pregnancies, etc—it is important to address these, with counseling if needed.
- Women's bodies are designed to give birth, naturally. There is no scientific justification for most standard hospital birthing procedures, and much of the evidence favors no, or cautious, intervention.
- A flush of hormones peaking after birth suffuse the brains of both mother and newborn, and also of dad, catalyzing profound neurological changes that enhance bonding.
- The feelings and consciousness of babies both *in utero* and at birth, have an impact on their entire life experience.
- A carefully prepared birth plan is an important element in fostering a supportive environment and supporting parents in asserting their rights and choices in the face of unexpected interventions.
- A midwife and doula offer invaluable support to Mom and Dad.
- While most births are hospital births, studies of birth centers show the superiority of fewer interventions, and homebirths with a skilled attendant show an even better record regarding complications and damage to the baby.

# 15: AFTER THE BIRTH—SPOTLIGHT ON DAD

*In 1972, it was rare for fathers to attend the birth of their children, but being a doctor, I had already seen one or two, so we chose the only hospital in Baltimore (Church Home and Hospital—where Edgar Allen Poe died) that allowed fathers in the delivery room.*

*We were having a late supper with friends, just finishing off hot fudge sundaes, when my wife's water broke. Contractions came fast, and I raced us down the Jones Falls Expressway into E. Baltimore, much faster than I usually drove. It was thrilling. She got checked in, and I drew a big smiley face (they had just appeared the year before) on her belly for the doctor to see. I took a photo of her, and the doctor when he arrived*

*Our daughter was born about 2 hours later. I recall the joking around between the OB and nurse, who were betting on whether she'd come before the nurse's shift ended at 11PM (she was born at 11:07). I got a lot of photos of her emerging, being held upside down in bright lights. I recall a lot of anxiety around her as-yet-unknown gender, especially when I thought the cord between her legs was a scrotum and said "It's a boy," only to be corrected in a few seconds.* —Jack

A generation or two ago it was rare for a man to witness a birth, and even if he wanted to, permission was rarely given. Today, in some places over 90% of men are present when their babies are born.

While traditionally women gave birth at home, in familiar surroundings, and with the support of a midwife or other women experienced with birth, today most babies are born in a hospital, and it is rare for a birthing mother to have a personal female labor companion. More likely, she will find herself with a harried maternity nurse looking after several women. This is changing as growing numbers of couples learn the value of having the support of a doula or midwife at hospital births. But most mothers, birthing in an alien environment, under the control of complete strangers, want a familiar face for moral support. But, why the father instead of an experienced woman? The extended family that predominated prior to World War II has been largely replaced by the nuclear family, where couples have only each other to turn to for comfort and support. Because birthing women are no longer given general anesthetics, they are awake—even though many prefer to have drugs so they don't feel the contractions—and wanting companionship from the person they feel should care the most—the father.

While many men are bored at some time during labor, or exhausted to the point of wanting to tune out for a while, especially during a long first stage when there seems to be little progress, most rate being present during labor and birth as among the peak experiences, if not *the* peak experience or turning point of their lives. Most also find the experience of birth quite overwhelming, and almost impossible to describe. One study found that two out of three spoke of the experience only in "glowing terms," and the vast majority of men (93%) were positive about it, *even if they had also been frightened or upset.*[43]

> *It was one of the most unpleasant experiences of my life, and I wouldn't have missed it for anything.* —Alfred

Many parenting books today give us the wonderful news that it is not only the mother that nature has primed to bond with their baby. Father's bodies also produce a rush of oxytocin and prolactin, those hormones that help them bond with their baby and be more deeply connected and sensitive as dads.

A mountain of studies show that the presence of the father helps the mother relax, both easing and speeding up the birth, and mothers report less pain and need less medication when their partners are present. However....

## The Other Side of the Coin

Michel Odent, MD, has long asserted that one of the main roles of health professionals should be to protect the *emotional* state of pregnant women, as this factors so very significantly in how the birth unfolds.

In the early eighties, Odent attracted attention by saying he was no longer happy with fathers in the labor room. Subsequently he clarified he wasn't against all fathers being there, but wrote of his experience at his hospital in Pithiviers, France: "For instance, we have noticed on many occasions that the presence of the man can inhibit the woman and that labour only progressed well after the husband had left the room. On the other hand we had many examples where the man was a positive factor."

Given all the research I had seen—and that you will find in most every parenting book—touting the benefits to mother, father and baby, of a father's presence at birth, I was a little surprised. Noting that this was his position almost three decades ago, I hypothesized that he would have found otherwise, by now. Here is his response to my query:

> *This is what I wrote in* Birth Reborn, *published in 1984. "At that time, the doctrine of participation of the father at birth was strongly established and what I wrote was at the limit of political correctness."*

> *At that time we only had the experience of 4000 or 5000 births with the participation of the father. More than 25 years later, having also the experience of home births, this is what I would probably write: "We have noticed that in general the presence of the man can inhibit the woman and that labour can only progress well after the husband/partner has left the room. However, the man is occasionally a positive factor."*

In a subsequent email, Odent wrote both of his "difficulties to digest theories," and that he is speaking from his experience of being involved in childbirth for more than half a century, since he was an "externe" (medical student with minor clinical responsibilities) in a Paris maternity unit in 1953, until today, involved in home birth in London.

So now I was more than a little surprised—and curious. How is it that his experience can run so counter to conventional thinking, practice, and research? My brain suddenly clicked into the multitude of reasons that could support his experience and, to current thinking, his "outrageous assertion." In fact it was now so obvious, I wondered how I didn't see it before.

## Father: Liability or Leverage at Birth?

I found that Odent had earlier stated:

> [T]he theoreticians of the 1970s [when the natural birth movement and birthing centers encouraged hospitals to consider the father] had not understood that in order to give birth, a woman must put to rest her neocortex and her "fight or flight system," i.e., maintain a low level of adrenaline. If they had understood this, they would have been more cautious before routinely introducing into the birthing place a male neocortex stimulated by a release of adrenaline. They would have understood that when a man loves his partner, his anxiety during birth is normal and that his adrenaline release is highly contagious.

A woman's womb and vagina are the sacred doorways through which a man conceives a child with his partner, and through which their child enters this life. Standard hospital interventions, such as the practice of strangers repeatedly coming into the labor room and examining the birthing mother's body, and forcing her to lie down with her legs up in stirrups and genitals exposed, can activate an unconscious rage or despair in a man. And, perhaps later, within the birthing woman, because her partner did not protect her from this violation.

These feelings, though they may never be consciously acknowledged, can cause long-term ramifications for the health of a couple's relationship. Also, the altered state of consciousness—a surrender to their body's process—that most women having undisturbed births move into during transition, or the final stages of labor, may be confusing or scary to a man if he is unprepared for this.

Some men are overwhelmed by the emotions and pain their partner is in— and their feelings of powerlessness and impotence in the face of this. Others relive their own birth trauma, consciously or unconsciously. Birth photographer, Anna Verwaal,[44] has vividly captured the pained look on many fathers' faces at birth. The mix of elation at the long-anticipated moment of the birth, the uncertainty of its outcome until the birth, and the re-stimulation of his own birth trauma may be triggered by his seeing a live birth, can cause a whole range of inner emotional turmoil that fathers simply aren't prepared for. This is a subtle, deeply relevant issue, not only for dads but for all who are present at births.

> *I got very sleepy at about 6PM, a few hours before Siena came out. I recall being puzzled and ashamed by the strong desire to lie down just when Meryn needed me the most. I later learned in a birth trauma workshop, with Ray Castellino, that it was likely a reenactment of the ether anesthetic that my mother (and I, through her) got during my birth.* —Jack

> *Seemingly strange spontaneous reactions, like suddenly feeling anger or suddenly feeling so sleepy that you can't keep your eyes open, are usually a sign that something deep is happening inside. It can be trauma, or it can be the body recalling/feeling the drugs that were given to the mother, which of course went right into the baby, via its umbilical cord.*
> —Suzanne Arms, personal communication

Many men, especially those who were circumcised as infants, experience symptoms of parasympathetic shock (i.e., the tendency to freeze, go numb, or feel paralyzed in the presence of threat) as soon as they enter into a hospital birth environment. While these men may not consciously remember the event of circumcision, their bodies never forget, and their physiology responds accordingly. Because the conditions of their child's birth remind them of the conditions of their own birth, they may freeze or go numb and are unable to stand in their power and enact their role as fierce protector during the birth of their children.

> *Birth can open wounds that birth can then heal. We should not assume that because labor is often so intense, we should keep men away from their feelings and buried body memories. Long time labor and delivery nurse, Anna Verwaal, from Holland, became a doula because she found she could offer better support in that role. She also became an outstanding birth photographer, and has noted that on many occasions a man's "breaking down" during his partner's labor, or right at the moment of delivery can, and often does, initiate a healing in the couple's relationship that also helps them bond more closely with their child.* —Suzanne Arms, personal communication

On one side of the scales we have:
- the importance of giving priority to a mother's emotional state, and the value to mother and baby (and so ultimately to father) of an "undisturbed birth," and
- the fact it is a peak (if not always pleasant) experience for Dad, and that when Dad is present at birth, he, too, receives a rush of hormones that support him in bonding with his baby.

On the other side we have:
- the high possibility of a man's experiencing emotional turmoil at this critical stage of the birthing process. He is hardly in a position to "be there" for his partner, or to protect and provide for, an undisturbed birth, and
- his presence possibly hindering rather than helping, disturbing rather than comforting her, and interfering with the natural progression of labor.

*Women are wide open, physically, hormonally, and psychologically, during labor. This renders them "porous" and affected by the energy of anyone in the room who has anxiety or fear or is just not feeling comfortable with her labor. This includes the father, mother, mother-in-law, child, nurse, physician, or midwife.*

*Her body registers what she feels and, if she catches that fear or discomfort, releases the hormones of anxiety throughout her body. This can slow or stop contractions altogether. We must assume that this also affects the baby's progress, too, for the baby is conducting its own labor as much as the mother's body-mind is.*

*For this reason, whenever attending a birth, if I found myself feeling anxious—sometimes because I was worried that labor wasn't progressing well, or that there might be a complication—I would leave the room and try to clear my feelings before returning. I didn't want to be the cause of the mother having a problem.*

*I have seen many men at births, in all kinds of situations—some where they felt very welcomed by staff or other family members, some where they did not, and others who simply felt awkward or distressed for seemingly no reason. Obviously they had reasons, but they might have been deeply buried, such as a fear for the baby's or the mother's wellbeing, or because of something that happened to them or to their mother when they were in the process of being born.*

*I've also seen men behave very strangely—given the sexual and intimate nature of labor. They, for example, began talking in a loud voice or wanted to turn on a television. Now, after years of reading about prenatal and perinatal psychology, and doing a lot more work on my own birth and the birth of my daughter, I understand that the intensity of labor restimulates memories, conscious and unconscious. However, that's not all bad.*

*Sometimes the presence of the father, regardless of how he's feeling or behaving, is really important to the laboring woman. His not being there, or wanting to leave the room, can bring up her feelings of abandonment and betrayal. That's one important reason to have someone there to support, not only the woman, but also her partner. A doula is the natural person to do that, if she (or he, since there are a few fine male doulas) sees it as her role to create a protective umbrella or shield around the birthing woman and the couple.*

*While in London in the early 1980s doing research about midwifery and photographing as many births as I could, I recall having dinner at the home of a "radical midwife" (that's what they called themselves). The midwife's father was a physician. The conversation naturally turned to the subject of birth. I vividly recall the midwife's mother, who was in her 60s, begin to talk about the birth of this daughter. The father had dropped his wife off in a labor room and, even though he was doing rounds in the hospital, didn't come back until after the birth.*

*Her voice began to rise in pitch as she recalled her feelings. She became so emotional that her husband suddenly tried to intervene, saying loudly, "There, there. I won't have you upsetting my wife this way." And she, even louder, almost yelling, cut him off, saying, "I'm upset and I have good reason to be!" Clearly, she'd been carrying those feelings ever since the birth and she had most likely never confronted her husband with what his not being there meant to her.*

*So, I am in favor, for the most part, of the father being present at the birth of his child—and if he is not the same person, for the partner of the mother, or friend of the mother to be there, too. The primary focus of attention must remain on the woman and her needs. However, someone needs to provide support for the father. And it can't be the woman in labor, although I've seen women try to do that—comfort a sibling or a husband in the middle of a contraction—such is the "need" many women have to take care of others.* —Suzanne Arms, personal communication

## No Magical Formula

While much of the literature talks about the importance of dad being at birth in order to get the "hormonal boost," the fact is that these hormones flow over the early days and weeks for dad, just as they do for mom. While they never approach the level that mom receives, nature does not neglect dad and the significance of his bonding with his baby, simply because he is not present at the birth.

Marshall and Phyllis Klaus, along with John Kennell, authors of *Mothering the Mother*, and famous for defining maternal attachment needs at birth, also give full credence to the significance of paternal attachment. The father's attachment will be increased if he makes contact with the baby in the first three hours after birth, and if he experiences the child undressed, for skin-to-skin contact, on a regular basis during the first three months.

Some evidence suggests that fathers who attend their babies' birth, *and are able to remain extensively engaged in the hospital scene afterwards,* stay more closely involved once the baby comes home. In the *days—and weeks—after the birth,* most fathers will crave to be with their partner and child. Not just to talk and look but most especially to touch, and hold, and cuddle. Witnessing his child's birth makes a man feel closer to his child, although it doesn't guarantee he will later be a good or involved father. Many other factors are involved, as we see in DDD.

As far back as 1974, Greenberg and Morris coined the term *engrossment*[45] to describe the kind of euphoric involvement that some men find with their newly born child during the *first three days* after birth. Most fathers feel this a profound sense of connection and interest, the moment they lay eyes on their newborns, and the process of getting to know and bond with their baby starts. Experiences can range from intense feelings of love, excitement, a desire to hold and touch and rock and kiss the baby, to pride and disbelief, virility and heightened self-worth, a powerful connection to mother and baby, and the need to count fingers and toes.

And so a father's presence at the birth and immediate contact with his baby is not a magical formula for guaranteeing, or even speeding up, bonding and attachment. Engrossment is a period when the process of getting to know and bond with his baby may be at its richest. And through this time, too, Dad is supported with the hormonal boost from Mother Nature, just as he was during pregnancy.

Many dads—and moms—feel a tremendous pressure to bond with their baby. It's important to know that it takes time—and usually more so for dad than for mom. It may be that for some men, the re-stimulation of their own birth trauma may actually detract from their ability to relax, be present to, and enjoy their newborn in the early days.

In summary, it is important to recognize that:
- whether or not he is present at the birth of his baby, Dad is supported with hormonal changes that help him in bonding with his baby, and
- Dad's presence at the birth is no magical formula guaranteeing bonding—it's a process that occurs with time, and engagement.

## Ambivalently Yours

Richard Seel, *The Uncertain Father*, noted that while today it is almost an expectation that fathers will be present through the labor, some men have ambivalent feelings. Some simply don't want to be there—not because they don't love and want to support their partner, but because they are afraid of how they will react if they see their partner in pain, or bleeding. They are afraid that they might fall apart and make a mess of things. While this rarely happens, it's an understandable concern, all the more so given the alien territory he will be in—and the stakes involved. In this case, a father's presence might hinder rather than facilitate the birth. Other men may simply not wish to see their wives in a private, vulnerable, and even embarrassing situation. These feelings are perfectly reasonable, and worthy of consideration well before the birth.

Given that most births take place in a hospital where the woman's need for an undisturbed birth can but minimally, if at all, be approximated (and her emotional needs rarely met), it may be that having Dad present, even if he is going through his own "thing" and not in a position to directly support her, is of some value. This is likely to be more so, the more he has prepared for the birth experience. His presence in this situation may not be any more disturbing to her than the situation already is, and in fact, his presence may be beneficial if only by virtue of his being the only familiar face in the crowd.

Odent cautions how dangerous it is to be a prisoner of theories, preconceived ideas, and doctrines. On reflection then, it seems best that a couple's carefully considered needs and preferences, rather than the latest trend, determine a father's involvement at the birth. And "involvement at birth" can come in many shades. A couple may decide that Dad can be there as long as, or as much as he chooses to be. Aside from being directly present during the full labor and birth, he can be right there, nearby, on call, to join his partner and newborn within moments of the birth, and to be with them through those all important minutes, hours, and days after the birth.

> *I suggest that couples, in preparation for birth, seriously consider exploring and discussing as honestly as they possibly can, what they know, and what they instinctively feel about the father being present, from the father's as well as the mother's point of view. It is hard, especially with a first baby, and with the dad's sensitivity to the fact that it is the mum's body so his needs come second. As birth facilitators/educators, I feel it is our role to support the father to feel that he also has permission to state his needs. It is good that things have now moved towards the father being there for himself, as much, or more, than for the mother. It's important that there is a good midwife or a doula present also, but a dad who doesn't want to be there, and who feels unsupported, is more likely to suffer than enjoy, be traumatised, and even become post-natally depressed.*
> —Adela Stockton, personal communication

## For an Easy Birth

In Part I, I wrote of Michel Odent's observation of "covert depression" and men's "need to escape" after having been present at the birth of a child. Some time later, Odent began attending home births with an experienced doula. In this context, his job was usually to encourage the man to stay busy in the kitchen or to identify topics of conversation that could distract him. Meanwhile the two women were alone somewhere in the house. "This," he writes, "is the best situation I know for an easy birth." He realized that in this situation, he did not see a single case of male postnatal depression.

> *I know a couple who did this for their third baby, who was born at home, after the father had suffered from postnatal depression both times following their first*

two babies' hospital births. The mother felt easier during labour, well-supported by her midwives, knowing that her husband was happy "pottering around the house" and minding the other kids. And the father coped much better during the postnatal period. —Adela Stockton, *Gentle Birth Companions*

Odent discovered that "where the man is continuously kept busy, not only is the birth easy, but also the father is in good shape and active the following days!"

Odent goes on to suggest that perhaps what is needed today is a modern variant of couvade behavior (in the anthropological sense of distracting tasks assigned to the father). Giving a task to the father may be a way to protect him from any extreme emotional reactions he might experience if participating in the birth; *and* perhaps a way to reconcile the need of a man to feel useful during childbirth, recognizing that women are best left undisturbed when giving birth.

Synchronistically, the example Odent gave of a modern variant of couvade, was in fact the task that fell to Jack during our labor, that of keeping busy setting up the portable birthing pool in our dining area—Siena arrived three days earlier than anticipated—and making sure the water temperature was maintained.

## But What's a Guy to *Do?*

Even in the absence of any knowledge of Odent's suggestion to keep men busy during birth, with approximately nine out of ten fathers now present at their child's birth, the pregnancy raises the expectant father's concerns as to *what* he is to do at the birth.

> For a man to whom "doing" equates with being, simply "being there" to support his partner can engender real fears. He must be of use—but how, and is he up to it? —Richard Seel, *The Uncertain Father*

Most men today, whatever their innermost reservations, appear in the delivery room. They believe that they should be present, to provide whatever physical and emotional support they can. While they may not be clear just what this will mean, it is generally understood to sustain morale, provide physical comfort, and help with breathing—or, in Patrick Houser's language, to "protect and provide for."

However, being the labor companion can be tough for many dads, given the male prerogative to *do* and the fact that this role primarily involves simply *being* there—fully present to his partner's changing needs through the labor. Assigning dad the role of coach ignores that the father, as well as the mother, is deeply involved in the process. And this may or may not, interfere with his ability to fulfill that role in the intended manner.

> *This is not to imply that it's really the men who suffer, but it is important to recognize that labor is often difficult for men, too.... She is becoming a mother, but you are becoming a father.* — Richard Seel, *The Uncertain Father*

The oft-espoused role of father as "coach" may not be helpful, as it can also reinforce the secondary nature of his role. If instead their roles are seen as complementary, the two can perceive themselves as working together to birth their baby—each doing what they are best able to do. For example, in the event of inappropriate intervention, it can be the father's responsibility to deal with the hospital staff. Again, while this sounds good and reasonable, and will work for some couples, it must be remembered that watching their partner in pain, especially if there are complications, is not something all men can view objectively.

> *What is clear is that the better prepared a father is for this significant life transition, including the birth itself, the better; regardless of what room he is in. He needs appropriate literature, classes, mentors, and forums where he can acquire gender-specific information and support for the most vital position he will ever have in his life. The influence he will have over the mother and child, from conception and before, will last a lifetime for all of them, so forethought, planning, and preparation are crucial.*
> —Patrick Houser, *Fathers-to-Be Handbook*

## Dad at Birth: To Be or Not to Be

Here then, is some controversial as well as more generally accepted information for a couple to ponder, and many questions for further consideration and research. At this point, it is up to each couple to weigh the pros and cons as they appear to them and, perhaps most importantly, to tend to their own inner guidance rather than be beholden to "theories, preconceived ideas, and doctrines."

And, if the decision is that the father will be at the birth, Dad, you will need support to be prepared:

- Learn all you can about the labor and the birthing process. The more informed you are, the more prepared you will be, and the less anxious you may be.
- Share your feelings about being at the birth of your baby with trusted friends or family members who will listen to you, and support you in being open with your concerns, without judgment or condescension.
- Most especially if you find yourself struggling with confusing, difficult, or frightening feelings—either prior to, or after, the birth, seek the empathetic ear of a trusted friend, doula, or counselor. Bottling these feelings up won't make them go away, but will get in the

way of you being present to your partner and baby. Indeed, your ability to connect with your feelings enables you to nurture yourself and your family.

- Review your own birth experience—so you are clearer on any unresolved issues you may still have—and seek counseling if necessary (see Chapter 20, 22).
- Plan to have a doula at the birth. This can relieve you of pressure to "be there" for your partner if you need some time out, keep you informed of what's happening, and protect you from the system pressuring you to coerce your partner to accept interventions.
- Have an experienced and trusted buddy outside the birthing room or on the other end of the phone to offer a reassuring presence or relief if needed.
- Figure out something to do (see "What's a Guy to Do, above)!

*One of the most inspiring births I have attended with a father fully experiencing the birth of his child, on all levels, was at a homebirth that continued for many hours, with little progress. The father, who was experienced with emotional release, took himself into another room and went through his own rebirthing process. Shortly afterwards the labor progressed, culminating in an intimately bonded and empowering birth experience for mother, father, and baby.*

—Anna Watts, *celebrationofbirth.com*

## After the Birth: Left Hanging at the Peak

Richard Seel observes that while a growing number of men want the birth of their child to be a special event for him as well as his partner, hospitals are based on hierarchies of power with doctors at the top, nurses in the middle, and patients at the bottom. In the delivery room, the father is even lower.

With most births taking place in a hospital, most fathers are forcibly separated from their newborn soon after birth, when mother is seen as needing rest. Given what we know today about the experience of birth and the importance of close and nearly continuous physical contact between infant and parents immediately after the birth, to include men at birth and then require they be separated from mother and child, makes no sense at all. This will be even more so as we consider the choice that some couples may make for the father not to be present at birth—but to hold and touch and be with his baby in the early hours and days.

> *It is hard to imagine a more curious way of treating new fathers.... If the father was not involved at all, his absence after the birth would be bearable. But to start a process, and then suspend it at its climax, seems almost gratuitously cruel.*
> —Richard Seel, *The Uncertain Father*

> *It always seemed to be three in the morning when I left the hospital after the birth of one of my children... Like a creature of myth you feel capable of anything... but, filled with the knowledge of your life-creating power, you discover that in fact you are impotent.... And as you wander aimlessly through those night streets until you arrive home or some other destination that ought to have meaning. But the real meaning is locked away in a bed in a ward in a building where you are not welcome. It isn't that reality is hard to come back to; rather that reality refuses to allow you in.* —Richard Seel, *The Uncertain Father*

While rooming-in options are a positive movement, a hospital is *not* the best place for people to get to know each other as a family. Home birth is an ideal option, but one only a minority choose. Birth centers that support parents in making a positive transition to their parenthood are a good in-between option.

> *Our first child, Hansa, was a breach birth. There were complications and she didn't make it. It was devastating to us. It took me five years to allow myself to fully experience my grief around this loss. I attended a two-day residential workshop on new ideas on pregnancy, childbirth, and parenting in Northern California. It was there that my tears finally came. I allowed myself to feel the grief. Only then was I able to let go and emotionally bond with my son who was then a 5-month-old fetus. When I returned home to my wife, we began preparation for his arrival in earnest.*

> *We read several books by Dr. Leboyer, Ina May Gaskin, and Jeannine Parvati Baker, took a birthing and parenting class, meditated, did yoga, went to inspect two hospitals with our midwife in order to determine how cooperative they would be with our Leboyer style, low stimulation birthing environment. We went to prenatal visits with both our midwife and our OB. We were very conscious of our diet and got frequent exercise. We spent the last few days before the birth at our isolated mountain cabin to relax and enjoy the quiet of Nature with few distractions.*

> *We arrived at Howard Hospital in Willits, a very small town in Mendocino County, California, at 5 AM. We were prepared with both a midwife and an OB at the hospital. A friend who was a Vietnam veteran posted himself as a guard in a corner by the door to prevent any unwanted "routine" medical invasions such as shots or heel pricks to obtain blood samples. We had done our homework and were pushing the envelope of natural birthing in a hospital environment.*

> *We had dim lights, a warm room, breathing support, and when Bodhi's head crowned the doctor let me hold his head as he emerged. I was so thrilled to be a part*

of this miracle. It was my job to give Bodhi his warm Leboyer-style bath as soon as his cord was cut. Lifting him off his mother's chest and gently lowering him in the warm bath, I felt the most exquisite joy of welcoming my beautiful son and our long-awaited healing.

Bodhi was born around 8 AM and we were ready to return home by 5 P.M. Our little apartment was warmed up and darkened for our arrival. We locked the door and stayed inside for nearly three days. A close friend prepared meals for us so we could focus on Bodhi and each other during that critical first period of bonding.

With my first son, I volunteered to be the diaper-changer, walker, and rocker of the crying baby at night. When I would arrive home after doing a day's work in construction, I would strap Bodhi on and go for a long walk. When we got home, dinner would be ready and we would have quality time together, then some quiet time reading or meditating. As Bodhi grew, he graduated to a backpack type baby carrier and we continued our walks. We even performed percussion jams in the park, with him on my back enjoying the entertainment. Bodhi is now a general contractor, a gifted musician, and a wonderful loving attentive father himself. We enjoy working together, playing music together and of course being a father-grandfather team.

Bodhi's daughter Kaia was born at home, underwater in a warm tub with extended family present. My wife Betty, a recently retired homebirth midwife, was there to assist. I consider these birth and parenting experiences to be some of the most rewarding in my life. In the late 1960s I knew I wanted to make a difference. Looking back now it seems I have. —Eric

**Key Points**
- Many studies report an easier labor and birth when the father is present. Today most men are present at the birth of their baby. Many report it as a peak experience of their lives—even if they had also been frightened or upset.
- Despite a cultural expectation that dads be present throughout labor, some men have ambivalent feelings.
- Some men are overwhelmed by their partner's pain and emotions. Their resulting feelings of impotence, and in many cases, their own re-stimulated birth trauma may lead to his presence at the birth a hindrance, rather than help.
- A couple should carefully assess their needs and preferences regarding Dad's involvement at birth, rather than following current fashion or research. Involvement can come in many shades.
- Whether or not present at birth, Dad is supported with hormonal changes that support bonding with his baby. Bonding is a process that occurs over time and with engagement.
- If Dad is to be at the birth, it is important that he be prepared. Dad must learn what to expect at labor and birth by talking with other fathers, reviewing his own birth experience, plus having a doula and a buddy on hand to be there for him, either outside the labor room or on the phone

# 16: After the Birth—Growing Together or Growing Apart

The transition to parenthood, perhaps especially the period running from third trimester of pregnancy through the early days, weeks, and months after a child's birth, is a time of rapid and profound change in a marriage, bringing new challenges, stresses, and tensions to a couple's relationship. Most couples are unprepared for what they encounter and have little or no support for resolving the issues they so suddenly find themselves facing. Many are troubled by growing breakdowns in communication, and changes in their sexual relationship. A passing comment can escalate instantaneously into a full-blown argument.

> *It is not only the experience of parenthood that is a closed book before birth; the sheer quantity of life that it takes up is also a shock. It can be frightening to find, after all the excitement and support available during the pregnancy, that suddenly it's just the two of you having to work it all out for yourselves, minute-by-minute and day-by-day.* —Source unknown

We looked at many of the issues that arise for a new mother and father after the birth of a child in Chapter 9—the tendency of the mother to rapidly emerge as the expert; the father's lack of training in qualities of nurturing; his struggles to balance work and fathering; the disturbing feelings that can emerge as his own insecure attachment is restimulated and he struggles with feelings of exclusion, rejection, and being superfluous; as well as with the structural obstructions he encounters as he endeavors to father his child. If you haven't read that chapter, we urge you to do so, before you read on.

Many mothers and fathers report a declining satisfaction with their marriage as they face the stresses that emerge as they move from life as a couple to becoming a family. Fifteen percent of new parents separate or divorce by the time the first child is between three and four years, and it appears that the time gap between formation and dissolution is narrowing. While the majority stay together physically, emotionally many, many more separate. Increased marital conflict and dissatisfaction have a negative impact not only on the wellbeing of mother and father, but also the child's development.

Understanding more about what causes marital strain during this period, is crucial to curbing the epidemic of men leaving. While in the following chapter we focus specifically on the challenges that arise for a man, and later we address more directly the socio-cultural and economic supports and interventions, here we focus on the information and skills that may be helpful on a more immediate level for the new parents.

## A Window of Growth

Becoming a parent affords the couple a unique developmental opportunity.

> *How would the world of childhood look if both fathers and mothers... entered on the process determined to make the most of the experience they knew would only come their way once, or perhaps twice, in a long lifetime?*
> —Adrienne Burgess, *Fatherhood Reclaimed*

When the new mother and father understand that the stresses of this transition time afford a window of growth for them individually and as a couple, they are more likely to survive and even develop a richer, more mature, and more fulfilling relationship.

A longitudinal study of partners becoming parents for the first time, conducted by Carolyn Pape Cowan, PhD, and Philip Cowan, PhD, semi-retired psychologists at the University of California, Berkeley, found the overarching issue to be the challenge of balancing individuality and mutuality, self-focus and commitment/obligation. How can two people establish a relationship of mutuality, interdependence, and intimacy, while allowing each to maintain a sense of uniqueness?

First, to reiterate, studies *consistently* point to the *quality of a marriage* being the best predictor of:

- both mother's and father's adjustments to parenthood,
- father's level of involvement as father and husband, and later, satisfaction with the marriage for both.

The Cowans found that while most couples experience a decline in marital satisfaction after the birth of the first child, some find that the new baby both brings them closer together *and* moves them farther apart. Parenting both enhances their sense of themselves and gives them a new, more solid identity as a couple.

- Many find that parenthood nudges them from being primarily focused on themselves, to a greater concern with others in their family, community, even the world, as issues such as peace and nuclear weapons take on a new urgency.
- Babies open men up to a concern with intimate relationships.
- The demands of juggling work and family roles stimulate women's investment in managing family tasks more efficiently and paying attention to their own personal growth.

> *I found that I had better time management skills after becoming a parent, and got more done. Before I was a mother, I wanted time to flow, to not be "restricted" by scheduling, but once I had children, I found that some pre-*

*planning of activities and chores helped the flow as well as helped me to get done the many extra tasks I needed to do.* —Barbara

In other words, the transition to parenthood can lead a couple to find a better balance of individuality and mutuality in their marriage.

*Note: If, for some reason, the birth does not go as planned, connection remains the key to healing—holding your newborn tenderly, rocking her gently, singing softly to her, stroking her tiny body, or gazing lovingly into her eyes. If you encounter any disappointments, losses, or complications during labor or shortly afterwards, be sure that you get support to process these emotions.*

## Conflict: Fuel for Growth

While we tend to assume increases in conflict are undesirable, conflict—interpersonal or intrapersonal—can be the fuel for personal growth and development. While conflict may be challenging, difficult, even painful, it is not necessarily bad. The Cowans found that it can be helpful if a couple can:

- accept that, for a time, some energy will be diverted from the couple's relationship to meet the nurturing needs of their newborn,
- understand that the stresses of this transition can lead to growth for them individually and as a couple,
- review their expectations of each other and of their relationship as a couple for this period.

Viewing the challenges of this transition time as opportunities for growth and development will mean different things to different people.

*My preoccupation with competence helped me get through the first few months; I like doing things well, and right. When I realized that there was a whole new set of tasks—changing diapers, washing diapers, taking a screaming infant and making him feel placid and sleepy, feeding him—when I realized all those things were new areas to master, I felt better....*
—A new parent, as quoted in Bronstein and Cowan, *Fatherhood Today*

## Why Is Transition Time Such a Tumultuous Time in a Marriage?

The most comprehensive study ever undertaken of the transition of a couple into parenthood, is by the Penn State Child and Family Development Project, funded by the National Institutes of Health, under the direction of Jay Belsky, PhD. The study ran for seven years in the mid 1980s, following 250 couples from their 3rd trimester of pregnancy until their first child was three years old. This study is reviewed here in some depth, as it appears to be as pertinent today as it was then—the issues appear to be basically the same. While being aware of the issues that commonly emerge for a new couple after the birth of a child will not resolve those issues, forewarned is forearmed.

The study found that most couples approach this period imagining a new baby will bring them closer together, giving them a new and deeper sense of "us." In time, this often occurs, but initially a child tends to push mother and father apart by revealing the hidden and half-hidden differences in their relationship.

It appeared that many of the gaps that emerge have their roots in biology and socialization: Nature and nurture have conspired to make men and women feel, think, and perceive in very different ways. While we saw in Chapter 8, mother and father appear to have equal, if slightly different, abilities and desires to nurture a child, Belsky found the birth of a child highlighted the fundamental male-female differences in their feelings, thoughts, and perceptions. Even couples that think of themselves as likeminded find their needs and priorities diverging dramatically. Differences in family background and personality mean that no two people share the same values or feelings or have the same perspective on life, and few things highlight these differences as pointedly as the birth of a child. And at the same time, a new child deprives a couple of many of the mechanisms they had used to manage differences.

> Belsky's study found that marital satisfaction influences parental competence. The more a marriage satisfies an individual's needs and desires, the less likely the individual to insert those needs and desires inappropriately into the parent-child relationship, i.e., to bring their personal agendas to their relationship with their children. For example, dads who feel ignored by their partner may become controlling and interfering parents; women may seek the closeness they feel with their husband in a kind of maternal hypersensitivity.

After their baby arrived, disagreements about who did what housekeeping had to be confronted because there was no money to hire help—and a lot more chores to be done. Couples who had previously avoided discussing differences in major values, or their differing opinions about whether the husband's or wife's work was most important, now found these issues came to the forefront. One or the other may have to put a career on hold, and differences in values can become paramount when facing the responsibility of shaping a new life.

> **Marital Changes—The Four Directions**
> Belsky found that marital change among new parents took one of four directions:
> - Severe decliners: 12 to 13% became so divided by differences that they begin to lose faith in each other and in their marriage.
> - Moderate decliners: 38% avoided dramatic marital tailspin but at the end of transition, were more polarized than at the start.
> - No change: 30% overcame enough of their differences to prevent a decline, but not enough to gain a new sense of closeness.
> - Improvers: 19% for whom the process of overcoming transition time's marital divisions brought them closer together.

The findings showing the direction of marital change among new parents is quite startling. While we want to believe that the experience of being a new dad or mom is, well, blissful, the statistics belie that fantasy. Since divorce rates are increasing, even higher numbers would likely be found in the decliner columns today.

*Our three-year marriage was strained prior to conceiving our son. We weren't living up to the projections we had created early on and had developed a dysfunctional dynamic of built-up resentments on both sides and an erosion of intimacy. We had a gridlock where I needed safety to connect and often didn't feel it in the face of her anger at the fact I was emotionally unavailable. She needed strength and acceptance from me and mostly felt judged and resented. We both brought big issues into the relationship and ended up disappointed.*

*In an effort to resurrect our sex life and save the marriage, we read and followed the advice of a book called* The Great American Sex Diet. *For a short time we had intimacy in our relationship again and this is when Michael was conceived. We had tried for a couple years prior to get pregnant with no success so this definitely brought us closer for a time. However, the years of prior resentment and dysfunction could not be erased and we slipped back into our old patterns.*

*There were also many months of additional strain in our relationship because my wife was confined to bed rest in the last half of her pregnancy (and she does not take well to being idle!). I felt prepared in that she is a doula/birth educator and I had been around many couples having babies for the first time. I even attended one of the first presentations Jack gave on the hypothesis of DDD, and was aware of much of my own wounding, including my parents' divorce. I had a strong desire to create a healthy family.*

*We had a difficult home birth, resulting in some bad tearing for my wife, but our son was fine and I was delighted to bond with him while my wife very slowly recovered from severe postpartum depression—alone at home with our son much of the time while I worked.*

*Despite the community of support that she had actively built, we felt quite alone in our new parenthood. Our friends without kids had no idea how hard it was and our friends with them were dealing with their own struggles. We were squarely confronted with being nuclear and not having family nearby to help us.*

*Our second son was born so quickly that she birthed him by herself in the bathtub while I was downstairs on the phone with our midwife seeing how close she was to arriving. Given the first birth, this was actually very empowering and healing for her. We had good support early on (the visit from Grandma, the meals from neighbors and friends) but soon after, we felt very alone. Two months later I was fired from my job and began confronting issues of depression and attention deficit disorder.*

*We failed to meet or change the expectations we had of each other and are now faced with the rubble of a failed marriage. We recently began talking about what it would take to move forward. Divorce has long been on the table but we are also looking at what might be possible as we each deal with our own issues. We are separately looking at ourselves and what we want for our lives and will see if we are compatible with the past stripped away and each of us taking responsibility for our own issues. Whether we stay married, or divorce and stay committed to co-parenting, something new will rise from the ashes.* —Ray

## Bridging the Divide

In each case, the direction of change was determined by the couple's ability to bridge the divide that emerged. This ability was determined by six specific capacities each partner brings to the transition that enables them to:
1. Surrender individual goals and needs and work together as a team,
2. Resolve differences about division of labor and work in a mutually satisfactory manner,
3. Handle stresses in a way that does not overstress a partner or the marriage,
4. Fight constructively and maintain a pool of common interests despite diverging priorities,
5. Realize that however good a marriage becomes post-baby, it will not be good in the same way it was pre-baby,
6. Maintain the ability to communicate in a way that nurtures the marriage.

Couples who scored high on four or more of these capacities, usually ended up in the improver's column. Those who scored low on four or more, ended up in one of the decliner columns.

Couples who knew, or learned, how to make these capacities work for them, usually saw their marriages grow stronger and richer. Those who didn't, often became unhappy and alienated.

Couples tended to grow closer when efforts to resolve the differences that emerged between them revealed their capacities for self-sacrifice, understanding, empathy, and compassion. Conversely, couples tended to grow further apart when previously unrecognized capacities for selfishness and stubbornness, emerged.

## An Unacknowledged Factor: Attachment

What Belsky's study did not note, is that an individual's ability to use these capacities will be strongly influenced by his attachment history. Those who are more securely attached, are able to adapt more easily to these unprecedented and unanticipated changes, while the insecurely attached will find themselves stressed severely. Just how strongly their attachment history influences their current ability to exhibit these capacities will be influenced by the level of "repair" work they have done. When couples are aware of their own attachment history, and how this plays into their ability to make these capacities work for them, they will become more resilient.

So please, take note, you can learn to make these capabilities work for you. You are not held by chains of your own history, whether they are of your childhood or last week's fight with your partner. Becoming a parent can be a wonderful opportunity to deepen your communication skills and connection with your partner, heal the themes of your childhood, and experience the joys of that era through your attunement to your own inner child.

---

### Changing Communication Patterns

Belsky found it common that a couple stopped communicating, and that half the time, *the change was permanent*. Additional factors that contribute to a decline in a couple's communications, as gleaned from Brott, include:
- having a baby to care for inevitably inhibits your ability to be spontaneous in heading to the movies or even to sit and talk;
- physical exhaustion inhibits the desire to hang out and talk;
- intimacy-promoting activities such as sex, or hanging out with friends, go through a general decline;
- with less opportunity to pursue outside interests, you may find yourselves with less to talk about; expectations and priorities change—often time spent with baby means less time with partner.

## United We Stand, Divided We...

Both parents are united by a common set of gratifications. Both find the baby irresistible; report parenthood makes them feel better about themselves, their parents, and their larger world; share a concern about the new work and financial pressures a baby creates, and about how parenthood will affect their relationship as well as their work.

When new parents fight, it is usually about one of five things:
- chores and division of labor,
- money,
- social life,
- work, and
- their relationship (who's responsible for the hole that's opened up in it).

Couples who manage to resolve these issues in a mutually satisfying way, generally become happier with their marriage, whereas those who don't, become unhappier.

While I expand on these issues that couples usually fight about in the box below, here I want to identify and highlight one of these issues, namely "relationship difficulties," both because the quality of the relationship is the foundation on which all the other potential divisions grow apart or together; and because of its pertinence to DDD.

## Relationship Difficulties: Maternal Preoccupation and Male Self-Focus

The Belsky study found relationship difficulties mostly focused on a decline in the frequency of sexual connection. Fatigue is partly responsible, as is the baby, who attracts the attention and affection his parents once directed towards each other; but in Belsky's view, the prime reason *new parents touch less frequently is that they feel less connected and less in tune with each other.* They feel estranged and lonely. And, again, differences in biology and upbringing often make men and women blame this on very different things.

The study identified the prime cause, from men's perspective, as *maternal preoccupation* with the baby. While most dads expected the baby to become the priority in the family, many were *stunned at how little attention or affection was left for them*—for their work, hobbies, concerns, or sexual desires. Often adding to this is the support that surrounds the mother—which leaves him feeling set aside and unimportant.

> *Not getting my needs met led to gradually growing anger. I became critical of my wife for not taking perfect phone messages for me. Then my criticism escalated to the point of verbal abuse. My wife stopped wanting to go our in*

*public with me, because she didn't want to be criticized in front of others. This led to increasing isolation.* —Ken

For women, the chief cause appeared to be *male self-focus*. Due to upbringing, and perhaps biology, a man's emotional energy and attention all too frequently flows inward toward his own concerns and needs. Shared experiences that pull a man out of this self-focus to concentrate on his partner's needs, can disrupt this flow. But because none of the transition's major events *demand* that he be there—for example, he does not have to be at the birth, breastfeed the baby—often his focus remains relatively undisrupted. As before his baby's arrival, he is preoccupied with his own wants and needs.

Regardless of where "blame" is placed—maternal preoccupation or male self-focus—both patterns are precursors to MPAS and to DDD.

---

**What Divides Us**
**Chores and Division of Labor**

This appeared as the major stress. While both expected their baby to create a lot more work, neither was prepared for what they actually encountered.

On top of this, mothers today expect and feel entitled to significantly more help from a man. And, men want to be more involved with home and children. Compared to their own dads, men today are more involved in baby and household chores. Yet new dads' reports of how much they're helping, don't match reports of new moms who don't feel they're getting the help they need.

Why the discrepancy? A wife measures what a husband does against what she does, and so often ends up unhappy and disgruntled. A man usually measures his contribution against what his dad did, and by this yardstick often ends up feeling good about himself and his contribution. His perception of his contribution is also influenced by the likelihood that he is, for now, the family's sole breadwinner, a role he equates with parenting that further makes the 20% he does at home seem like 200% to him. And then, too, as one of the dads in Belsky's study says:

"I expected to do more, I really did. But then I started thinking. Since Brenda's breastfeeding Jenny, Brenda should get up with Jenny. Then, pretty soon, "getting up with Jenny is Brenda's job" became "Jenny is Brenda's job."

Then, too, as we saw in gatekeeping, a mother's resentment of the contribution her partner makes, either in quality or quantity, can lead to his giving up and doing even less.

**Money Worries**

Parenting changes men and women's self-perceptions in very different ways. Pre-baby, both identified themselves as workers, rather than as spouses or parents. After baby's birth, women (including working women) began identifying themselves more and more as parents, while men identified relatively more to the worker role. Many a man's thinking about money is dominated by his impulse to conserve and enhance financial resources. Mother, too, might turn out the lights when leaving a room and "brown bag" it. But seeing herself primarily as nurturer, her chief concern is her baby's wellbeing, and this may lead her to make economic choices that conflict with her husband's. New cute baby clothes may be a priority for her, as a sound investment in her baby's presentation to the world.

**Career and Work**

While today's employed mother expects parity or near parity on division of labor, her adherence to this ideal often leads her to expect something much deeper—marital parity. She expects her partner to share emotional responsibility for their child and family and to share in any career sacrifices. Few men remain steadfast in sharing this ideal. Because of cultural conditioning, most are psychologically and emotionally unprepared to be the full partner their wife wants and expects.

**Social Isolation**

Recreational activities—movies, restaurants, visiting friends—decline by some 40% during the first year. New mothers tend to suffer more from isolation than fathers, but both tend to feel isolated and cut off. While some men will put this down to their partner's obsession with the baby, "she won't leave her alone," women are just too exhausted to go out—and may put that down to their husbands unwillingness to help.

*Going out with a baby means preparing for diaper changes on the run, carrying extra clothes for weather changes, finding a comfortable space for baby to sleep (even on mom or dad). The rebozo (sling) and Mexican culture made it easier for us to go out when we only had one baby, but my husband and I had an agreement—at the point at a social engagement that I would feel overwhelmed, I would signal him, and we would go home.* —Barbara

> **What Unites Us**
> Belsky found that there was as much agreement about the transition's gratifications, as there was about the stresses listed above. But just as men and women perceive the stresses differently, often they also perceive transition gratifications differently. Both:
> - Agree the transition's most exquisite gratification is the baby. Often, when new mothers talk about why the baby is so wonderful, they speak the language of love, and of a new dimension of the feeling that they did not know existed before. With notable exceptions, few men were as swept away by feelings of love. Most were swept away for more traditional male reasons—seeing him as a terrific new playmate, —a wonderful new cement that strengthens their feelings toward wife and family. While both used different verbal styles to describe their feelings about their baby, when they talked about him, both *smiled;*
> - Report parenthood makes them feel more mature, more grown up. But these words meant different things to men and to women. Usually, to a man this meant feeling more responsible about his work.
> New mothers also equated maturity with responsibility, but they usually meant the responsibility of shaping a new life. Others felt awakened to larger concerns, such as environmental issues;
> - Experience a new sense of family. This is the one gratification that both mothers and fathers experience in the same way. The new child gives a couple a biological connection that they had not had before, a connection that brings them closer because their partner is no longer just their partner, but parent of their child;
> - It brought them close to their own parents, giving them a better appreciation of what their parents had given them and what they had gone through to give it.

## The His and Hers Transition

The Belsky study found that differences in *upbringing* give both dad and mom contrasting ideas of what it means to be a parent, and differences in *biology* contribute to a different relationship and feelings toward the baby. A possible third difference: evolution, which programs both to prioritize parenting in different ways.

Jane Lancaster, PhD, a human evolutionary ecologist believes:

> ...*a woman is "wired" to pull a man into the family because of her limited reproductive capacity—she can only produce so many eggs a month... each child represents an enormous biological investment to her....*

> *The reason men often resist a woman's demands to settle in is that their reproductive capacities have produced quite a different kind of evolutionary programming. A man can continue reproducing well into his seventies and emits millions of sperm in a single ejaculation. Therefore, he is "wired" to regulate his biological investment in any single child because that child represents only one of hundreds of potential offspring.*

Once the baby arrives, the differences usually present such widely different priorities, needs, and perspectives that in most marriages, not one but two transitions develop, a His and Hers. While both become parents at the same time, they don't become parents in the same way.

Most of the profound changes that occur, especially in the early phase, happen to women, making her transition more tumultuous than his. Some are good... her love affair with her child (a downside being when mother's love affair with her child fully consumes her, so that she shows little or no love or affection for her partner.)

> *At the moment I became pregnant, I lost my sexual desire, which I only got back in the third trimester of pregnancy, and then lost again for the first months of mothering. I felt strongly (some faulty feminist influence I think at this point) that I didn't need to cater to my husband's desires or be sexual when I didn't want to be, so I just left him hanging during those periods. Frequent sexual play was one of the patterns of our relationship until then. And the biggest thing was that we didn't talk about this. We were still pretty affectionate, but it was mostly just hugging and cuddling.* —Barbara

Chronic exhaustion creates a vulnerability to unpredictable mood swings. When not worrying about exhaustion, parental competence, or emotional volatility, she may be worrying about the physical changes to her body, the loss of her figure.

Meanwhile men may worry more than their partners do about work and money. They worry about fatigue, in-laws, chores, and their wives. On the whole, his transition is more even-keeled. New dads took weeks and months, not hours (as is so with two-thirds of women) to form a strong attachment, making it easier to maintain emotional balance (of course, as we saw earlier, a factor here is that dads just don't have as much hands-on time with their baby, and certainly not as much one-on-one time).

## Our Transition

The different characteristics of Her and His transitions resulted in both developing different priorities and needs.

Bearing and caring for a child absorbs tremendous amounts of maternal energy; working full time on top of it, as more than half of new mothers currently do, absorbs still more. This strongly influences his and her needs and priorities. Note that several of these are key causative factors in DDD.

## Mother's Priorities:

**A reasonably equitable division of labor:** A top priority, she wants a husband who will relieve her fatigue by taking an active role with home and baby—a man who will be her partner, not just helper.

**Spousal understanding and empathy**: She wants a husband who understands her profound attachment to the baby well enough to know why she may sometimes neglect him emotionally and physically to be with the baby; and who understands how powerful her feelings toward her baby are, and helps her maintain emotional balance.

**Emotional involvement:** She wants to feel that in his own way he is as involved in their new family as she is. She wants him to sit and listen when she wants to talk about her anxieties and frustration, to play and care for their baby instead of returning him to her in 10 minutes, to check the fridge to see if anything is needed before heading to the store. To repeat: she wants a partner, not helper.

## Father's Priorities:

**Work:** This appeared as top priority for dad. The study found that even in this relatively egalitarian age of the eighties, most men believed the family's financial security to be a husband's primary responsibility. More recent studies indicate a significant shift, in that today this is seen as more of a shared responsibility.

**Affection and Attention:** While he recognizes his workload has increased dramatically and the baby is now the chief priority, he wants, as before baby, some affection and attention for himself, a reasonably active social life, and some freedom to pursue his hobbies and sports interests. A couple's ability to reconcile these conflicting priorities was the chief hallmark determining whether this transition time brought them closer together or drove them further apart.

I cannot help but imagine that, had Jack and I at the time been able to articulate these priorities so succinctly, we would have been 1) not caught unawares and 2) better able to negotiate a smoother transition time.

*Note: There were no primary caregiving dads in the study, which is not surprising given this phenomenon has emerged more recently. It seems likely that some of these priorities would change in the case of a primary care-giving dad, i.e., be determined by who is primary caregiver rather than by what gender.*

## For a Richer, Stronger, Warmer...

Essentially, from Belsky's findings, if you want your marriage to grow richer, stronger, warmer... after the birth of a child, here's what you need to do:

**Dad:** recognize that your wife's need for physical and emotional support far outweighs your needs at this time, surrender some of your autonomy, and step more deeply into the marriage to provide her with that help and support.

While concurring with this, we believe it is important to recognize that this can be very, very difficult for a man if he has not had his own infancy and childhood needs met, and he finds these—likely unconsciously—restimulated to the point of disabling his ability to be present.

**Mom:** recognize that your husband's desires for some attention and affection are also legitimate needs, and learn to control your feelings about their baby so that you can meet him at least halfway in these desires. You also need to recognize that he will see the support he offers differently than you do, and meet him halfway on this issue by giving him some of the gratitude he expects for his commitment to your new family.

> *The hundreds of small acts of self-sacrifice, consideration, and understanding necessary to arrive at agreement also give such homes another characteristic: mutual empathy.* —Carolyn Pape Cowan, PhD, and Philip Cowan PhD
> *When Partners Become Parents*

**Mom and Dad:** We would add, get support. Don't rely fully on your partner to meet your nurturing needs—whether it is for understanding, fun, empathy, or engagement. You each need a buddy, perhaps another new or an experienced parent who can empathize and laugh with you. Similarly, do not anticipate that you and your partner can meet your baby's nurturing needs alone. It does indeed "take a village" (see Chapter 28).

### Findings of a 2011 Report

A 2011 report by the National Marriage Project at the University of Virginia and Center for Marriage and Families at the Institute for American Values,[46] looks at what accounts for the success of the more than one-third of married couples that continue to thrive even after a baby comes along.

The 10 key factors linked to increased odds of successfully combining marriage and parenthood include a mix of newer and more traditional marriage values. Factors more closely associated with the newer, "soul-mate" model of marriage include shared housework, good sex, marital generosity, date nights and having a college degree. Factors more closely associated with the older, "institutional" model of marriage include shared religious faith, commitment, the support of friends and family, a sound economic foundation provided by a good job, and quality family time.

Note that again, equality in shared housework emerges as a predictor of marital success for today's young married parents. The report notes that while in the 1960s and 1970s, many husbands and wives took a more individualistic approach to marriage, that didn't work out so well, as illustrated by the divorce revolution. This report finds that in today's marriages both wives and husbands benefit when they embrace "an ethic of marital generosity." This means making regular efforts to serve their spouse in small ways—with a cup of coffee, a back rub after a long day, or going out of their way to be affectionate or forgiving.

## Focus on the Good—The Importance of Appreciations

It became very clear early in the study that couples who are able to focus their attention on what unites them and produces mutual joy, usually end up with a better, happier transition. The transition gives a couple many new and potentially deeper points of connection. There is the baby and the biological link she creates between husband and wife; the new sense of unity, of family they experience as they join together to nurture him; and the enormous satisfaction of knowing that the two partners are growing together. However, to take advantage of these new points of connection, a couple must first learn how to deal with the new differences and divisions of the transition. Mutual delight in the baby won't do much for marital satisfaction if the parents spend most of their time fighting about who diapers, bathes, and dresses the baby.

And, to come full circle, our attachment history, and the repair work we do, strongly impacts our ability to connect with others and to deal with any differences and divisions that arise (we look at this more closely in Part III).

## An Unacknowledged Factor

Interestingly, and not altogether surprisingly, while neither the Cowans nor Belsky talked directly in these studies about the re-stimulation of unmet infancy needs, many of their findings reflect the attachment themes as identified by Sue Johnson in *Hold Me Tight*: feeling unimportant or not valued by a partner; feeling excluded and alone; feeling abandoned at a time of need, or being unable to depend on a partner; longing for emotional connection; feeling anger at a partner's lack of responsiveness; and experiencing the lover as a friend or roommate.

> *There are very few ways to cope with our pain when our primary needs for connection are not met.* —Sue Johnson, PhD, *Hold Me Tight*

Other attachment themes that Johnson identifies are: feeling hopeless and lacking the confidence to act; dealing with negative feelings by shutting down and numbing out; assessing oneself as a failure as a partner, as inadequate; feeling judged and unaccepted by the partner; trying to cope by denying problems in the relationship and attachment needs; doing anything to avoid the partners rage and disapproval; using rational problem-solving as a way out of emotional interactions.

> *We often miss each other's attachment cues. We don't see the longing for emotional comfort or connection: we move into action mode, solving logistical and practical problems but leaving our lover alone and hurting. Or we fail to send out a clear call for the comfort we need.... And when we cannot find love and connection, the emotional chaos deepens.*
> —Sue Johnson, PhD, *Hold Me Tight*

More recently, the Cowans have directly addressed attachment themes in their work with couples. In their more recent book, *When Partners Become Parents*, they look at how early attachment experiences of parents with their *own* parents (the grandparents) play out in their style of parenting their babies and children, and how the quality of attachment they have developed as a couple (can they rely on each other to be there for them when they are upset, needy, or frightened?) plays a role in how they respond to their children.

This explicit identification of the connection between the re-stimulation of low childhood attachment levels and unmet infancy needs of the parents, with their present-time experiences that are triggering feelings of abandonment, as well as the way couples can work together to resolve these issues, is another welcome sign of change on the horizon.

## Chapter 16: After the Birth—Growing Together or Growing Apart

**Key Points**

- Most new parents are unprepared for the changes and challenges they encounter after their baby's birth.
- Most imagine a new baby will bring them closer together, in time this often occurs, but initially the child tends to push the two apart.
- Many couples report a declining satisfaction with their marriage as they move from life as a couple to life as a family. While most stay together physically, many more separate emotionally.
- Understanding the stresses of this transition enhances the likelihood of their developing a more mature and fulfilling relationship.
- Many of the differences that emerge have their roots in biology and socialization.
- The success of this transition is largely determined by their ability to bridge the divide that appears. This is determined by such factors as their ability to surrender individual goals and work as a team, realize a good marriage will never be good in the way it was pre-baby, and to maintain their ability to communicate well.
- The more securely attached the parents are, the better they are able to navigate the changes.
- Many relationship difficulties focus on a decline in frequency of sexual connection. A prime reason new parents touch less frequently is because they feel less in tune with each other. Men identify the cause as maternal preoccupation, women as male self-focus. Regardless—both are precursors to MPAS and DDD.
- Most of what divides a couple are chores and division of labor, money worries, career and work, and social isolation. What unites them is the baby, feeling more mature, a new sense of family, and a deeper connection with their own parents.
- Men and women have differing priorities at this time. Hers is a reasonably equitable division of labor, spousal empathy, and his emotional involvement. His are work, affection, and attention.
- Dad needs to recognize his wife's need for physical and emotional support *at this time* far outweigh his needs. Mom needs to recognize this can be very difficult for him if he himself was insecurely attached. Both need to recognize when and if his unmet infancy needs are restimulated to point of disabling his ability to be present, and *to then seek support*.
- Mom needs to recognize her partner's needs for attention are legitimate and meet him at least halfway. Neither can rely on the other to meet all their nurturing needs—whether for fun, engagement, affection, or empathy.

- Recognizing the connection between the re-stimulation of their unmet infancy needs with present-time experiences that may trigger feelings of abandonment, a couple can work together to resolve these issues. A third party can be engaged for counsel and support—sooner rather than later.
- Couples who can focus attention on what unites them and produces joy, usually make the transition much more easily.
- Our own attachment history and the repair work we do, strongly impacts our ability to connect with others and deal with the inevitable challenges of becoming parents—together.

## 17: AFTER THE BIRTH: SPOTLIGHT ON DAD

While a vast body of research has focused on the transition from woman to mother, little attention has been given to the transition from man to father. There is very little support for men confronting the emotional demands of becoming a father unless they are so distressed as to seek counseling or therapy. Even for the small number of men who enter therapy, few therapists address the realities of insecure attachment and the cascade of feelings and emotions that the birth of a child engenders. This is unfortunate, as preparatory information and support—prior to, as well as after, the birth—can greatly facilitate a man's transition to fatherhood and a couple's recognizing and resolving problems before they become insurmountable.

> *Going from man to father is one of the most dramatic changes you'll ever experience. It'll force you to rethink who you are, what you do, and what it means to be a man. Your relationships—with your partner, your parents, your friends, your coworkers—will change forever as you begin to reevaluate what's important to you and reorder your priorities. Some parts of the man-to-father transition are sudden; one day it's just you and your partner, the next day you've got a baby... there are individual variations, but for everyone, it's a gradual, ever-changing process that will last your entire lifetime.* —Armin Brott, *Father for Life*

Most fathers turn to their wives, not to other men, to help them cope with their feelings about fathering. It's not manly to ask other guys for help, especially on such a personal matter. The trouble is that even if his partner wants and intends to be supportive, it is very difficult for her to really appreciate her partner's reality, and so many men end up feeling inadequate and isolated. Feeling this way makes it tough to be a good dad—or husband.

> *If new fathers knew, or were reassured that it was normal to experience even wild emotional swings, and that the birth of a child restimulates issues from their own childhood, they might not be driven into flight or fight.* —Martin Rubin, MD

> *It is mind-blowing to discover that the incredible, deeply moving feelings experienced in being at the birth and becoming a father are not enough to carry you through to do the job you want to do.* —Chris Maple, PhD

Talking with other new and experienced dads about the fears he faces, he can find relief in learning he is not alone, and that his response is "normal." Hopefully those he shares his feelings with will not encourage him to "get used to it," but rather to recognize the opportunities transition time offers a man.

## Touchy Issues:

Here we look at some of those issues that many a new dad may be reticent to talk about with others. Can it be that in an era of supposed openness and sexual emancipation we are more open in exposing our bodies than exposing our feelings?

## Who Do These Breasts Belong To, After All?

> *Breasts are sex objects in our society. Most men in the West find them sexually stimulating both to sight and touch. They are still tabooed from general view, and their constant exposure in advertising, magazines, and films only serves to reinforce this taboo. They play an important role in close relationships and touching of the breasts is an important expression of intimacy. Some men see breasts as "theirs"—almost as property.* —Richard Seel, *The Uncertain Father*

Breastfeeding looms large for many a new dad. Before the baby is born, most expectant fathers are supportive of their partner breastfeeding, and while after the baby is born, they still feel the baby does best with breastfeeding, they begin feeling more ambivalent about it. Even those dads who support their partner breastfeeding may find themselves embarrassed and resentful when she breastfeeds in public—baring "his" breasts to other people.

For many men the breasts are an important part of lovemaking. As Seel observes, this makes for complications, as the breasts are often—usually—taboo after childbirth for quite sensitive reasons: perhaps she doesn't want them touched; or they leak if they're touched. He feels they've become the baby's exclusive property, and this further contributes to his feeling rejected and left out.

> *Within months of the birth of our fourth baby, my husband began expressing a deep jealousy. When he saw her breastfeed, he commented how he wished he were the baby. I became tired of being obsessed over sexually and my affections demanded. If I refused, he became very angry, kicking things, yelling at me, or retreating into chronic depression. He felt the children had taken his spot (in the bed). I felt his self-worth was dependant on whether or not I gave him lots of affection, and desired him sexually. I have become terrified of being intimate with him and go to great lengths to avoid it because he is so demanding.*
>
> *Before we had our first child, we were a team, doing everything together. Now I feel like I'm drowning, alone. I just can't keep up with it. I wish he would just grow up and start acting like a man instead of a neglected and abandoned little child. I ask very little of him for fear of his becoming angry.* —Marnie

Feelings of jealousy or resentment in the face of the intimacy and exclusive nature of the mother-infant breastfeeding relationship, may be eased when father understands that the experience is not entirely positive for the mother, who can be left exhausted and drained by the infant's need to be fed around the clock.

> *I recall, from the one time I tried it, the sweet taste of my first daughter's milk, but I don't recall any re-stimulation from seeing her mother's nursing breasts for the year before she was weaned, as I was pretty out of touch with my wounding and my sexuality. I never got to taste my second daughter's milk, 21 years later, because our sexual connection was so tenuous. Meryn's breasts were already in such demand and "on call" round the clock for Siena, she was feeling "sucked dry" and I was feeling scared and abandoned much of the time, though not consciously enough to talk about it as directly as I wish I had now. This was the formative period for our hypothesis that we weren't going to be able to verbalize for another 2-3 years. See Jeannine Parvati Baker's "Primal Sex: Bosom Buddies and Other Lovers," in Appendix B, which seeded the idea for me. —Jack*

Pamela Jordan and Virginia Wall found that a father's positive perception of the couple's relationship is associated with a more positive approach to fathering.[47] It can be very difficult for a man to maintain a positive view of the couple's relationship when the mother's nurturing and attention, often abruptly with the birth of the baby, shifts dramatically from her partner to their baby. Around the clock breastfeeding plays havoc with established routines and with "planned" periods of togetherness. Dads can feel robbed of their mates. Mom may think her partner is obsessed with sex when what he really needs is reassurance that she still loves and values him.

> *My wife and I tried very hard to conceive over a period of ten years. We even went through nine in vitro fertilization procedures before deciding to pursue adoption. There was a lot of physical and emotional trauma for both of us from these procedures and from our difficulty in becoming parents.*
>
> *When our son arrived it felt like things really shifted. We were both determined to give him the best of everything we could provide, especially physical and emotional bonding. I had missed out on nursing with my mother, so I had a special desire for our son to have this nurturing experience. My wife was also determined to bond with our son as deeply as possible. She used a supplemental nursing system (SNS) to augment the milk she was able to produce on her own. As soon as possible after he was born, she put our son to her breast, and began their nursing relationship, which lasted several years.*
>
> *For a while, I was very happy just to see them being so close and we were all feeling the joy of having a close, loving family. I felt like I was holding the space for them to nurse and bond. I assisted in preparing the SNS and became the night parent, changing our son's diapers as needed and assisting my wife in any way I could.*

*I began to feel a sense of withdrawal from the affectionate sexual intimacy my wife and I had become accustomed to before the birth. I rationalized that it was important for me to put my "selfish desires" on the backburner.*

*However, I was not able to deny that I was envious of our son having taken over the intimacy I was accustomed to having with my wife. I felt cut out, and realized that I wanted some of that yummy breast, too, so I asked for it. My wife was happy to give me a taste. She let me suckle her breast occasionally and I got some of the experience I had been longing for. I was touched that she was willing to share herself in this way with me.*

*I was able to feel into my wife and my son as they were nursing and enjoy the warm feelings that they both were experiencing. Sometimes I would hold both of them while they were nursing. She appreciated my help and we were able to maintain our connection. By supporting their nursing relationship it felt like I vicariously got something I had missed in my own infancy.*

*Gradually our sexual relationship began to blossom again, but only after a lot of deep emotional processing (Process Coaching—see Appendix E). We knew our journey through infertility had been rough but we were not prepared for the confrontation with our hidden emotional issues that ensued once we became parents. We learned to hold space for each other's expression of hurt feelings, while not taking it personally. The trust deepened and we were able to bring healing to the fear of intimacy and wounding that it would stir in each of us.*

*Eventually we realized that choosing healing as a way of life continued to deepen our connection to ourselves, each other and our life as a family. In this context, we are, and continue to be, healing partners.*

*I used to think that we would struggle and work hard to heal and that eventually we would reach a point where we would be healed and everything would be okay. Now I realize that healing is an ongoing process without end, where love is summoned and the experience of becoming more whole continues to unfold.* —Eric

Jordan and Wall emphasize the importance of recognizing that the father's need for intimate connection within the adult partnership can minimize his experience of the baby as an intruder and increase his support for breastfeeding. When the mother can recognize and appreciate the father's need for intimate connection, and that it is very difficult to cope with his pain when his need for connection is not met, she can respond to her partner with reassurance that she still loves him. This can minimize the risk of MPAS by letting him know she needs him as an intimate, husband, and father to her child, and that her love for him has not been replaced by the baby.

*My wife and I married with the intention of being parents together. We were closely connected, and spent every free moment engaging with each other. We*

*teamed up well to prepare for a planned home birth, attended Lamaze classes together, and joyfully participated in the birth of our daughter.*

*I had expected to feel left out of the close bonding between mother and child, and was delighted to have my own strong bonding with my daughter. But despite my best intentions, having a new babe in arms, and a babe in bed, dramatically changed our relationships.*

*Most notable was that our lives now had a new center of attention. Practically every shared conversation was focused on the progress and care of our daughter. I vividly recall waking up in the morning, starting to share a thought or idea and getting only partly into a sentence before being interrupted. If the idea was important to me, I had to wait the entire day until I was home from work and our daughter was asleep to complete my sentence and continue the conversation. This was very frustrating and led me to share much of my inner life with other friends. Increasingly it intruded on the intimacy that my wife and I had treasured, and we began the long process of gradually distancing ourselves from each other. We remained together as committed co-parents; but the intimacy of our personal relationship never returned.* —Ken

> **Oral Needs**
>
> The World Health Organization[48] recommends breastfeeding for a minimum of two years. Few children in the Western world get anywhere close to this amount. Premature deprivation of the oral needs we were designed to have satisfied through suckling at the breast, results in a host of oral substitutes in infancy: pacifiers, thumb sucking, and transitional objects to replace contact with the mother such as "blankees" and stuffed animals. This is amplified by further separation from the nurturing arms of mother by substituting cribs, strollers, and a variety of plastic carrying devices that deprive the infant of all-important touch and warmth.
>
> In adult life, nail biting, smoking, overeating, drinking, etc., replace pacifiers and thumbs as we persist in our unconscious attempts to get unmet oral needs met. Our deep oral cravings are fueled by advertising that prominently features images of voluptuous models with the very breasts our mouths were denied. Much of our consumer society is built on substituting material "things" for our unrecognized unmet oral needs—a futile attempt to fill our inner void. A trendy drink, new shampoo, or the latest model car will somehow make it all better. From advertisements for basic commodities to the girlie magazines many teenage boys have under their mattress, breasts are a proven sales tool.

Fathers may not understand that breastfeeding is not always easy for mom, who can be left exhausted. Jordan and Wall found that most fathers have little understanding of breastfeeding beyond the fact that it is good for babies. While new fathers as well as mothers need support to share both their positive and negative feelings about breastfeeding, education and support for breastfeeding is directed almost exclusively to the mother. Including the father can foster a parental relationship for breastfeeding and the father's willingness and ability to encourage and support his partner.

> *Feeling loved and secure makes us kinder and more tolerant people.*
> —Sue Johnson, PhD

The essential value of breastfeeding is not just about nutrition, but rather the whole bonding and attachment process that unfolds from the complex of behaviors involved in breastfeeding, as well as the close intimate physical contact from carrying and sleeping with infants. It is this bonding process that we simply cannot afford to lose—it is a critical preventive factor in curbing the tide of the next generation of men leaving.

## Sex AB (After Baby)

There are many reasons why sex after childbirth can be difficult. It can take many weeks for a woman's body to recover fully from her labor, and the altered hormonal balance after birth lowers many women's interest in sex. The new mother may have little libido, while at the same time experience vaginal dryness related to estrogen. She may feel "all touched out" from the demands of breastfeeding and physical care of their baby. The new father may feel repulsed by his partner's leaking breasts, or less-than-trim figure. She is likely exhausted, sees few opportunities for relaxed lovemaking, and may be uncomfortable with the way her body looks after birth. Parenting books tend to imply that the problems will soon pass.

> *But psychological scars are often deeper than physical ones, and the feeling of violation experienced by many women can take much longer to get over. The woman whose body was taken over and controlled by obstetricians may fear sex as yet another assault and violation, which she is simply unable to cope with—especially with the stress of adjusting to a new role with a new baby.*
> —Richard Seel, *The Uncertain Father*

Seel goes on to note that many, perhaps most, women find their whole attitude towards sexuality and the physical aspects of lovemaking radically changed after childbirth, and this change lasts for many months or years, and is sometimes permanent. This lack of interest is much more common than is usually recognized.

Seel speaks directly to the fact that many couples have to face the fact that he wants it, she doesn't. Being aware of this likelihood prior to the baby's arrival, can at very least lighten the "personal" element in the equation. The more a man can understand that the rejection is not personal, not a rejection of him per se, but a sign of a change in the nature of the relationship between his partner and him, the easier it can be to accept. But this remains a real problem for most couples, since the man's affectional/attachment needs are not being met in the same way the mother's are through contact with the baby. Most men want sex after the baby is born—and they want it very much, but since it's often not an option they try to find other means of getting their affectional needs met. As we saw earlier, if a man can realize that this present-time need is really based on longings from unmet childhood needs, he will be much better able to compensate for them now.

A man may come to realize that he may want sex as much for the cuddling, consolation, and reassurance that he has not been completely displaced by the baby, but many will not recognize this component without it being explained. While a wife may not be interested in intercourse, she may be happy about cuddling, and if they talk about it, his needs may be partly met in this way, and the intensity of his abandonment issues may be reduced significantly. Seel suggests that more close contact with friends, massages, playing with affectionate pets, etc., may be preventatives for the urge to have an affair—a common outcome when this issue is not dealt with consciously.

## Affairs and Other Compensations

Several studies, including Masters and Johnson's famous work on human sexuality, have suggested that many men start affairs just after the birth of their child. Seel observes that while on the face of it, this seems a particularly callous thing to do, the new father wants physical contact; he needs to express himself and his feelings through the medium of touch. He is denied access to the one person he really wants to be with. "So he turns to someone else—a woman friend, maybe. His vulnerability appeals to her—brings out her maternal instinct, if you like—and when he turns to her for physical support she is there to help him."

Because our culture has collapsed the sensual into the sexual, most men equate closeness and intimacy with sexual intercourse, even if the new father's main desire is for non-sexual contact, many men also have a strong feeling of potency; they have before them proof of their ability to create new life. Given the increased awareness of their own sexuality, which many men have after birth, and the unavailability of their partner, it is hardly surprising that some find themselves "tumbling into affairs" almost by accident and almost against their wills.

Some men find themselves drawn to other women, not because they want to be unfaithful or break off the relationship, but because they feel hemmed in by the now imminent responsibilities of becoming a father. While some men may actually have an affair, for most it remains simply a vague feeling of desire.

## About an Affair

Post-traumatic stress disorder (PTSD) symptoms often result for the victim of infidelity. Traumatic wounds are especially severe when they involve, in the words of Judith Herman, professor of psychiatry at Harvard Medical School, a "violation of human connection." Affairs do not have to be sexual. Some are primarily emotional. Infidelity is any emotional or sexual intimacy that violates trust. Some psychologists believe that there is no greater trauma than to be betrayed by the very people we count on to support and protect us. And of course, the trauma parents experience when their partner is unfaithful, is transmitted to the children.

Jennifer Chalmers, PhD, co-author of *Surviving an Affair*, notes that while a betraying spouse rationalizes that they had to look out for themselves, and it may appear that their actions benefit themselves in the short-term, it has disastrous effects on members of their family.

> *...to add infidelity to a troubled marriage turns a problem into a disaster.*

Yet an affair has become, to many, an accepted way to exit or to challenge a relationship. I am deeply concerned about the reverberations of these betrayals through our families and communities. The repercussions of infidelity run deep, don't "go away" with the ending of the affair or the dissolution of a marriage, and spread far beyond the immediate family.

> *When the betrayer and the betrayed are parents, marital infidelity is never a private affair.* —Ana L. Nogales, *Parents Who Cheat*

When children of any age—six, sixteen, or twenty-six—learn of a parent's infidelity, they often react with intense feelings of anger, anxiety, guilt, shame, sadness, and confusion. They usually find it extremely difficult, if not impossible, to trust that someone they love will not lie to them, reject, or abandon them. They very often learn not to put their trust in love, nor the possibility of their forming faithful, lasting relationships.

Note, these are the very same lessons that we learn as infants when our needs are not met—we cannot trust anyone, love is uncertain, and human attachment is a dangerous proposition. Affairs then, compound the problem identified as the primary causative factor in MPAS and DDD.

Yes, there are times when a couple's relationship will simply not be able to survive the challenges of life after birth of a child. Given the impact of infidelity, not only on our partners, but also the lifelong imprint on our children, please seek counsel if you feel you may be "at risk." At the very least, do all you can do to separate with kindness and compassion, with maturity and respect. An affair can never be an honorable way to end a relationship.

## Enhancing the Father-Infant Connection

> *It broke my heart that my husband refused to have one-on-one time with my second baby, after he had been so present with the first. It's true, the second boy was a higher needs child, fussier, calmed best when in-arms or at the breast; but my first had been a colicky baby his first few months, and as I said before, my husband did*

*wonders with him. He absolutely refused to stay alone with my second son, even when the baby was asleep, once telling me—but what will I do if he wakes up? His refusal to engage with our boy pushed us farther apart. I felt unsupported, that I was in it alone, and I was also just experimenting with how to calm our child. I didn't have the answers, but I did have the breasts. I also believe that the tension in our marriage was one of the reasons our son was so fussy.* —Barbara

As well as spending time parenting with his partner, the new dad needs one-on-one time alone with the baby. He, like Mom, needs time and space to develop and master basic care-giving skills and to read his baby's cues. This is how Mom builds confidence and competence, and Dad needs to do likewise. This will help Dad feel that Mom does not have exclusive rights to the baby, and will foster sharing of parenting responsibilities. Many dads claim bath time as their own—bathing with baby in the tub and finding it a fun and helpful way to connect with their newborn.

Jordan and Wall report that some moms need encouragement from others to legitimize dads' parenting alone like this. Some perceive their desire to have time away from the baby as selfish and neglectful, but in fact it's invaluable to her, too, to take time for self-nurturing.

## And Then, There's My Beautiful Baby

Further compounding a man's confusion around sex and sexuality, is what many a dad will perceive as sexual feelings for their baby. Most dads are unprepared for just how physical interacting and caring for a baby can be. Most parents feel a physical pleasure toward their baby's bodies, and these pleasures may sometimes be experienced as fleeting sexual feelings. Some men will experience arousal, and "normal" or not, this can be frightening. But please Dad, don't withdraw your attention from your baby. Touch equals connection, so keep playing, cuddling, and bathing with your baby. If you're seriously worried that you cannot manage your feelings appropriately, get help.

**Key Points**
- There is little attention or support available to dads facing the emotional demands of making the transition from manhood to fatherhood, yet this can be a highly significant factor in easing this passage.
- Few counselors address the realities of insecure attachment and the cascade of feelings and emotions the birth of a child engenders, yet this can greatly facilitate this transition time.
- Issues a new dad may be reticent to talk about with others include: feelings of resentment or jealousy in the face of the intimacy and exclusive nature of the mother-infant breastfeeding; changing attitudes of his partner to sexuality and lovemaking; his longing for touch; and fleeting sexual feelings towards his baby.
- Preparation for the issues that may emerge, and heart-centered communications are important for Dad—and Mom.
- Recognizing a father's need for intimate connection within the adult partnership, can minimize his experience of the baby as an intruder and increase his support for breastfeeding.
- Some men start affairs after the birth of a child. Infidelity is any emotional or sexual intimacy that violates trust. Seek counsel if you feel "at risk." To add infidelity to a troubled marriage turns a problem into a disaster.
- Dads, as well as moms, need one-on-one time alone with their baby to develop basic skills, competencies, and their own unique ways of connecting with their baby.

# 18: Facing Our Own Unmet Childhood Needs and Self Love

*Holding this baby in our arms, we hold a whole world of possibilities—a microcosm of the future. Unlike us, older and captives of our time, she is ready and new. Let us infuse her with our hope and our affection at the start of her great adventure of life. "O Nobly Born!" This is how every new baby should be welcomed. It will be a deep reminder for the rest of her life that she is a beautiful and noble being.* —Laura Huxley, *The Child of Your Dreams*

There is another face of life after the birth of a baby that we rarely read about in any of the parenting books, and rarely—if ever—hear spoken about: the re-stimulation of parents' unmet infancy and early childhood needs. It is a face of parenting that, in large part, remains outside the conscious awareness of most adults.*

The way we feel towards our babies has a lot to do with how we ourselves were treated when we were babies. While it is known today that many adults have experienced more blatant forms of physical or emotional abuse for many of us the trauma was more subtle. For example, many of us were left to cry alone and uncomforted—it was believed that crying exercises a baby's lungs, and babies don't have real feelings anyway.

*Today we know that newborn babies experience discomfort, pain, and shock in the same way adults do, and have the same range of emotions as adults. Early experiences, positive or negative, in the pre- and perinatal period can have lasting effects, leaving traces on neural pathways of the brain and affecting the ways in which we view ourselves, and those around us, and our world. They become the basis of many of our behavioral patterns as adults. Whenever someone is neglectful or hurtful, it is because life has hurt them or let them down. More than likely, they suffered as children. Our insensitivities towards our children, the mistakes we make as parents, are reflections of things that hurt us when we were children—just as the love and patience we pass on springs from the love we received.* —Robin Grille, *Heart-to-Heart Parenting*

Most of us experienced feelings of abandonment or rejection as babies or children. Many of us are unconsciously carrying repressed feelings of rage or terror, and may find ourselves feeling resentful, even hostile towards our

---

* Robin Grille's *Heart-to-Heart Parenting* is the only parenting book we know that consistently weaves throughout every chapter, from pregnancy through the early years of parenting, the re-stimulation of unmet infancy and early childhood needs that emerge for many a parent. Brott's *Father for Life* is an immensely readable book written for dads, and also addresses this issue, though not in the depth of Grille.

children. While we have no conscious memory of abandonment or rejection, unless it is resolved, we will carry it in our body as implicit, or emotional memories that we won't remember, but we'll never forget. If our own childhood emotional needs weren't met, it can be very painful to be faced with meeting the needs of our own babies. We might find our children's dependency unbearable. It is hard to give what has not been given to us.

Whenever we feel overwhelmed by the demands of caring for our baby, and we notice ourselves disliking our baby or even being angry with him, it is likely that the emotional memory of some unresolved issue is being stimulated.

> *My wife sent me the link to your "Why Men Leave" article. My experience matches yours closely enough. How easy it is for me to leave! Having a perspective of unmet needs as a hold in my makeup may help to remind me to come back to myself and make a cleaner choice. I've done loads of work, and fatherhood continues to be the seminar that keeps on bringing up the pain. I know life is a classroom, and reactions are an opportunity; I'm just tired of the real vigilance it takes to come back to my heart, time and time, and time again.*
>
> *In a second note: Fatherhood has pushed my buttons more that I can tell you. Mostly it feels like torture. The more I react, the "righter" I want to get about how wrong my sons are (ages 5 and 21 months, I'm 45). Victimhood, resentment, shame, anger—I'm willing to try on your concepts regarding the origins of this internal tangle. I get so out of balance so regularly I know it goes deeper and pre-rational.* —Carlson

The good news is that every difficult moment in parenting is an opportunity to heal and grow. Sometimes our child's acting out is a response to our stress or marital conflicts. Sometimes it presses our buttons because it triggers our unresolved issues. However, we are *not irreparably damaged*. A wealth of information from neurobiology reveals that healing is possible and that it involves experiences that stimulate the growth of new neural pathways in the brain.

We look at this in more depth in Part III, but for now, know that allowing ourselves to *feel* these feelings in our body—not to simply think about them—and giving these feelings some healthy form of expression—writing them down, talking with a friend, or perhaps a counselor or psychotherapist if they feel overwhelming—can free us of these past hurts.

> *If you are not used to disclosing your emotions, doing so might feel uncomfortable at first, but it is worth taking the risk and extending your comfort zone a little. When you express your feelings and receive emotional support, you will notice how much more space you have for your child afterwards, and how much more loving you feel. Emotional maintenance is essential for parents if we want to keep renewing the joy of being a parent.* —Robin Grill, *Heart-to-Heart Parenting*

## Self Love

With parenting, as with all things in life, it helps tremendously if we feel *good* about ourselves. Yet almost every one of us—to varying degrees—feels that we are *not* OK.

To the extent that we do not value ourselves, our wellbeing is compromised, as is our ability to connect with others.

We absorbed messages about our worth, our goodness, from our primary caregivers—usually our parents. If left in a crib alone to cry, we began to doubt our own instincts. Most of us were taught to question our own truth—our instincts, feelings, and needs. We came to ask what *should* I do rather than what do I *want* or need to do. We came to feel that there was something wrong with us. These messages are strengthened to an unprecedented degree by the media—and by our peers and a culture that is driven by the media. This keeps us in a constant state of anxiety. We pretend that we are OK, but there is something in almost all of us that feels that we are not. It takes tremendous effort to maintain the false façade that we believe we are OK, in the face of our self-doubt.

To overcome this, we need to address the beliefs that in some way we're not good enough, and to understand how they got there. We need to ask if these beliefs are really true—do they even make sense?* Practice saying what you really mean and stating your needs in situations that are safe; and spend time each day exploring what is true for you—and what is not.

We need to understand that every child on this earth is born, as we were—worthy, loving, and lovable. Whatever the details, whatever led to our feeling not OK, needs to be lifted into consciousness. We need to distinguish between blaming our caregivers and simply acknowledging the truth of what was, and the associated feelings we still carry—of anger, grief, whatever. Our parents were the products of the beliefs of their day. Today, we are responsible for our feelings and for what we do with them. It's relatively easy to understand this intellectually; it's something else to really *get* it, to know the truth of it in our bones. We need to develop the conviction that we *are* good, loving, and lovable. This belief needs to grow until it becomes conditioned as our new belief, the belief we spontaneously act from.

When we develop that sense of goodness within ourselves, we act out of a constant and spontaneous belief in our own worth. Then everything changes. We have all had experiences like this, when we felt *good*—and we began to ask where were all these nice people before? Of course, they were there all the time, but our defenses were keeping us from experiencing them in this way. So

---

* For specific tools to do this, see "The Work" of Byron Katie, such as in her book, *Who Would You Be Without Your Story?*

developing this sense of innate goodness—of love—within ourselves is very important. Without it, we live in a constant state of vulnerability and fear—fear that the truth of who we are—will be exposed, and the fear that we will be recognized as lacking, as "less than." Our wellbeing is compromised—as is our ability to connect authentically with our partner and child.

## Attuning to the Frequency of Love

Love is a tangible energy, a frequency that can be felt. Attuning to the frequency of love requires first taking full accountability for the situation we are in, and recognizing that our reality is a result of what we are bringing to it, rather than what's happening—or has happened.

We can attune to the frequency of love, like tuning to the frequency of a radio station. When you feel unlovable, imagine adjusting the dial back to the frequency of love. It helps immensely to create a reality in which you are lovable—both in your mind, and in attuning to people and places with whom and where you feel lovable (and avoid those that don't!).

The first step is to be mindful of the frequency we are tuning into. And when necessary, gently turn the dial back to love. Often we first need to call on *compassion*, deep self-acceptance. The more we practice, the easier it gets. And what finer a way can there be to use our time and our mind?

## Nurturing the Adult Couple Relationship

> *Physical and emotional closeness actually calms our nervous system and helps us to find balance again, physiologically and emotionally. To a wounded partner, a lover's comfort is as desperately needed and powerful as any drug. Sometimes we do not offer compassion because we are scared and we think that our emotional response will somehow weaken our partner further. We do not understand the power of the love we have to give.* —Sue Johnson, PhD, *Hold Me Tight*

Precisely because this is such a sensitive period, and a period when we may first find ourselves coming face-to-face with any early unmet needs, it is a vitally important time to recognize and honor the need for self-love as well as "emotional maintenance" with our mate. This may mean making adult couple time a high priority when their baby is asleep, or perhaps spending short periods away from their baby on dates, leaving her with a close friend or family member. But it can also mean simply "being there" for each other.

> *Neglect will kill love. Love needs attention. Knowing your attachment needs and responding to those of your lover can make a bond until "death do us part."*
> —Sue Johnson, PhD, *Hold Me Tight*

Recognize the importance of making time for meaningful connection and intimacy. A little authentic, heart-to-heart connection can go a very long way. It can be found in snuggling together to read, listen to music, or watch movies. Or in walking hand-in-hand at a favorite place in nature, baby snuggled comfortably in a carrier on dad's chest. No, it is not the same. But the fact is:

> *Having a baby calls for changes across many dimensions of our lives—personal and interpersonal. Life will never return to the way it was. You and your partner are stepping into a new era of your life, individually and as a couple. Some couples never manage to get things together again, a rift forms that becomes impassable. Others find new dimensions and a hitherto unknown richness and meaning in their relationship.* —Anonymous

Remember:
- what is key is not so much our early attachment experiences as how we, as adults, reflect on and learn from these experiences;
- being in a stable relationship with a supportive spouse; a loving relationship can literally rewire our brain;
- having a baby affords a window of opportunity for healing and growth.

## Caring for Self

Self-love is evident in self-care. Taking good care of yourself is absolutely central to your ability to care for your family. The bottom line is that if you are not caring for your self—when you are feeling victimized and burned out—you are not in a place to reflect in any helpful way on your own early attachment experiences, or to do your part to nurture a loving relationship with your partner (it really does take two to tango). And you are certainly not in a place to resolve any differences that may emerge between the two of you, or to give your best to your child, or even to simply enjoy your newborn or young child.

> *Relationships only work well when you're simultaneously committed to full intimacy in the relationship and to your own creative development.*
> —Gay and Kathlyn Hendricks, *Conscious Loving*

As most of us have received little or no training for healthy self-nurturing, this is a skill we need to learn. And it isn't always easy. We may feel—even be told—that we're being selfish if we say "no" to others, and then we may feel guilty. In caring for our children—and our relationship with our partner—we cannot neglect our own needs. It takes courage and clarity, but it's the best way to prevent stress and create a truly nourishing environment for you and your family.

One of the most commonly reported challenges people find in caring for themselves, is that they simply don't have the time—or money. Of course, this may be especially so when we are caring for very young children. And, yes it can be wonderfully nurturing to have a massage, take a week in Hawaii, share a meal in a favorite restaurant, or even have someone wash the dishes for you. However, it is also possible to have or do all these things and *still* not feel nurtured. Feeling nurtured is in large part a matter of intention and attention.

You can take an hour's walk through the most beautiful place in the world and get to the other end feeling no better—and possibly worse—than when you began. Or you can get to the other end feeling grounded, centered, deeply content, and "in heart." Yes, the weather can make a difference, as can whatever you have on your feet, but the primary determinant will be your intention and attention. Do you spend the time ruminating over all you have to do? All you have not done? Or how X is ruining your life? Instead, can you set that aside for a period to connect deeply with your breath, to feel the life force moving through your body, to notice the gentle breeze moving across your face, the warmth of the sun on your back, the feel of the earth beneath your feet, the vastness of the sky above you, the sounds of the leaves rustling in the wind, the scent of an oak tree? You get the idea.

*Choose love, not fear. —A Course in Miracles*

In this way it is so much more about intention and attention, than what you happen to be doing at the moment. And yes, when what you're doing is washing the dishes—yet again—it can require a very conscious shift of attention to focus on the pleasure of the feeling of the warm water on your hands, and the pleasure of stacking clean dishes to dry. It's a great skill to develop—most especially if you go gently with the practice, and keep it fun. Just start over when you forget—and that may be often, but the lapse will become less frequent with time.

## *Simplify*

As you become clearer about your own worth, and the value of self-care, you will likely become more thoughtful about, and sensitive to, the people and places and situations that are healthy for you, and those that are not. You may find yourself thinking about how you can simplify, letting go of things—physical and emotional—that clutter up your life and deplete your energy. These may include pent-up worries; unexpressed emotions; toxic people—people who drain your energy, criticize you, pressure you to be someone other than who you are; and situations, as well as "stuff" and activities you don't really need. Paying attention to the impact of different people and places and situations on your energy is an important element in self-care. Be thoughtful about the people with whom you surround yourself—and your child; and about the places and activities to which you give your time.

Be honest. If you're tired, let people know. Take the phone off the hook. Put a sign on the door. Keep visits that are best short, short. "Thank you for coming, and we need to rest now." If possible, hire someone, perhaps a teenager or an elderly person, to help you to wash the dishes, do the laundry, or shop for you.

Sometimes when we are exhausted it can seem there is nothing we can do to care for ourselves. At those times, it's invaluable to have a list of things that nurture you—whether it's stroking the cat, gazing at the clouds, cruising a hardware store, reading a novel, pounding a few nails, polishing your nails, or skinny dipping.

And perhaps place a "magnet map" of inspiring images, somewhere that you will see often. These may be images you draw yourself, photos, or pictures cut out of magazines. Use images of nurturing people, places, things, and activities. Dwell on it every day, even if only for a few minutes here and there.

## *Meet the Buddha in Your Baby*

Don't underestimate the immense opportunity that your baby's presence in your life, affords you.

> *Feelings are contagious. If you let yourself be still, open, and watchful around your new baby, you might find that his simple, utterly non-judgmental attention, his Buddha-like calm and disarming innocence, will transport you into a similar state of mind.... Once you have found these moments of fathomless peace, your nervous system is more likely to remember the pathway to it. In our hustle and bustle we forget how to access this natural state: babies can remind us—if we let them. Spend quiet time together, often, and you'll find you are nourished by this experience as much as baby is nourished by you.*
> 
> —Robin Grille, *Heart-to-Heart Parenting*

Today, neurobiology confirms what we intuitively know: nurturing emotions can nurture self as well as other. In fact, it appears that learning to access and maintain a state of nurture (see Chapter 18) is not only personally satisfying, it may also entrain others into that same state. When we touch someone while in a loving, coherent state, our heartbeat can even register in the other person's brain waves, activating a profound merging and sense of wellbeing.

Of course, even babies are human and as such may not always appear before us with Buddha-like calm and disarming innocence. And of course these may just be the moments you most need to calm the rhythm of your own nervous system.

One of the easiest, most immediately accessible tools for doing just that may be the Quick Coherence Tool from Heartmath. Practicing this when you are already in a relatively good place enables you to draw on it more easily when you really need it. It's a wonderful exercise to practice at intervals throughout the day—when you're walking with your baby, washing those diapers, or falling asleep. With time, it's a state you will find yourself accessing more and more readily and naturally. In fact, it will set a whole new baseline for how you can "be" with yourself.

> **Quick Coherence™ Tool**[*]
> The Quick Coherence Tool is a simple, easy way to interrupt the stress response and quickly bring your body/mind system into coherence, or an energetically organized state.
>
> Step 1: Heart Focus. Focus your attention on the area around your heart, the area in the center of your chest. If you prefer, the first couple of times you try it, place your hand over the center of your chest to help keep your attention in the heart area.
>
> Step 2: Heart Breathing. Breathe deeply but normally and feel as if your breath is coming in and going out through your heart area. As you inhale, feel as if your breath is flowing in through the heart, and as you exhale, feel it leaving through this area. Breathe slowly and casually, a little more deeply than normal. Continue breathing with ease until you find a natural inner rhythm that feels good to you.
>
> Step 3: Heart Feeling. As you maintain your heart focus and heart breathing, activate a positive feeling. Recall a positive feeling, a time when you felt good inside, and try to re-experience the feeling. One of the easiest ways to generate a positive, heart-based feeling is to remember a special place you've been to or the love you feel for a close friend or family member or treasured pet. This is the most important step.
>
> [*]From Heartmath, *Heartmath.org*

*We were introduced to Heartmath's training through friends of Joseph Chilton Pearce (author of* Magical Child), *when Joe invited us to Thanksgiving dinner at his home in central Virginia shortly after we became neighbors in 1996. I had heard about Heartmath from another close friend several years earlier, but it was pretty far out there even for me, and stretched my latent scientism prejudices. Joe's reports from his frequent long visits to their center in California, impressed me, as well as the quality of the neuroscientists and other health professionals on their staff and advisory board. That got me past those hang-ups.*

*A few weeks later we did the Heartmath basic training along with a group of friends. I loved the introductory video, the instructors' explanations, and the nurturing space they created for the small group of us at another friend's farm home. But—when we got to Step 3 (above), and I tried to recall an experience of complete acceptance and nurturance—I came up with nothing!*

*After struggling for a while, I got angry at what I perceived as the program's assumption that everyone had a wealth of such experiences to draw upon. I later realized that my anger was covering up the profound sadness this realization brought up.*

> *Nevertheless, I got value from the program and a few years later, had an opportunity to try out Heartmath's early version of the biofeedback device (now marketed as the emWave). It measures heart rate coherence,\* and displays it on a computer screen. I was astounded at the waveform shift I saw on the screen when I went into an appreciative state.*
>
> *That moment inspired me to learn how to create appreciative states, and a dozen years later, I can say I'm getting much better at that than my previous "default" setting of finding the flaw with everything within my purview. I am now regularly doing "rampages of appreciation" and people around me are commenting on how much more openness this practice is allowing in me.* —Jack

Doc Childre, founder of Heartmath, finds that most people usually love only as the mood arises or if the day is going especially well. However, at any point we have the opportunity to recognize that there are two different perspectives to a situation—especially stressful ones. The heart offers an opportunity for solutions, while the head often imprisons us in hurt or anger. When responding to life from the heart, we feel secure, listen to the hearts of others and ourselves, and believe there is always a way to understand and find solutions to problems.

By relearning to generate loving and appreciative feelings, heart rhythms return to balance, adaptability increases, and creative exploration and learning resumes.

Feelings of anger, worry, frustration, or stress cause heart rhythms to become disordered or incoherent. The brain then operates less effectively. Frustration, anger, boredom, self-pity, or anxiety can take over.

Research at Heartmath reveals that the mind represents only a portion of available human intelligence. Our perceptions, mental and emotional attitudes, creativity, immune systems, reaction time, and decision-making abilities are all directly related to the health of our heart.† Heart intelligence, or intuition, resides at a higher octave of intelligence that is introduced to the mind through the heart frequencies of love, compassion, appreciation, etc.

It is on these grounds that Pearce, in his foreword to Childre's *Teaching Children to Love,* asserts love to be our principle survival intelligence—but like all intelligences, it must be developed. The good news is that it is a learning we can undertake at any time in life—and the more we practice, the easier it becomes.

---

\* Coherence refers to an orderly heart rate variability (HRV) pattern—a measure of the beat-to-beat interval.

† Heartmath offers a range of resources for both children and adults for activating the core values of the heart: *Heartmath.org.*

> *To love effectively, we must consciously practice addressing life with love...
> experiencing and expressing love are the peak moments of fulfillment in life....*
> —Doc Childre, *A Parenting Manual: Heart Hope for the Family*

What better time to practice than with our own baby Buddhas?
Most importantly, whatever you do, do not add any of the above suggestions to an already existing list of shoulds! Take anything that resonates with you as a means of enhancing your ability to access and sustain a sense of personal wellbeing. This is the wellspring from which you can reach out to joyfully connect with your loved ones and the world around you.

## Key Points

- The way we feel towards our babies has a lot to do with how we were treated when we were babies.
- If our own infancy/childhood needs were not met, it can be painful facing and meeting the needs of our own babies—it is hard to give what has not been given us.
- When we find we are overwhelmed by the demands of caring for our baby, or disliking or being angry with her, it is likely an emotional memory of an unresolved issue is being restimulated.
- Allowing ourselves to *feel* these feelings in our body, rather than simply thinking about them, and giving them healthy expression—journaling, talking with a friend or counselor—can free us of past hurts.
- Because this is such a sensitive time, it is important to recognize the need for "emotional maintenance" both as individuals and as a couple.
- Make time to nurture your relationship with your partner. A little authentic heart to heart connection can go a long way.
- With parenting, as with all things in life, it helps to feel good about ourself. Self-love is evident in self-care, and essential to our ability to connect with and care for our family.
- Self-nurturing is, for many adults, a skill to be developed. A commonly reported difficulty is absence of time or money. However its possible to have time, and money, and still not feel nurtured. It's largely a matter of *intention* and *attention* than what you are doing in the moment. In addition, simplify your life, letting go of things that clutter it or deplete your energy. Keep a list of simple ways you can nurture yourself—stroke the cat, entrain with your baby's Buddha-like nature, pound a few nails, polish your nails—and just do it.
- Feelings of anger, worry, and stress cause disordered or incoherent heart rhythms, and the brain to operate less effectively. Generating loving and appreciative feelings, heart rhythms return to balance, and creativity and learning resumes.
- It is on these grounds that Joseph Chilton Pearce asserts love to be our principal survival intelligence—but like all intelligences, it must be developed.
- Use the Quick Coherence Tool, a remarkably swift and simple way to interrupt the stress response and bring your body/mind to coherence.

# Part III

# Healing the Wounds:

## Rewiring for Connection

# 19: Addressing the Legacy of Unmet Needs

Today, thankfully, you can find a good number of books guiding parents in the art and science of attachment parenting. While these books focus on how parents can foster a strong bond with their infant/child, virtually all overlook the equally significant factor in the equation—the *legacy of unmet needs* that parents carry from their own childhood, and the ways that these needs will be restimulated with the birth and caring for an infant and child. Even if we put all the right blocks in all the right places according to the attachment parenting practices, without addressing our own attachment needs—both those unmet from our own childhood and also our valid needs for attachment with loved ones as a mature adult—our best efforts to parent well will be thwarted.

Returning to Robert Karen's classic, *Becoming Attached*:

> [U]nreflective parents don't realize what is happening to them. They may love their baby, talk about it in glowing terms… be diligently concerned with the baby's feeding, sleeping, and physical comfort. But when attachment needs arise, they find themselves being impinged upon by an intolerable sense of threat. For to be fully open to the baby's emotional needs is to become re-acquainted with oneself as a baby, to re-experience the pain of being totally dependent and desperately in love and yet being shut out and unwanted. People construct their defenses in order to prevent being engulfed by such feelings. But when one becomes a parent, the buried unresolved pain is shaken loose, the defensive wall is breached, and the new defensive efforts are required, which, in the case of the dismissing parent, means keeping the baby and its needs at some distance.

In the closing section of the book, "Legacy of Attachment in Adult Life," Karen goes on to look at the ways parents' own attachment styles are passed on to their child, and also how parents can work through any insecure attachments of their own childhood so as to not pass them on to their children. It is now well established that the key quality of secure, autonomous adults is not that they had secure attachments with their parents, but rather, they have an open and coherent way of reflecting on their attachment style.

> To the extent that they felt wounded by a parent, they had managed to work it through, so that they were no longer either rigidly cut off from their true feelings about that relationship or still embroiled with hurt, rage, and blame. Somehow they had arrived at the point where they could let the past rest and move on with their lives….

> *What is key is not simply what our early attachment experiences were, but how we think and feel about them now—that is, how we represent them in our mind, what our internal model of the world is like, and whether we can allow ourselves to access painful memories and open them up for inspection.*
> —Robert Karen, PhD, *Becoming Attached*

> *I was the second child, and many more of my unmet needs were restimulated after the birth of my second child. I was not prepared for this, since it had not happened with my first.... I have sometimes wondered, did I unconsciously help to create the scenario that was so much more difficult after the birth of our second child, as it matched my own experience in infancy?* —Barbara

Some people appear able to go beyond what they experienced with their parents because they had other relationships in childhood that kept an alternate perspective alive in them: the kindness of a relative they saw even only *occasionally*, a teacher who took a personal interest in them, or a friend of their parents who provided a healthier parenting model. For those children who do not experience alternative models, the task is much more difficult, and psychotherapy can be beneficial.

## Primary Elements in Breaking the Cycle of Unmet Needs

Karen notes three variables that appear to be the primary elements in breaking the cycle of emotional abuse:
- having had a loving supportive figure available in early childhood,
- having undergone in-depth psychotherapy, and/or
- being in a stable relationship with a supportive spouse.

Therapy can enable a person to be self-reflective in a way that was impossible before, and to better appreciate the mental states of other people—both key ingredients of a secure adult. This can also take place outside the therapy room. Close friends and spouses can serve this function, when the trust is such that they can disclose things to one another and explore them in ways they haven't before.

As Alicia Lieberman puts it, "With a love partner one can go over and over the kinds of things that one's mother and father didn't respond to well, and if the partner responds well, its like a release and one can finally lay old conflicts to rest." Karen alludes to a possible fourth element in breaking the cycle of abuse, in stating:

> *Selma Fraiberg believed that having a baby is also a key developmental stage for adults and that it, too, represents an opportunity for change. Having a baby can offer a new perspective on one's own childhood—what one felt, what one's parents must have felt, how psychologically delicate the process is, how inevitably imperfect.* —Robert Karen, PhD, *Becoming Attached*

In other words, finding oneself dealing with the emotional challenges of parenting can be a transforming experience.

> ### What Therapy Can Do
>
> Because the word "therapy," and even more so, "psychotherapy," has such negative connotations for so many people ("it's only for crazies"), I want to reprint Karen's succinct listing of just what therapy can offer. The field of coaching, which was just developing when Karen's book was published, offers many of the same advantages but without the stigma some associate with therapy.
>
> Therapy [and coaching] can:
> - Provide a new model of what a close relationship can be;
> - Teach one to reflect on feelings, events, and the patterns of one's own behavior in a way that one was unable to do before;
> - Compensate to some degree for nurturing experiences one never had as a child;
> - Provide the guidance, persuasion, and pressure one needs to break an addictive pattern and attempt something new,
> - Be an opportunity to face some unpleasant facts about how one really operates in relationship;
> - Provide a safe context where that portion of self that has always been ready to relate in a new, more trusting, more direct and healthy way can emerge and take what may be its first tentative steps; and
> - Offer a safe haven where feelings of shame no longer present such a terrible barrier to self-exploration.

Karen identifies core feelings of shame, of not being worthy of love, as another early attachment theme that may play a part in adult relationships; and can pose a critical barrier to the entire working through process.

## Shame and Guilt

Bobbie Burdett, a life and wellness coach, believes that along with fear, shame is the biggest impediment to human wellbeing and lifestyle change, and a difficult subject to address because the very nature of shame is one of hiding. It's accurately been called the "ugly stepchild of emotions." We don't want to talk about it, let alone experience it, so it stays hidden—and runs the show.

The extent that we don't see it, understand it, and can't talk about it, is the extent to which it rules our lives. It's a silent epidemic that is slow to come out of hiding. Burdett says that it's very important to recognize shame because it's at the core of much of what gets us stuck and unable to achieve what we want. And there's research that backs this up. Burdett makes the point that shame is normal. We all experience it. It's universal in all cultures and all societies. Our experience of shame is the same, but what we do with it varies widely. The only people who don't experience shame are those who are incapable of empathy. Shame is normal but it's extremely painful, so we cover it up with lightning-fast responses of other emotions—the same responses that we exhibit when our survival is threatened: we fight, flee, freeze, and/or appease. We do anything rather than accurately name it and experience what we are actually feeling.

This powerful emotion stays hidden because we fear disconnection or banishment. We fear words or looks of disgust, contempt, or turning away. At the core of shame is our fear that we are unworthy of being cared for; we are unworthy of connection. Sometimes it's unconscious and other times it's painfully conscious.

Burdett asks us to think about how most societies control its members. In one form or another, the greatest punishment is banishment, ostracism, or some form of disconnection. In the United States, other than capital punishment, what is the most severe punishment for any crime? It's solitary confinement, the ultimate disconnection.

The reason this is the ultimate punishment has to do with how we are neurologically hardwired. The human brain is "a social organ." We need connection with each other to survive. There is nothing that strikes more deeply at our existential fears than of being involuntarily alone. So it's only natural that we keep hidden that which we fear will lead to disconnection (contempt, disapproval, disengagement).

Of course, there is a big catch. The more we keep stuff hidden, the more invulnerable we pretend to be, the more resentful, angry, isolated, and alone we are. The more we protect against what we don't want, the more we create it. We give up our power and our ability to connect with others when we can't confront and accurately name our experience, compassionately accept our humanity, and move on.

Very often shame and guilt are used interchangeably. But they are distinctly different emotions with radically different results.

Shame and guilt are both "self-conscious" and "moral" emotions—self-conscious in that they involve the self evaluating the self, and moral in that they presumably are intended to play a key role in fostering moral behavior. But it's here that the similarity stops. While often looking similar, the results in how we respond to these two emotions are usually quite different.

Simply put, guilt says "I *did* something wrong." Shame says, "I *am* something wrong." Guilt is focused on specific behaviors, while shame is focused on the self. The underlying assumptions are that guilt is fixable (behavior can be changed); shame, however, is not (an unworthy self is unredeemable).

Research has clearly shown that there is a consistent link between shame, anger, and hostility.[49] Conversely, guilt tends to motivate individuals to accept responsibility and may actually inhibit anger and hostility. Shame is more painful and more difficult to describe and cope with than guilt. With shame, there is an experience of feeling inferior and physically small and a sense of being helpless or out of control. Because of the perception of lack of control, shame leads to more desperate actions toward ourselves and/or others.

*When in a class I was taking with Dan Siegel, MD, "Relationships From the Inside Out," he made a passing comment that brought it all together for me. He said that the inception of shame is disconnection. That's where shame starts. That's what causes it. When our needs are not responded to in a coherent manner, we disconnect not only from the other, but we also disconnect from ourselves!*

*As infants and children, we are exquisitely aware that our survival depends on our caregivers. This awareness is hardwired through evolution. When caregivers aren't able to give us what we need—for any reason—rather than see them as inadequate (because they are like gods to us) it is much safer to see the cause of our suffering as the result of our own inadequacy—what we have done, or who we are. When there are problems between the parents, the child usually believes that it's something the child has done, or worse yet, it's who the child is, that has caused the parents' problem.*

*Besides the unintended shaming results of our actions, there is the purposeful shaming that is so often used to control others. It's astonishing to realize that somewhere in our survival programming and in the cultural belief system, there is a built-in assumption that if we shame ourselves (our children and loved ones, or whoever) enough, it will result in the connection and behavior change we desire. As a society we believe that if we shame those closest to us, they will be moral, upstanding people who love and care for us. But here's the problem. Shame never works! Ever! Never has and never will! There is never any good that comes from shame. In the long run, that strategy always backfires.*

*When disconnection occurs repeatedly over time, we form an individualized, complex, survival response (sometimes called a "control pattern"). It governs our lives and how we see the world, and how we see ourselves. Some work harder to prove themselves until they are completely burned out. Others are angry, bitter, or violent. Some hide from view. Some are depressed and hopeless. Some develop skills like humor, intuition, intelligence, or physical prowess to cover the subterranean feelings of vulnerability and unworthiness.*

*In that moment when I saw so clearly how shame is created, it all made sense. If disconnection causes shame, then connection heals it!*

*To heal our relationships, we need to be aware of shame—our own and our partner's. As Sue Johnson so beautifully says: "If we can see our protective dances with each other, name them, and reconnect coherently with each other's needs, we can build empathy, trust, safety, and connection. By creating a relationship of connection and trust, it literally heals the people in it."*

*Disconnection creates shame. Connection heals shame. Empathy, for one's self and others, is the antidote to shame. It's as simple as that.*

—Bobbie Burdett, coachbobbie.com

For most of my life I've been plagued by what I later learned were "shame attacks"—feeling awful for no reason, catastrophizing, excessively worrying, especially in the middle of the night, etc. I started being conscious of them in college, and they followed me through medical training, and on through my becoming accomplished in my field.

I have much to be proud of with what I've made of my life, yet at the core, until recently, I've always felt like something was wrong with me. Confusing self-esteem with self-worth, like mixing up guilt and shame, had caused a lot of confusion in my life.

Like most people, I had assumed that self-worth and self-esteem were the same thing, until Pam Leo created a milestone in my self-understanding by explaining why I felt such conflict between different parts of myself.

Pam showed me how it was possible to have high self-esteem simultaneously with low self-worth. She explained how self-esteem is a cognitive function of the cortical brain, the thinking, reasoning part of us that uses language as its primary tool.

She explained that self-esteem is connected with guilt—the primary mechanism for lowering self-esteem. Self-worth is a function of the limbic brain—the emotional, non-verbal part of us that often runs the show (without being recognized). I had only recently gotten a full appreciation of the limbic brain from reading the NY Times best seller, *A General Theory of Love*. Suddenly my limbic system became my friend!

Pam then pointed out how shame is the fuel that powers low self-worth, depression, and probably addiction and violence. Shaming is done by parents (often unconsciously) or other authority figures, and is part of the normative abuse of most conventional parenting methods. This is why she created connection parenting.

I suspect many people, like me, with self-worth issues, learned to excel in school and over-achieve in order to compensate for the inner gnawings of low self-worth. I'm clear it's behind my decision at about age five to become a doctor like *my daddy—I wanted to earn his love and respect since I had not gotten it emotionally via the parenting practices of the 1940s.*

*I raised my self-esteem by piling up many accomplishments, but it didn't touch my self-worth quotient, because esteem and worth are experienced in different parts of the brain for entirely different reasons. Self-esteem is "doing-related." Self-worth is "being-related." As Jean Liedloff put it so well, meeting humans' mammalian needs for movement and touch leads to an infant feeling "worthy and welcome."* —Jack

## Becoming Your Own Person

Both Peter Fonagy and Mary Main, experts in adult attachment, believe that the primary quality distinguishing securely attached from anxiously attached adults is their capacity to understand their own attachment needs and styles, their capacity to understand what makes themselves and others tick. The healthy adults they studied were found to be better able to recognize their own inner conflicts and have a sense of why their parents behaved as they did. If securely attached adults had an unhappy attachment history, they seemed to have understood and worked through it, at least to the extent that they could speak about their parents without getting "into a stew," often demonstrating insight into the effects their negative experiences have had on them, as well as some forgiveness or understanding of their parents' behavior.

In contrast, those who were "dismissing of attachment" seemed unwilling or unable to take these issues seriously, and disliked or distrusted looking inward. They tended to speak of their parents in idealized terms, dismissing the impact of early hurts or claiming that they "built character." Those who suffered terrible separations at an early age appeared indifferent to affection or hurt. They warded off crucial parts of their feeling worlds, so as to no longer feel the pain of rejection or longing for love. Others spoke as if feelings of hurt and anger they had as children were as alive in them today as they had been 20 or 30 years ago. Anxious adults either failed to have insights into themselves or offered explanations that were platitudinous, self-deceptive or self-serving.

Thanks to Freud, many of us are aware that despite our unconscious protests and longings, we often choose relationships that repeat our early experiences, no matter how unsatisfying they were. Bowlby explained this as a natural bias in favor of what we already know—no matter how painful or unfulfilling the relationship may be, it offers the "security" of being familiar (the "familiar misery").

> *[It is] an unconscious commitment to those we worshipfully loved as children. No matter how much they hurt us, we don't want to give them up.... We can't let go of the mother or father who didn't love us the way we needed to be loved.*
> —Robert Karen, PhD, *Becoming Attached*

Karen observes that in our society, attitudes towards parental flaws tend to flow in one of two directions, which "not surprisingly echo the two major styles of anxious attachment." There are those who believe we should never speak ill of our parents—they gave us life, they cared for us, and to complain reflects ingratitude and betrayal.

In Karen's experience, people who hold this view rarely have an open, warm relationship with their parents. There may be the dutiful visits, the gifts… but the feeling is absent. He sees this as the result of their rigidly defending against feeling any anger and notes that they often have difficulty experiencing other feelings as well. And then there are those whose response to their parents' failings is that of unrelenting anger and blame. Holding on to anger is another impediment to mourning, it prevents the grown up child from feeling the loss of what he never had.

> *His anger, in effect, shields him from his sadness and also, paradoxically, keeps him enthralled with the very parent he hates and blames and denounces.*

While agreeing that wounds must be fully experienced at some point in your life, carrying them like a banner is not a symbol of strength and maturity.

> *Eventually one must separate, in the positive sense of becoming one's own person, which means not just letting go of the unconscious neurotic tie to the parent, but letting go of the wound that perversely sanctifies that tie and letting go of the ways in which one's behavior with others (including one's children) replicates it.*

## Perfection Is Not a Requirement

Karen closes his book with an important lesson from adult attachment research:

> *We cannot change our childhood. But we can let go of the defensive and obsessive postures formed at that time. We can make sense of what has been repressed and forgotten. We can re-experience dissociated feelings with a new appreciation for ourselves as we were as children, for the situation that existed at the time, for the parents who may have caused us to suffer. And we can successfully mourn our losses. If we've managed to hold onto an alternative model, and if we are wise or lucky in love, we may be able to work through our childhood experience in the context of a marriage or something like that. If the grip of the past is too strong, we may be able to work it through in therapy. In either case, if we remain conscious of ourselves and of the pull of early models, even if hang-ups of various kinds remain, as inevitably they must, we have a better chance of creating satisfying relationships with our mates and secure relationships with our children. To that extent it seems that in emotional life, much as in history, we are only doomed to repeat what has not been remembered, reflected on, and worked through.*

## Neurobiologically Speaking

Human infants are born with approximately 25% of the brain's patterns already formed. The remaining 75% are formed through accumulated experiences during the growing years. The most important of those experiences have to do with an infant's relationships. Without adequate connection, touch, and stimulation, the brain literally doesn't form in a complete and healthy way. The pain of *lack* of connection is real; scientists now know that emotional pain operates on the same circuitry as physical pain. It really hurts, even though we might find amazingly creative ways to not feel it.

As we have seen, the early imprints of optimal bonding and attachment involve the mother producing an abundance of the "love hormone," oxytocin, which promotes connection and provides a blueprint for initiating and sustaining loving relationships. During this early formative period, our nervous systems learn whether to trust or fear, and whether to thrive or survive.

Thanks to revolutionary discoveries in the field of neuroscience, scientists now have a greater understanding of neuroplasticity—how the brain can change throughout a person's life. Now we know that the power to direct our attention has within it the power to shape our brain's firing patterns, as well as the power to shape the architecture of our brain itself. The brain can be rewired, and this change is directed by our mind's focus and attention.

Taking this a step further, Dorothy Mandel, PhD, brings the heart into what is known about the brain, and points out how the heart, with its endocrine capacity, orchestrates many reparative processes.

Intentionally accessed heartfelt emotions play a major regulatory role on multiple levels—a regulatory role that is fundamental to optimal hormonal balance, and to neuronal rewiring of dysfunctional patterns. Heartfelt emotions, such as appreciation and caring, generate highly organized heart rhythm patterns that have a regulatory effect on multiple systems in the body.

The oxytocin produced in the heart is associated with these heartfelt emotions and has the power to speed the healing of wounds, reduce inflammation, diminish the harmful effects of stress, diminish the sensation of pain, and increase social bonding by rewiring and/or strengthening the neural pathways.

Mandel has put together a conceptual framework, the "neurobiology of nurture," and a process that she refers to as the "restorative response of the heart," that repairs, restores, and re-regulates our nervous system by intentionally accessing emotional pathways that affect positive changes of heart rhythm and hormone production.

She has found that nurturing touch, and the emotions of appreciation and love, can reignite the essential and restorative chemistry of affiliative bonding at any point in our lifespan.

Accessing what Mandel refers to as "states of nurture" not only counters the harmful effects of stress, but also provides a means of mood modulation and emotional self-regulation—a rewiring of neurological pathways that, when practiced, can supersede the neurological wiring of trauma. Learning to create and anchor physiologically and emotionally pleasurable states in the body—such as those referred to by Mandel as the "oxytocin-mediated states"* of inner peace, safety, and wellbeing—and learning to access them at will, allows us to progressively reclaim this state as the nervous system's new baseline.

Put simply, in attuning to, and using the chemistry of heartfelt emotions, we can actually rewire our neural connections,[50] and in so doing, reclaim our ability to nurture, trust, and thrive.

We open a whole new window to healing when we recognize that nurture can be an *intentionally accessed* state of being that has profoundly positive effects on physiology and psyche. The heartfelt emotions of love, appreciation, and caring, are *restorative* in nature. Giving *or* receiving nurturance activates a cascade of restorative processes and neurochemicals, including oxytocin.

Nurturing can involve physical processes such as caring touch and sexual fulfillment, and emotions such as love, joy, appreciation, caring and altruism. Consciously accessing these emotions, even through guided imagery, can powerfully alter body chemistry into restorative and pleasure-producing modes. And the more that oxytocin is accessed, the more it stimulates its own production.

Now let's go on to look more closely at our own earliest formative experiences, and how we may reflect on these so as not to be caught unaware and headed down the path to DDD. It's important to look at these experiences so that we will be better able to live up to our heartfelt aspirations and pass the good, not the bad, of our legacy on to our children.

Keep in mind while reading the following chapters, the *significance of centering our intention and attention* in a place of love, not fear. Accessing or reliving childhood history can be either a painful re-immersion that reinforces the existing pain; or a compassionate, "witnessing" experience when viewed from that part of ourselves that holds both the pain and the intent to heal an experience frozen in place for many years.

---

* Oxytocin-mediated states are also associated with enhanced immune function, and functional and intuitive intelligence, increases in social memory and learning ability, regulation of body temperature and digestion, decreases in pain perception, and accelerated wound healing.

### Key Points

- While there is much attention given to the importance of parents fostering a secure bond with their child, there is little given the importance of addressing the legacy of unmet needs that parents carry from their own childhood—and how these can be restimulated with the birth and care of their own infant.
- If we can be conscious of ourselves and the pull of our own unmet needs, even if some hang-ups remain, we have a better chance of creating satisfying relationships with our partners and secure attachments with our children.
- We pass our own attachment styles on to our children. A key quality of secure-autonomous adults is not that they had secure attachments with their parents, but that they have an open and coherent way of reflecting on their attachment style.
- A key quality distinguishing securely-attached from anxiously-attached adults, is their capacity to understand what makes themselves and others tick. Anxious adults either fail to have insights into themselves or offer explanations that are platitudinous, self-deceptive, or self-serving.
- While guilt says "I *did* something wrong," shame says, "I *am* something wrong." Guilt is focused on behaviors, shame on the self. While guilt is fixable (behavior can be changed), shame feels like it is not (an unworthy self is unredeemable). While there is a consistent link between shame, anger, and hostility, guilt tends to motivate individuals to accept responsibility and may actually inhibit anger and hostility.
- Reviewing our childhood history can be a painful re-immersion that reinforces the existing pain; or a compassionate "witnessing" experience that recognized both the pain and the intent to heal.
- Heartfelt emotions such as appreciation and caring, and other intentionally accessed heartfelt emotions, play a significant role in the neuronal rewiring of dysfunctional patterns. Through the heart, we can actually rewire our neural connections and in so doing, reclaim our ability to nurture, trust and thrive.

## 20: Reflecting Back on Our Own Childhood

As a child, my parents—both strong willed, assertive, and also working and living full time together like Jack and me—fought. They argued. It was never physical, and by no means their primary mode of communicating, but it was very frightening to me, seeing those who were my world, at war with each other. At the time of Siena's birth, I had spent years working with my inner child to heal the despair she carried as a result of this fighting, the despair she felt that things can ever be any different, that she could never return to the "paradise" that she carried somewhere inside of her; but still, remnants of that despair lingered. While I had grown immensely in my ability to distance myself from them, to observe those feelings rather than become them, they continued to need my monitoring, my love. And, too often, sabotaged me in fulfilling my dreams.

Now a parent myself, I was horrified that Jack and I were doing as my parents "did" to me, *while* cognizant of the impact of this on our daughter—as my parents had not been. I reminded myself that this cognizance is itself a step along the evolutionary ladder, but still, our discord brought me pain. Our many years of work with exploring the very subtle ways in which we seek to dominate and be dominated, left me excruciatingly aware of every little transgression into blame/shame/attack. I worked with it through practicing compassion for my self, and striving to model constructive and loving ways of resolving conflicts as they emerged between us. We no longer did the protracted fighting that we did before Siena came, but we could surely be mean to each other on occasion. I so yearned to consistently model that loving, caring relationship that I aspire to, and to honor the depth of my desire not to pass my wounding on to her.

> *The more we understand ourselves, the more likely we are to see our children for who they really are instead of mistaking them for ghosts from our past. The more we recall, the less likely we are to confuse our baby's needs and communications with our unmet needs.* —Thomas Verny, MD, *Preparenting*

Our own childhood history, replete with its unique blend of both vividly remembered and long-forgotten joys and sorrows is, for most, a primary determinant of our parenting style. How we care for our children often reflects how we ourselves were parented as children.

> *Thus, the well-nurtured seem to act kindly towards their children as a matter of reflex, while those who tyrannise their children are re-enacting their own oppression.* —Robin Grille, *Heart-to-Heart Parenting*

The quality of our parenting—and the joy we experience in parenting—is in large part dependent on our willingness and ability to reflect back on our own childhood and learn from it. Without an awareness of the themes of our own early years, we will find ourselves reacting to our children out of our own early unmet needs, and embodying the same dysfunctional behaviors that our parents—albeit unintentionally and unwittingly—inflicted on us.

> *Our childhood experiences are so deeply ingrained in our bodies that they permeate our thoughts, feelings and behaviors without our realizing it…. In particular, our automatic responses that erupt under stress are often faithful representations of how we were once treated.*
> —Robin Grille, Heart-to-Heart Parenting

Those of us who have a history of secure attachment will, in all likelihood, find that our nurturance flows freely. Even during pregnancy, those of us who experienced more emotional warmth from our own mothers are better able to establish an affectionate relationship with our unborn baby.

On the other hand, those of us who were abused or neglected as children will tend to abuse or neglect our own children, or act in ways that frighten them, *unless* we have sought help for healing our trauma. To the extent that we can be conscious of the source of our feelings and motivations as we relate to our children, we will be able to respond in an appropriate and healthy manner, rather than react unconsciously and inappropriately to their needs.

Our willingness and ability to examine our personal history, consciously evaluating the values, qualities, and patterns we hope to both pass on to our children and also those we hope to leave behind, plus our willingness and ability to make the changes that will enable us to meet the authentic needs of our children, will determine both the quality of the bond we form with them, and their evolving sense of self—as well as our effectiveness and the joy we experience as parents.

## The Adults We Have Become

From the moment of our birth, we are rewarded for certain behaviors and discouraged, even punished, for others. And so it is that some aspects of our selves are strengthened and others weakened, for we quickly learn the value of hiding or disowning those parts of ourselves that are not rewarded. These rejected parts become our disowned selves, energies that are repressed but not destroyed. In Jungian terms, our disowned selves are a part of our shadow. Our individuation and experience of wholeness—and our ability to parent well—requires our integrating these disowned parts into our conscious awareness of self.

While today we recognize that large numbers of people have experienced blatant physical, sexual, or emotional abuse, for many of us, the abuse was much more subtle: being left to cry alone and uncomforted, fed by bottle rather than breast, or isolated in a crib or plastic carrier rather than held in-arms. Such neglect is more insidious and difficult to recall than blatant abuse because we carry few memories of what *didn't* happen (because we didn't have anything to compare it with). These normative abuse practices, which Karen Walant first described in *Creating the Capacity for Attachment*, often pass unnoticed in many people who assert, "I had a wonderful childhood" or "I don't have any childhood issues!"

As we've seen, these negative experiences form our childhood wounds and factor significantly in the adults that we become. Much of our personality is structured around protecting ourselves from the pain associated with our wounds. The unconscious defenses—such as the denial and repression of emotions—that we developed to avoid feeling the pain associated with these unmet needs, have become a large part of our personality, or our "act." While most of us live our lives unaware of the disowned child within, it distorts our perception of reality and puts distance between us and our world.

These aspects of our inner child can be detected by an intense, often uncharacteristic emotional reaction to persons or situations. Indeed, often these aspects are so outside of our awareness that we can *only* recognize its presence by observing our dysfunctional behaviors—such as when we act compulsively, or under- or overreact.

## Our Inner Children—How They Appear in Our Relationships

Much of the conflict in our relationships stems from our lack of connection to our inner child. Early neglect and abuse are often translated into the belief that we are somehow bad, not worthy of love, or that people cannot be trusted. While as adults we may carry no conscious memory of that neglect or abuse, we may find ourselves unable to trust others or to develop or sustain intimate relationships. We may live trying to please or impress others, to prove our worth. We may withdraw from relationships, and from many forms of self-expression, feeling we will never be understood. Frequently, when we respond to another with anger or withdrawal, the driving force behind our outburst is the unmet needs of our inner child.

> *Remember, no feelings are ever wrong or bad. All the feelings you have are for good reasons, and by dialoguing with these parts with great compassion, you will be able to discover the information these feelings have for you.*
> —Jordan and Margie Paul, *Do I Have to Give Up Me to Be Loved by You?*

Healing and connection becomes possible whenever we can acknowledge the hurt feelings or needs of our inner child. Being able to put feelings, especially unwanted feelings into words, allows us to make them available for review, reflection, and transformation.

## Connecting with Our Inner Child

We can learn to give our inner child the love, the acceptance, the validation—whatever it might be that she wanted and didn't experience as a child—ourselves, rather than take actions that further separate us from the love we want.

Connecting with our feelings and childhood experiences can be facilitated by our awareness of the child-like personalities that reside in every adult—aspects of our inner child.

Hal Stone, PhD, and Sidra Winkelman, PhD, in *Embracing Our Selves*, identify three aspects of the inner child that are of particular importance—the **Vulnerable Child**, the **Playful Child**, and the **Magical Child**.

Stone and Winkelman believe that the most universally disowned self in our civilized world is the **Vulnerable Child**. Yet this child may be our most precious sub-personality, the one closest to our essence, the one that enables us to become truly intimate, to fully experience others, and to love. Unfortunately, she has usually disappeared by the age of five. As with all our inner children, while we may abandon her, we cannot destroy her. She lives within us—hurt and needy. Her unmet needs translate into limiting and self-destructive behaviors.

The **Vulnerable Child** embodies our sensitivity and fear. Her feelings are easily hurt and she generally lives in fear of abandonment. We have buried her deep within ourselves so that she will not be hurt. It is common for parents to support this repression by rejecting the child's vulnerability, by asserting that life demands *strength*. Many men have an even harder time than women in contacting their Vulnerable Child because it is less socially acceptable for men to be vulnerable.

Made conscious, the Vulnerable Child can often tell us who can be trusted and who cannot, by her ability to recognize the people who have disowned their Vulnerable Child and can therefore hurt others, intentionally or unintentionally. In contrast with her ability to end an unrewarding relationship, the integration of the Vulnerable Child into a relationship can encourage unparalleled intimacy and depth.

According to Stone and Winkleman, when we disown our vulnerability we identify instead with our fantasies of omnipotence. Any quality admired by society can become the grounds of our omnipotence—good looks, social standing, achievements in life, etc. However, if we let the subpersonality that develops around the omnipotent voice take over, the opposite energy will not be far behind. As high as the omnipotent voice flies, that's how low the frightened voice will fall.

We need to be able to access our assets and use them wisely, but a certain feeling of self-satisfaction is a signal that we have gone too far and begun to identify with the omnipotent voice. It does not take long before the opposite voice will take over—the frightened child within will wonder if we can back up those promises. The more we identify with the omnipotent voice, the more frightened our inner child becomes. Power is illusory as long as it depends on our superiority and the disempowerment or inferiority of others. True empowerment, ironically, requires embracing both power and vulnerability.

The ***Playful Child*** is just what the name implies—playful. She is generally easier to reach than the Vulnerable Child, because we are more likely to permit play than tears and pain. Many adults who are spiritually identified have access to the Playful Child but not to the Vulnerable Child, and tend to confuse the two.

Usually shy, the ***Magical Child*** is the child of imagination and fantasy—an invaluable ally in our connecting with our own children.

Adults who ignore their inner child have trouble playing, being spontaneous, being in touch with their feelings—even enjoying themselves. Out of touch with the needs of their inner child, they often suffer from stress-related diseases or chronic illness. These adults will have difficulties parenting, as their abandoned inner child resents the attention given to others and falls into an inner child sibling rivalry syndrome (see Chapter 12). Pent-up rage pours out as harsh punishment or violence. These adults especially can benefit from inner child work and self-parenting.

Lucia Capacchione, in *The Creative Journal for Parents*, offers some wonderful exercises for accessing and healing the inner child through art and writing. No special talent required! The exercises appear to be simple, yet are profoundly revealing, helping us connect with our true feelings and needs. This is vitally important as we begin to reflect on our experiences, beliefs and values, and develop our own style of parenting and partnering.

Capacchione suggests that both parents do this dialogue on a regular basis (every few days or so) throughout the pregnancy and after the baby's birth. The answers will be different each time. It may seem there are many inner children; they are just different aspects. Capacchione urges us to simply accept whatever comes, regardless of how irrational it appears: the inner child is about feelings and intuition, not reason and logic.

*Caution:* this kind of work is important for all of us, and especially important for survivors of abuse. If you feel that you had a particularly difficult childhood or experienced abuse as a child, or if you feel overwhelmed by your feelings at any time while doing this work, consider seeking professional help. It is important that you do not process this material without support.

> **Inner Child Chat: How Do You Feel?**\*
>
> Materials: paper, felt-tip pens.
>
> Purpose: To experience the inner child; to give voice to the inner child's feelings and needs in words.
>
> Technique:
>
> 1. With your *non-dominant* hand, let your inner child draw a picture of itself. Don't worry about aesthetic merit or artistic ability. Be a little kid again. Let the image emerge spontaneously on the page without planning it. If you find yourself being critical of the drawing, simply be aware of the fact and continue drawing anyway.
> 2. Write out a dialogue between yourself and the child who appeared in your drawing. It doesn't matter what the child looks like or what age it appears to be. Your adult-self writes with your dominant hand. Your inner child may wish to print and the printing may be very awkward. If so, just be patient and allow it to write as slowly as it needs to. Ask your inner child to tell you about himself or herself:
> Name and age
> How it feels
> How it feels about your pregnancy
> What it wants from you.
>
> \* Adapted from both *The Creative Journal for Parents* by Lucia Capacchione and *Creating a Joyful Birth Experience* by Lucia Capacchione and Sandra Bardsley

## Reparenting Our Inner Child

Reparenting recognizes that we all have subpersonalities within us that correspond to a family. As well as inner children, we have Inner Parents.

Reparenting your inner child[51] is a process of recognizing the child who lives within you by:

- Listening to your deepest emotional needs;
- Learning to be a nurturing and protective parent to yourself;
- Communicating your needs to your partner or other support persons in your life;
- Clearing the way to being a better parent to your child.

The role of the inner parents is to care for and protect the inner child. How our inner parents relate to our inner child is shaped by how our parents or caregivers treated us as a child. If they were loving, our inner parent will likely care for our inner child lovingly. If they were critical or neglectful, we will likely relate in a similar manner to our inner child.

Capacchione identifies three aspects of the inner parent: the ***Nurturing Parent***, the ***Protective Parent***, and the ***Critical Parent***.

***The Nurturing Parent*** listens to the inner child's feelings and needs and responds to them with loving care. When our inner child is physically tired, our Nurturing Parent will see that we get more sleep, urge us to take time to play, to be creative, or to care for ourselves—physically, emotionally, mentally, and/or spiritually.

We can learn to be a Nurturing Parent to our own inner child from role models we grew up with. It may have been a parent or relative, a teacher, or neighbor. For some of us, it may have been a nurturing figure from a movie or book.

---

**Developing an Awareness of the Nurturing Parent Within—Inner Child Chat, What Do You Need?**[*]

*Materials:* paper and felt tip pens.

*Purpose:* To find out what your inner child needs in order to feel loved and cared for.

*Technique:*

1. Using two different colored pens, do a written dialogue with your inner child asking what it needs right now. The Nurturing Parent asks the questions with your dominant hand and the inner child responds with your non-dominant hand. Ask your inner child what it needs in order to feel loved and cared for.

2. Draw a picture of your inner child being cared for by your Nurturing Parent within.

3. With your dominant hand, write a letter from your inner Nurturing Parent to your inner child. Think of it as a love letter in which you tell your inner child how you feel about her. If you haven't been taking care of your inner child, perhaps some apologies are in order. Tell the child how you will take care of her.

*Optional:* Have your partner read your love letter to you. You can also tape record your letter and play it back to yourself.

Alternatively, take time to recall your own experiences of nurturance as a child. It can be very helpful to take the time to write them down. Who really nurtured you as a child, as a teenager? Who cared for you when you were sick or upset? Who listened to you and comforted you? Who encouraged your talents and interests? What did you learn from these people? Share these with your partner, as you develop your own definitions of a Nurturing Parent.

* Adapted from *Creating a Joyful Birth Experience* by Lucia Capacchione and Sandra Bardsley

---

Many adults who had no or little nurturing in childhood, find themselves nurturing others in adulthood—many will find themselves in the helping professions. Capacchione refers to them as "parentified children"; in childhood, they had to take on adult roles and be caregivers to their parents. They learned caretaking behavior, but not necessarily healthy nurturing. It may look like nurturance, but often feelings of resentment, abandonment, and low self-esteem lie beneath the caretaking. It is extremely important to recognize the difference between caretaking behavior and real, genuine nurturing. It is essential that you know—or learn—to nurture yourself. You cannot give to your child or your partner from an empty cup.

**The Critical Parent** is the voice in our head that tells us we are inadequate and will never be good enough. It shames us, blames us, and berates us about "everything and anything"—our body, our house, our car, our marriage, or our children. Told repeatedly that we are worthless, we behave accordingly and look to others to make us feel worthwhile. When we become parents, the Critical Parent can emerge full-force. Enmeshed in feelings of unworthiness, we may be so desperate for our children to like us that we find it impossible to set boundaries. As long as we remain unaware of the Critical Parent within, we often dump its messages onto others, most often our partner and children. Never being able to do enough, and accepting unrealistic expectations as realistic, can cause tremendous stress that endangers not only our own wellbeing, but ripples out to those around us. Becoming aware of the voice of the Critical Parent, we can recognize it for what it is, and refuse to give it the power to define who we are. We can learn to say no—even NO—to the Critical Parent. And instead, turn to the Protective or Nurturing Parent within.

**The Protective Parent** is an advocate for the child, ever alert for people and situations that threaten the inner child's wellbeing. The Protective Parent is not concerned with seeking others' approval. Without the Protective Parent, we can easily be taken advantage of or abused. We cannot take care of ourselves when facing over-demanding people or situations, and we cannot offer our children a good example of limit setting and boundaries. And so the pattern will be handed down, generation to generation. Cultivating a strong Protective Parent within, we can say no to others who don't respect our wishes or needs.

Connecting with our own inner child and our Nurturing and Protective Parent, we are better able to nurture and care for ourselves as individuals. Whenever we catch ourselves feeling even a slight glimmer of sadness or grief, we can pause, and bring our attention to that feeling—being present to that feeling, with all that we can muster of deep self-acceptance and loving kindness, and compassion. This is what it wants—for us to feel, accept, and love it.

Having discovered our inner child, we can share our vulnerabilities with each other. Being willing to tell the truth about how we feel and what we want, and to empathize with the wants and needs of others, we are better able to resolve any conflicts in our relationships and so foster a more loving atmosphere in the home—and let's not underestimate it—*on the planet.*

## Acknowledging and Transforming the Pain

What is crucial in healing is not the wounding but our attitude towards it. Once we can identify our unmet needs, we can develop healthier ways of dealing with them. Re-viewing the old is not re-living the original pain but acknowledging it and transforming it. The focus is not on *how* or *why*, but on the beliefs we took on at that time and how they continue to affect us.

> *I just finished reading your article "Why Men Leave." The first thing that struck me was the issue of non-bonding. We all experience losses; we all cope with these losses in various ways. Some of our coping mechanisms work; some work for a while; some have stopped working for a long time but we continue to use them. I recall the expression, "Pain is necessary for growth; suffering is optional!"*
>
> *I also have done a lot of work dealing with* perceived *losses (I believe this modifier is important). When I perceived a loss as a child, I didn't have an effective means of dealing with it. My coping mechanism was to deny that I had feelings, because I had experienced physical pain as a child when I had expressed my needs in the only way I knew: by crying. When my needs were not met, I judged myself to be unlovable! (This is usually referred to as low self-esteem, but I find ownership of my self-judgment to be an effective means of getting my power back!) This self-judgment resulted in all sorts of ineffective behavior, such as not asking for what I wanted, but the judgment had been made at such an early age that it was out of reach of cognitive scrutiny.*
>
> *By looking at my problem behaviors, I was often able to identify the hidden causes behind them. Once identified, I deliberately started grieving for the losses I had experienced as an infant. I phoned what I judged to be nurturing women from some of my support groups, and actively grieved for my losses. I believe that this grieving process helped me to forgive myself for my critical self-judgment. I am still a flawed human being, but today I am much more effective in being engaged with others.* —Alvin

> *You can cry and rage forever but if you are not willing to take 100 percent responsibility for your pain, you will be stuck with it forever.*
> —Jordan and Margie Paul, *Do I Have to Give Up Me to Be Loved by You?*

> *Responsibility for all that happens is the hallmark of a Healer seeking complete wholeness. If I am having an experience, I am ultimately the one responsible for generating it. When I know myself as both the one having the experience, and the one creating it, I close the circle and experience the essence of wholeness. This means if there is hurt, I am both the victim and the perpetrator. If there is love, I am both the lover and the beloved. Taking responsibility empowers me to make a difference.*
> —John Pateros, *Healing to Wholeness, Healer's Guide*

We blame as long as we perceive ourselves as victims and see power residing outside of ourselves. Healing requires forgiving our parents, siblings, schools—whomever—for what they did, or did not do. Forgiveness does not condone or excuse, but releases otherwise locked-up energy patterns. Healing requires we accept that we have the power to heal ourselves.

> *As kids who have been hurt, it is really hard to see your parents as anything other than parents...to see them as people means we have to allow them the mistakes and fumbles that they made during our childhood. Sometimes, when you have only your hurt and anger to hold onto, you are afraid to let it go. When you do let it go even in a small degree, there is not an empty space, as I had always feared! It gets filled with understanding and knowledge of your parent as a real person. I wish my father could see me as a real person instead of a source of pain. At this point I cannot keep holding on because it is costing me, and in turn my children, too much pain...too many moments spent crying that would be better spent cuddling with my kids.* —Amy

Healing is possible when we connect with our feelings. Our willingness to learn from our feelings, rather than to ignore them, means being ready to learn to love, rather than to ignore or judge the wounded parts within us.

---

### The Six Steps of Inner Bonding*
### Step 1: Willingness to Feel Pain and Take Responsibility for Your Feelings

Move into the present moment and focus within, tuning into your feelings—the physical sensations within the body. Choose to be mindful of, and pay attention to, all distressing feelings rather than protect against them with substance and process addictions. Make a conscious decision that you want to take responsibility for your feelings.

### Step 2: Move into the Intent to Learn

Invite the compassionate presence of Spirit into your heart to help you learn what you may be doing or thinking that may be causing your pain, or what may be happening externally that needs your attention. In Inner Bonding there are only two possible intents in any given moment:
- to protect against pain and avoid responsibility for it through trying to control yourself and others, or
- to learn about what you are doing or thinking that may be causing your pain so that you can move into loving yourself and others.

When you are in the intent to learn, you are a loving adult. When you are in the intent to protect and avoid you are operating from your shame-based ego-wounded self, or child-adult. In Step Two, you welcome and embrace all your feelings with compassion.

> **Step 3: Dialogue with Your Wounded Self and Core Self**
> Discover the thoughts/false beliefs from your wounded self that may be causing your shame, fear and pain; release anger and pain in appropriate ways; learn about the past that created the false beliefs; nurture your wounded self; explore what may be happening with a person or event that is causing the core feelings of loneliness, heartache, heartbreak, helplessness, or grief; explore your core Self and what brings you joy.
>
> **Step 4: Dialogue with Your Higher Guidance**
> Ask your Higher Guidance (whatever that is for you): What is the truth about the thoughts/false beliefs I may have uncovered in Step Three? What is the loving behavior toward my Inner Child in this situation? What is in my highest good? What is being kind to myself? Open and allow the answers to come through you in words, pictures or feelings. The answers may not come immediately, but if you have a sincere desire to learn, they will come.
>
> **Step 5: Take Loving Action**
> Tell yourself the truth and take the loving action that came through from your Guidance in Step Four; put God/Spirit into action. Consciously move into gratitude for the guidance that is always here for you.
>
> **Step 6: Evaluate Your Action**
> Check in to see if your pain, anger, and shame are getting healed. If not, go back through the steps until you discover the truth and actions that bring you peace, joy, and a deep sense of intrinsic worth.
>
> *© Margaret Paul, PhD, used with permission, Innerbonding.com.*

When we are able to express our anger or disappointment about any mistreatment we received as children, we are less likely to pass this abuse on to our own children. Psychologists working with mothers who were indifferent and neglectful towards their babies, invited the mothers to talk about their own childhoods. As these mothers connected with their own pain, they began to cry. Immediately after this emotional release, they spontaneously cuddled their babies. Their nurturing energies had been locked behind a wall of unexpressed grief.[52]

When we can be honest with ourselves about our unmet childhood needs and connect with how we felt as children, when we feel safe to share our experiences of loss or abandonment, when we can grieve openly and release the grip these repressed emotions have on us, we can connect more readily with our inner child, and more authentically with our own children, breaking the chain of abuse otherwise passed from generation to generation.

Healing experiences can be accessed through many venues: the field of expressive arts—which includes journaling and creative arts—is itself enormous.

> *Guided imagery or visualization techniques can be a powerful tool for healing. The power of empathy and compassion allows us to bring the experience of love, acceptance, and deep connection to those aspects of ourselves that were never before touched in this way. The times you have offered these experiences to others have attuned your soul to them—through emotionally rich imagery you can allow them throughout your entire being.* —Emmett Miller, MD, *Deep Healing*

As seen, healing is also accessed through loving relationships, counseling, or psychotherapy; still others will find respite in spiritual pursuits. Different forms of bodywork can be helpful in moving through body armoring to access and release repressed emotions. Regardless of the healing modality chosen, it will inevitably involve some form of reparenting.

## Deactivating Triggers

Wounded in the context of relationship, ultimately we will be healed in the context of relationship.

Robert Karen identified being in a stable relationship with a supportive spouse as a primary element in breaking the cycle of emotional abuse or neglect. He noted, too, that an additional element may be having a baby—the new perspective a baby can offer on our own "inevitably imperfect" childhood. Many new parents are eager to embrace this transition time as a window for growth, but as we have seen, despite their best intentions, many rapidly find themselves caught spinning in a downward spiral, each perceiving the other as the "enemy." In such a situation it is impossible to create the safe haven of emotional connection that affords a space for healing and growth.

A first step in moving out of the "enemy camp," is understanding that what is happening when we get triggered is that we are reacting to something that is really an implicit memory from the past, i.e., a memory that may surface as uncomfortable bodily sensations and emotions rather than anything we can recognize as a "memory." And, probably no one sets off your "buttons" as well as your partner.

Harville Hendrix, PhD, in *Getting the Love You Want*, speaks about the phenomenon whereby, unknowingly, we choose to be with someone who is similar to a member of our family-of-origin where there are usually unresolved issues. This occurs at a sub-awareness level; something about the person's energy feels familiar to you, and you are drawn to him or her in the hope of resolving the leftover concern.

> *Then, these issues start to play out. Suddenly, there's a situation that upsets you. Your reaction is quick and automatic. Very often, the expressed emotion is one*

*of frustration or anger. But these are reactive, or secondary, emotions. Underlying these are more basic emotions like hurt or a sense of unworthiness. While it feels like whatever has just taken place is what is upsetting you, in reality, something from the past has been "hooked into" and set off.*
—Karen Sherman, PhD, *Mindfulness and The Art of Choice*

Sherman offers an example of how this might actually "look":

*Years ago, I worked with a young couple where the woman had childhood issues of a father who was never present. He worked all the time and wasn't able to give her much attention. Her spouse was not only aware of this history but very sensitive to it. On one occasion, he had to go away on a business trip for several days. Then, it turned out that the company tacked on a second trip, which would mean he would be gone an especially long time.*

*Knowing how distressing his wife would find this long absence, he spent the entire day at work trying to rearrange plans, find different flights, and figure out some way to alter the amount of days he'd be gone. But nothing was possible. He called me and asked what to do. We discussed how to present the situation to her, reassuring her how important she was to him, the extent to which he went to try to change things, the efforts he would make to stay in touch with her.*

*Nothing he said mattered—she went ballistic! Was she reacting to her spouse? No. She was, without realizing it, re-experiencing the old painful feelings she had when she felt like an abandoned little girl.*

*Here's another situation: I worked with a couple where the wife felt that the husband was very insensitive to her needs and that she just didn't matter to him. He worked very hard to be more aware of her. Things definitely did improve.*

*Then, in one session, they came in very upset and here is what he reported: he had gone to their son's basketball game without her because she had gone to the doctor, not feeling well. After the game, he called to inquire how the exam went and how she felt. I privately thought, "That was good." He also let her know he and another family would be going out to dinner with the kids so he'd be late in getting home and inquired if she'd want to come. I privately thought, "That was good."*

*Even she admitted, "So far, so good." But when he got home and went upstairs to check on her (more points for him), he said, "There was that expression on her face." She was extremely upset with him. Why? Because he hadn't asked if she wanted him to bring home a slice of pizza!*

*When we worked on this feeling, though she initially felt it really was because he didn't care about her, she was able to hook it back to an experience with her mother not paying attention to her. There were many such episodes, implicit memories, with stored energy that got triggered when her husband did something that felt similar.*

*Sometimes, things get even more complicated because each partner has issues from the past that get set off in the present by things their mate does or says.*

Fortunately we can learn to work with these reactions and heal the underlying wounds or "triggers.

### Working with Reactivity in Relationships*

This process is adapted from an exercise in *Mindfulness and the Art of Choice*, by Karen Sherman, PhD.

This exercise is to be read prior to any exploration of it with your partner. Both partners need come to an agreement that they will try the exercise the next time either partner is having a reaction. It is very likely that, at least in the beginning of working with this model, i.e., until both partners are skilled in listening rather than reacting, one will have a reaction and the other will respond defensively.

The steps outlined here are offered as guidelines, to be adapted as appropriate for your needs. The model is outlined by presenting a sample couple, Samantha and Chris.

**Best-case scenario:**

1. Sam is having a reaction (a reaction is quick and automatic and really seems to be an over-reaction to what has happened).
   Chris takes a deep breath to ground and center.
2. Chris then gently states, "I can see this is really upsetting (frustrating, angering, saddening) you."

This is an important first step. Sam's wounded child needs to feel validated, understood. *It does not matter if Chris agrees with Sam's reaction.* At this point, it is his wounded child who is having the reaction; that is to say, it is the emotional part of the self. Therefore, *logic is of no value!*

3. Once Sam's wounded child has calmed down, Chris gently inquires, "Is it possible that something upset your wounded child? Can you share it with me?" This is a variation of the Adult Self experience in being loving and accepting.
4. It is important that as Sam shares whatever the experience is, Chris is fully present, i.e., not distracted and doing anything else, but rather, making eye contact and perhaps gently touching her.
5. If Chris thinks Sam is done speaking, rather than ask, "Are you done?" say, "Tell me more." The latter is much more inviting and sends the message that, "I am here for you." The intention here, is to offer comfort and connection.

It may be that the reactive partner is not comforted. When people are emotional, they cannot think logically. It will be helpful for the other partner to discuss how he could be more responsive. *It is important to wait until things have calmed down before trying to do this.*

Very often, the common reaction to feeling attacked is to leave the room. If Chris chooses to do this, it will be extremely helpful to state, "I am leaving only to calm down; I am *not* leaving you."

**Alternate 1 (When Chris gets grabbed by Sam's reaction):**
1. Chris recognizes that Sam was having a wounded child reaction. After Chris has had a chance to calm down, if he did attack Sam, Chris should first acknowledge that he got grabbed and apologize.
2. Chris then says, "As I had a while to think about things, I realized how upset you were. I do want to work on this with you. Can you tell me more about what you were experiencing?"
3. Proceed with Steps 3–5 as above.

**Alternate 2 (When Sam realizes she has had a triggered reaction):**
If Sam realizes that her reaction was from her wounded child, it is more likely to lead to some healing with Chris's help.
1. Sam approaches Chris to let him know she's had a chance to think about the incident and realize that she got grabbed, her buttons set off, and that her wounded child was having a reaction.
2. Sam apologizes and asks if Chris is willing to help her work through the process.
3. Sam explains what set her off; that is, what she *perceived* that was upsetting. For example, was it the way something was said? Was it a facial expression? Was it a gesture? Was something not done that was anticipated?
4. Sam shares what feelings were aroused.
5. Sam relates what old situations this reminded her of.

If Chris is not offering Sam the type of nurturing she would like, she asks for what she needs.

Remember, others are not mind readers; but if asking for what is needed finds your partner willing to give it, it is because you *do* matter to him. Remember that the difference between your past experiences and *now* is that, as a small child, you did not have the ability to ask for what you needed. The very act of being able to do so now is part of the healing process. Also, there is a healing that takes place that is very unique just by virtue of the fact that it is coming from such an emotionally significant person.

## Parenting Our Children

Neither Jack or I were raised by "continuum parents," and we carry within ourselves those very same wounds that we hoped to minimize in Siena. While our intentions were great, when stressed and needy, we fell into reactive patterns and communications. Blaming, shaming, shifting responsibility—however subtly we may have done it, it was there. Siena's presence made me not only more aware of those patterns, but also more committed than ever to changing them. And not "tomorrow" or "when I get time," but now. What was very wonderful was that her spirit, the beautiful natural child in her, called forth the natural child in me, affording me a wellspring of energy to draw on in healing my own wounds.

> *Our children make us better parents, and also better people; and in this regard they give us as much as we give them.* —Robin Grille, *Heart-to-Heart Parenting*

As parents, we will discover that different ages and stages of our child's growth and development are more difficult for us than others. The difficult times will likely reflect times that were difficult and painful for us as a child, the stages at which we ourselves were wounded.

> *I had thought that I had prepared well and worked through my attachment issues before I started parenting, only to discover that I would frighten or terrorize my dear older child when he was two. The behavior seemed to sneak up on me, until I stopped, named it, and vowed to work it through so I could eliminate it. Even then, I continued to act inappropriately and unacceptably towards him in moments of high stress, lashing out instead of recognizing that his behavior was expressing unmet needs. I was struggling to work through my past quickly enough to not affect my children, while I was in a marriage that was falling apart, with a partner who was also acting out addiction and abuse.*
>
> *My pattern was a bit different with my younger son; he had tantrums until he was five or six; I would react by tantruming myself, covering my ears and yelling for him to stop. Much later, my work in Early Start gave me the gift of supporting parents of 2-year-olds with tantruming behavior and teaching them how to meet their children's needs; too late for us, perhaps, but a kind of penance/healing nevertheless. Interestingly, my children and I remained securely attached despite my bad behavior.* —Barbara

Here we note again that perfection is not a requirement. Barbara found that, despite her earlier efforts to work through her childhood trauma, it was restimulated with the parenting of both of her children. Perhaps key to her secure attachment to her children was her resolve to work through the issues that emerged—through getting triggered—in parenting her children, and their resulting sensing of these intentions to better herself. Also, her earlier work on resolving her trauma helped her through these early years of parenting, as she found herself confronted with yet another layer of the onion.

Gentle and compassionate self-inquiry and self-exploration can evoke our empathy and understanding, of both our children and our own reaction, enabling us to better respond to both our own inner child and our biological child: "What was happening to *me* at the age that my child is now?" "How did that make me feel?" "What did I do?" "What did I really need and long for at that time, from significant others in my life?" "How would I have felt if my need for _____ had been met?"

Release and healing can be accessed simply by imagining, envisioning, or "experiencing" ourselves receiving *now* what we needed and wanted, but never received. And don't forget, in all this, the magical and playful child who also lives within. These aspects can find new life and expression in the company of our own biological children.

> *One of the greatest gifts of parenthood lies in the way our children, just by being themselves, can help us to see where our wounds are. The way to transform our relationship with our children is to heal ourselves.*
> —Robin Grille, *Heart-to-Heart Parenting*

Sometimes one or other of us will be more able to parent our child than the other. When we have taken the time to share our childhood stories and feelings with each other, we have a window into how it felt for our partner as a child, at different times in his or her life, and are more likely then to extend to our partner understanding and compassion when they falter or fall. Recognizing our own vulnerabilities as well as our strengths, we can be more forgiving with ourselves and seek support when we encounter those rugged stretches of our own childhood, in parenting our own child.

The following terms and tools offered by Pam Leo, *Connection Parenting*, are designed to support parents in developing the skills needed to build the connection and strong bonds children need to thrive. Drawing on these terms and tools can be equally valuable to us in our endeavors to deepen our abilities to connect with different aspects of our self, with our partner—or with the world around us.

Leo says that we will always know when connection is re-established. When children feel connected, they make eye contact with us, they talk to us, and they welcome our touch.

## Connection Parenting (and Partnering) Terms and Tools[*]

*Connection*—feeling loved and listened to.
*Disconnection*—feeling hurt and unheard.

The goal of connection parenting is to meet proactively our children's need for connection. Leo has found that whenever the optimal level of connection gets too low, children communicate their need for more connection through their behavior. She offers two tools for connection, which she has found, again and again, are the only tools we need.

When a child's behavior is challenging, use tool #1.

### Tool #1: Connection

Provide children with a consistent, loving connection through eye contact, loving touch, respect, listening, and spending time working and playing together.

Whenever we question how to respond to a child's behavior, we ask ourselves, "Is this response connection or coercion?" Look for a way to respond to the behavior without creating a disconnection. Connect before you correct.

### Tool #2: Reconnection

Sometimes a child's behavior pushes our buttons and we react before we connect. We can tell when our reaction has caused disconnection. A child who feels hurt and/or unheard will either:

*Attack*—cry or scream, or
*Retreat*—won't make eye contact, won't talk to us, and rejects our touch.
As soon as we realize our reaction has created a disconnection we reconnect with tool #2.

### The 3 Rs of reconnection are:

*Rewind*—acknowledge our hurtful behavior ("What I said was hurtful"),
*Repair*—apologize and let the child know he did not deserve our behavior,
*Replay*—respond with love and listening.

Now, we suggest that you read over the above terms and tools, substituting Leo's use of the word "child" with "your partner." Do you see that these tools and terms are as applicable in making connection with our partners as with our children? And, it can't get much simpler.

Remember that as you refine your skills in this area, as you learn the language of love, you are offering a most wonderful gift to not only yourself and your partner, but also to your children, and to their children... and in fact, what better gift could you offer the planet?

---

[*] *Connection Parenting*, Pam Leo, reprinted with permission, connectionparenting.com.

## Key Points

- How we care for our children often reflects how we ourselves were parented as children. Without an awareness of the themes of our own early years, we find ourselves reacting to our children out of our own unmet needs, and embodying the same dysfunctional behaviors our parents—albeit unwittingly—inflicted on us.
- To the extent we are conscious of our own personal history, the values and patterns we want to pass to our children, and those we want to leave behind, we will be able to meet the authentic needs of our children, and strengthen the bond we share—as well as the joy we experience as parents.
- Connecting with our early experiences is facilitated by an awareness of the child-like personalities that live in each of us—aspects of our inner child. Unconscious defenses—such as the denial and repression of emotions—that we developed as children to avoid feeling the pain of our unmet needs, become a part of our personality or our "act," and distort our perception of reality. These shadow aspects of our inner child can often be detected by an intense emotional reaction to a person or situation.
- Early neglect or abuse are often translated into the belief that we are somehow bad, unworthy of love, or that people cannot be trusted. Healing is possible when we acknowledge the hurt feelings and needs of our inner child, so making them available for review, reflection, and healing.
- Reparenting our inner child is a process of recognizing our inner child by listening to our deepest emotional needs, and offering nurturance and protection.
- What is critical is not the unmet needs of our childhood, but our attitude to it. The focus is not on how or why, but on the beliefs we took on, and how they affect us today.
- When can express our anger, disappointment, or grief about any neglect or abuse we experienced as children, we are less likely to pass this on to our own children.
- Healing experiences can be accessed through many venues—counseling, loving relationships, bodywork—the field of expressive arts, which includes journaling and drawing—is itself enormous.
- A stable relationship with a supportive spouse can be a key element in breaking the cycle of abuse and neglect. Likewise, a baby can offer new perspective on our own "inevitable imperfect" childhood.
- Despite best intentions, many couples find themselves in a downward spiral, each perceiving the other as "the enemy."

- Suddenly a situation upsets you, you react automatically with anger or frustration. But underlying these are more basic emotions such as hurt or a sense of unworthiness. While it feels like the current situation is what's upsetting you, it's likely something from the past is "triggered." Compassionate self-inquiry can change the course.
- When feeling loved and listened to, we feel connected. When feeling hurt and unheard, we feel disconnected. Consider whether your comment or action or response will foster connection, or disconnection.
- The 3 Rs of reconnection are Rewind—acknowledge our hurtful behavior; Repair—apologize and let the others know they did not deserve our behavior; Replay—respond with love and listening.

# 21: Healing Childhood Trauma—One Approach

The importance of healing old traumas, so we can be fully present as parents, cannot be overstated. Here we want to recap some of what we have said, and share some additional insights and tools as offered by John Pateros and Betty Idarius of the Process Coaching Center in northern California (see Resources). We have seen that most of the deeper traumas we have experienced in life happened very early—during conception, gestation, birth, and infancy. In these early stages of growth and development, we were completely vulnerable and dependent on our environment, especially our parents, for love, sustenance, and our very survival. We learned to suppress or repress any feelings that were not well received by our parents as a way of insuring that love and sustenance would not stop. That sent the traumatized feelings into our shadow where they remained hidden—until triggered, or restimulated, by a present-time circumstance.

Pateros and Idarius underscore the fact that *triggering is useful*, because now there is an opportunity to become reacquainted with the parts of us that are still feeling what was previously suppressed. These early traumas continue to be triggered in the *hope that* some healing will finally occur. We have emphasized the likelihood that many events around pregnancy, the birth of a child, and the first few weeks and months of caring for an infant are typically ripe with triggers of our *own* early unmet needs. Pateros and Idarius accentuate the point that bringing help to these very young triggered parts of ourselves typically results in deep and profound healing:

> *Our own healing then frees us up to be more lovingly present with our partner and newborn.*

They offer an example of a new dad who was very triggered when his newborn son became the focus of his wife's attention.

> *He was used to receiving more of this kind of attention from his wife; however, her role of mother superseded her role of wife and companion. He felt hurt and angry, and yet guilty about expressing it. So he "stuffed" the feelings and became distant from both of them as a reflexive way of avoiding the pain of what was triggered in him.*

> *His healing began by writing in his journal about his experience of alienation. He recognized that what he was feeling was familiar—something he had experienced earlier in his life. Noticing when we are spontaneously triggered into an early developmental stage is the first step in healing. Some of the signs that a very young part might be triggered are: mental confusion; an inability to verbalize what we are experiencing; deep neediness; aloneness; a generalized fear that the world is not a safe and loving place; an inability or reluctance to*

experience intimate loving connections with others; and very commonly, a sense of numbness or shock.

Traumas are held in our body, and our body is where the healing of these traumas happens.

> This dad was familiar with Process Coaching (see Resources) and used one of the most direct (and perhaps easiest) ways to heal and integrate past traumas, which is simply to embody and love the energy of the feeling where it occurs in the body. However, an old coping strategy kicked in when he first began; the story in his mind started up again about the present-time triggering circumstance and the loss of special attention from his wife. He knew, however, that the triggered feelings were not really about the current circumstance, and that resolution would happen from his working his own healing process.
>
> By dropping himself out of the story, and its conditioning in his mind, he was able to directly meet the real issue—the energy of the feeling itself. The information held in the unconscious "felt sense" that he was feeling in his body, was now available to him. He was able to feel what was really going on—just this previously denied, unwanted energy that he was now embodying. Feeling the energy of an emotion in the body enables us to experience the feeling directly, on its own terms. He was successful in loving himself and his triggered part, and was overjoyed at his new ease of presence with his family in the circle of love.

Pateros and Idarius urge us to realize that we, too, can do this for ourselves. They suggest that when you are aware that you are triggered, begin by inquiring about the energy in *feeling* terms; the easiest way to do this is to ask yourself about the location and sensations of the energy. "Where am I feeling this in my body?" is the first question. After you find the location of the energy, breathe some space in and around this place in your body so the feeling can be present more comfortably. You then can ask yourself questions about the sensations, "Is this energy more tight or loose?" "Warm or cool?" "Hard or soft?" "Sharp or dull?" "Is it still or moving?" Etc. With curiosity, notice the sensations of the energy in your body.

> When you use the mind in this way, you avoid the conditioned pitfalls of having to deal with a story you've been telling yourself. Our new dad was able to let go of the story of being neglected by his wife, as well as the story of what had happened to him as a young child. The story had served its purpose of helping him find the energy of the feeling in his body. He knew that the story is not the actual experience; it's only a model of the experience. The experience of the feeling's energy in the body is what is real. There is no victim or perpetrator in this direct approach; there are no judgments. There is only the energy that's

*been triggered and the feeling of its sensations in your body. Once you have explored the sensations of the energy, you can begin to make friends with it.*

Their experience as Process Coaches has led Pateros and Idarius to the unequivocal belief that love is the true medicine of healing. It's our love for the feeling parts of ourselves that enables us to find and heal them. They are encouraging: if a Judgment Release (see Process Coaching, Appendix C) seems like it would help, go for it. Or you can simply find something about this energy that is lovable and begin by loving that. Your love will expand as you welcome the energy and find appreciation for it being here in you. This is the easiest way to help it feel your love.

*Sometimes, when feeling into the energy of a feeling, an image of a child part of you will come up. This might be a memory of an event that actually occurred, or simply an image from the unconscious mind. Use the image as a metaphor for the feeling. Imagine you are there with the infant, loving him or her just as you would the energy. In this case, you are working with an image that represents a feeling, not the story.*

*You'll know you're on the right track when you can feel into the feeling and say something like this: "Ah, my most excellent life force energy! Thank you for being here, I love you. I want to be with you. I want you to be with me—always."*

*When we move toward the energy in body with unconditional loving acceptance for it just as it feels, right now, the feeling will respond positively. It's as if this child part of us is finally getting the love and acceptance that it's been yearning for all these years. Very often deep emotional movement arises and new information comes spontaneously.*

*The healing medicine here is your honest love and trust for yourself and all of your life force energy, just as it is right now, no matter how badly it had been judged or repressed in the past. Healing happens whenever real love shows up for a feeling part of self that has never received love before. And we now have the opportunity of being the bearer of the love that we have been yearning for.*

If working on your own at first seems daunting, it also can be very helpful to find a body-centered professional (see Resources) who is experienced in helping people heal childhood trauma to hold the space for your process.

*The gift of learning how to show up lovingly for all of your feelings is truly life changing. As you learn to embody real self-love, your quality of life improves, and the benefits will be not only for yourself, but also for your spouse, your children, and your entire world.*

## Journey into Life

As we have seen, the experiences that we had during conception, gestation, and birth have far-reaching effects on us, often becoming unconscious generalized attitudes towards life. For instance, an infant who had a traumatic birth may feel that the world is not a safe place. This belief will be held unconsciously as the person grows and matures with a profound effect on how they experience life and what they project onto their sense of "objective reality." It is helpful to explore the possible traumas we, as an incarnating child, may have experienced during this time. With this understanding, we are better able to recreate new experiences so that the early trauma can be healed.

Mom and Dad: In exploring your own birth trauma, Pateros and Idarius suggest some questions you might ask yourself: Was your conception planned or unplanned? Was the pregnancy wanted or not? Was abortion contemplated? Were your parents together in a committed relationship based in love for each other? Were you born at home or in a hospital? Was the environment sensitive to you, the newborn infant? Were the lights low? Was the air warm? Sounds soft? Was there gentle touching, skin-to-skin? What was the emotional state of your mother during labor and birth? Was she given anesthesia? Was the birth vaginal or cesarean? Were there complications? Were you breastfed or bottle-fed? Were you kept close to your mother with plenty of skin contact, or were you often separated and left alone to "cry it out"?

> *After answering these questions, take a moment for a deep breath or two! There may be some triggered feelings coming up. If so, it's good to notice what you are feeling and be with those feelings before continuing.*

Pateros and Idarius have found that a powerful way of bringing healing to these traumatic experiences is to help this young part of you by "redoing" the experience(s). In redoing a "movie" of your being born, see yourself as the fetus still in the womb—as if you are watching a movie on the screen of your imagination. Then go there and be present with that aspect of yourself as if you're on the set of a movie.

Say hello, and ask what the fetus wants to experience, instead of what has been going on. Ask the fetal-you for the specifics of what your ideal birth would be like. For instance, "Where do you want to be born?" "Who do you want at your birth?" "Who would you like to catch you when you are being born?" "What would your ideal parents be like?"

You as the infant can now have the journey of being born to your new parents and into your new childhood. Now imagine that you *are* the child about to be born and your adult self is nearby to make sure this goes exactly the way you desire. Allow yourself to have this new experience.

They suggest that, in general, an ideal journey could go something like this:

*As you are still in the spirit world, you look down and see your new mother and your new father. They meet and fall in love with each other and decide they want to bring a child into the world as the culmination of that love. That child is you! You can see them loving each other and coming together to conceive you. You can feel the joy of the love and happiness they feel being with each other.*

*The love they have for themselves and for each other draws you toward them, and you enter the body of your mother. Your first sensations of incarnated life are like an explosion of love and connection. Soon you feel yourself traveling down and into your mother's waiting, expectant womb. You implant yourself and nestle into the rich, nurturing warmth of her womb.*

*After a while you sense a rush of joy and excitement that completely encompasses you. Your parents are so happy when they find out you are here with them!*

*As you continue to grow and be nurtured in the lush surroundings, you hear the sounds of her voice and your father's voice, and you feel the feelings of being completely safe and cared for. You float in an ocean of love, completely supported by the amniotic fluid. You are feeling at one with your environment and so very, very peaceful. You often sense your new parents expressing their love for you and the excitement they are feeling about your soon-to-be birth.*

*The time draws near for the journey of birth. The contractions now begin and you feel like you're being hugged and gently squeezed. They come more and more quickly now, as you feel yourself moving down the birth canal. You can feel the joy and anticipation in the air outside, and inside of you as well. The lights are low in the room. The air is warm. Everything is just right, awaiting your arrival.*

*With each contraction you move farther down and soon you begin to feel the opening of your mother's cervix and you move down even more. Now she's pushing and you are feeling pleasantly bumped and squeezed. Some more pushing and another bump or two, and now gently you come out into the loving arms of the one who catches you. Your cord is left intact for now, and you are immediately given to your mother, who gently brings you up onto her warm, soft bosom.*

*You can now hear clearly the sweet sounds of your parents' voices full of joy and excitement. "It's a girl (boy)!" Everyone is so happy to see you! Welcome, sweet baby! We are so happy you are here! We are so happy to have you with us! You are truly our bundle of joy!*

*You can hear your mother's voice in particular, and your father's, too. You feel the warmth of your mother's skin. The smell of her is so sweet as you lie in her arms, on her skin, so happy to finally be together. You are covered with a soft blanket while still on her chest, feeling warm and cozy.*

*As you feel the desire, you nuzzle up to her breast and begin to suckle. The warm, sweet milk comes into your mouth and you feel it as pure love moving into you, filling you completely. You relax even more, feeling nourished and sweetly held by your mother. She is your world and you are hers. She feels you and responds lovingly to your every need. You feel wonderfully good to finally be here with her and in your new world! Your father is here, too, always nearby supporting and helping you and your mother in whatever ways you both want.*

*With your mother still holding you, and your father next to you both, you are in your true home and beginning your childhood. This new childhood is your right childhood, the childhood you truly deserve, the one you imagine unfolding from this healed journey from conception to birth.*

Pateros and Idarius urge you to take as much time as you need now to fully feel the new experience. When you are ready, notice that there are two of you, the grownup and the child, and become the grownup again. Look into the face of the newborn and see your beauty, innocence, and greatness. And feel the love. Spend as much time with each other as you wish. When you are ready, hold the child close to you—so close that you absorb the child into yourself—one, whole, complete being. Take some time to relax even more deeply and notice what you are experiencing now.

Here we have looked in some detail at one of the many modes of healing early trauma. In the following chapter we look at several other stories of healing, and healing modalities.

## Key Points
- Healing old traumas enables us to be more fully present as parents. As children, we learned to repress any unacceptable feelings. These can be triggered or restimulated by present time situations. These triggers can be welcomed as an opportunity for recognition and healing of our past hurts.
- Traumas are held in the body, and healed in the body. When being triggered, inquire "where am I feeling this in my body?" "How does is feel?"
- When you notice the sensations of the energy in your body, you can begin to make friends with it. Bringing love to these parts of us, is in itself healing.
- Experiences during conception, gestation, and birth have far-reaching consequences. Understanding any trauma we experienced as this time, can allow us to recreate new experiences—thus healing the early trauma.
- Explore your early life with questions such as was the pregnancy wanted; were there complications during the birth; were you breastfed or bottlefed; were you often left to "cry it out"? Be present to any feelings that emerge.
- Guided visualizations in which you see and imagine yourself receiving what you wanted and needed, but did not get, are then one way to "redo" the experience.

# 22: Stories of Healing

*In this chapter we share several of our readers' own healing stories as illustrations of the diverse paths this journey can traverse.*

## The Power of Emotional Release, Chris, Mendocino Co., California

These first two stories are by friends who lived nearby when our daughter was little. We have stayed in touch over the years and I admire their commitment to healing.

> *I had a major increase in my level of physical distress immediately following my daughter's birth in 1990 when I was 43. Looking back, my body was in a state of rigidified terror. I had painfully frightening headaches. I had no idea what it meant to be a father and the early experiences I had as a child with my father were terrifying.*
>
> *Upon returning from piloting a bomber during WWII, my father was lost, career-less and in emotional chaos—my parents had terrifying fights that I witnessed. "Terrifying" may seem an extreme word, but having gone back—since the birth of my own child—through to release the emotions of the shuddering impact that witnessing that violence had on my tiny, one-and-a-half-year-old body, I believe that "terror" is the correct word. My wife (see next story) and I did this healing work of discharging our distressed emotions using Revaluation Counseling/co-counseling (see Resources). I do not have direct memories of the fights, but my mother told me about them when I was age nineteen.*
>
> *Also, I was separated from my parents for long periods as they traveled to South Carolina for pilots' training school prior to my dad going to fight overseas. I know my mom was scared about my dad going to war so I'm quite sure her fears kept her from being able to connect closely with me. I have a letter from an aunt who admonished my mom to hold me. As I was growing up—like most children—I was usually shut down and put down whenever I tried showing my emotions. So, as an adult I was very confused about the way feelings work. The effect of this in the family I grew up in was serious enough that my older brother took his own life.*
>
> *Today I understand that the lack of deep bonding with my mom and dad made my parents' fighting unbearable because there was no one to whom to turn with my fears, no place of safety or nurturance. My experience of life with my mom was as a deserted wayfarer on the sea of life with no anchor and no connection*

*of any kind. She was an object in my young world but not a source of nourishment, safety, or physical, palpable love.*

*Before and following my daughter's birth, I suppressed my constant triggered internalized terror of memories of their fighting, by compulsively working 80 hours a week. I truly felt when I left the house in the morning, I was unable to be part of the deep bonding process that was occurring between my wife and daughter—after all, my role was the breadwinner and a male.*

*I remember looking at them with a fond longing as I internalized over and over the notion that this goodness was not for me and I was doing the "right thing" by leaving for work.*

*Several incidents occurred in my early years of fathering, that I believe were caused by the violence I witnessed, and the emotional disconnection I experienced as a young person. As a new dad, I was totally unaware of my emotional blocks. I've now done quite a bit of personal emotional work in this area with co-counseling, and so, although there is still grief around what I missed as a child, I am no longer in the grip of the terror. I can look at these memories somewhat objectively and rationally and not blame myself for the failed bonding and suppressed emotions. One evening, my wife was out attending a weekly class so I was our daughter's caregiver, after a long day and many weeks of overworking. She chose that night to cry endlessly. I believe now that she was trying to discharge emotions around the traumas of her birth. There were no other immediate sources of physical discomfort for her—she had been fed, diapers were clean, and she was relatively well rested. She was at last feeling safe enough with me to try freeing her body of the tensions of birthing. I tried everything I knew, and that had worked before, to try to console her. Nothing was working to calm her down. After about an hour or more of this, I sat her rather abruptly on the couch so that we were face to face and I began to tell her that I couldn't handle any more of this. She was 10 months of age at the time.*

*She did stop crying but I was so hugely disappointed for the abrupt and rather harsh way I handled this. I can become grief stricken even now if I put attention on this sad memory. Fortunately, my wife walked in the door immediately after this and I was relieved of duty. I now know that if I had had someone to call whom I trusted with my emotions, I could have gotten some emotional support for myself and continued to listen to her as she released all of the feelings she needed to. I could have done this without having had to stop her tears. Unfortunately, I did not know this nor did I have such a person in my life at the time. Ironically, the class my wife was attending was all about getting and giving this kind of emotional support—the simple process of two loving, intelligent humans taking time to listen well as each pours his or her heart out, one at a time, to the other.*

*The night I was unable to listen to my daughter cry endlessly occurred because I hadn't had a bond with anyone as an infant myself, to whom I could turn and release endless tears of my own, tears that would have relieved and healed me of the terror of the violence I had witnessed. I had no nurturing mommy to run to.*

*Had I such a bond with my mother, I could have run to her to seek comfort and release from the various ensuing traumas of growing up.*

*Another very upsetting episode for me as a new father came unexpectedly one late afternoon upon returning home from work, fatigued, and probably feeling some significant effects of the way I had been excluded in the deep bonding process with my daughter. This one is even more difficult to disclose. My wife greeted me soon after coming in the door with a demand that I be more responsive to her desire for closeness. My body was wracked after giving all I had to give at work, on top of the regular terror-based bodily tension I had grown accustomed to. I resisted her demand in some way, but she refused to give in—of course, not knowing what I was experiencing. I came "unglued"— shrieking and exploding in total rage—picking her up by the shoulders and walking down the hall toward our bedroom and down a few steps over which we stumbled and fell, me on top of her and she lying on her back. I proceeded to shriek and beat on her. I don't remember which parts of my body I used but when I pulled back she had black eyes and bruises. To feel such a beast come out of me was very frightening. She was very badly hurt and very terrified as well. It took us a very long time to feel any sense of recovery from this experience. Now, almost two decades later, I sometimes still work on it in the regular co-counseling sessions I do. We received some excellent emotional support soon after this event, which helped us a great deal. But it's still very difficult to share this story with others.*

*I believe these events were the result of the failed bonding and emotional disconnection that is prevalent in our culture. Hardly any of us truly has a partner (spouse or otherwise) that we can literally pour out our emotions to. Across the board, setting up a partnership like this with another parent is the single most valuable activity a prospective or new parent can undertake. If we pursue an emotional bonding process with other adults in this elegant manner, a great deal of tied up emotional energy can become available, enabling better bonding between adult and infant.*

*The lack of bonding with my mom and dad formed many of my later disconnecting behaviors. Their existence stands in contrast with a very strong appreciation and even deep feeling of love that I have always felt for my beautiful daughter.*

## *Constantly Recommitting,* Barbara, Mendocino County, California (partner to Chris)

*I was almost 41 when I gave birth to my daughter in 1987. I very much wanted to birth and raise her in a very different way than I was—born premature, several weeks in an incubator, bottle-fed, and later severely physically abused. I doubted my abilities and feared I would not be a good mom, since statistics said children of abusive parents were 75% more likely to pass on the abuse to their children.*

*Despite our care and intentions, the labor and birth were difficult. I had heard the moment of birth was the most joyful experience a woman can have. I was in pain (we had to be induced) and so exhausted I was just glad it was over. This added to my fears of being a good mom.*

*The bonding process wasn't an instant hit like I heard others experienced, but it grew each day. I was greatly relieved and did all in my power to nurture this precious bond growing between us. I was not aware of how my switch in attention from Chris to our baby was affecting him. I guess I was too tired to notice. I was very traumatized and swollen, having had an unusually large episiotomy. I can clearly remember that the last thing I wanted was a penis anywhere near that area of my body for at least a year.*

*Although I was soon deeply in love with my baby I had no reserves for anything or anybody else. I was an older mom, breastfed for close to five years, and was also running a business out of our home. I was not told about taking vitamins or supplements that might have helped my body recover more quickly. As I was nursing, as much as I loved it, I would sometimes cry from exhaustion. I felt very alone with this, as my husband couldn't help me even if he wanted to. He was working long hours and if I wasn't with my daughter I was trying to manage my business.*

*Chris and I grew further apart. My health had been deteriorating. I was getting weaker and weaker. I was eventually diagnosed with multiple chemical sensitivity or environmental illness. I was so weak and exhausted. I nurtured our daughter and tried to "take care of" my husband, but my soul wasn't there. It was a task performed out of duty and respect. I also did it in hopes of avoiding criticism or his anger. I was both too exhausted to be able to handle it and too fearful of his confrontations or upsets, due to my abusive past. Maybe without the abusive history or unrelenting physical exhaustion, I could have been more resilient or thought of more creative ways to deal with our frequent upsets.*

*I felt more isolated after the birth of our daughter. I used to hold small dinner parties or go to lunch with close friends. Now I had no time or energy. In addition, I was the first in my circle of friends to have a child. It took quite a few years and numerous upsets for us to adjust to this new reality and reconnect on a deeper level. Also, I became less flexible in social settings. I used to be gregarious and accepting of all types of people and personalities. Now I didn't like people if they were grouchy or anything less than totally accepting of my child. I avoided other moms if they showed any tendencies to be controlling with their children. All this contributed to my feeling more isolated and more dependent on my husband for social gratification than before.*

*Although we were having our personal difficulties, he was one of the few people I trusted to have the same parenting values as I. Now with my increased isolation and social dependency on Chris, something that used to be minor took on much greater significance. We always went to his family for holidays and they didn't like me. He was deeply committed to trying to build a closer relationship with them and was critical of me and wanted me to try harder to make my relationship with them work as he viewed me as the one with more psychological skills to do so. I resented this and felt betrayed. I was jealous of the effort he put into trying to get close to them. I wanted him to put that effort into getting closer to me.*

*We were caught in that old sex versus nurturing/cuddling struggle. He needed sex to feel closer because at that time it was the only way he could connect with his body enough to soften from the isolation caused by his extreme overwork. Then maybe he could feel connected enough to give me the kind words and gentle touch I craved. But I didn't feel sexual—especially if we'd been isolated or if he'd been critical or angry with me. I wanted kind words and cuddles, not sex. Because we were caught in this limbo, neither of us got what we needed so we stayed stuck and felt separate from each other.*

*There were numerous times when we came close to divorce. I think what saved us was not wanting to hurt our daughter and our own pure dogged tenacity and perseverance. We both had a strong commitment to working things out and taking responsibility for our personal growth. Unfortunately, we were both deeply traumatized as children. Fortunately, we recognized this, and knew that we could do something about it. We both took time regularly to discharge our old built-up distress using co-counseling (Revaluation Counseling—see Appendix C), sometimes on a daily basis with close friends and co-counselors—to cry and shake and rage and whatever it took—to work on our past hurts instead of staying stuck in our present condition of blaming each other for our situation. It helped us immensely to be continually reminded of the "false reality" of our current upset (i.e., our believing the other person was really doing something to us to cause our upset feeling) rather than realizing our behaviors were triggering early unexpressed intense feelings from past traumatic experiences, and we could reduce their grip on us by the release of emotions in the safety of our co-counseling sessions and thereby become more present to each other.*

*I want to say it's a miracle we kept our relationship together, but it wasn't. It was our very hard work and continuous effort to be honest with ourselves and each other, and to constantly recommit to each other, that has kept our relationship alive.*

Around the time these stories were written (nearly five years before the completion of the book) Chris and Barbara undertook some intensive couple's co-counseling work together at a retreat intensive, and along with the support of their ongoing co-counseling, are now closer than ever before.

## *Remembering What's Truly Important,* Greg, New South Wales, Australia

When we moved north in Australia, Greg and his wife were some of the first people we met, and their kids attended the same school as our daughter.

*In September, 2004, a flyer promoting an evening program titled "Why Men Leave" caught my attention. To be fair, I was originally attracted to the fact that the facilitator was Jack Travis—an author of several wellness books I was then reading. I remember thinking, "Why Men Leave? Well that doesn't apply to me. I am still with my family!" I decided not to go.*

*A little later I decided to go online and read Jack's article of the same name. This piqued my interest just enough to want to attend the workshop.*

*At the workshop, I sat and listened to people share their experiences. As I listened I suddenly realized—I did leave my family! Maybe not physically, but I definitely left emotionally.*

*My father left his wife and three children when I was five years old. This was something I vowed I would never do to my own family. I guess this is why I didn't leave physically.*

*My wife and I had always had a fantastic relationship and friendship. We spent most of our time together before we had children. When our first child arrived it was very noticeable that the time my wife and I had together was a lot less. I felt less important to her and it seemed she was always with the baby. When my son was seven months old I started a new business. While my wife remained totally focused on our son, my attention turned increasingly towards my work.*

*When our second son arrived two years later, my wife and I began sleeping separately. With two young children who woke many times to either be breastfed or comforted, I reasoned at the time that it would be better if we both were not sleep deprived. I was tired of being woken so many times a night and this affected my performance at work, and I was really moody with my wife and my son. It wasn't initially a permanent decision. I just wanted a few nights rest and eventually it stayed that way. I wasn't aware of how I felt about it, I guess I had really distanced myself from my feelings; they were too painful.*

*All my decisions and actions seemed to come from my head rather than my heart. An example of this is when my second son was booked in to have an induced birth, my wife came home and told me she had booked a Monday because she liked and trusted the doctor who was on that day. I got so annoyed with her because Monday was my busiest day and it would be inconvenient to reschedule all my patients. I made her change it to Tuesday (my day off), because that would be more logical. Looking back I am so ashamed of my selfishness, and I know she still is very emotional about this event.*

*By the time our daughter was born 18 months later, I now, in hindsight realize that I had emotionally left my family. I felt alone and rejected by my family. I was not coping well with the demands of fatherhood; I didn't play with them much or get involved in their daily activities. I focused on being a great provider.*

*Gradually our relationship began to worsen. I felt my wife was disappointed in me as a father and husband. She wanted me to bond more with our children, especially our eldest son, and I had no idea how to do this. I had different views on parenting than she, I was more traditional and she was very "new age." We argued a lot about the children, finances, work, and her social commitments. I felt her family and friends got more of her love and attention than I did and I was jealous. In my heart I loved my wife and the children immeasurably, but my day-to-day interactions with them did not reflect this. I disconnected from my family and made my work my prime focus. When people ask me how I felt at this time, I don't truly know—I guess I must have let work distract me from feeling.*

*About five years ago my wife came to me one day and said she wanted us to separate. When she said these words I went straight to my head and started to logically work it out. I had no real initial emotional reaction that I was aware of. I said "OK, let's divide up the stuff and work out all details." After about half a day of letting this sink in I actually began to feel a huge sadness and loss. I loved my wife and my children and I didn't want to lose them. I realized I would have nothing meaningful in my life if they were gone. I would have given up my career and all the money in the world to just keep them. That was a huge realization for me.*

*I did whatever counseling and workshops that were needed to work out our issues. I knew my wife was working on our relationship mainly because of the children, but I was doing it for us. It has been a challenge for me to re-connect to my family, and at times I still have to remind myself of what is truly important. Working hard and earning money is how I have shown my love and support to my family. My patterns are strong, but I find myself continuing the challenge to break them.*

*Every day provides a new opportunity for me to do this.*

## *Giving What You Didn't Get,* Kim, Dallas, Texas

Kim is a recent addition to our circle of friends and colleagues. She provided us with this story of healing that began with her pregnancy, and led to her founding Co-Active Parenting™ (see Resources).

*When I became pregnant with my daughter, I was simultaneously thrilled and in fear! Although I wanted a natural birth, like many first-time mothers, I ended up having a C-section. Looking back, this was the beginning of my journey of self-empowerment and the eventual healing of my most intimate relationship.*

*Even though I felt amazed, excited, and often blissful being with my baby, two things were overwhelming me in those early months of being a new mom. The first was the strong emotions that were triggered from having a C-section. It sparked years of repressed feelings of regret, shame, guilt, and frustration, and brought them all barreling to the surface.*

*I wasn't even aware that these feelings were in me, and it caused confusion about what was going on with me. I started to realize that my birth experience unearthed feelings of powerlessness. On the surface, I thought I was making my own birth choices, but my fear of not doing it "right" opened the door for others to take control. I did not have faith in my body's innate ability to give birth in a natural way or confidence in my decisions. In the end, it was my upbringing, my culture, my doctors, family, friends, and my husband who determined and guided my choices. I was left feeling a deep sense of sadness, lack of confidence, and disempowerment.*

*The second issue that was sparked, as a new mom, had to do with my deeply held beliefs about* men; *beliefs that I unconsciously overlaid onto my husband. Every time he would go to work, I had mixed feelings—on one hand, I was eager to have him away so I could devote attention to my daughter. On the other hand, I was resentful and angry when he was not there. Why was I feeling this emotional battle inside? I was surprised when I named what I was feeling: Men are never there when you need them. When they are around, they are uncaring, selfish and controlling. (In case you might be wondering where my beliefs came from, my mom still says that "men suck.")*

*Even though I was actually pushing him away, I was reacting as if my husband couldn't be counted on for support. I felt unsupported, overwhelmed, and alone, the same way I felt as a child with no one there supporting me. As I was being triggered, he withdrew more and worked more. We were disconnected, without intimacy, and continued growing further and further apart.*

*I coped by discovering and nurturing my connection with my daughter. As time went on, I bonded with her and began healing my childhood wounds through my parenting. When I held her, I imagined being held. Through singing to her, I found my voice. Through guiding her, I learned my values and priorities. As I listened to her, I felt heard. As I allowed her to express her feelings, I learned how to feel and express my own. Every time I validated her experience, I felt more alive. It was she and I! I was devoting all my attention to her. She was getting her needs met and I was healing at the same time.*

*With that mindset, I unconsciously continued pushing my husband away physically and emotionally, while expecting him to support me in all the "work" I was doing in caring for "my" daughter. I was in conflict; I wanted his support, but found myself feeling angry towards him. It really took a toll on our relationship. I knew that I couldn't continue living this way. I might as well have been a single parent, but I didn't really want that. Even the parenting part was a struggle for me, and I wanted to do a good job at it. I envisioned creating a nurturing family environment. That's when I made a commitment to find another way, and began my research.*

*Among the information I discovered was the importance of early attachment from both mother and father. It opened my eyes and gave me a deeper understanding of our own unmet needs as children, which continue to have an impact into adulthood. It is difficult to give what you did not receive!*

*Because it is difficult to give what you didn't get, I had to build a foundation from scratch! For example, I learned to connect with people I could trust, and with whom I found safety. Through different modalities, I learned to feel. I found role models that exhibited the love, fun, patience, and compassion that I wanted. Through school, research, reading, and practicing, I empowered myself with more confidence and then empowered my daughter. I used the challenges with which I was faced as opportunities for healing and growth.*

*Because of my commitment to shifting my perspective and changing my behavior, my family is now thriving. We are consciously "participating in living as a community," contributing to each others' wellbeing, and being mindful of our individual responses to what comes up. Thankfully, both my husband and I were committed to having a harmonious family unit, and this is what has saved our marriage.*

*My experience has motivated me to develop* Co-Active Parenting™ *to empower other parents to create an authentic bond with their children and nurture a strong family connection. You can start nurturing your own strong family connection even before your first pregnancy—and it's never too late to start.*

## *Bringing Healing to the Triggers,* Betty, Ukiah, California

Betty, our midwife almost two decades ago, shares her healing journey that led her to become a coach and teacher of Process Coaching (see Resources).

*During 30 years as a homebirth midwife, I learned that our experiences in utero, birth, and early childhood lay the groundwork for the quality of our lives, as well as our experience of the universe. Unmet infant needs do not disappear. During pregnancy and birth, as we become parents ourselves, this big bag of past wounds we carry is primed to be triggered and reenacted.*

*Of course, we want to be the best parents we can possibly be. Advice abounds on how to do everything "right," yet this only puts more pressure on us—we're bound to fail our expectations.*

*I believe our most important preparation for birth and parenting is bringing healing to the wounds in ourselves. Otherwise we are destined to reenact them unconsciously and pass them on to our children. Yet in order for real healing to happen, it has to be from a place of loving acceptance of ourselves and our experiences, rather than from fear or pressure to be different than we are.*

*How can we break the cycle of wounding reenacting more wounding, especially since the wounds needing our attention reside in the unconscious, not in the conscious mind that is trying desperately to bring order to these uncontrollable events of birth and parenting? In my case, it took the experience of infertility to wake me out of my coping mechanism of turning away from my painful feelings.*

*When our son was born, via adoption, it was one of the happiest days of my life! I wanted to nurse him—give myself fully to him. It was as if I was nursing my own inner child, giving myself what I hadn't gotten as an infant. Loving and nurturing him gave me so much! And my husband was willing to support us emotionally and physically.*

*We wanted to give our son the best we possibly could, and we knew that meant bringing healing to the triggers that parenting was bringing up for us. We knew we needed to shift our experience from unconscious coping into loving presence for whatever feelings were triggered.*

*Process Coaching was the key for helping us make that shift. We learned how to be our own healers, and how to lay the groundwork for healing to happen in the quickest, easiest and least painful way. We learned that real healing meant showing up with real love.*

*Any triggered feeling is an invitation to show up for a part of self, a child part, and bring it the love that it's never had. I am the healer bringing the medicine to a part of myself—and the one receiving the love. It's easy to relate to these feelings when we think of them as child parts of ourselves, rather than unwanted, unpleasant feelings. Our conditioning has been to judge these feelings, yet it's the judgments that make them feel unpleasant, not the feelings themselves. The same loving parenting that we want for our outer child, we can give to our own inner child parts. By bringing love to all our previously lost parts of self, my husband and I are modeling real love for our son.*

*I remember the overwhelming sense of anguish when I found out I wasn't going to be able to conceive a child. The anguish gave way to rage, grief, and feelings of abandonment by whoever was in charge of this universe! These feelings weren't new—they had been there for a long time, just triggered by my current situation.*

*With Process Coaching, I learned how to stay present with all of my feelings— the anger at feeling abandoned by God as a child, the fear of the unknown, the deep sense of being alone, the grief of all the loss that I had experienced as a child. I learned how to feel the energy of these feelings in my body, with loving acceptance, as if I was loving a child part of myself. It took practice to embody a new, healthier approach towards my feelings, and it's been well worth it. I have been able to nurture a deeper love in myself than I had ever known, and a wholeness of being that continues to unfold. It's the greatest gift I can give to me, my partner, and our son.*

*I am dedicated to bringing unconditional loving acceptance to the deepest parts of me, and to helping others do the same. My journey has taught me that only by experiencing real love inside us can we each create the truly loving world we desire.*

## Reverberations of Birth Trauma, Suzanne, Bayfield, Colorado

One of the earliest leaders of the natural birthing movement in the 70s, Suzanne Arms shares her story of her daughter's and her own birth.

*I would have had a much easier time giving birth to my daughter, had my mother told me what her life had been like and how she felt about my conception, pregnancy, and birth. There was trauma at each phase of my "primal" period, and that trauma was stored in my body, in my very cells, where it remained and contributed to great unhappiness in my life. My birth-related trauma directly contributed to the pathological level of fear of birth that I carried into labor. It made me fearful and tense and caused my labor to be extremely painful and complicated, despite my having wanting a natural, unmedicated birth and having taken birth classes to prepare for that. It also caused me to be passive and feel helpless.*

*The trauma I carried had other causes and dimensions. As I later discovered, my father did not want another child—me. His negative feelings about my existence had nothing to do with me, yet they affected me. He carried an unhealed trauma from childhood and PTSD from being a combat vet in WWII, which caused him to feel abandoned by my mother when she gave birth to my older brother (who committed suicide on my 21st birthday).*

*In addition to the traumatic imprint on me from my father, there was the high level of stress that my mother had throughout her pregnancy with me. She was alone, because my father was in combat. She carried both the ongoing fear of a possible German invasion of our country plus her fear of losing my father. Evidence now abounds that war hurts everyone involved and usually leaves trauma that extends down into the next generation. So war-related trauma and birth trauma exacerbate each other and shape entire generations.*

*In addition, there was definite trauma associated with my birth which, had I known about before entering labor, I could have understood and let go of at least some of my fear of dying. Only years later did my mother tell me that she went into labor with me on the one night of the week that her doctor told her not to go into labor, for it was his night to play poker with his friends. After waking up from the narcotics she was given, and finding herself having the urge to push, the nurse told her to stop pushing.*

*The narcotics carried a physical imprint of trauma for me, and the trauma my mother experienced when she was ordered to stop pushing, but could not stop created another form of trauma in me, because the nurse placed a menstrual pad against my mother's vagina and pushed my head back with every contraction, and forcibly held my mother's legs together (a fairly common practice in US hospitals at the time).*

*I was pushed back during the pushing phase for so long that, when the doctor finally arrived and allowed me to be born, I was nearly dead, and she did not get to see or hold me for three days. I have discovered that much of my fear of death has to do with my mother's fear that I would die from the nurse holding me back in the birth canal, plus the fear that she carried from having lost a baby just before she conceived me.*

*Her fears went straight into me. They combined with my own feeling of abandonment from the three days in the hospital nursery, alone in a crib, listening to crying babies, being attended by strangers, and forced to take artificial formula. This experience was compounded by the sense of being totally abandoned when I got home from the hospital and made to sleep in a separate room, and bottle-fed on a schedule.*

*We each have our own story and our story shapes our future. Knowing this early part of my story helped me understand myself better. Doing various forms of healing—mental as well as physical and emotional—over the course of many years, doing a piece at a time, has given me great insight into my own emotions. It has definitely lessened my morbid fear of death.*

*What have been the long-term effects of working to heal my own birth trauma? First, it has given me understanding and compassion for the trauma that my daughter carried from her birth that resulted in all kinds of drugs to speed up labor and anesthetize me. This led to her getting "stuck" in a posterior position in the uterus and needing forceps to be born. I can understand some of my daughter's patterns that are likely related to all the drugs she got through the umbilical cord, and then having to be mechanically pulled out, rather than making the journey to successfully birth herself, as every baby is designed to do. Birth is, after all, a developmental process for the baby as well as the mother!*

*Second, while I still carry the "imprint" in my body from all those early traumatic experiences, I have felt much freer in my creativity and in my ability to finish projects, without collapsing whenever I'm confronted with obstacles, as was my long-term pattern. My reaction to facing obstacles used to be to push, as if with my head, against a brick wall and when pushing didn't get the results I wanted, then I would collapse into hopelessness and almost catatonic depression, which lasted for weeks. Many a project went that way and, although I ultimately picked myself up and resumed my work on a project, it cost me a lot of energy and needless suffering.*

*Third, I have gained a great deal of compassion for the emotional struggles most people born today go through, which are rooted in feelings of hopelessness, helplessness, and lack of self-worth, stemming from early trauma they have probably never even looked at, much less understood. What I know from my personal experience of addressing and making healing from birth trauma a priority in my life has made me a stronger advocate and activist for biologically natural, normal birth for every mother and baby, for co-sleeping and "wearing" babies and fully breastfeeding them, for leaving baby's genitals intact. Also for helping mothers and babies heal any trauma that they may have from conception, pregnancy, and birthing their own child.*

*We are fortunate to live in a time when evidence and practices to prevent and heal birth trauma abound! Now our work is to spread the word to parents and professionals that birth trauma can usually be prevented and most often healed, to the benefit of everyone—families and society alike.*

## Opening Up Our Ability to Connect

In the remainder of Part III, we offer synopses of books from experts in the field of couples' communication, each selected because of their highlighting the importance of connection over mere problem resolution skills or behavioral change. Their books are replete with examples and information we can't begin to cover here. Our hope is that with these brief introductions, one or more will offer the insight, inspiration, and guidance that will entice you to read—and engage with their work.

But first, longtime colleague at the Wellness Resource Center in the 70s, Bobbie Burdett, who subsequently counseled us through more emotional "crises" than we would like to think about, here shares her experience as a wellness coach—helping people heal from the pain of disconnection. This is of special relevance to consider, before we head into the following synopsis from authors in the field of couples' communication.

While many of the couples' communication exercises presented in this book can serve to "reshape and rewire" us for connection, some people may not have the neurological equipment to facilitate this. As Bobbie says, we can *want* to connect with others, but if we don't have the neurological equipment to be able to feel them and empathize with them, it's pretty hard to do. Recent discoveries in brain science show us that the brain's and body's sensory and interpersonal capabilities are intimately connected. People who have a greater sensory awareness, also have greater abilities to empathize and connect with others. When, as infants and children, we feel the pain of disconnection too much, we can literally turn off those neural circuits in the brain. When we shut off the hurt, we also shut off our sensory acuity, which in turn shuts off our ability to sense and empathize with others. As we disconnect from the pain, we also disconnect from others.

Bobbie talks about how, with focus and attention, and repeated small steps, we can create new neuro-pathways in the brain and literally open up our ability to connect.

> *By consciously increasing first our sensory acuity, it can help us reawaken our internal world; then we can increase our ability to empathize and appreciate the internal world of others. We can change our brains in ways that wake up the parts of the brain and body that are necessary to deeply connect with others.*
>
> *An example can be seen in my coaching work with "Adam." He came to me with the goal of having a friend—perhaps even a partner. He came from an abusive, addicted family and had learned to shut himself down so that he wouldn't be hurt, which also prevented him from feeling close to people. Adam had never experienced true friendship. Without needing to explore the causes, which would be outside the purview of coaching, he was able to change his brain*

within 16 sessions over 5 months using the simple techniques of present-time awareness practices.

I shared with Adam very briefly how the brain works and what happens when we need to shut down part of it to survive. I asked him if he would like to do an experiment. He was intrigued and very curious to see what would happen.

I could see that Adam likely wasn't able to connect with others simply because the neurological equipment needed to connect was disengaged. Following what I'd learned from Dr. Siegel's writings (see Mindsight: The New Science of Personal Transformation[53]) and classes, I suspected that if Adam increased his sensory brain connections through a mindfulness practice, he would be more able to empathize and connect with others. I suggested that Adam do a simple walking exercise every day, even if for only a few minutes. In brief, it was to focus attention as totally as possible on one sensory channel at a time for short periods. He was to direct as much attention as possible—first to his breath for a few minutes as he walked, then to what he saw, then to what he heard, then what he sensed in his body. Finally, he was to bring them all together and see if he could hold awareness on all of them at one time. Adam practiced the exercise every day. His sensory life was unfolding, albeit in very small steps.

After about two months, our conversations started gravitating to his primary goal—connecting with others. By this time, his brain was changing. He now had more fully engaged sensory abilities that would allow him to connect with others. Now when he was talking with others, he was engaging all his senses. He reported that he noticed that he was talking less and people were more interested in him. After he reflected more on what was happening, he said he was actually able to feel himself and others at the same time. He was listening with his whole self and by doing so others wanted to connect with him. He could not remember a time in his life when he had had that kind of experience.

This is the connection for which humans are hardwired. Dr. Siegel calls this experience Mindsight—a delicious connecting experience of combining **insight** (the ability to be aware of your own mind and the mind of another) and **empathy** (the ability to feel your own mind/body and the mind/body of another)—that is often described as an experience of "feeling felt" by another. It's an integrated mind/body experience that is deeply satisfying and healing. Sue Johnson writes about this kind of connection and helps couples to understand and feel each other more deeply in Hold Me Tight (see Chapter 25).

Adam and I continued coaching for about six more weeks as he honed his communication skills. When we terminated our coaching agreement, he not only had one close friend, but he had a whole group of friends. Every year, at Christmas, his card lets me know how our work together has changed his life.

*Adam changed his brain using his focus and attention. Through repeated small steps he created new neuro-pathways in his brain and opened up his ability to connect. We can want to connect with others, but if we don't have the neurological equipment to be able to feel them and empathize with them, it's pretty hard to do.*

Adam used the Sensory Walk to help his brain wake up. Bobbie finds that other kinds of exercises, practiced regularly, can have similar effects. Many people use meditation or mindfulness practices such as sitting for a period of time and calming the mind by noticing the breath. Other practices such as yoga, tai chi, or chi kung (qigong) are also helpful. All help to awaken new neuro-pathways.

For clients with little time, Bobbie suggests they experiment with turning any daily activity that doesn't require a lot of mental focus into a mindfulness exercise:

*One busy mother turned her resented daily sweeping task into her mindfulness exercise. She decided to sweep with total mindful attention to each sensory experience in the task: the feel of the broom in her hands, what she heard, what she saw, what she smelled, the motions of her body, while also noticing her emotions and thoughts without getting caught by them. Each time she swept, she tried to notice something she hadn't noticed before, while holding awareness of what she'd noticed previously. Within a week, she couldn't wait for her sweeping task each day. She reported that it was her favorite part of the day. It calmed her mind and restored her body as she became more aware of her sensations. She emerged from sweeping ready for an evening of connection with her children.*

Bobbie emphasizes that there are many ways to increase one's sensory awareness; it's up to each person to find what works for them. Reading about it won't do it. A simple practice that you do regularly is what's needed. Find what most appeals to you and set up the supports that help you stay with it long enough to reap the benefits. By working with how we are hard-wired to connect, instead of working against it, it makes the process so much more enjoyable and workable for the long haul.

Once we are feeling more alive and able to connect, then we can learn the skills for connecting, such as deep listening, reflecting, and communication skills.

**Key Points**
- **The Power of Emotional Release:** Traumatized as a young child, Chris discovered co-counseling (Revaluation Counseling or RC). This is a process of healing through discharging our distressed emotions. It entails a simple process of two loving, intelligent humans taking time to listen deeply as each pours his or her heart out, one at a time, to the other.
- **Constantly Recommitting:** Chris' partner, Barbara, also traumatized as a child and similarly committed to healing, regularly discharged old built-up distress using co-counseling, sometimes on a daily basis with close friends and co-counselors—to cry and rage and whatever it took—to release past hurts and instead of staying stuck in blaming her partner for her situation.
- **Remembering What's Truly Important:** Greg did whatever counseling and workshops were needed to resolve his issues with his partner. It was a challenge for him to re-connect to his family. Everyday provides new opportunity for him to remind himself of the importance of this connection.
- **Giving What You Didn't Get:** Because it's hard to give what you didn't get, Kim had to begin from scratch. She committed to creating a nurturing family environment. She found role models exhibiting the parenting she wanted to emulate, and through study and practice, used the challenges she faced as opportunities for healing and growth.
- **Bringing Healing to the Triggers:** With Process Coaching, Betty learned how to stay present with all of her feelings—the anger, the grief of all the loss that she had experienced as a child. She discovered by experiencing real love inside her, she can create a truly loving world.
- **Reverberations of Birth Trauma:** Suzanne's personal experience of making healing from birth trauma a priority in her life, made her an advocate and activist for natural births and attachment parenting practices, and for helping mothers and babies heal any trauma that they may have from conception, pregnancy, and birthing their own child.
- **Opening Up Our Ability to Connect:** Some people simply don't have the neurological equipment to "rewire" for connection, and discovered how, with focus and attention, and repeated small steps, we can create new neuro-pathways in the brain and open our ability to connect.

# 23: SYNOPSIS: *DO I HAVE TO GIVE UP ME TO BE LOVED BY YOU?*

*I first encountered Jordan and Margaret Pauls'* Do I Have to Give Up Me to Be Loved By You? *in the early 80. Jack and I used their work in our series of seminars for helping professionals, "From Domination to Partnership." All quotes in this chapter are by the Pauls unless otherwise indicated.*

After many years of marriage and long careers as psychologists and marriage counselors, Jordan and Margie Paul concluded that traditional therapies, based on problem solving and changing behaviors, didn't produce sustainable results. People went back to their old patterns even after their problems had seemingly been solved. The Pauls came to recognize that the changes that had been made rarely affected the quality of the relationship. Couples were still not emotionally intimate—in other words, not feeling emotionally connected. They concluded that it is critical that we seek to understand and overcome the powerful hidden motives that drive our present behavior. In other words, the intent, purpose or unspoken motive behind what we do.

In *Do I Have to Give Up Me to Be Loved By You?* the Pauls underscore the importance of our understanding the themes of our own childhood. Because so many of the beliefs, fears, and protections that underlie our interactions with others originated in our earliest years, we need to revisit our childhood, not to find excuses or to assign blame, but to respect the important reasons behind our protections. As we have seen, most of our pressing issues, while seeming to be the product of present circumstances, in fact derive their power from childhood experiences. The parts of us that cannot stay open in the face of fear are really different ages of wounded children we carry within us. They "pop out" as soon as their fears of rejection, abandonment, domination, or engulfment are activated, responding to the fear by getting angry, giving in, withdrawing, or resisting. We will return to the inner child a little later, but for now we will focus on our adult reactions—driven by our inner child—to conflict, and the choices we make in the face of this conflict.

The Pauls' theory is based on the idea that all responses to conflict stem from only two intents—the **intent to protect** or **the intent to learn**. It's not the conflict, but what we *do* in the face of the conflict, that leads either to difficulties and distance or to freedom and intimacy—in other words, to disconnection or connection.

Here is an example many of us will be able to relate to: David wants to make love. He reaches out to Barbara when they get into bed and begins to caress her. Barbara sighs and turns her back to David, indicating that she's not interested. David feels disappointed, hurt, and anxious, but rather than experiencing his feelings and becoming open to learning about his own fear and the beliefs that are causing them, he gets mad at Barbara. David's anger hurts and frightens her, but rather than opening to learning about how to take care of herself in the face of David's anger, she either gives in to him or shuts down completely, effectively shutting him out so she won't be affected by his feelings. The disconnection is painful, palpable. Any resolution or understanding requires shifting intent from protection to learning.

The Pauls named their approach Intention Therapy. It focuses on:
- understanding and respecting the one intent that creates almost all difficulties in our relationships—the intent to protect ourselves against pain, especially pain of being disapproved of or rejected,
- helping people understand and take responsibility for their fears and protections rather than on solving the presenting problem—for example, teaching one person to come home on time and the other to forgive tardiness focuses on the problem but not the underlying fears and protections.

## The Path We Travel

The path we travel in any particular conflict will be determined by the intent we align with. The Pauls have brilliantly outlined the map of this territory with the chart that appears on the following page.

The chart notes both the conditions in which exploration may be effective, and the areas that may be explored in order to understand both the issue of the conflict and our protective intent. Before reading on, where we will look in a little more depth at the highlights of this journey, you might want to take a few minutes to locate those parts of yourself that hang out in Intent to Protect, and preview the road you will travel if you avoid personal responsibility and act out controlling behaviors—noting the negative consequences that inevitably follow.

Then try out the path of the intent to learn. Through assuming personal responsibility, you pass through the territory where you will learn about self and other, and arrive in the final resting place (at least until the next conflict) of intimate love and evolving relationship.

Of all the many, many conflict resolution techniques I have explored—personally and professionally—over the years, this basic question "Am I defending and protecting, or loving and learning?" is always the one to which I return. Checking in with the body to determine which mode I'm in can, in itself, create a profound shift—a breath of release, an opening of the heart. It is so simple—though, as you will see, it's not always easy.

## The Intent to Protect

We protect when we are upset. We are protecting ourselves against having to experience some pain we fear, just as David and Barbara did above. Our protections, learned in childhood, become automatic, instantaneous and for the most part, subconscious.

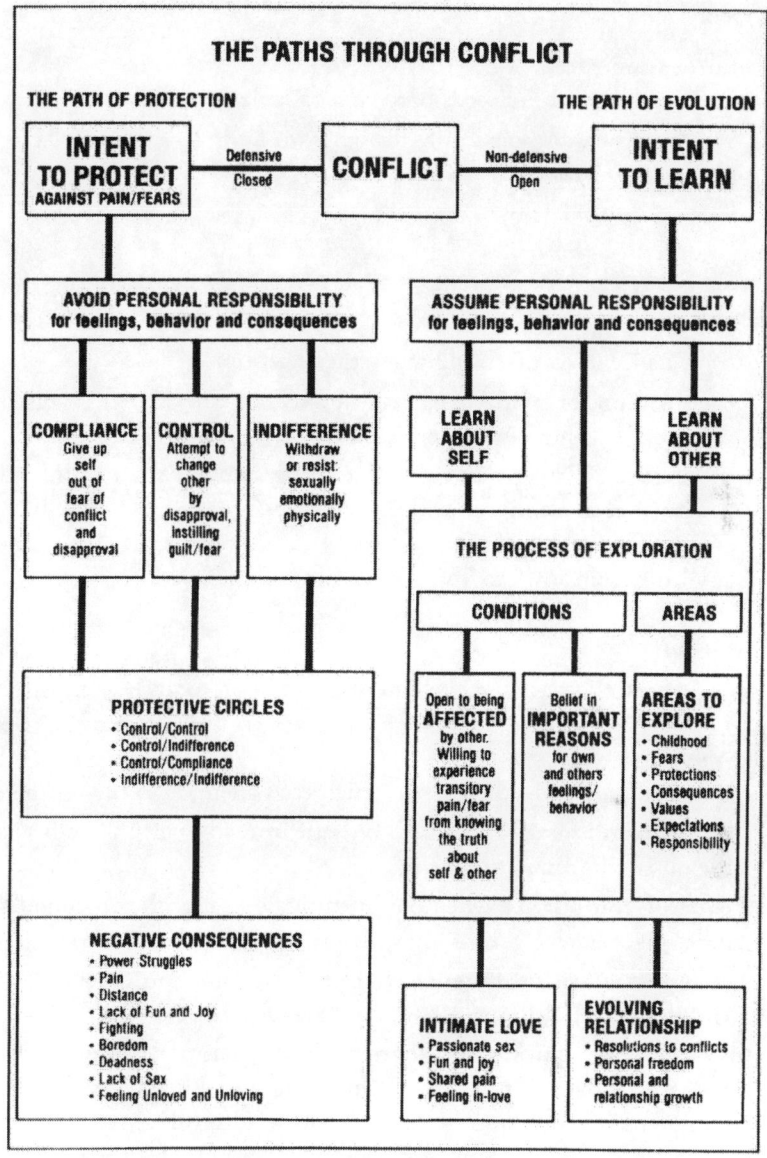

© 1983, 2002 Jordan and Margaret Paul, used with permission.

*The primary intent of a protective response is **not against another**, but **for yourself**.*

When in protection, we:
- become defensive—closed, hard, unavailable and cold,
- avoid personal responsibility for our own feelings, behaviors, and any resulting consequences,
- are closed to learning.

***The Pauls identify three categories of protection, or controlling behaviors:***
- compliance, or conforming to another's wishes;
- overt control, or trying to change another, whether it be through anger, accusations, complaints, tears, lectures, or lies; and
- indifference. This appears as our seeming indifference to avoid either disapproval or being controlled. We withdraw or resist sexually, emotionally, or physically; and can shut out our partner by means of anything from work to TV, sports, mediation, or depression.

## *Protective Circles*

When one partner protects, and the other responds protectively, i.e., when both partners are in "protect," a protective circle is created. Protective circles may take the shape of:
- a circle of **control-control**, in which each attempts to change the other;
- **control-indifference** in which one attempts to change the other, and the other withdraws or resists;
- **control-compliance** when one attempts to change the other and the other gives in and goes along with the controller's demands;
- or **indifference-indifference** when each becomes indifferent, withdrawing and living essentially separate lives.

These power struggles quickly turn lovers into adversaries. Attempts to solve the presenting or apparent "problems"—be it a lack of fun and joy, boredom, or feeling unloved (or unloving)—will inevitably fail until we recognize them as the inescapable symptoms of protective circles. Resolution requires we shift our intent from protection to learning.

## *Moving from Protection to Learning or Exploration*

*It is our increasing awareness of the futility and unhappiness of our protective choice that eventually leads one (and then both) of us to want to learn.*

You probably don't need the Pauls to tell you that if you are fighting with or feeling withdrawn from your partner, moving from protection to learning mode and starting an exploration feels nearly impossible—it requires your being vulnerable, reaching out. It's safer to wait for your partner to reach out to you. The Pauls have found that many people wait too long, settling for a distant relationship or divorce rather than risk being vulnerable.

Before we can move from protection to exploration, we must acknowledge our present intent, asking:

- Is my primary intent to be safe or to be loving?
- Is my primary intent to be right, to avoid the pain of being wrong and disapproved of?
- Do I want to know myself and my partner? Do I want to get closer?
- Is it worthwhile, right now, to open myself to unpleasant feelings for the sake of intimacy, or would I rather remain distant and safe?

We cannot be protected (closed, hard, defensive) and open to learning (open, soft, curious) at the same time. The two are mutually exclusive. Whichever intent is stronger at the moment will prevail.

## The Intent to Learn

The Pauls believe that our natural state is that of *curiosity*, and an intent and openness to learning inevitably emerges from that state. The intent to learn is evidenced in a willingness to:

- be vulnerable and open,
- feel our feelings directly rather than through the filter of our protections, and
- explore why each of us is feeling and behaving as we do.

When we want to learn, we are non-defensive: open, soft, curious, warm, available.

This openness to loving and learning opens the door to intimacy. Unprotected, we feel curiosity, compassion, sadness, or excitement. While sadness may at first appear to be misplaced in this listing, a moment's reflection will reveal that when we feel sad, we remain soft, and non-blaming, and so more open to learning.

*When we are open and willing to learn, everything changes.*

When both partners really want to learn about themselves and each other, exploration—simply spending time talking to each other about things that matter—can begin.

### *Exploration or Learning*

The goal of exploration is acceptance and intimacy.

Sincere exploration requires:
- a willingness to experience the transitory pain and/or fear that may accompany knowing the truth about ourselves and another;
- the belief that feelings, thoughts, and behaviors are always motivated by very important reasons—our needs, hopes, beliefs and fears.

When we believe there are very important reasons for behavior, we stop accusing our partner of being wrong and the door is open to understanding and respect. Engaged in exploration:
- we give up blaming our partner and assume personal responsibility for our behavior and any resulting consequences;
- we want to learn more about ourselves;
- we use our feelings to help us discover more about ourselves.

Helpful questions may include:
- What important reasons does my partner have for behaving that way?
- What part do I play in this?
- How is my partner's behavior affecting me (is it threatening me, or irritating me)?
- Why does it affect me that way?
- What personal issues does it stir up?
- Why is it so important to get my way—to be right?
- What fears, expectations, beliefs, lie behind my feeling threatened or irritated?
- How does my anger, irritation, or indifference affect my partner?
- How does s/he respond?
- What are the consequences?

Wanting to learn about our partner, we can ask:
- What are your fears?
- Why are you so afraid?
- Why do you see things the way you do?
- What are your unmet expectations?
- Why do you get angry when you're hurt or disappointed?
- What are your fears of not being in control?

Explorations are cooperative efforts to understand. When protected, we simply go around and around without real understanding or resolution.

The focus of the exploration is not a search for solutions to our problems or a commitment to change behavior.

*We search for new understandings, which give respect and dignity to behavior.*

Resolution and meaningful changes will automatically follow. Explorations are complete when both feel understood and loving toward their partner.

*When we explore until we understand each other we finally reach the most cherished state: feeling accepted and accepting, deeply respectful of self and of partner. This is the doorway to intimacy.*

## Our Feelings—Indicators of True Intent

The Pauls draw our attention to the difficulty that most of us initially face: our intentions are usually chosen on an unconscious level, and chosen so automatically that we don't even know that we've made a choice to protect or to learn. Protections are subtle and deeply ingrained, and so moving from an intent to protect and into an intent to learn can be very challenging.

The difficulty is that our protections are not easily recognized.

*We can't see our partner actually run into his or her hideaway; instead we see and feel coldness, anger, and other signals. The partner who has retreated often has as much trouble recognizing when he or she has run for cover.*

Our feelings are clear indicators of our true intent. Protected, we either feel angry, irritated, hostile, and resentful, or empty, removed, and indifferent. We may believe our partner is "making" us feel bad. Our partner will see us as defensive—cold, critical, tense, unyielding.

Communication *always* occurs on two levels: *what* is being said about the issue (money, sex, etc.), and *how* it is being said. Regardless of the words used, it is the tone of voice, body language, and facial expression that reveal *intent*.

It is the *how* that reveals the intent, and that *always* determines the course and outcome of any interaction. We always react (although usually subconsciously) to the way we are being spoken to. We react not to the words, but the intent behind the words.

The crucial first step is simply to recognize our protectiveness, to recognize when we are closed, hard, defensive. And congratulate rather than condemn ourselves for noticing. This in itself sets you on the path to learning. When we believe it's wrong to be protective (calling it weak, hostile, cold, unfeeling), we make it harder to see our own or another's protectiveness.

*The only outcome we are looking for, when we are in a true intent to learn, is to become a more loving human being.*

## Understanding *Why* We Protect

*Accepting that you and others have good reasons for your feelings and behaviors moves you out of judgment and into the heart of compassion, where loving and learning can grow.*

Sincere exploration rests on the assumption that all of us have very good reasons for feeling and behaving as we do. Understanding these reasons help us to better understand each other and to have more self-respect. Labeling behavior as "sick," needy, or neurotic, disregards the very important reason—the learned self-protective strategy underlying the behavior.

> *Working on a relationship often means working on protections rather than just on issues.*

Whether dealing with our own or another's anger, it can help to remember that anger is generally a self-protective strategy, covering up more vulnerable and primary emotions and feelings such as hurt, frustration, deprivation, fear, rejection, failure....

> *It will be easier to look at your protective behavior if you do not judge it as wrong or bad but rather look at it in the light of what works to create intimacy and joy.*

Conflict in personal relationships usually involves one or both of the partners' early childhood "buttons" or "triggers" being set off by the present situation. These highly sensitive issues usually engender strong feelings and we subsequently go off into reactive patterns. Resolution is dependent on our understanding more about ourselves and our partners. We all use a variety of ways to keep ourselves from feeling the real emotions generated by a particular conflict. For example, as anger is an easier emotion to tolerate than fear, many of us protect ourselves from facing our fear by feeling angry. Whether we are threatening our partner with our rage, dissolving in self-pitying tears, or using calm and rational logic to debate a point—we are being self-protective, in that we are not wanting to learn.

## Our Inner Child

As noted earlier, our wounded inner children "pop out" in the face of fear—whether it be fear of rejection, abandonment, domination, or engulfment—and respond to the fear by getting angry, giving in, withdrawing, or resisting. All the while, wanting love.

> *When fear blocks heartfelt feelings, it does not mean you are a bad or unloving person, or that you do not love yourself or another. It only means that fear is reigning. Heartfelt feelings are silent, and your behavior is not loving at that moment. Similarly, when heartfelt moments predominate, it does not mean that your fears are not there, only that they are not getting in the way of your heartfelt feelings, in any moment.*

When fear arises, we usually zip straight into our protections. Staying open in the face of fear may mean tending the scared child within, discovering loving action toward yourself that would heal the fear; or it may mean accessing a higher power.

As these wounded selves are tended to our natural, or core Self, can emerge. Conflicts are easier to work through when partners understand both their own and their partner's extra-sensitive issues and their origins.

Accepting the proposition that each of us has good reasons for our behaviors, we are more open to learning about ourselves and the other, and being genuinely interested and curious, we begin to shed light on the blind and deaf spots in our communications. Here we have it again:

*Seeing conflict as an opportunity rather than as a calamity puts it in a new light.*

*Until we develop a powerful, loving adult self, capable of staying in charge in the face of fear, we will continue to collapse into our learned protective behavior when our fears are activated.*

Whether the connection is to a Nurturing Parent, or a spiritual guide, by connecting to a source of love and wisdom beyond the limits of our wounded self, we can begin "embracing rather than being" our wounded self.

## Blocks to Moving from Protection to Learning

Protective responses run deep, and protective circles are activated in an instant, so that it can be difficult to go directly from a conflict into an exploration. Over time, with practice, protections lessen and we move more easily from protections to learning. The usual pattern is to move on the Path of Evolution when we're feeling strong, and dive back to the Path of Protection when frightened. If, in that moment, we can't shift from protection to learning, remember that simply being aware of the path we are on, and our reason for choosing it, is a big step and an indication that you have already changed.

If you're anything like Jack and me, you will find many a time when you feel certain you are in "intent to learn," and so you begin to dialogue and resolve the upset with your partner, only to find wham, you are right back into protect and defend mode. Even now, though we think we "should know better," we still get caught, though we are much more skilled (as one would hope) at reclaiming the state of mind to recognize we are—within seconds or minutes of our beginning the dialogue—in protect mode—and call a timeout. And, of course, we are much more able to identify when we truly are in a place of loving and learning, or of protecting and defending, before we head full pelt down the wrong track. These reactive patterns are so deeply embedded, it takes a lot of practice and persistence—and forgiveness—to reclaim a place of loving and learning as our "natural state."

The process for reaching resolution is the same for an issue. When we let go of the anxious search for solutions in favor of fascination with the process of, then we can explore—not how to change or what to change to—but *why* things are the way they are, and what is getting in the way of each of us having what we want.

## When He/She Remains Closed

If your partner refuses to talk or continues to blame you even when you have remained open for a long time, you can only accept your partner's choice, after making it clear you would like to continue to explore when he or she is ready. Releasing the pressure, in itself, can be helpful.

> *Most people leave relationships convinced that the other person is at fault, never understanding their part in creating the difficulties. If they can't see that, however, divorce is merely the prelude to another marriage in which two protected people make life difficult for each other.*

Exploration of a conflict does not guarantee change. If there are no changes, even after repeated explorations, the Pauls offer these options:
1. We can continue to try to get the other to change with some form of controlling behavior, which will only result in a deeper power struggle;
2. We can accept the situation and attempt to find ways to take care of ourselves in the ace of the situation as it is;
3. We can leave. This is an option when the situation is intolerable and we realize it isn't going to change. However, in the Pauls' experience, most people leave before having fully explored the situation or looked for better ways to take care of themselves. They propose that the time to consider leaving is when you are able to consistently stay open in the face of conflict, but your partner remains closed, and the situation is harmful or intolerable.

Caution: Before determining that your partner really is not open to learning, thoroughly check how open *you* really are. This is not easy to do, as friends and even a therapist may not see the way you really are with your mate.

> *A major question that often arises is "What if the other does not open to learning about himself/herself?" That certainly is a possibility. All you can do is open the door for learning. In a disconnected interaction, that door is blocked. With a connection to your feelings, there is a greater possibility that the other person will walk through that door. Although he or she may miss a golden opportunity by not taking advantage of the open door, you have made it a little safer for him or her to walk through it later.*

> *However, it is also possible that the other may never be interested in self-knowledge. You cannot have control over another person's choices—all you can do is perhaps influence him or her with your openness. If another person does not open, you will not be intimate with that person, but you will have achieved something perhaps even more valuable—the self-esteem that accompanies staying connected to your feelings.*

## Key Points

- Intention Therapy, developed by Jordan and Margaret Paul, perceives all responses to conflict as stemming from only two intents—to learn or to protect. The intent we choose determines whether we further disconnect, or connect.
- Protections were learned in childhood, as a means of protecting ourselves against experiencing pain or fear.
- Our wounded inner child "pops" out in the face of fear—whether it be of rejection, domination, engulfment—and we react to *protect*, with anger, resignation, withdrawal or resistance.
- Conflict usually involves one or both partners' early childhood triggers being set off. As our wounded selves are tended to, our natural or core self can emerge. Conflicts are easier to work through when partners understand both their own and their partner's extra-sensitive issues.
- Labeling behavior as sick, needy or neurotic disregards the learned self-protective strategy underlying the behavior, and needing our compassion and attention.
- In protection mode we are defensive—unavailable; avoiding personal responsibility; closed to learning.
- In learning mode, we are curious, non-defensive, available, warm—vulnerable and open to exploring why we are feeling and behaving as we are.
- The key question is always: Am I defending and protecting, or loving and learning?
- When both partners are in protect, lovers quickly become adversaries. Resolution requires shifting intent from protection to learning.
- When we are open and willing to learn, everything changes.
- Working on a relationship often means working on protections rather than just on issues.
- Simply being aware of the intent we are in, and our reason for choosing it, sets us on the path to learning.

# 24: Synopsis: *The Unexpected Legacy of Divorce*

I was struck by the Pauls' comment at the closing of the preceding chapter that most people leave a relationship before having fully explored the situation and without looking for better ways to take care of themselves and their families. I realized that a crucial element in fully exploring a possible separation should include the impact of any such decision on the children. And so I set out to learn about the impact of divorce on children. The resulting information is of particular importance to new parents, given that an estimated 80% of divorces occur in the first nine years of marriage.

*The Unexpected Legacy of Divorce* by Wallerstein, Lewis, and Blakeslee,[54] literally fell into my hands. This book is the only long-term close-up study of divorce conducted. It brings to light the nature of our "divorce culture," illuminating the largely unrecognized and unspoken reality that when children of divorce become adults, no less eager than their peers who grew up in intact families for passionate love, sexual intimacy, and commitment, they are badly frightened that their relationships will fail, just as their parents did.

> *Note: For parents who have divorced, please remember the importance of distinguishing between guilt and regret. Guilt is what we feel when we knew better and didn't act on what we knew. Regret is the sadness we feel when we learn something new that we wish we had known earlier.*

Today a quarter of adults under 44 in the US are children of divorce. This means that today in the US alone, millions of people are struggling with the residue of divorce in their personal lives. Until a few decades ago, marriage was considered a lifetime commitment. Almost overnight, changes in family law in the late sixties in California and other states determined that couples were now able to end unhappy marriages without proving fault or pointing blame, and could, presumably, go on to make happier marriages. Almost without exception, most assumed that the lives of our children would improve as well.

In reality, no one had any idea of how the next generation would be affected. *The Unexpected Legacy of Divorce* dispels the myths that if the parents are happier, the children will be happier too; divorce is a temporary crisis because children are resilient and resourceful; and divorce automatically rescues children from an unhappy marriage. High conflict marriages often lead to high conflict families after divorce, with no relief for the children. Divorce may rescue children from a violent or cruel marriage or a marriage of unremitting high conflict, but these situations fall in the minority. For most children, divorce is a watershed event that permanently alters their lives. The world is newly perceived as a far less reliable, more dangerous place because the closest relationships in their lives can no longer be expected to hold firm. Few parents realize that their children can be reasonably happy despite a failing marriage.

And divorce isn't simply one failed marriage. A child does not experience one huge loss of an intact family, then stability and happy marriage. The experience is not one, not two, but many more losses. As parents go in search of new lovers and partners, each throws the child back into turmoil, and the impact of repeated loss is cumulative and children learn that love is fleeting.

Still, the myths persist. For example, since so many children have experienced their parent's divorce, kids nowadays don't worry so much. It's easier. If I feel better, so will my children. There is no stigma. It's no big deal. And children raised in bad intact families are no better off.

Wallertstein affirms that each child experiences divorce "single file." Just because others are suffering, it doesn't reduce their suffering. At a breakup, children are frightened, angry, terrified of being abandoned by both parents, and feel responsible for the divorce. Most are taken by surprise. Few are relieved. As reported earlier (chapter 7), children of divorce experience more depression, learning difficulties, and social challenges—and adult children of divorce have more psychological problems than those raised in intact families.

> **Qualitative versus Quantitative Research**
>
> Quantitative researchers have criticized Wallerstein, et al.'s research because of her reliance on a nonrandom sample, the absence of a comparison group from her design, and her "impressionistic approach to aggregating and reporting data"; however all styles of research have their limitations. Paul Amato's investigation, reported in *Reconciling Divergent Perspectives* concludes that while the impact of divorce on *all* children may not be as strong as Wallerstein claims, other research generally concurs with her findings.
>
> *The research literature concurs*: divorce negatively affects the lives of many children, and that compared with children with continuously married parents, children with divorced parents reach adulthood with lower levels of psychological wellbeing, have more problems forming and maintaining happy and stable intimate relationships, a greater likelihood of seeing their own marriages end in dissolution, and weaker ties to parents, especially fathers. Research also concurs with Wallerstein's reporting that the strongest consequences of marital disruption do not appear until offspring confront the challenges of early adulthood.
>
> Wallerstein herself acknowledges that *divorce is not universally detrimental to children*, and that many children of divorce reach adulthood as "compassionate, courageous, and competent people." Many conquer their anxieties about relationships and form happy and stable unions. She has also stated, "Children raised in extremely unhappy or

> violent intact homes face misery in childhood and tragic challenges in adulthood." As Amato concludes, Wallerstein does not give priority to these qualifications because her overriding goal is to learn about the inner world of these children as they matured, to 'see the world through their eyes'. This detailed, qualitative methodology is well suited to portraying the difficulties these children have in establishing healthy adult relationships and "capturing the richness and complexity of each person's experience." Seen in this light, her analyses represent useful descriptions of the "complex patterns of events, emotions, and experiences through which divorce can undermine children's sense of wellbeing and later functioning in close relationships."

## Divorce: a Long-term Crisis

Wallerstein et al reveals the veiled reality that divorce is a long-term crisis affecting the psychological profile of an entire generation. After divorce, childhood is different, adolescence is different, adulthood—with the decision to marry or not and have children or not—is different. The whole trajectory of an individual's life can be profoundly altered by the divorce experience. From the viewpoint of the children, divorce is a cumulative experience. At each developmental stage, children of divorce reassess their understanding of divorce. They will rehash it when they are grown and have children of their own. The major impact does not appear during childhood or adolescence but in adulthood as serious romantic relationships move center stage. As this study reveals, when the time comes to choose a life mate and build a new family, the effects of divorce crescendo. In adulthood, it affects their personality, ability to trust, expectations about relationship, and their ability to cope with change.

People raised in "good enough" intact families, who feel loved by their parents, rarely doubt that they have choices and that they'll be able to choose when the time is right. Despite the high incidence of divorce around them, those in the study who were raised in intact families never doubted they would marry a good person and have a stable life with children. Those from an unhappy marriage that stayed together brought more guarded hopes and expectations. They may have had a hard time deciding to marry, but they also had experienced a model of people who stayed together "through thick and thin" to protect their children. Adults from troubled marriages that stayed together came to marriage with serious concerns that they would repeat their parents' experience, along with a firm resolve to keep that from happening.

They used their parents' marriage as a model that they could shape to their liking. They did not doubt the very possibility of a happy marriage, even if their parents had failed to attain it, and deliberately used their parents' example in the early years of their own marriage when it's deeply reassuring to have an external model of stability.

Wallerstein found the power of this symbol was revealed when much older parents decide to divorce. One might think that the grown children of such couples might feel sad but not devastated. After all, they're adults. They're not losing the protection of an intact family, familiar surroundings and other supports. But grown children, too, are profoundly distressed. Divorce sends shock waves through their world. Suddenly they're propelled into examining their own relationships and worrying what and whom they can rely on and for how long. Despite their passionate hope for a good marriage, children of divorce carried a much higher expectation of failure and only a sketchy sense of how to go about protecting their relationships. Some decided to stay away from loving, or only get involved with those they didn't care about so they wouldn't get hurt. Others chose not to feel. They had concluded, logically, that nothing is stable.

Wallerstein discovered that most children of divorce find themselves barren of good memories of how a man and woman live together. At adolescence, the significance of the absence of an internal template of a couple relationship became a central impediment blocking their developmental journey. While parents may have thought their divorce was wise, for the child it meant: if they failed, I can fail too. Seeing more and more failed relationships, reinforces the belief that failure is inevitable. From the outset, they were more anxious and uncomfortable with the opposite sex, and it was harder for them to build a relationship and allow it time to develop.

The contrast between children of divorce and children from good intact homes as they reached adulthood and went in search of love, sexual intimacy and commitment was striking. Adults in their twenties from reasonably good, or even moderately unhappy intact families, had an understanding of the demands and sacrifices required in close relationship—and memories of how their parents struggled and overcame differences. They had developed a good general idea about the kind of person they wanted to marry. Most importantly, they didn't expect to fail. Adults from divorced families were at a greater personal disadvantage. Anxiety about relationship was the "bedrock of their personalities and endured even in happy marriages, as they lived in the shadows of their fears of disaster and sudden loss, of abandonment, betrayal, rejection."

Fortunately for many, these fears were conquered by their late twenties and thirties, but only with struggle, courage, and perseverance, and learning from their own failed relationships. Many emerged stronger for their struggles. They did not take relationships lightly, and most maintained a reverence for good family life. Two out of three adults in the study had decided not to have children and cited divorce as the main reason. They had little confidence in their ability to raise a happy child. Others were afraid a child might destabilize their marriage. Most thought long and hard about parenthood before taking the plunge. Those who chose to parent, committed to providing their own children with what they missed. They retained some serious residues—fear of loss, of change, that disaster would strike—and were terrified by the mundane differences and inevitable conflicts found in every close relationship. Others went on to repeat the same mistakes their own parents made. Others led lonely lives, afraid to get involved in relationships that they thought were doomed to fail.

## Is There a Best Time? The Hidden Costs

Of course, there is the frequently asked question: is there a best time to get a divorce? Wallerstein's answer: "It depends" ....on a host of factors, including the quality of marriage (is it violence or boredom behind the decision) and the quality of the post divorce family over the long haul. That said, the youngest children tend to suffer the most. At an age when they need constant protection and loving nurturance, their parents are in turmoil.

Many parents today determine, post-divorce, to put their children first and so protect them from many of the adversities touched on above. Yet, Wallerstein cautions, the prevailing advice—don't fight—does not protect children from experiencing the same sorts of difficulties in adulthood as do those raised in less cooperative families. It doesn't protect children from feeling anxious when they grow up and go in search of love and intimacy. The safety net that good post-divorce parenting provides in childhood is irrelevant in adulthood. The sense that a loving, faithful lasting relationship remains out of reach is a residue of divorce unrelated to the conflict at the breakup.

*The impact of the parents' divorce echoes and crescendos in adulthood whether the parents were civil or not.* —Wallerstein, et al.

Years ago Erik Erikson concluded that childhood and society are vitally connected. What does it mean that a million new children a year are added to our "march of marital failure"? As this study reveals, it's happening so fast we scarcely notice, and affecting us all in ways we don't understand. Yes, we adults have greater freedom and more opportunity than perhaps ever before, but there is a hidden cost. Many children, and adults, are not better off. It appears that after most divorces, one of the couple feels much better while the other feels no better or even worse.

Of course, there is another cost. Children of divorce learn those very same lessons that infants and children learn when their very early needs for attachment are not met—people cannot be trusted, love is uncertain, and human attachment is a dangerous proposition. Divorce then, compounds the problem of dads leaving—of couples separating. Indeed, it compounds the problem of their even hoping that they can experience a lasting relationship.

## Moderating the Impact

How can we maintain the advantages of divorce but protect children and help parents mute the long-term effects of divorce on future generations? Wallerstein's recommendations echo the message in *Why Dads Leave* and will not be new to you, but bear repeating. First, we need efforts to strengthen marriages. We need to fully understand the nature of contemporary man-woman relationships, to appreciate the difficulties modern couples confront in balancing work and family, separateness and togetherness, conflict and cooperation. Second, is the need to address the imbalance between demands of workplace and needs of family life—we need changes in corporate and public policy to consider their impact on families and buffer some of the stresses, especially in the early vulnerable years. And we need to help prepare the young for marriage—how to choose a partner and build a relationship—especially as growing numbers of young adults are without role models. While it is uncertain whether educational intervention can replace the learning that occurs naturally over many years within the family, premarital education and marriage enrichment classes and marital counseling can all help.

What does Wallerstein say to parents contemplating divorce? She is neither against divorce, nor does she assert that divorce is always detrimental to children. She simply urges that we face the complexities full on, and make any decision in full view of the realities: Consider staying together for the sake of the child, examine what you have as a family, and take a realistic look at what divorce entails.

> *Dr Phil McGraw ["Dr Phil"] spoke of this on a recent [television] program when he was working with a couple on the verge of divorcing. His emphasis was on the importance of the parents together exploring every possible avenue to resolving the difficulties in their relationship, prior to making the decision to divorce. Then, if they did decide to separate, they could say to their children, with absolute integrity, that they were sorry, they had explored every possible avenue for staying together and now knew that for there to be harmony in the family, they needed to divorce. This reminded me of the Pauls' observation noted at the beginning of this chapter—that most people leave a relationship before having fully explored the situation. My ex-husband and I were one of those couples. It's a regret I now carry. At the time, I didn't know any better.* —Meg

In closing, the young adults of this study offer hope and promise for future generations. Despite their firsthand experience of seeing how marriage can fail, they sincerely want lasting, faithful relationships whether in marriage or in a lasting cohabitation. No single adult in this study accepted the notion that marriage is going to wither away. They want stability and a different way of life for their children. They accept divorce as an option but believe divorce in a family with children should be the absolutely last resort. Those who are happily married feel blessed—and eager to rewrite history, not repeat it.

Better still, let us do all that we can to ensure that our children do not need to rewrite this aspect of their lives.

## Key Points

- An understanding of the repercussions for children of their parents separating, is of special relevance to parents, given that some 80% of divorces occur in the first nine years of marriage.
- Myths about the impact of divorce are rampant: if the parents are happier, the children will be happier; divorce is a temporary crisis because children are resilient and resourceful. For children of divorce, the world is newly perceived as a far less reliable, more dangerous place because the closest relationships in their lives can no longer be expected to hold firm.
- The myths persist: So many children have experienced divorce that kids today don't worry so much. It's easier. There's no stigma. It's no big deal. And children raised in bad intact families are no better off. Right? *Wrong*....
- Each child experiences divorce "single file." Just because others are suffering, it doesn't reduce their suffering. Children of divorce experience more depression, learning difficulties and social challenges, and have more psychological problems than those raised in intact families.
- After divorce, childhood is different, adolescence is different, adulthood is different. In adulthood the effects of divorce crescendo, affecting their ability to trust, expectations about relationship, and ability to cope with change.
- The contrast between children of divorce and children from good intact homes as they reach adulthood and go in search of love, sexual intimacy and commitment, is striking. Adults from divorced families are at a significant personal disadvantage.
- The prevailing advice—don't fight—does not protect children from experiencing the same difficulties in adulthood as do those from less peaceful families. The safety net that good post-divorce parenting provides in childhood is irrelevant in adulthood—the sense that a loving, faithful, lasting relationship is out of reach, remains a residue of divorce.
- Adults have greater freedom and more opportunity than ever, but at a hidden cost. Many, children *and* adults are not better off.
- Despite seeing how marriage can fail, studies show that young adults sincerely want lasting, faithful relationships, whether in marriage or in a lasting cohabitation. They accept divorce as an option but believe divorce in a family with children should be the absolute last resort.

# 25: Synopsis: *Hold Me Tight: Seven Conversations for a Lifetime of Love*

*It was only recently that I discovered* Hold Me Tight: Seven Conversations for a Lifetime of Love, *by Sue Johnson, PhD. This book added yet another dimension to mastering this all-important, lifelong challenge of creating harmonious relationships. What especially excited me was her placing conflict within a frame of attachment and bonding.*

*This chapter is a synopsis of the especially relevant parts of her book. Unless otherwise indicated, all quotes are by Sue Johnson's.*

Having been successful with treating individuals and families, Johnson found herself at a loss when counseling warring partners—they didn't want insights into their childhood relationships, nor to be reasonable and learn to negotiate.

> *Love, it seemed, was all about non-negotiables. You can't bargain for compassion, for connection. These are not intellectual reactions; they are **emotional** responses.*

Johnson was mesmerized by the intensity of the struggles warring couples evidenced, and the way they often spoke of their relationships in life and death terms. Determining to simply stay with the couples' experiences and let them teach her about the underlying dynamics of romantic love, she found that there were key negative and positive emotional moments that defined a relationship. With the help of her thesis advisor, Les Greenberg, she developed a couples' therapy that was based on these moments, Emotionally Focused Therapy or EFT (not to be confused with the more widely known Emotional Freedom Technique).

The results from EFT were amazingly positive, but Johnson wasn't satisfied. She felt compelled to discover the *why* of the intensity behind the emotional dramas. Why did EFT work and how could they make it even better? Finally, in the midst of a charged dialog with a colleague, she was struck by the realization that romantic love was all about attachment and emotional bonding—our wired-in need for someone to depend on, a loved one who can offer reliable emotional connection and comfort. Love relationships were emotional bonds, representing an adult's innate need for safe emotional connection. A revelation! Bowlby's identification of the innate needs of infant and children for bonding and attachment, here applied equally to adults.

Primed with this framework of attachment and bonding, Johnson began to see the drama surrounding distressed couples in a different light; their intense emotions were part of a survival program created by millions of years of evolution. She was thrilled, but found little agreement for this premise among her colleagues—after all, adults should be self-sufficient, and able to control their emotions. It is only dysfunctional people, those who are "enmeshed" or "codependent" or "merged," who need or depend on other people. Therapists, colleagues admonished Johnson, are supposed to encourage people to stand on their own two feet.

She recognized that this was just like Dr Spock's advice on handling children—picking up a crying child creates a weakling: "Trouble is, Dr Spock was dead wrong when it came to kids. And so were my colleagues when it comes to adults."

## An Attachment View of Adult Love

While today it is widely accepted that children have an absolute requirement for safe, ongoing, physical and emotional closeness, the attachment view of adult love is "radically out of line" with our culture's established social and psychological ideas of adulthood: that maturity means being independent and self-sufficient.

It appears that we are emotionally attached to, and dependent on, our partners in much the same way that a child is attached to a parent for nurturing, soothing, and protection. EFT focuses on creating and strengthening this emotional bond by identifying and transforming the key moments that foster an adult loving relationship: being open, attuned, and responsive to each other. More on these key moments a little further on.

## Can I Count on You?

*We are never more emotional than when our primary love relationship is threatened.*

Johnson has found that most couples' fights are really protests over emotional disconnection: our anger, criticism, demands are really *cries for connection*. They are our attempts to draw our mates back in emotionally, and to re-establish a sense of safe connection. The fact that EFT has helped over 85% of those couples who have practiced it to make significant changes in their relationship—and that these changes appear to last—would seem to indicate she's got something right!

*Underneath all the distress, partners are asking each other: Can I count on you—depend on you? Are you there for me? Will you respond to me when I need, when I call? Do I matter to you? Am I valued and accepted by you? Do you need me, rely on me?*

Johnson finds the idea that these demand-distance spirals are all about attachment panic is still revolutionary to many psychologists and counselors. Learning problem-solving or communication skills, becoming aware of our unmet early needs, or taking timeouts, are ineffective unless we address the fundamental need for connection and the fear of losing it. In other words, unless they show us how to connect or stay connected.

## The Attachment View of Adult Love

The attachment view offers a new frame for viewing relationships. Very simply, it told Johnson:

1. The powerful emotions that erupted in her couples' sessions were not irrational. Partners acted as if they were fighting for their lives because they were doing just that. The need for safe emotional connection is wired by millions of years of evolution, and potential loss of connection activates a primal panic response.
2. Attachment needs and emotions underlie negative interactions. When safe connection seems lost, partners go into fight or flight mode. Both are terrified. Trouble is, once the pattern is activated, it spirals and confirms their fears. Rational skills don't work because they don't address the need for emotional connection. The pattern can only be quieted by a partner's moving emotionally closer—to both hold and reassure.
3. Key moments of change are moments of safe attunement and connection, moments of secure bonding when both partners hear each other's cries for connection and respond with soothing care—these moments change everything. They answer the pressing question: Are you there for me?

Note the remarkable similarity between these adult needs for attunement and connection—and how they are met—with that of our babies and young children.

> *Babies feel connected to you when they understand that you hear their voice, that you take in how strongly they are feeling, and that you are willing to respond... if only to stay near them. The most powerful tools of healing are available to any mother or father, in fact to any loving adult. Listening. Holding. Gentle rocking. Singing. Any or all of these ways to connect with your baby can change their world for them. Neuropsychologists tell us that loving human touch can trigger the secretion of feel-good brain chemicals, such as oxytocin.* —Robin Grille, *Heart-to-Heart Parenting*

Johnson found that as clients learned to view their emotions, needs, and conflicts through an attachment frame, and learn how to reach for moments of connection, they began to understand their own unspoken longings and "irrational" fears, and could connect with their partners in a new way. Learning that there was nothing "wrong" or "immature" about their longings and fears, they did not have to deny or hide them.

## Key to Lasting Love

The basis of EFT are conversations that are aimed at encouraging a special kind of emotional responsiveness that Johnson has found to be key to lasting love for couples.

This emotional responsiveness is marked by three main components:
**Accessibility**: Can I reach you?
This means staying open to your partner even when you have doubts and feel insecure, struggling to make sense of your emotions so that they are no longer overwhelming, and tuning in to your lover's attachment cues.
**Responsiveness**: Can I rely on you to respond to me emotionally?
This means tuning in to your partner and showing how his or her emotions, especially attachment fears and needs, impact you; and sending clear signals of comfort and caring when your partner needs them. Such responsiveness touches us emotionally and calms us on a physical level.
**Engagement**: Do I know you will value me and stay close?
Emotional engagement means the very special kind of attention we give only a loved one—gazing at them longer, touching them more, being *emotionally present*.

Johnson offers the acronym A.R.E, and the phrase "Are you there, are you with me?" as an easy way to remember the three components of emotional responsiveness.*

## In the Absence of Emotional Safety

Losing connection with our loved ones jeopardizes our sense of security. We all experience some fear when we have arguments with our partners, but for those with secure bonds, it's a momentary blip, the fear quickly dissipates. For those with weaker bonds, the fear can be overwhelming. Swamped by "primal panic," we are likely to react in one of two ways:
1. We become demanding and clinging in an effort to draw comfort and reassurance from our partner (notice me, be with me, I need you), or
2. We withdraw and detach in an effort to soothe and protect ourselves (I won't let you hurt me, I'll act cool, try to stay in control).

Our chosen strategy—becoming demanding and critical, or withdrawing and shutting down—partly reflects our natural temperament, but mostly it reflects the lessons we learn in the key attachment relationships of our past and present.

---

* Men and women express their attachment needs and fears differently. While men typically talk of feeling rejected, inadequate, and a failure, women talk of feeling abandoned and unconnected. Women appear to have one additional response to distress, the "tend and befriend" response. Women reach out more to others when they feel a lack of connection.

Because we can learn with every new relationship, our strategy is not fixed. This means not only, as can we be critical in one relationship and withdraw in another, it also means, as Johnson's work is testimony to, that we can learn new and healthy patterns of relating and connecting.

Take a moment to consider: can you identify with playing out either or both of these patterns with your partner? Can you see how these patterns push you further and further apart from the very one you are trying to connect with?

Either reaction initiates a spiral of insecurity that pushes us further and further apart.

It is amazing how deeply these reactive patterns are entrenched in our circuitry. I can recall more times than I would like to own, when I am fully aware that what I am doing is not going to get me what I want—reconnection—but it's almost like I'm caught in a vise that keeps me reacting in ways that I can see, even while in the midst of the conflict, won't get me what I want. I am withdrawing and detaching, and this is pushing Jack further and further away from me. What I need to do is soften and turn toward him. It can seem so hard. To choose love rather than fear. But oh, what a beautiful shift it engenders.

## Demon Dialogues

New beginnings start with knowing how we create the trap we are in, how we have deprived ourselves of the love we need. Strong bonds grow from resolving to halt the cycles of disconnection.

The facts of the fight (whether it's about who should change the diaper, about your sex life, or your careers) aren't the real issue. The issue is the strength and security of the emotional bond with your partner. It's about **accessibility, responsiveness,** and **emotional engagement**.

Researchers have identified several such damaging patterns, and Johnson names the three most basic of these, the "Demon Dialogues." By far the most dominant is the Protest Polka, wherein one partner becomes critical and aggressive, the other defensive and distant. John Gottman (see Chapter 27) has discovered that couples caught in this pattern in the first few years of marriage have more than an 80% likelihood of divorcing within 4–5 years. It is not the level of conflict, but a lack of emotional responsiveness that is the best predictor of how solid a marriage will be five years into it.

When we can see that the negative patterns we are caught in—the Demon Dialogues—have a life of their own and are hurting us both, rather than just focusing on the other's last response and reacting to it, we can begin to recognize that in fact, the enemy is not our partner, but the spiral we are caught in.

Negative patterns are triggered when one partner tries to reach for the other and cannot make safe emotional contact. When we can appreciate that we are both victims of the dialogue, and are able to show more of ourselves, to risk sharing deeper emotions, the conflict can soften, and we can feel a little closer. We all get caught in one or all these negative interactions, but in less secure couples, they become habitual responses.

Johnson tells us that reconnecting requires allowing our emotions to move us into new ways of responding to each other. This also requires we take risks, showing our softer sides. When, as withdrawn partners, we can confess our fears of loss and isolation, we can talk about our longings for caring and connection. This takes great courage but can serve wonders in "moving" our blaming partner into responding more tenderly and sharing his own needs and fears.

*It was as if both people suddenly stood face-to-face, naked but strong, and reached for each other.*

These moments move a couple into a new kind of loving responsiveness, safety and closeness—in other words, connection.

*Hold Me Tight* is replete with examples of how couples move in and out of these patterns. In the interim before you can purchase her book, play like a detective. See if, in the very brief synopsis below, you can identify the patterns that most threaten your current love relationship, and sentence by sentence, step by step, decode a remembered interaction between your partner and yourself. Can you recognize the hidden cries for connection, and how the pattern itself, not your partner, is the enemy? It will help if you can step back and do this with some humor, as well as heart—for your loved one and yourself and your misguided efforts to connect. Remember—it's the wiring. This is heavy stuff. Take it lightly. Note the likelihood is that we also play these patterns out with our children! OK, here we go.

**1. Find the Bad Guy:** this is a dead-end pattern of blaming each other for the distressed relationship. It keeps us miles apart and blocks re-engagement. While the purpose is self-protection, the main move is mutual attack, accusation or blame. It begins when we feel hurt by or vulnerable with our partner, and out of control. We blame in an attempt to get control, to be Top Dog.

When loving ways of connecting are the norm, we can reach out to each other after we've cooled down. But once the pattern becomes habitual, the attacks and hit-backs get stronger and stronger.

The secret to stopping the pattern is recognizing no one has to be the bad guy. The accuse/accuse pattern itself is the villain, and you and your partner the victims. When we recognize proving the other wrong just pushes us further and further apart, we can begin to break the cycles. We can begin talking about what happened without it being anyone's fault. Getting this attack-attack dance under control is a first step towards building connection.

**2. Protest Polka:** Commonly recognized as a Demand-Withdraw or Criticize-Defend pattern, Johnson renamed this the Protest Polka, as she sees it as a reaction to, or protest against, the loss of secure attachment.

The Protest Polka is all about trying to get a response.

*Attachment relationships are the only ties on Earth where any response is better than none. When we get no emotional response from a loved one, we are wired to protest.*

One partner reaches out, albeit in a negative way. The other steps back, and the pattern repeats. One partner is demanding, actively protesting the disconnection; the other is withdrawing, quietly protesting the implied criticism.

Characteristic expressions include: "These days he is always busy, always somewhere else. Even when he's home, he is on the computer or watching TV. I am shut out," and "I get mad. He just doesn't seem to care, so I smack him. I'm just trying to get a response from him, any response." "I'm not sure I matter to him. It's like he doesn't see me. I don't know how to reach him." "If I didn't push and push we would never be close."

Johnson points to the wealth of attachment themes playing out here: feeling unimportant or not valued by a partner; experiencing separateness in terms of life and death; feeling excluded and alone; feeling abandoned at a time of need or being unable to depend on a partner; longing for emotional connection and feeling anger at a partners lack of responsiveness; experiencing the lover as a friend or roommate.

When caught in a pattern of protest and pursuit, we talk of being enraged, frustrated, or upset, and this is what our partner sees. But this is only the most *superficial layer* of what is going on. Characteristic expressions include:

- "I can never get it right with her, so I just give up."
- "I don't matter to her. I come somewhere after the kids, the house, her family. Even the dog comes before me! I just bring home the money. So I end up feeling somehow empty."
- "I feel numb. Don't know how I feel. So I freeze up and space out."

Johnson skillfully deciphers the themes here, too:

- Feeling hopeless and lacking the confidence to act;
- Dealing with negative feelings by shutting down and numbing out;
- Assessing oneself as a failure as a partner, as inadequate; feeling judged and unaccepted by the partner;
- Trying to cope by denying problems in the relationship and attachment needs;
- Doing anything to avoid the partner's rage and disapproval;
- Using rational problem solving as a way out of emotional interactions.

In our society, women are usually first to pick up on distance, and more in touch with their attachment needs. So they are usually the pursuing, more blaming. Men, taught to suppress emotions, and also to be problem solvers, usually take the withdrawn role. Problem solving skills ignore the hot attachment issues that underlie the pattern. From an attachment perspective, the issue is emotional distance, and most problem solving skills don't address this.

Johnson explains how, if I appeal to you for emotional connection, and you respond intellectually to a problem rather than directly to me on an attachment level, I experience this as "no response." I want emotional confirmation and caring, not advice. She finds that while men may say they don't know how to respond on an emotional level, they do when they *feel safe*, most often with their children.

> *The tragedy here is a man may be doing his best to answer his wife's concerns by offering advice and solutions, not understanding that what she is seeking is emotional engagement.*

Sound familiar?

It is important to recognize that social beliefs keep us ensnared in the Protest Polka—most especially so when looking at the whole issue of connection/disconnection with respect to disappearing dads.

The single most destructive belief Johnson identified is that a healthy, mature adult is not supposed to need emotional connection, and so is not entitled to this kind of caring.

Unable to name and accept our own attachment needs, which are activated perhaps as never before in the transition to parenthood, we cannot send clear messages to others. As she says, it's so much easier to say, "Why won't you talk to me?" than to open up and ask that our need for loving connection be met.

> *To achieve a lasting, loving bond, we have to be able to tune into our deepest needs and longings and translate them into clear signals that help our lovers respond to us. We have to be able to accept love and to reciprocate, emotionally as well as physically.*

> *Above all we have to recognize and accept the primal code of attachment rather than attempting to dismiss and bypass it. In many love relationships, attachment needs and fears are hidden agendas, directing the action but never being acknowledged.*

Of course as you can see, the Protest Polka is not just danced by lovers, but by parents and children and anyone with close emotional ties to another. Steps in stopping the dance include catching yourself in it and discovering the patterns; recognizing the hidden calls for connection in the pursuit or the withdrawal; seeing the pattern, not each other, as the enemy; learning how to step to the side and create enough safety to talk about attachment emotions and needs.

If a safe, loving bond is to stay strong and grow, couples have to be able to repair moments of disconnection and step out of common dead-end ways of dealing with them that actually exacerbate disconnection by destroying trust and safety.

**3. Freeze and Flee** or **Withdraw-Withdraw**: This usually happens when couples feel so hopeless that they begin to give up and put their needs and emotions in the deep freeze, becoming numb and distant, with both stepping back to avoid hurt and despair.

Locked in self-protection, each is trying to act as if he or she doesn't feel and does not need. This is what happens when the pursuing critical partner of the Protest Polka gives up trying to get the partner's attention, and goes silent. Partners typically are polite to each other, even cooperative on pragmatic issues, but the love is gone. There is no emotional connection. This extreme distancing is a response to the loss of connection and sense of helplessness to restore it. The real problem is the hopelessness that colors it. The basic cues we see in infants and parents, and in lovers, such as prolonged gazing and physical caressing, become muted, then nonexistent.

## Sincere Apology

Sometimes people try to handle relationship injuries by ignoring them, but unresolved traumas do not heal. They require confrontation and healing. It can be very hard to show the core of our hurt to the one who hurt us; the pain is best understood when we relate it to our attachment needs and fears. Until the injured partners see that this pain has been truly recognized, they will not be able to let it go. For the injuring partner to take ownership of how they inflicted the injury and express regret and remorse, they will need to listen to and engage with their lover's pain, showing it has an impact on them. Sincere apology will always necessitate the injuring partner staying emotionally present and acknowledging the wounded partner's pain and his/her part in it. There is no room here for defensiveness or justifications. When the injured partner is able to accept the apology, the couple is on a new footing, and trust can begin to grow again.

While forgiveness is often spoke of as a moral decision, and that letting go of resentment is the right and good thing to do, the decision "to forgive" will not alone restore faith in the injuring person and in the relationship. What is needed is a healing conversation that fosters not just forgiveness but also the willingness to trust again.

Johnson encourages us to reflect on how difficult it is for us to apologize, even in small things. Can you recall a time when you voiced your regret in any of the following ways:

The four-second "where is the exit" apology. "Yes, well. Sorry 'bout that. What shall we have for dinner?"

**The minimizing responsibility apology.** "Well, maybe I did that, but..."
**The forced apology.** "I guess I am supposed to say..."
**The instrumental apology.** "Nothing is going to work till I say this, so..."

These token apologies can sometimes work for very small hurts, but otherwise they only increase the wounded person's pain.

**A sincere apology** might include statements along the lines of:

"I pulled away. I let you down."

"I didn't see your pain and how you needed me. I was too lost, afraid, angry, preoccupied. I just shut down."

"I didn't know what to do. I got all caught up in feeling stupid and worrying about doing the wrong thing."

Elements of a sincere and genuine apology include 1) the injuring partner making it clear to his partner that he feels and cares about her pain; 2) his explicitly telling her that her hurt and her anger are legitimate; 3) his owning up to exactly what he did that was so hurtful; 4) his expressing shame. He tells his partner that he too feels dismayed and disappointed by his behavior; and 5) his reassuring her that he will now be there to help her heal.

Sincere apology is "not just a statement of contrition, it is an invitation to reconnect."

## New Beginnings: Engaging and Connecting

Having identified the trap we are in and how we are cutting ourselves off from the love we need, and resolving to halt the cycle, we can begin rebuilding the bond. Just as with the Protest Polka, this, too, will likely be a dance—two steps forward and one step back.

Building and sustaining a secure bond requires the ability to tune into our loved one by deliberately creating moments of engagement and connection, actively furthering a sense of closeness. Stepping aside from our usual ways of protecting ourselves and acknowledging our deepest fears can be hard, even painful. Yet if we don't let our partner see our attachment needs, the chances of getting these met are minuscule. We have to send the message loud and clear for our partner to get it. If we are feeling unsure of our relationship, it is harder to risk being vulnerable, even to the point of denying the emotions and needs exist. If we have generally found others to be safe havens and we have a close bond with our lover, it is easier to keep our emotional balance when we feel vulnerable, connect with our deepest feelings, and voice that attachment longing that is always part of us. Engaging and connecting then requires asking "What am I most afraid of?" and "What do I most need from you?" It involves being able to openly and coherently speak your needs in a way that invites your partner into a new dialogue marked by *accessibility, responsiveness, and engagement* (A.R.E).

## Attachment Needs and Problem Solving

Sorting out attachment issues from practical problems so that you can easily resolve the practical problems as a team, is a key part of keeping your love strong. Couples who learned to reach for each other and create a secure bond rapidly become skilled at solving the everyday problems that plagued their relationship—they were cooperative, open, and flexible. "Mundane problems were no longer the screen on which their attachment fears and unmet needs were played out."

Johnson encourages couples to take an ongoing problem, such as a wife wanting her husband to be a more involved parent, and first have an A.R.E. conversation around the issue, sharing the attachment needs and fears that the topics raise. That done, they can move into defining the pragmatic problem, and consider solutions together. Here is her report of one such conversation:

> *Janet used to complain to her husband, Morris, that he never helped in setting limits for their son; Morris would promptly dismiss her concerns and withdraw. Now she begins by expressing her vulnerability. "I don't feel like I am being a good mom here," she says. "It is so hard for me to really set limits for the kid, and I feel like I flip between being a harridan and a wimp. I get overwhelmed by it all. It never ends, setting rules, dealing with his evasions, talking to the school, driving him to all these appointments. I get angry, but it is because I really need your help here. I can't do this all by myself. I know you withdraw in frustration, but when you do that, it leaves me alone and overwhelmed. Can we please find a way to do this together?"*
>
> *Morris, who now feels reassured that his wife values and depends on him, hears her and responds to her distress. They acknowledge that they both get overwhelmed by the demands of parenting and need each other's support. They define the problem as their son's over-involvement with a fast-living set of friends, and they decide jointly to set some limits. They talk specifically about how to support each other in conversations with their son when he does not respect these limits.*

Think of a problem-solving discussion that always ends up in frustration for you and your partner. See if you can write down your attachment needs and fears that are operating just under the surface during this discussion. How could you express these to your partner? What could he or she do to help you with them? If you got this help, how do you think this would affect your discussion?

A conversation about how to parent together is manageable. A dialogue that slips into desperate abandonment, rage *or* hopeless evasiveness will never end in workable solutions. The essence of good problem solving is being able to stay focused and flexible. Emotional safety promotes a team approach and creative problem solving. Countless studies link emotional safety and secure connection to our ability to assert our needs, empathize with others, tolerate ambiguity, and think clearly and coherently. It makes sense to take care of the hot bonding issues hiding out in pragmatic problems first before trying to find workable solutions. Sometimes, just clarifying the emotional music that is playing when a topic comes up, changes the problem itself.

If we, as a species, are to survive at all on this fragile blue and green planet, we have to learn to step past the illusion of separateness and grasp that we truly are mutually dependent. We learn this in our most intimate relationships.

### Key Points
- Emotionally Focused Therapy (EFT), developed by Sue Johnson, is sourced in the understanding that romantic love is all about attachment and bonding—our wired-in need for someone who offers reliable emotional connection and comfort.
- We are emotionally attached to our partners in much the same way that a child is to a parent for nurturing and protection.
- This attachment view of adult love is radically different from our culture's established ideas of adulthood, where maturity equates with independence and self-sufficiency.
- We are never more emotional than when our primary love relationship is threatened. Wired by millions of years of evolution, any potential loss of connection activates a primal panic response.
- Most couples fights are protests over emotional disconnection: our anger, criticism, demands are attempts to draw our mates back in emotionally and to re-establish a sense of safe connection.
- Attachment needs underlie negative interactions. When connection seems lost, both are terrified. Rational problem solving doesn't address the need for emotional connection. What's needed is a partner's moving emotionally closer—to hold and reassure.
- Learning there is nothing "wrong" nor "immature" about our longings for connection, we no longer need to hide them.

- EFT focuses on creating and strengthening this emotional bond by identifying and transforming key moments that foster an adult loving relationship: being open, attuned, and responsive to each other.
- The facts of a fight (whether its about diaper changing or your sex life) aren't the real issue. The issue is the strength of a couple's emotional bond. It's about accessibility, responsiveness, and emotional engagement.
- Negative patterns are triggered when one partner tries to reach for the other and cannot make safe emotional contact. When we can soften and share our deeper emotions, recognize our mutual need for caring and connection, and sincerely apologize, we can talk about what happened without it being anyone's fault.
- Sincere apology includes communicating: you care, the others hurt is warranted, owning up to your hurtful actions, expressing shame for your behavior; and reassurance you will help your partner heal.
- Key moments of change answer the pressing question: Are you there for me?
- Note the similarity between adults needs for connection—and how they are met—with babies' needs for connection.
- Building and sustaining a safe, loving bond requires 1) couples learning to repair moments of disconnection and step out of habitual dead-end ways of dealing them that exacerbate disconnection by destroying trust and safety; and 2) the ability to tune into our loved one by deliberately creating moments of engagement and connection.

## 26: Men's Secret Shame

*I initially had reservations about reprinting this piece from Jed Diamond's* Mr. Mean: Saving Your Relationship from The Irritable Male Syndrome,[55] *namely, that it may appear to put the burden of "making it better" on the woman, by suggesting that mothers, who already have their hands full raising children, should actively mother her man. However, Jed wrote this specifically in response to women's requesting "what can I do to help him," after reading* The Irritable Male Syndrome. *I believe it is of great value in furthering an understanding of the dynamics between men and women.*

Five kinds of shame that men experience, which women (and men!) may not recognize, are:

### 1. The shame of competition and rejection

Males often remember, with a great deal of shame, walking across a room and asking the "cute" girl to dance, only to be turned down and having to walk back to his seat feeling that all eyes are on him and imagining people saying to themselves, "loser, loser, loser." This is the essence of male shame. There are other situations in life when we are again in competition with other men for the favors of a woman. Being rejected can trigger earlier memories and we feel the flush of shame.

And our shame deepens as others witness our retreat.

### 2. The shame of her "size" and "power"

Most women are not aware of the power they hold over men just by being female. Think about this. All of us are born from the body of a woman, but only men (in heterosexual relationships) have an intimate relationship with a person who is the same sex as the mother.

All men have a body memory of being small and totally dependent on a woman who is big, strong, and imposing. He may appear big and strong as an adult, but inside he still feels vulnerable. He never forgets that it was a woman who held his life in her hands, whose displeasure might cause her to abandon him to his death. This creates an inherent sense of shame that men feel when they are around women, but it's a shame that neither the man nor the woman is conscious of him having.

### 3. The shame of wanting to return to the comfort of infancy

There's a joke that men spend nine months trying to get out and the rest of their lives trying to get back in. It's often used to illustrate men's preoccupation with sex, but it may hold a deeper truth. Women trigger men's desire to return to the safety, comfort, and warmth he remembered as a child—even back to the memory of being in the womb. I remember many times in my life feeling crushed by my battles in the world and wanting nothing more than to return to the comfort and warmth of childhood. But the thought was so frightening and shameful, I immediately blocked it out.

If I could have allowed the thought to surface it might have been something like this: "It's so damn hard being a man in the world, always competing, always fighting my way to the top, always struggling to make a living and support a family. I just want to rest. I want to crawl into my wife's arms and let her hold me. But if I ever let myself do that I know I'd never want to leave. I'd forfeit my manhood, she would hate me, cast me out, and that would be the end of me. I've got to erase that thought and never let it return."

This shameful longing seems to be universal. As anthropologist David Gilmore writes in *Misogyny: The Male Malady*, men throughout the world have "unconscious wishes to return to infancy, longings to suckle at the breast, to return to the womb, the powerful temptation to surrender one's masculine autonomy to the omnipotent mother of childhood fantasy."

## 4. The shame of men's dependency on women

In *Fire in the Belly: On Being a Man*, psychologist Sam Keen talks about his hidden dependency on women. "If the text of my life was 'successful, independent man,' the subtext was 'engulfed by *woman*.'" Keen goes on to describe the ways in which the archetypal *woman* (and hence all real-life women to a significant degree) rules our lives. "The secret men seldom tell, and often do not know (consciously) is the extent to which our lives circle around our relationships to *woman*.... She is the audience before whom the dramas of our lives are played out. She is the judge who pronounces us guilty or innocent. She is the Garden of Eden from which we are exiled and the paradise for which our bodies long. She is the goddess who can grant us salvation and the frigid mother who denies us."

It's no wonder there are times when we "hate" the woman we feel so dependent upon. We long to let ourselves melt into her arms, but our shame causes us to deny our need and project our anger on to her. If we can't accept our own needs to be nurtured and cared for, we will have a difficult time feeling love for the women in our lives.

## 5. The shame of women's words

Often women assume that men are "tough" and their words won't hurt him. In part, this is a result of our inaccurate gender assumptions. Many believe that women are more delicate and easily hurt, and men are stronger and can take more punishment. The truth is that a man is very vulnerable to women's words. He is likely to cover his pain because he feels ashamed to admit that what she said may have cut him to the core.

Patricia Love and Steven Stosny remind us that "Words hurt. Words destroy. Words can kill a relationship." In *How to Improve Your Marriage Without Talking About It*, they detail some of the most common things that women say that trigger shame in a man, including:

- Correcting what he says, "It was last Wednesday, not Thursday."
- Giving unsolicited advice: "If you would just make the call you'll feel better."
- Implying inadequacy: "I wish you had been at that workshop with me" (not because he would have enjoyed it but because it would have "corrected some of his flaws").
- Focusing on what he didn't do, not what he did: "It would have been better if you'd said 'I'm sorry' to begin with."
- Using a harsh tone: "I'm so tired of this!"
- Condescending: "Someday maybe you'll learn to pick up after yourself."
- Making "you" statements: "You make me so mad I can't think straight."
- Expecting him to make you happy: "If we just did more fun things together...."

As with fear-triggers in men, women often aren't aware of the things they say that trigger shame in a man. Women are generally much more facile with words than men and are more used to verbal jousting. They often wound without meaning to because they aren't aware of the power of their words.

## Women: What You Can Do to Help Reduce Shame in Men

### *1. Put yourself in his shoes*

The most important thing you can do is to be aware of the "put-downs" that men have suffered and continue to suffer in their lives. Just putting yourself in his shoes and having compassion for his experience can go a long way towards healing. You don't have to figure out what to say... talking can often trigger shame in men. You just have to feel with him and accept that his irritability, anger, withdrawal are not meant to hurt you. They are often the best he can do at the moment to protect against shame.

### *2. Watch your words*

You can also notice the ways that you have contributed to his shame by things you may have inadvertently said. You need to watch that you don't shame yourself when you notice hurtful things you may have said to him. Just apologize sincerely when you do it and increase your awareness so that you don't do it again. You also need to stop saying things to friends or family that are shaming towards your man. Sharing your negativity may offer temporary relief and make you feel closer to a girlfriend, but it will undermine your relationship with your man.

### *3. Help him accept being touched and nurtured*

We all long to be held, touched, and nurtured. Yet men, even more than women, are touch-deprived. This begins in childhood because boys are touched less, and less lovingly than girls. As we grow up, we often associate being "manly" with being tough, independent, and self-sufficient.

Nothing could be further from the truth. We all need to be held and nurtured from the day we are born until the day we die. As Sue Johnson says, "Contact with a loving partner literally acts as a buffer against shock, stress, and pain." Help him learn to touch and be touched. It will go a long way to reducing his shame and creating a closer bond between you.

Write down some things about shame. How have you been shamed in your own life? What aspects of shame may be affecting the man in your life? What things have you done that may have inadvertently contributed to increasing shame in him? Are you willing to do what you can to change things?

**Key Points**

Five kinds of shame that men experience are:
- The shame of competition and rejection—situations where a man is again in competition with other males for the favors of a female—can trigger earlier memories causing a man to shut down as he relives the flush of shame.
- The shame of her "size" and "power." All men have a body memory of being small and dependent on a woman who is big, strong, and imposing. As an adult, he still feels vulnerable.
- The shame of wanting to return to the comfort of infancy. The safety, comfort, and warmth he remembered as a child—even back to the memory of being in the womb.
- The shame of men's dependency on women. This can cause men to deny their need and project their anger on to women.
- The shame of women's words. Men are not so "tough" that her words won't hurt him, and he will be ashamed to admit it.
- What women can do to help reduce shame in men:
  - Put yourself in his shoes. Compassion for his experience helps heal.
  - Watch your words. Apologize when you say hurtful things.
  - Help him accept being touched and nurtured. Men, even more than women, are touch-deprived; and often not as tough and independent as they pretend to be.

# 27: Building a Friendship with Your Partner

*This chapter is a synopsis of commentaries written by Bobbie Burdett (coachbobbie.com) for the Wellness Inventory Online (wellpeople.com)*

## Living with Unresolved Conflicts

Another important perspective on how to forge a safe and supportive emotional connection with your partner comes from the work of John Gottman, PhD, author of *The Seven Principles for Making Marriage Work*.[*]

Gottman's research with thousands of couples over the last 30 years indicates 69% of all relational conflicts are *not* resolvable, due to differences in family-of-origin and cultural rules, personality, lifestyle, or personal values. But, while a problem may not be solved, how we deal with it predicts whether we'll have an intimate and happy union. Gottman believes that the secret to a happy relationship is building a *friendship*. Now this is good, and makes perfect sense, because if friendship isn't about *connection*, what is it?

First, see below an overview of his findings. As you read through each of these, notice how they foster connection.

## Build Rather Than Fix

The primary factor in predicting marital longevity and satisfaction was the ratio of positive interactions to negative. During conflict conversations, if the couple enjoyed five positive interactions for every negative one (ratio of 5:1), or better, then the partners had the best chance for happiness together. In normal conversations of exemplary couples, the ratio was observed to be about 20:1.

> **Your Interactions: Positive or Negative?**
> Think over the past 24 hours. What do you think was the ratio of positive to negative interactions between you and your partner? What was the ratio in those early days of romance with your partner?

Friendship is borne of fondness, respect, and admiration. *If how we interact conveys respect and appreciation, even if we don't agree, a relationship can thrive.* The Big Four that run counter to friendship are criticism, contempt (the worst because it engenders shame), defensiveness, and stonewalling (ignoring). Even if partners resort to these negative patterns from time to time, the relationship can thrive if partners allow themselves to be influenced by the other person. So,

---

[*] Unless otherwise indicated, all quotes are by John Gottman.

even though you sometimes get critical and defensive, if you are ultimately able to take in what the other is saying and learn from it, the relationship is likely to thrive. When these negative patterns are permanently entrenched in a relationship, it doesn't bode well.

So the message is: Be mindful of where you place your attention. Focus on what you like—not what you don't like. You get more of what you focus on. Build on the strengths—don't focus on fixing the weaknesses. Build positive experiences in the little everyday interactions rather than relying on those special dates and expensive gifts.

---

**Appreciations**
- Take a few minutes to write down what you appreciate, respect, or admire about your partner.
- Watch for little opportunities to let your partner know you appreciate her. Start by listing some that you could tell your partner right now. Don't unload the list all at once. Spread it out artfully in the course of your daily interactions.
- Do this for at least two weeks.
- Keep adding to the list.
- Write in your journal, or share with your partner or with a friend, what you notice as a result of doing the experiment.

*So often, both mother and father feel unappreciated in their roles, and battling the feelings as new parents that, in whatever way, they are not doing well enough. A remedy may be found in sincere appreciations: if not of what was done today, of what was done yesterday. There can always be some good to find, and to acknowledge. If only people knew what a difference it makes to appreciate others, they would never stop doing it.* —Chris Maple, PhD

---

Gottman found that the key to intimacy lies not in personal disclosure or in the long "heart-to-hearts," but in the small, daily interactions that we may not even think about that promote intimacy. This led to his identifying what he calls "bids for connection."

Bids for connection can range from a direct request to spend time together, to the slightest touch. They may be a look, gesture, little comment, question, or even a criticism or complaint. We make bids for each other's attention all the time. Our happiness together depends on how we respond to these bids from our partner, and how our partner responds to ours.

Daniel Siegel, MD, in *The Developing Mind*, refers to this form of exchange as "reflective dialogue." Very simply, if the response is appropriate to the bid, correctly reflects the bid, and the bidder has the feeling that she's been correctly understood, a positive *connection* has been made. There is a resulting *coherence* in the brains of both bidder and responder. It just *feels good* to have our spoken or unspoken requests for connection met positively. It's a feeling of completion. Gottman identified three responses to bids for connection.

1. **Turning-toward:** The receiver of the bid responds positively with humor, respect, attention, or a sense of joining in. Over time, this response builds trust and respect and develops stable, long-lasting relationships, rich in good feelings for each other.
2. **Turning-away:** This involves ignoring another's bid or acting preoccupied. If this is a regular response, it is very destructive to relationships.
3. **Turning-against:** This response is often belligerent or argumentative, involving ridicule and/or hostility. It's very destructive. It doesn't engender friendship, respect, or admiration. Most relationships are not likely to last long with this kind of chronic response.

Take a few minutes to review the three styles of response, and rate on a scale of 1 to 5 how typical you consider each to be: a) from yourself to your partner, and b) from your partner to yourself.

If you and your partner are engaging in this together, you may want to exchange notes, being careful to use these observations as an opportunity to learn and grow, rather than protect and defend!

Bids may be verbal and nonverbal, such as touching, facial expressions, gesturing, or vocalizing (laughing, sighing, etc.).

## 1. Turning-toward Responses:

These let the other know that they are being welcomed, understood, or joined. Here are some examples:

Sue: "This stupid computer! I'm sick of this job!"

Peter: "Sounds like you need a break. Go get a cup of coffee and I'll find the number for tech support."

David: "I can't believe that you were so late!"

Carolyn: "Sorry. I get that you're mad. Do you want to talk about it?"

April: "I don't suppose you'd ever think of going for a walk with me."

Dale: "I might. Hey, I've got an idea. Do you want to go for a walk?"

Fuzzy bidding is bidding that is not easily identified by the receiver. It may be the result of our attempting to avoid vulnerability or emotional risk; having poor communication skills and an inability to express our self clearly; speaking in negative ways that are hard for others to hear or accept; or failing to acknowledge our needs in the first place. If we can't acknowledge our own needs, we cannot expect another to understand them. A specific request like "Let's get a babysitter for this Saturday night and go to that little inn our friends told us about," is far more direct than a vague "We should do something romantic sometime," or "We never do anything fun!"

Fuzzy bidding means that our partner, most likely, won't even *recognize* our bid for connection. Cody realized that Melissa often made bids by asking him questions or presenting problems about their business. He usually responded with irritation. When he viewed those same interactions with his new awareness of bids for connection and responded accordingly, it made a big difference in their relationship.

Bids in the form of criticisms, complaints, or laments are hard to recognize as bids for connection. Building a positive relationship requires mustering the patience and compassion to turn toward the other with heart.

## 2. Turning-away Responses:

Some of these are simply the result of "mindlessness"—responses that are outside of our immediate awareness. They include:

- **Preoccupied:** she wants to share her day and he wants to watch the news, so he ignores what she is saying.
- **Disregarding:** he tells her about a new car he wants to buy and she rambles off in a soliloquy about what color it should be, completely derailing his excitement.
- **Interrupting:** she tells him about a fear she's grappling with and he interrupts by talking about a new project he's beginning.

Looking back over the course of a typical day, can you identify any commonly recurring Turning Away responses in your own relationship?

## 3. Turning-against Responses:

- **Contemptuous**: he gives hurtful, disrespecting comments, or put-downs, e.g., "You? Lose weight? I doubt it!"
- **Belligerent**: she is provocative or combative, looking for a fight, e.g., he: "You look tired, dear." She: "I wouldn't be if you got off your computer and helped me."
- **Contradictory**: he is ready for an argument, e.g., she: "I just got a great book about homeopathy." He: "My friend says that stuff is all just a bunch of voodoo."
- **Domineering**: she attempts to control him by getting him to withdraw, retreat, or submit, often with a negative parental tone, e.g., "Now dear, that really is no way to behave."

- **Critical**: he makes broad-based attacks on her character, using global terms like "always" or "never," or statements of blame or betrayal, e.g., "The problem with you is that you always let people down!"
- **Defensive**: she creates a sense of separation by disavowing all responsibility, thus discounting his reality, e.g., "I don't care what you say, I didn't do anything wrong!"

> **Turning Which Way?**
>
> Looking back over the course of a typical day, can you identify any commonly recurring Turning Against responses in your relationships? Which are those you most use? What do you perceive your partner as most using? If sharing, do your perceptions match? What can you learn from this?
>
> When met with either "turned against" or "turned away" responses, the bidder may quickly give up bidding in that same way or, in the case of the former, settle into a repeating negative pattern based on the concept that "negative attention is better than no attention at all."
>
> I am not suggesting that we can turn toward our partner all the time. If we want to build a long-lasting emotional connection, we need to turn towards our loved one's bids as much as we can, while also caring for our own needs.

## Marital Masters

*Marital masters are the folks who are so good at handling conflict that they make marital squabbles look like fun. When they disagree, they're able to stay connected and engaged with each other. Rather than becoming defensive and hurtful, they pepper their disputes with flashes of affection, intense interest, and mutual respect—and seem to have access to their sense of humor even when they are arguing.*

Like marital masters, to increase our relating abilities, we can build open affection, kidding around, surprises, and humor into our interactions. The more positive responses we deposit into our relationships during the good times, the more we have to draw on during difficult times. Remember, changing established patterns takes time. By repeatedly *turning toward* our partners, we're literally building those neural networks into our brains, i.e., strengthening our tendency to do so with ease and ultimately, habitually.

A question Pam Leo, in *Connection Parenting*, urges we ask when relating to children is, "Will this serve to connect us or disconnect us?" One of the best practices partners can cultivate is asking this simple, self-applied question before choosing how to respond to their mates.

## And, Making Repairs When We Blow It

Gottman's research has dispelled many long-held myths about what makes stable and happy intimate relationships. He found both that couples who fight frequently and couples who avoid conflict can be as stable and happy in their relationships as those couples who confront issues and calmly talk things through. He found that the agreement between people *about how they deal with problems* was more important than their style of relating. In other words, if both people preferred a vigorous fight now and then, they had a better chance of being satisfied with their marriage. However, if one person preferred to avoid conflict and the other person preferred a good argument to clear the air, it required a lot more understanding and compromise to have a happy marriage.

## Flooding

We all get upset with our partners from time to time. Sometimes it results in a very intense emotional state that psychologists call "flooding." Flooding alters our physiological functioning and hampers our ability to think. The most immediate cue is the heart rate. It can increase by 30 beats per minute within the space of a single heartbeat. Muscles tense, causing labored or decreased breathing. And the ability to think clearly is severely reduced: the thinking part of the brain literally gets put on hold, the emotions take over, and we respond with knee-jerk reactivity to something our partner says or does.

If emotional flooding is a frequent experience in a relationship, intimacy is difficult to achieve and there is a higher likelihood that the relationship will end. It's tiring to be in a constant state of alert. It simply wears you out.

When your brain disconnects from the thinking function, your body is flooded with adrenalin. You are in a primal, survival mode. You can't think straight and your bodily senses are obliterated by your intense emotions. Think of a cornered animal and you're approximating what is going on emotionally within. If this is happening with you and your partner about arriving home later than promised, do you think you have a prayer of coming to a reasonable conclusion to a discussion about time management?

What can you do?

Here are some suggestions:

- Call for a timeout to allow you to cool down. Don't even think about trying to resolve anything while either of you is flooded.
- When you are both calm, share with each other how it feels when you are emotionally flooding. If you can think about it as a neurological process, then the problem becomes your brains, not your selves. This distinction can do wonders for your understanding and respect.
- Together, devise a signal that will indicate that you're starting to flood and you need some time out.

- It takes 20-30 minutes after a flooding experience for the brain to reconnect and the adrenalin levels in the body to drop, so allow at least this much time before resuming your discussion.

*Take whatever time you need! There is no point resuming discussion until you are both back in balance. Sometimes we think we are and start in, but have to call for a retreat when we find we are not as ready as we thought we were. Meryn's bag of tools for returning to balance range from taking a walk, a swim, or gardening, to meditating, or stroking the cat. Jack withdraws to read a book, pound nails, watch a video, or talk to a supportive friend. Knowing what works for you is a big step forward. Doing this is great role modeling for your children.*

- Men are much slower to return to calm than women, they tend to experience flooding more intensely than women, and are more easily overwhelmed by marital conflict. So, allow for this!

Be mindful about how you begin a discussion, and you'll be more likely to have a productive ending.

A common pattern seen in relationships was described by Daniel Goleman in *Emotional Intelligence*:

*As I was entering a restaurant on a recent evening, a young man stalked out the door, his face set in an expression both stony and sullen. Close on his heels a young woman came running, her fists desperately pummeling his back while she yelled, 'Goddamn you! Come back here and be nice to me!'*

Women are usually the initiators of discussions about marital problems, and discussions invariably end on the same note they begin. If initiated harshly, flooding is more likely, and the end result is likely to be some variation of the above scene. So be attentive to how you initiate a discussion, consider whether it will serve to connect rather than disconnect, to promote loving and learning, rather than protecting and defending.

Men tend to maintain their distress longer by recycling their negative thoughts, impeding their ability to think clearly.

If you continue mentally rehashing what you are angry about, your brain will remain disconnected from its clear thinking part, and you won't be able to process the information and make a sound decision about how to proceed. You need to change to your emotional channel and get your brain connected again.

Channel changers include: physical activity such as exercise or hard work, something requiring total concentration like a complex game, or the escape of TV or movies, or meditation, deep breathing, or talking with a skillful friend or coach. Use whatever works for you to soothe yourself into a calmer state of mind and body. Support your partner in doing the same.

Now you can take stock of the situation and evaluate what you need to do to re-establish closeness. Gottman calls them "repair attempts."

## Repair Attempts

The magic words, "I'm sorry," often do wonders. Sometimes it's just a touch, or a look, or an unrelated subject, e.g., very often both partners completely miss each other's repair attempts, and this can cause a lot of undue mental and physical stress.

The elements that are necessary for repair are the same that are necessary for connection; generously pay attention to and appreciate each other and build a friendship as the basis of your relationship. It's never too late for a repair attempt. And most often, the repair can actually build a stronger connection.

With awareness and practice, you can strengthen your ability to keep your brain integrated.

## Balancing Integration and Differentiation

Integration, the ability to come together in supportive interactions on a daily basis, and differentiation, the respect for each other's individuality and private needs, are two important elements of relationship.

If there is too much emphasis on integration, a relationship becomes "enmeshed," with both people liking and disliking all the same things. Individuality is discouraged and compliance is the spoken or unspoken rule.

If there is too much emphasis on differentiation, connection and intimacy are discouraged. You then have two individuals sharing the same space, but little else.

Consider the balance of the differentiation and integration in your partner relationship. Does this feel good? What would you like more of: integration or disintegration? Can you talk with your partner about this?

A healthy balance of differentiation and integration fosters the most stable and satisfying kind of relationship.

## What Next?

While these last three chapters have focused on developing a healthy emotional connection within couples, it is important to be aware of the unrealistic expectations many of us have developed—relying too heavily on our partner to meet virtually all our needs for connection. We need to also develop and sustain a loving connection first with ourselves (see Chapter 18), and also with people beyond our immediate family constellation. If we are not connected with ourselves, we cannot authentically connect with another. Self-connection begins with self-care.

**Key Points**
- The secret to an intimate relationship is friendship. If our interactions convey fondness, respect and appreciation, even if we don't agree, a relationship can thrive.
- Criticism, contempt, defensiveness, and stonewalling (ignoring) run counter to friendship.
- The key to intimacy is in the small daily interactions, and how each responds to "bids for connection" from the other that range from a direct request to spend time together to the slightest touch, gesture, question, even complaint.
- Responses to bids are **turning-toward** (letting the other know that they are welcomed, understood); **turning-away** (ignoring another's bid); **turning-against** (argumentative, defensive, etc.).
- Long-lasting emotional connections are built on turning towards our partner's bids, while also caring for our own needs.
- The more positive responses we deposit into our relationships in the good times, the more we have to draw on in the difficult times.
- Agreement between partners about how they deal with problems—a vigorous fight or a calm discussion—is more important than their style of relating.
- We all get upset with our partners on occasion and experience "flooding"—an intense emotional state that increases heart rate, tenses muscles, and hampers our ability to think clearly. This is not a time for a rational discussion, but for taking the time you need to return to calm.
- Repair attempts re-establish closeness: A sincere "I'm sorry," a touch, or a look, can work wonders.
- A healthy relationship requires attending to the balance of integration, the ability to come together in supportive interactions; and differentiation, respect for each other's individuality and private needs.
- Interpersonal boundaries are invisible limits of each partner. In healthy relationships, the permeability of each partner's boundary is self-regulated. In unhealthy relationships—by the other.
- Finding the balance between being interested and supportive, respectful of their process, and clearly and kindly asserting our own needs and wants, matures through the practice of "noticing" and making small moves—almost unperceivable daily adjustments that become big improvements.
- Healthy emotional connections are supported by connections with beyond the immediate family—and with self. Self-connection begins with self-care.

# Part IV

# An Ounce of Prevention Is Worth 1.78 Tons of Cure

# 28: ATTACHMENT PARENTING: AN OUNCE OF PREVENTION...

> *Everything about the newborn—her abject vulnerability and dependence, the genetically programmed distress call the moment she is separated—is geared to remaining in contact with her mother, and to a lesser extent with her father, at all times after birth.* —Robin Grille, *Heart-to-Heart Parenting*

Today neuroscientists explain how the hormones of loving connections between parent and infant literally nourish the child's brain and stimulate the growth of new networks of connections in the regions of the brain associated with regulating emotions. While we used to think that genes determined everything, today we know that early life experiences can activate or deactivate genes. And, as we have seen, brain growth is shaped by early childhood experiences. In the absence of loving connections, the emotional centers of the brain fail to develop properly. When a child experiences something distressing or frightening, such as being left alone to "cry it out," cortisol levels spike. If she is not comforted soon afterwards by a loving adult, cortisol levels remain high. If this happens repeatedly, brain cells can be damaged. Failure to establish a secure attachment doesn't affect all children in the same way. Some react by becoming depressed or aggressive, others become shy or withdrawn; still others are overly driven and competitive.

> *Let's raise children who won't have to recover from their childhood.*
> —Pam Leo, *Connection Parenting*

Children who have a healthy and secure connection with their parents are more likely to:
- cope well with stress,
- have satisfying relationships,
- have healthy self-esteem,
- have good mental health,
- reach their full intellectual potential,
- have fewer discipline problems,
- have fewer problems separating from parents when it is developmentally appropriate.

Building blocks that facilitate healthy attachment between parent and child include:
- nurturing the unborn as an aware and sensitive individual,

- a gentle, natural (intervention-free) birth,
- skin-to-skin contact,
- breastfeeding,
- saying no to circumcision,
- co-sleeping,
- holding and carrying the infant (babywearing),
- decoding and responding to the infant's cues,
- the parents' loving, consistent presence during the pre-verbal years.

It is important to recognize that these are merely the building blocks. The quality of attachment that forms between parent and child is based on the caregiver's *responsiveness, dependability, and warmth*. The most important message we can give our infants during the first year is that they can trust the people around them; that their environment is a safe, benevolent one; that their parents, especially the mother, are close by and attentive; and that they are deeply loved.

Having been primed by Jean Liedloff's *The Continuum Concept*, and William and Martha Sears' *The Baby Book*, each of these building blocks fell together to create a practical approach for us to raise a child. It felt good, right, **exciting**, to contemplate nurturing our baby in this way. You, however, will not be alone if your immediate response is that attachment parenting is impractical, exhausting, and going to make for a spoiled and overly dependent child.

## A Monumental Undertaking

The fact is that raising a child today is a monumental undertaking—regardless of parenting style; and *the stresses can be minimized* when parents fully meet their children's nurturing needs. While attachment parenting may appear more consuming than the expeditious-seeming alternatives, to the degree that you can adopt and adapt these practices, *the benefits far outweigh the costs*, and in the long run it's much easier. Adopting even one of these practices—the building blocks of attachment—will deeply impact a child's wellbeing. And, of course, the more the better.

Let's look more closely, first at this seemingly outrageous proposition that the stresses can be minimized with attachment parenting, and then at the equally controversial issue of fully meeting a baby's needs. Later, we explore how, in the absence of the village, you, your partner, and baby may be able to embark on this journey of healing and wholeness together.

## Oh, Sure, It's Easier!

- **A gentle, natural birth:** A natural, i.e., intervention-free birth is usually quicker, less painful and has fewer complications than a medicalized birth. A natural birth favors the greatest flow of those wonderful hormones perfected by Mother Nature intent on helping mother, as well as father and baby, fall deeply in love.
- **Co-sleeping:** Snuggled alongside mom or dad's body, their baby sleeps soundly. There is no being woken by an infant's cries from another room, and no arguments about who should get out of a warm bed in the dark of the night to fix a bottle and comfort a crying baby. Mother draws her baby to breast and, most often, both drift back into sleep without having ever fully woken. There is no need for the large range of paraphernalia needed to equip a baby for sleeping alone—cribs, cradles, night lights, "blankies," music boxes, pacifiers. And no need for stuffed animals when the baby has Mother or Father's body to snuggle with. If sharing the bed with your baby simply doesn't work for you, options include having your baby sleep in a "sidecar" connected to your bed.

*It was around 11 PM on the evening of Siena's birth when we finally found ourselves in bed, together, all three of us. Exhausted? Yes. And reveling in the wonderment of it all, the deep joy and satisfaction I felt in my whole being as we lay nestled together—Jack, this tiny little being who had entered our life, and me, "newborn-as-a-mother."*

*It was not always easy. I remember nights lying awake, feeling squashed between husband and daughter, not daring to move lest Siena wake. I was exhausted. I wanted to be left to myself. But those moments fade into insignificance seen alongside the deep pleasure that fills my heart as I look to all the other minutes and hours and nights we have shared.*

*Siena is now five years old. We three still sleep together—other than on those nights she has friends for a sleepover—and are in no hurry for this to change. It feels so right, for all of us. If the day has been a tough one, here now, we are all at peace with each other. If the day has been a special one, here we lie in deep contentment with each other. Either way, I am deeply grateful for her presence, here, now with us: The fascination of this experience has never waned for me. I love to wake to her sleeping alongside me: The sound of her breathing, the touch of her body, so trusting, so precious, so close. This is a part of parenting I would not have missed for the world.* —Meryn's journal

- **Skin-to-skin contact:** Direct skin-to-skin contact helps a baby regulate her own temperature, metabolic rate, hormone and enzyme levels, heart rate and breathing, and attunes the baby and parent, deepening their connection and ability to interpret the baby's needs.

*The morning after Siena was born, I nestled her, naked on my bare chest, and felt the softness of her tiny body, so trusting, merging with my heart. I had never imagined I could love someone so much. I lay there, in wonderment—her innocence, purity, and presence both inspiring and painful to behold in contrast to my own recollections of my infancy.*

*I had done a similar thing with my first daughter when she was a month or so old—21 years earlier. Of all my memories of both girls, these primal moments of bonding stand out as the most profound.* —Jack

- **Breastfeeding:** Breastfed babies are sick less often, thanks to the immunological properties of breastmilk. They wake less often in the night, have fewer earaches and stuffy noses, and being healthier, tend to be happier and cry less. Money, time and effort are saved in not buying formula. And the milk's composition, temperature, and cleanliness are left to the expert—Mother Nature. For formula-feeding parents, these matters are often a cause for worry and argument. Outings for the breastfeeding mom and baby don't require purchasing, cleaning, packing, and carrying bottles and accessories. A 2009 study in *Pediatrics*[56] revealed that if 90% of US families could comply with medical recommendations to breastfeed exclusively for 6 months, the United States would save $13 billion per year and prevent an excess 911 deaths, nearly all of which would be in infants.

    If for some reason you cannot breastfeed your baby, remember that what is important is to nourish your baby emotionally as well as physically. Hold your baby while feeding her. Avoid leaving your baby to lie down with the bottle propped beside her, a style of feeding devoid of the all-important human connection. Rotate your baby right side to left side, just as if breastfeeding. Make eye contact and talk with her.

*My husband and I received the long-awaited call from our baby's birth mother that she had begun labor. It had been a long journey for us to this point. We quickly packed our things, got in the car for the two-hour drive to the birth center, made a quick stop to pick up the donated breastmilk that I would use as a supplement to my own milk for nursing.*

*We arrived just an hour after Benjamin was born! The labor had been exceptionally short. He was handed to me as we walked into the birthing room. Everyone, including his birth mother, gave a sigh of relief now that he was in my arms. That moment stands out as one of the happiest of my life! Our baby boy was here! I was a mother!*

*I immediately sat down to put him to my breast. I had prepared myself for nursing our son by using a supplemental nursing system (SNS) to supplement the milk that I would bring in myself. Since I hadn't gone through pregnancy, I didn't have the quantity of milk ducts to meet all of his needs. However I was able to bring in a good amount of the milk he needed by having him nurse at the breast. The rest was provided by the SNS filled with donated breastmilk from women I knew and trusted, or goat's milk formula that we prepared ourselves.*

*The blissful feeling of having my baby at my breast was indescribable! It was liquid love that flowed from me to him, and the love was returned as I sensed his deep wellbeing. Because my son was adopted, I felt our bonding to be especially important. I was overjoyed that he was receiving the very best that I could give him.*

*My husband prepared the SNS daily as we needed it. It was a family endeavor. He did whatever he could to help out. We all thrived on the nurturing love that flowed between us all.* —Betty

- **Babywearing:** Holding or carrying a baby in arms, sling, or backpack enhances parent-infant bonding, reduces crying, promotes night sleeping and day waking, and promotes learning and cognitive development. With the baby in a sling, hands are free to cook, pick up the phone, garden, wash the car, or take the hand of another child. There is no need to make special arrangements for the baby's sleep, no scheduled naps to be enforced; she wakes and sleeps easily and according to her needs rather than an artificially determined schedule.

    When out and about, slings, frontpacks, and backpacks give far more mobility than a stroller, which turns every door and stair into an obstacle course and makes a walk on the beach or off the beaten track a virtual impossibility.

*When she was little, I loved the mobility and freedom the sling gave me to take Siena most anywhere with me. One particular time I recall was up on the gently sloping south-facing roof of our cabin in California. I was rigging up a solar hot water system and she was peeping out to watch whatever I did. Her powers of perception are exceptionally strong to this day.*

*Once while we were walking along a road, I vividly recall seeing only Siena's finger and part of her hand pointing out of the sling that Meryn was wearing, at a patch of wild blackberries—her first solid food I believe. She loved them. This was long before she could speak, but it was clear what she wanted. Being up at chest level, instead of down at ground level, sucking in dust or fumes, made it possible for her to participate in our world much sooner than otherwise.* —Jack

- **Decoding and responding to the baby's cues:** The most powerful enhancers of brain development are the quality of the parent-infant attachment and the responsiveness of the care-giving environment to the cues of an infant.

*Children are delightful to be with when we meet their needs and nothing is hurting them. Whenever a child responds negatively to a reasonable request, we look for the hidden hurt or unmet need. Once we acknowledge everyone's needs, we can work on problem solving.* —Pam Leo, *Connection Parenting*

- **Loving, consistent care:** The consistent availability of a caregiver builds confidence and helps a child learn to trust herself; and attachment enhances development. When caregivers change, it is impossible to prepare the very young because they cannot communicate verbally. "I love you," or "I'll be back later," means nothing to them. The despair of the young one who feels deserted, is real despair, even if the desertion is no more than a parent's routine departure for work.

*Benjamin was carried in a sling as we went through our day. He let us know loud and clear that putting him down was not what he wanted. Being in his sling next to our bodies, he was relaxed and happy. Holding him in-arms felt right to both of us. He also slept with us in our family bed. It felt so natural and wonderful to be this close.*

*As a practicing homebirth midwife, I still had a few births to attend after Benjamin was born. While I was busy at the births, Benjamin was held by the grandmothers and other family members who were awaiting the birth. He fit in perfectly!*

*Our son is now twenty years old, a young man coming into his own. Time goes by so quickly! I look back on those early months with fond memories, and gratitude that we shared the closeness that we did. We remain close with our son to this day; a gift, I believe, of the precious bonding that we all experienced when it mattered most.* —Betty

## Spare the Rod, Spoil the Child

*There used to be the notion that constantly indulging a child's need would make her spoiled; she would demand more and more. It is quite the opposite... it is not indulging a need that matters; it is fulfilling it... once a need is fulfilled there will be no more inordinate demands. No one wants more than they need, unless of course, they demand more to fill up an early lack.*

—Arthur Janov, *The Biology of Love*

In indigenous cultures that raise their children with respect for their mammalian needs, there is no concept of a spoiled child. Having their every need for nurturing met, they develop a deep sense of security and wellbeing. Newborns are nursed, held, or carried from the time of birth. As toddlers, they join their mother as she goes about her daily chores or they play with siblings and friends of all ages. At night, the families sleep together. The children of these indigenous cultures are remarkably poised and self-confident, and remain so as they grow into adolescence—the outcome of having received so full a measure of the security and affirmation of belonging in the early years.

Attachment parenting responds *appropriately* to a baby, spoiling responds *inappropriately*. While the overindulgent parent's possessiveness keeps a child from doing what he needs because of the parent's own insecurities, a stage of healthy dependence is necessary in order for a child to become securely independent.

> *In no way is mother beguiled by such nonsense as the notion things must not be too easy for the infant, lest s/he think the world is a bed of roses. She knows that frustration does not build concepts in the brain. Concepts build through assimilations (the ability to accept and digest new experience), and successful accommodation (new patterning to handle dissimilarities and make new muscular coordinations of response)… the mother knows that the infant is prompted from within by an enormous drive that goes ahead of ability… and there are frustrations aplenty in that.* —Joseph Chilton Pearce, *Magical Child*

Attached babies, feeling responded to, connected, and valued, cry and fuss less—and so have more time to learn and grow in positive ways. The absence of a needy, whiny child makes parenting less exhausting, more practical—and the joys are multiplied a thousandfold. And attached parents develop a sensitivity that allows them to see things from the child's perspective, and "discipline" is eased as it becomes something you do *with* rather than *to* a child.

Operating from a core of fear or anger rather than trust, "disconnected" children are more difficult to discipline. Securely attached babies become children who *care*, for other people and the world. Accustomed to being fulfilled in interpersonal relationships, they develop a strong capacity for intimacy. Then, too, parents develop confidence sooner, enjoy parenting more, and develop a sensitivity that carries over into other aspects of their life.

If we do not offer our children a secure foundation in the early years, the costs can be tremendous, financially and emotionally. This means that the caregiving choice will best be one of two alternatives: 1) a parent(s) stays at home and provides continuity of care. Or, if this seems impossible, 2) a warm, intelligent, experienced person who can offer the *continuity* of nurturing care needed by the young.

## The Perils of Daycare

When we lived in villages and tribes, there were always willing hearts and hands available to care for the young ones, but in our highly specialized environments, living among mostly strangers, with likely both mom and dad in the workforce, the issue of daycare looms large.

The National Institute of Child Health and Development published a study of 1100 children in daycare, in ten US cities, in 2003. This comprehensive investigation into the effects of daycare (30+ hours a week) on child development, confirmed that the more time children spent in daycare arrangements, the more aggression, disobedience, and conflict with adults they showed when entering kindergarten.

These patterns remained, even after the study had controlled for many features of the children's families and the quality and type of daycare. The study found that spending a lot of time in daycare predicted more truly aggressive and disobedient behavior, not just more assertive or independent behavior. Significant changes were noted in children who had as little as 12 hours of daycare a week.

Similar observations have been made in both Australia and Britain. One study showed children's cortisol levels doubled in the first nine days in daycare, and remained high five months later.[57]

An across-the-board review[58] shows that emotional, social, and behavioral measurements were significantly higher for children in maternal care. In fact, the type of non-maternal care was irrelevant—whether babies were cared for by daycare centers, babysitters, or older siblings, those in non-maternal care (even high quality daycare) scored lower on behavioral and emotional scales than those being cared for by their mother. While most daycare workers are caring people, daycare centers are notorious for low wages, resulting in high turnover. Children feel a greater attachment to parents, and most parents feel a more intense investment in and commitment to their child. Interestingly, boys fare more poorly than girls in daycare.

Children's early relationships with primary caregivers are particularly profound because they shape the neurochemistry of emotion and their entire nervous system, including the brain. This means that whenever possible, at least one of the parents should serve as primary caregiver at least during the child's pre-verbal years.

> *At the absolute minimum, I suggest three to six months of parental care in the period after birth. This is the mandatory period anyone needs to develop parenting skills, to bond with the baby, and to influence the infant brain as only a parent can.* —Thomas Verny, MD, *Pre-Parenting*

Verny suggests that when children are in non-parental care, parents can compensate to some degree if they remain aware of their children's emotional and neurological requirements—a primary requirement being quality and consistency of care—and consistently and lovingly compensate in evenings, weekends, or whenever they can.

Many parents probably feel caught between a rock and a hard place, in the sun. The following chapter outlines creative ways that some parents are adopting to enable them to serve as primary caregivers to their children for at least the first six months, and better still through the pre-verbal years.

If you have no other option but daycare, continuity and constancy of care are important.

> **Types of Daycare by Preference**[*]
> 1. A warm, intelligent, and experienced person caring for the child in the child's home;
> 2. The same quality of person caring for the child in that person's home;
> 3. The same quality of person caring for no more than two children under 18 months or no more than three from 18–36 months in her own home;
> 4. Non-profit center-based care with the same caregiver/child ratios as above, and the total number of children fewer than 10;
> 5. Profit-oriented center-based care, carefully selected to match the above.
>
> [*] *From the* aTLC Blueprint, Section G: *Identifying and Meeting Children's Innate Needs (see Appendix D)*

Nannies usually come at the cost of a high turnover rate, and this is even more so in daycare centers where overworked caregivers are responsible for many children at once. No amount of specialized training can substitute for the emotional connection between parent and child.

The more that we are able to *be there* for our young ones in their early years, receptive and responsive to their needs, the easier and more joyful our life, and theirs, can be. It is true that in many non-Western cultures children are not raised exclusively by their mothers but rather by a number of other people, including other mothers and older siblings. Classic attachment theory implies that these children would suffer some degree of maternal deprivation, but there's no evidence this is the case. While some studies suggest that a group of loving caregivers (compared to just one) will also enable them to thrive, the observations of other experts such as Thomas Verny, MD, support the notion that children can bond with more than one individual, but not with everyone who comes along. Though children in distress may turn to a range of available adults, true bonding and intimacy occurs with mother, father, and perhaps a few select members of the inner family circle.

## Nurturing Ourselves and Our Partner

While doing our best to fully meet our baby's needs within the nuclear family, it is vitally important, for ourselves and our children, that we find ways to nurture ourselves and feel emotionally supported. Otherwise we can find ourselves doing all the "right things"—holding and carrying the baby, sleeping with the baby—but our baby is restless, we are experiencing her as "demanding", and we are exhausted, even depressed. It is natural at times to feel all or any of these things....

> *The strain that many parents suffer in trying to be closely involved with their children comes from their attempt to do what it takes a village to do—without the support of the village. In order to nurture, the parent must be nurtured.*
> —Robin Grille, *Parenting for a Peaceful World*

Connie Allen, author of *Joyous Child, Joyous Parent*, has discovered three significant areas in which attachment parenting often goes astray, where parents unknowingly create needless effort and struggle for themselves and unintentionally limit their child's emotional wholeness.

The first is in *not taking care of themselves*. They believe their primary objective is to meet their child's needs to the exclusion of taking good care of themselves. This results in parental exhaustion, an almost exclusive focus on their child, and the loss of true fulfillment and joy. Children need parents who take good care of themselves, parents who are nourished body and soul, who take time to be with their friends, to exercise and eat healthy food, and to laugh and play. They then have more energy to meet their child's physical and emotional needs, to love their child wholly and authentically, and to create a happy marriage. All of these are essential for a child's emotional wellbeing.

The second is *failing to set empowering limits* with their child. These parents believe that their child must be happy no matter what, and give in to their child's demands when they shouldn't. As a child grows beyond infancy, he need parents who provide structure, which includes limits, in order to feel safe and secure in life. As much as a child may cry or beg for something he wants, deep inside he longs for the strong parent who does not give in to his demands that exceed his parent's limits.

The third is *failure to work together as a team*. Often moms are more familiar with the principles of attachment parenting and believe they know what is right for their child, ignoring the father's feelings of being left out or his doubts about the mother's approach to parenting. Dads often don't realize the vital role they play in their child's life and the information they have about raising their child. They give in to the moms' beliefs instead of trusting their own ideas and perspectives. Attachment parenting only works when *both* parents participate equally, and are happy with their approach to childrearing. One of the greatest gifts parents can give their child is a happy partnership between Mom and Dad, a partnership in which the ideas and feelings of both parents are equally considered and included.

To best meet our children's emotional needs we must take care of ourselves, set empowering limits, and nurture and honor our relationship with our partner. Then, Allen asserts, we will have joyous children who grow up within joyous families!

Mother and father are *the world* to their baby. When parents are upset, exhausted, tired and irritable, their distress will spill over onto their baby or child. Of course, this is true of stresses between any two people, adults included. Hopefully, however, as adults, we will have the skills to maintain our own center even in the face of another's distress, or at the very least we will have built defenses that protect us from the full blast of another's upset. Knowing how hard this can be for us as adults at times, imagine how it is for a baby, who is wide open emotionally, literally knows no boundaries, and is acutely sensitive to what is going on around her.

We all get tired and cranky at times, we all get both physically and emotionally depleted, even when we don't have a little one to care for. And it is not true that your every upset or burst of anger will damage your baby. What is true is that *frequently* the best way to help your baby be calm and content is for you to feel that way, too. This requires that you take good care of your own emotional, as well as physical, needs. If our own needs are not being met, we have no resources to offer our children.

## Good Feelings, Bad Feelings

Most of us were raised to believe that there are good feelings and bad feelings, and that it is not OK to express the bad ones. Control was the name of the game. We were told to "Stop crying. There's nothing to cry about." "Don't be afraid. There's nothing to be afraid of." "Don't be angry. That's not nice." Most of us will find ourselves passing on these same messages to our children. Human beings are *feeling* beings, and to be fully human is to experience and express the full range of emotions, from happiness and joy to anger and grief.

We tend to believe that if we are feeling sad or mad, or if we "lose it," we are bad or doing something wrong. Cheri Huber, in *Time Out For Parents: A Guide to Compassionate Parenting*, proposes that the feeling of "about to lose it" is a gift; "it is the self signaling itself that a need is being neglected." This means that when we get to the point of screaming, it does not make us a bad person, but a person who is out of touch with our feelings. Having been denied a basic need for too long, our reactions become huge.

Huber offers several simple processes for attuning to and responding to our own needs. Of course it takes practice to get in touch with and accept our feelings. She outlines a simple process whereby we stop and take time-out to be present to our self, to our breath, to our feelings, to our experience of the moment.

She recommends taking a few minutes each day as an exclusive "time-out" period to stop and listen to the voice within, and to create the inner peace that our deepest self longs to experience. Once the process has settled into our consciousness, it becomes easier in times of stress to pause and create the space for us to fully experience ourselves—and only then to move forward.

Anger can be particularly difficult to accept and express because the cultural prohibitions on expressing anger are so insidious. Passive aggression has become standard operating procedure. However, anger-energy is powerful, and suppressing its direct expression will not make it go away. Like every other emotion, it needs to be acknowledged. Suppressing it can lead to serious physical and emotional diseases about which whole books have been written.

Being mad at your boss or partner is one thing, but finding yourself feeling angry at your baby is another. It can be frightening. It's important to recognize that some level of frustration and anger are experienced by virtually every parent.

First, know that it's OK to feel angry.

*The longer you can keep yourself attentive to the physical domain without acting out your anger, the more you'll learn about yourself. Although the mind can and will keep you endlessly agitated if you feed it with rationalizations and explanations, or reruns of the event you've just endured, the body itself seeks equilibrium. Observe the body long enough and without a lot of mental intervention (easier said than done) and you'll notice a change in those reactions.*
—John Travis and Regina Ryan, *Wellness Workbook*

Second, it's OK to express it—but not to dump it on your baby. If possible, leave the scene. Find some way to let off some steam—several deep, full breaths may be all you need to gain perspective. Or take a fast walk, beat on your bed with a tennis racket, tear up a phone book and ceremoniously throw it into the trash can. Monitor yourself to determine whether yelling or beating on something helps you get clear or not. If it doesn't, don't use it. Aerobic activity or talking to a tree or a willing friend are helpful ways to deal with the raw edge of anger.

Be aware that almost always, under the anger, is sadness or grief that typically has its roots in some unmet need. Getting in touch with the underlying emotion, the unmet need, can in itself be immensely valuable in shifting the energy towards healing rather than hurting.

Third, you may need the help of resources like those synopsized in the previous chapters on communication skills, or described in Appendix F, such as co-counseling, Process Coaching, or EFT—with or without a practitioner. Whatever your path, please follow it, for your sake and for your baby's. You will know when you have expressed or connected with your anger effectively because you will feel softer, and more open and powerful.

When we are centered, i.e., inwardly attuned, our partners and our children know it and we enjoy feeling that way. When we find ourselves off center, however, sometimes the best we can do is accept that that is where we are. And as Huber reminds us, it's from that place of acceptance and compassion that we can best model for our children the ways we hope they will treat themselves and those they love.

## Helping Hands

When your cup is full, your heart opens. It can be challenging to balance your baby's need to be with you, and your baby's need to be with someone who is emotionally available and present to him. This is where it is so much easier if your baby has been able to bond with more than one or two people, and you have a network of support around you. Reach out to find like-minded parents and other caring people. It may not be easy—but it will be so worth your while. Ideally, you will have begun this process before baby arrives, but if not, it's never too late to start. When we are feeling loved, supported, when our own cup is full, parenting is a pleasure, and our children are happier, and more content. When we are tired or frustrated—or better still, *before* we get to point of being tired and frustrated—we need another pair of hands, someone who can hold our baby, wash the dishes, feed the dog.

> *[W]ith more helping hands around, the task of parenting becomes less of a burden and more of a pleasure. When you feel securely held in a web of loving friends and family, you are better placed to help your child feel secure. When your social needs are met it shows in your demeanor, your mood, your tone of voice, your expression; even the way you hold your child is different. The good vibes you emanate are immediately picked up by your baby, and this helps him to feel contented.* —Robin Grille, *Heart-to-Heart Parenting*

## Key Points

- The hormones of loving connection between parent and infant literally nourish the child's brain and stimulate the growth of networks of connections in the brain associated with regulating emotions.
- A healthy and secure parent-child attachment optimizes mental, emotional, and intellectual health and wellbeing.
- Building blocks to healthy attachments include: nurturing the unborn as an aware and sensitive being; a natural (intervention-free) birth; skin-to-skin contact; breastfeeding; avoiding circumcision; co-sleeping; holding and carrying the infant; responding sensitively and promptly to the baby's cues; the loving, consistent care of primary caregivers in the pre-verbal years.
- Raising a child today is a monumental undertaking—regardless of parenting style; stresses can be minimized when parents fully meet their infants nurturing needs.
- In indigenous cultures, there is no concept of a spoiled child. Having their every need for nurturing met, they develop a strong sense of security and wellbeing that they carry into adolescence and adulthood.
- Healthy parenting responds appropriately to a baby; spoiling responds inappropriately. A stage of healthy dependence is prerequisite to a child's becoming securely independent.
- Attached babies, feeling responded to, connected and valued, cry and fuss less—and have more time to learn and grow in positive ways. Operating from a core of fear or anger, "disconnected" children are more likely to develop behavioral and emotional problems.
- Children's early relationships with caregivers shape the neurochemistry of emotion and their entire nervous system, including the brain. Whenever possible at least one parent best serves as primary caregiver in the pre-verbal years. Otherwise, a warm, intelligent person who can offer the continuity of care that is needed.
- Most of us, as children, learned that there were good and bad feelings, and to control our "bad" feelings. "Stop crying." "Don't be afraid." Repressing feelings is physically and emotionally unhealthy.
- The feeling of "about to lose it" as a signal of self neglect, and time to tune in and respond as best we can in the moment to our own needs. Even acknowledging them, can help.
- It is vitally important as parents to find ways to be physically and emotionally supported—or we have no resources to offer our children. Ideally this support will be in place before the baby comes.
- With helping hands, parenting is less of a burden and more of a pleasure—and parent and baby are more content.

## 29: IN THE ABSENCE OF THE VILLAGE

*Classic attachment theory and the new findings in neuroscience seem impossibly, outrageously exacting in the modern world.... Given the extraordinary demands placed on mothers in the modern era, how can they meet prescriptions for the selfless, constant mothering required to establish secure attachment and actualize the full potential of a child's brain? Research on bonding and attachment implies that good mothers must stay at home or permanently damage their children. For most of today's moms, the bar is too high.* —Thomas Verny, MD, *Pre-Parenting*

Blending what we now know about what's needed to optimize our children's health and wellbeing with the complexities of modern life—from the loss of the village to the dissolution of the extended family, along with the frequent need for both parents to work and/or the strong desire for many men and women to remain in the workforce *and* be a mother or father, leaves us with a burning question: *how do we manage to give our children what they need?*

The all-important simply being there can appear as an impossibility to most parents.

Along with the complexities noted above, an additional and less-acknowledged factor contributing to the seeming impracticality of attachment parenting is our having become accustomed to an incredible degree of freedom to pursue our own personal interests, and a high level of material comforts. Perhaps we can have all these things, but we may need to do with a little less in some areas, for a limited time, if we are to provide our children with the care that optimizes their wellbeing.

When a parent sincerely considers serving as primary caregiver through the early months and years of their child's life, the question may not be only "how can we afford it?" but also "how much do we want it?"

*Children are—or can be—a source of enormous pleasure, wonder, laughter, awe, and love. Commitment to one's developing child is as important as any career for the limited time we are privileged to be parents, and an invaluable investment in the future of our children, families, and society.*
—Isabelle Fox, *Being There*

Today, growing numbers of men and women are saying their families are as important as their careers, or more so, and are choosing to serve as their children's primary caregivers.

It may be possible for us to "have it all"—the joys of parenthood, the stimulation and ego gratification of career, and the material benefits of two incomes—but not concurrently, if we are to be responsive to the innate and legitimate needs of our children. In the absence of the "village" our children, in order to thrive rather than merely survive, need us, mother or father, to serve as primary caregiver at least during their pre-verbal years, i.e., the first two or three years.

Given this, let's look at some of the ways parents—in the absence of a supportive social milieu—are fulfilling their desire to serve as primary caregiver for their child through the early years.

## How to Meet Our Children's Needs for a Primary Caregiver

### *I. Sequencing*

Sequencing, a term described by Arlene Cardozo in *Sequencing: A New Solution for Women Who Want Marriage, Career, and Family*, allows growing numbers of women to enjoy both career and family to the fullest—by not trying to do it all at once. These educated career women are choosing to sequence their adult lives into three stages. For example: full time career, full time mothering, and then reincorporating career into their lives in new ways so family and professional life may complement each other rather than conflict. It seems reasonable to assume, given what we are learning from dads serving as primary caregivers, that this equally applies to men.

Sequencing parents see education and career as additional to, rather than a substitute for, their right and responsibility to care for their children, and recognize that by placing their child in surrogate care they deprive themselves of an experience they can never again have. They are challenging the assumption that hired caregivers can replace the loving care they can give their own children.

Sequencing is allowing them to "have it all"—career and family—by not trying to do it all at once. Differing substantially in age, income, geographical location, and professional background, many struggle with doubts and conflicts before making their decision. Some options, such as an at-home father or feminist at-home mother, may seem scary because there are so few models for them. While they may initially struggle with the loss of identity and rewards of the workplace, and feelings of isolation and loneliness, this is usually limited to the transition period because along with these feelings they bring home from their professional life problem solving skills, positive open attitudes, and the determination to make a success, in their own terms, of their home-based mothering years.

> *I loved having the primary role of nurturer. I was also initially scared of losing myself, and even more of boredom in the caretaking role, which is one reason I was so grateful for the rebozo (baby sling) and breastfeeding, which allowed me to get out and about, and be social when I had small children, instead of being "stuck" at home. I also never intended to stay in this role past the time my children were five or so; it was a choice for a period of time in my life. I am also grateful I did not have to deal with pumping and leaving my babies during the breastfeeding years.* —Barbara

With the mother sequencing, many couples report a feeling of cohesion, both in their marriage and as a family, a feeling there's time for them to share activities together, and fulfillment in knowing that they are the central, core figures contributing to their children's emotional, social, and intellectual wellbeing.

Cardozo has identified the factors that contribute to a sequencing mother's sense of happiness and satisfaction, and feelings of self-esteem and fulfillment. Looking at these factors listed below, these would apply to any parent—mother or father—choosing to stay at home with their child.

These factors include:
- a very clear sense of who she is and why she is at home raising her family;
- a supportive husband who values what she is doing;
- a community—even a neighbor or mentor—that reinforces her own values;
- her making a very clear distinction between children and work of the house with minimum of time spent on housework and maximum of time on family; and
- her recognition that she must have time to develop and maintain interests apart from family—even if this means 30 minutes a day to read or write—rather than clean house—while the baby naps.

When a woman interrupts her career to raise her children she is saying a career is an important part of me, but not all of me. I will do my work well but I won't give it my life. In Cardozo's words, "She is restructuring her personal priorities in opposition to the prevailing definition of professionalism, which today has come to mean not just career-involved but career-consumed." Again, these factors can apply equally to those dads who want to serve as a primary caregiver to their child.

## II. Working at home, or part-time

Beyond putting a job or career on hold for a period of time, other choices include working part-time, or working at home. Sometimes it makes economic and emotional sense for one parent to stay at home; or mother and father may consider split-shift work. Similarly, single parents can team together, each caring for the children of both while the other works.

## III. Cooperative and communal arrangements

Other options include arrangements where a single parent lives with another family that has a young child and receives living accommodations for caring for both children, or two or three families occupy adjacent living quarters in a large house or neighboring homes or apartments, sharing child care. Other care possibilities are relatives, or several families pooling financial resources to employ a full-time caregiver; or alloparents—secondary parents who have a special and ongoing relationship to the child, whether they are grandparents, other kin, or close friends.

Throughout time, mothers have depended on others for help with childrearing. The same is true for many other species. Co-operative parenting exists among wolves, tamarinds, marmosets, and elephants. In *Mother Nature* anthropologist, Sarah Blaffer Hrdy concluded that the best predictor of a mother's commitment to her infant is the amount and quality of support available to her. These studies highlighted the value of alloparents.

> *When Siena was about four years old, we moved to an intentional community in rural Virginia where we shared 500 acres, mostly wooded with a small lake and a river frontage, with about 60 adults and 25 children of all ages. Most members shared our values of individual freedom, cooperation, and camaraderie within a diversity of lifestyles and belief systems. Monthly meetings to handle the business of the farm were run by consensus—an eye-opening experience to participate in.*
>
> *It was a great place to raise children. Our home was in a cluster five, all but one of which were occupied by kids near Siena's age. The kids ran freely between the houses, and in the summer would all go to the little lake to swim, or play in the shallows of the river, dragging along any convenient parent.* —Jack

Robin Grille, in *Parenting for a Peaceful World*, urges us, most especially if separated from our biological families, to gather around us a "loyal, tribe-like co-operative parenting group." Friendship, common vision, and values can forge bonds as strong as biological ties. Pointing to modern-day mothers groups as a step in this direction, he reminds us that in the safety and familiarity of a small group of people with shared values, your child can become attached to people other than mom and dad.

### Creating Community

Today we know that something like 75% of abused children grow up to be adults who abuse their own children—passing this pattern of abuse on to the next generation. What we do not recognize is the abuse we carry as a result of our being raised in the nuclear, or more recently, the single parent family, and how we have internalized the oppression engendered within the isolation of those unnatural family structures. Beliefs, such as we have to do it on our own, the importance of "looking good," it's not OK to ask for help—and the tremendous feelings of isolation so engendered—are deeply imprinted and passed on.

Having been raised within the nuclear or single parent family, while we have the hurt, the longing for something more, for community, many of us have no internalized model or skills of connection, and so blocks emerge. We find we don't know *how* to be in connection/community. Many of us have tried, in some way, to be part of a more communal life process, only to experience failure on some level, to find it not to be as we dreamed and wanted. As we attempt to create community, we unconsciously begin recreating the familiar and therefore "comfortable" family dynamics we grew up with. Isolation behaviors are so built into our habits that they can erode our very best intentions to create connections/family. Unaware of the source of the difficulty, we will tend to blame ourselves for our failing.

*Even though we may not succeed as hoped, we will be passing something different on to our children who will see at least our desire, intention, and willingness to connect. And we have to keep going, awkwardly, clumsily groping our way—or we will never make the change.* —Chris Maple, PhD

## IV. Assets and borrowing

Isabelle Fox, in *Being There*, suggests looking at existing assets—savings accounts, stocks, and bonds—that could allow a parent to stay at home. Another option is borrowing money. We often borrow money for a car, home, or college tuition, but rarely consider a loan to allow parents to invest in their child by one of them staying at home. Some parents start a college fund for a child, often before the child is born, but the money may be of little use to a young adult with a poor attachment history. Saving money before the child is born, just as many save for homes and vacations, allows a parent to stay at home when the newborn arrives.

## V. Living more simply

Another option is living lower on the consumer chain—at least for a short time. With one spouse at home, payments for substitute care and the many work-related costs are eliminated. Many couples report that scaling down their standard of living provides their children with not only mothering, but also more fathering time. Many discover that living with less material values leaves them happier and freer, and they feel good passing these values onto their children.

While I sense some parents looked enviously at Jack and my working at home, where we could be full-time with Siena, or said with a sigh "you are so lucky to be able to do that," many of them could do likewise, were they willing to live more simply. Several years of living in a Quaker community in the mountains of Costa Rica, with a commitment to "voluntary simplicity" or living lightly on the earth, taught us how to live well on an average income of under $20,000. Yes, there have been "sacrifices," but every one of them worth it to have this time together, and the memories and experiences of these early years that will live on in our hearts forever.

## A Critically Important Role Choice

The prevailing social and economic climate undermines and disempowers parents, making it very challenging for them to give children what they need. Meeting our children's need for bonding and connection may appear to be more and more implausible, not because parents don't care, but because of an absence of appreciation of the vital role of parenting a child, and a lack of communal support.

Regardless, growing numbers of men and women are affirming both fathering and mothering to be a critically important role choice. Their decisions are prompting others to recognize that, in fully meeting our children's needs for continuity of care, parents contribute to the happiness of the next generation and generate the social and human capital that is essential to the wellbeing of our culture—and our world.

Significant changes will occur only as the social, economic, and political fabric of our culture provides meaningful and substantial policies and practices that give value and support to the role of parenting. And it is this to which we will now turn.

## Key Points
- Given what we know both about what's needed to optimize our children's health, and the complexities of modern life—how do we manage to give our children what they need?
- Growing numbers of women and men are choosing to serve as their child's primary caregiver through the early years, and also to accrue the rewards of career—but not concurrently.
- These parents are doing this by, for example: sequencing (enjoying rewards of both career and family—but not simultaneously); working at home, or part-time; cooperative and communal arrangements; using assets or loans; and/or living more simply.
- Factors contributing to sequencing parents' happiness and satisfaction include: a clear sense of who they are and why they are doing this; a supportive partner who values this; community; time to maintain their own interests, if only for 30 minutes a day.
- Those affirming parenting to be a critically important role choice for the future wellbeing of our children are prompting others to recognize to do the same.
- The prevailing social and economic climate makes it very difficult for parents to give their children what they need. Truly significant changes will occur only as the social, economic and political fabric values and supports the role of parenting.

# 30: Valuing the Art and Science of Parenting

The principles fostering optimal development are at best seriously compromised, at worst virtually impossible, for most of us to sustain in the one-parent or even two-parent families of today. The healthy development of the mother-infant bond—and the father-infant bond *and* the adult-adult relationship—must be addressed recognized as an issue vital to the wellbeing of our communities and our world.

> *Since we are all directly affected by the way children are cared for around the world, we should be concerned that all children are nurtured and educated, that both their physical and emotional needs are met. It is inverted logic to think that any society cannot afford the cost of supporting its parents to stay close to their children through their early years. What we cannot afford is the cost of not doing this.* —Robin Grille, *Parenting for a Peaceful World*

## Cost-Benefit Ratio

The cost to society per year from criminal behavior, drug use, and high school dropouts for a single youth ranges between $1.7 and 2.3 million.[59] Using Robert McFarland, MD's calculations, Lloyd deMause estimates that, while it would cost $5 billion a year to run parenting support centers in every US municipality, there would be a net savings of $750 billion/year through reductions in social violence.

Preventive and early intervention programs have proven repeatedly to be universally effective, and shown that improvements in parental sensitivity help children to become more emotionally secure. When mothers have solid support services—whether from extended family or an outside helper—the likelihood of secure attachment is enhanced. Secure attachment develops more readily when the mother learns how her emotions, based on her own childhood experience, can get in the way of providing responsive care. This is more important than the mother learning better techniques of childcare.

Social support enables parents to be more responsive to their children's needs. Lack of support from community, or from her partner, is particularly destructive to a mother's capacity to be emotionally responsive to her baby. Mothers who do not feel *emotionally* supported are more at risk of committing child abuse. It would seem reasonable to extrapolate the same to a father's capacity. Another special significance of these studies is their highlighting the fact that support for parents needs to address their *emotional needs*.

*People respond in remarkable ways when they feel that someone is there to help them.* —Robert Karen, *Becoming Attached*

Karen believes that implementing programs that take attachment needs seriously:

> *[W]ould offer us a different quality of life, where we would be taking care of human needs that most societies attended to before the industrial era: strengthening the family, which is the best institution we have for meeting the needs of children; enjoying a greater social cohesion, with less cause for segregation and fear. And perhaps we would be rendered less wistful by reports about loving primitive tribes.*

## Why Denial?

Today we know that newborns experience discomfort, pain, and shock to the same or a greater degree than adults do, and have the same range of emotions as adults. Early experiences have lasting effects, leaving neural pathways in the brain affecting the ways in which we view ourselves and our world.

As far back as 1951, in his report commissioned by the World Health Organization on the mental health of homeless children in post-war Europe, Bowlby underscored the quality of an infant's/child's connection to loved ones as key to personality development and to their ability to connect with others.[60]

As noted earlier, research in the 80s validated Bowlby's predictions of the relevance of attachment theory as applied not only to the wellbeing of children, but also to parenting styles and to adult love. Literally thousands of studies have documented the importance of these attachments—and yet it is only now that we are seeing the significance of attachment theory, most especially as it applies to parenting style and adult love, filtering into the fringes of any mainstream parenting books.

Certainly, Bowlby's report and the aftermath of the research it engendered, has revolutionized child care practice around the world, influencing adoption, hospital and social work policies, and the parenting practices of many a parent. Yet there are enormous gaps and we have a long, long way to go before every child receives the welcome to the world that is the surest way to foster their optimal development as infants and children, and the adults they are to become.

Arthur Janov, in *The Biology of Love*, stated that if we are to avoid substance abuse, depression, and violence, and if we are to populate this world with healthy human beings, we need to take great care in pre-birth and in the early hours and months after birth. Today, this would be substantiated by not only neuroscientists, but accepted by a growing number of helping professionals working within the field of birthing and infants and children.

> [The early hours and months after birth are] *when the brain is forming new synapses and dendrites; its communication system is developing that will allow the child to be more than competent in many spheres, physical, artistic, and intellectual....*
>
> *I am impressed by... how simple it is to accomplish.... It is far easier than building prisons and mental hospitals to take care of the errors we have already made in childrearing. What most of us write about is how to fix the compensating mechanisms of early lack of love. We fix the migraine sufferer, the rapist, the drug addict, the voyeur, the hypertensive, the teeth-grinder, and the depressive. We need to start addressing causes before there is a deviated, abnormal brain system that forces deviated behavior.* —Arthur Janov, *The Biology of Love*

Given what we know, how is it that we are continuing to do what we do? Can it be that what is needed to raise a well child—and a well world—is in conflict with prevailing personal and social needs and interests, such as the importance of careers, our right to "our own lives," the importance of the almighty dollar? These priorities are reflected not only in a parent's inability to remain at home to care for her child, but also in the business world's refusal to deal with lengthy parental leaves, flex-hours, and options like job-sharing. And social and political structures, with few exceptions, give only lip service to the art and science of parenting.

Why is it that we live in denial of the wounding that most all of us have been subjected to? Can it be that the underlying reason for this denial is because the message activates a pain in the collective consciousness that is so deep that most people simply cannot contemplate it. It is simply too painful, too despairing, for most people to let in. As Suzanne Arms writes:

> *We live in denial about what babies experience for two reasons. If we were to look at babies and allow ourselves to feel what they are feeling when they appear to be in distress from things we do to them, then we would not be able to continue doing what we do. Second, if we stopped denying a baby's capacity to suffer, we would then have to face the feelings we carry deep within ourselves of the trauma we experienced during our own birth and infancy.*

Are we willing? Clearly, while it is not a territory that many will venture into, the response of the early readers of this book (and the article that preceded it) indicates that many are willing to do just that.

> *We are the generations, alive today, who understand the profound effects of early pain and trauma on the neonate. We understand the violation perpetuated by denying the infant's need for body-to-body contact, mother's breast, and protection from circumcision. We understand the lifelong physical and psychological consequences that result from birth and beginning-of-life trauma. We also are the generations who can do something about bringing an*

*end to these unnecessary trauma-inducing practices and the inherent pain and suffering inflicted upon infants and children. And, in that process of protecting others, we heal our own trauma, ourselves, and future generations.*
—Marilyn Milos, founder, NOCIRC*

## Valuing the Art and Science of Parenting

*Constantly making lists of things to do… not valuing mothering as a job… feeling I have to produce to be of value. If I valued mothering more… if it had gotten into my bones… if I was around people who valued it…. if mothering was valued as a role* and *I felt permission to live it—it would have made a huge difference. I got it intellectually, but that wasn't enough.* —Maggie

Today the connections between a well child and a well world are laser-clear. Yet, although the US ranks second worldwide in per capita income, it does not make it into the top ten in any significant indicator of child welfare. Until we, as a society, recognize and give value to the art and science of parenting as being of utmost importance to the wellbeing of our nation and world, and offer educational, economic, and social practices and policies that support all families in preparing for optimal gestation, birthing, and parenting,† substantial change will not occur.

Many people are still convinced of the value of "rugged individualism," and some will even claim that attachment parenting is un-American because it promotes cooperation and interdependence instead of independence.

Practices and policies fostering the healthy bonding and attachment between parents—mothers and fathers—and babies, are the surest way to prevent child abuse, neglect, and antisocial behavior in older children, not to mention turn the tide of men leaving. These policies include out-of-hospital, independent birth centers specializing in natural childbirth; financial incentives to all mothers who breastfeed for at least six months; a parenting leave system that supports parental choice; financial incentives to at least one parent to be primary caregiver of the baby during the first three years; postpartum care for families through the first year and longer if necessary; incentives for job sharing and flexible hours; and both childhood development education and relationship building programs in schools and adult learning centers. It is vital that prenatal and postnatal engagement with mothers *and* fathers be expanded to cover healthy relationships, parents' attachment history, father involvement, and collaborative parenting in ways that "make sense" to both sexes.

The Fatherhood Institute notes a great variety of ways in which relationship education and support can be delivered, with increasing reliance on electronic

---

* National Organization of Circumcision Information Resource Centers
† See the *aTLC Proclamation and Blueprint* (Appendix D).

and other outlets. Both men and women like to receive relationship and parenting information via television and the Internet, and there is considerable commercial potential for existing and new programs to address the relationship issues that emerge during the transition to parenthood.

All these initiatives need to be backed by community-based group support networks for parents, early intervention and home support services, and family-friendly community environments that welcome children and encourage family and intergenerational activities.

While advocating for these changes on every possible front, we cannot merely wait for them to occur. It is imperative that we begin now to nurture our children's natural tendency for living a compassionate, cooperative, and creative life. We can begin today by developing and sharing our visions and dreams, and practicing in our homes and introducing into our communities, the values and principles that will guide and inform such a humane and sustainable world.

> *I went to see the new Spielberg movie,* War Horse, *last weekend. A powerful film about an amazing horse and a young man who loves him, but one that contains footage of World War I and the violence and gritty filth of war. It's not a film for children, yet parents are bringing even toddlers. I was sitting next to a boy who couldn't have been 5 years old, who was there next to his father. I cringed and looked over every time there was a noisy, violent scene on the screen, hoping to see the boy's father put his arm around him protectively and hold him close and whisper comforting words or shield him from that part of the film. But the father was engrossed in watching. As gently as I could, I whispered: "You may want to comfort your son, as I think he's afraid." The father, feeling attacked by a stranger, and a woman no less, responded: "He's my son and I know what to do for him." I nodded. But I noticed after that, that most of the time when there were noisy, violent scenes, that father would put his arm around his son, and tuck him closer to him, and sometimes even whisper in his ear.* —Suzanne Arms

## The Changing Face of "Family"

While we talk about the importance of valuing the art and science of parenting, and supporting families in raising children, it is important to recognize that what constitutes family is itself changing rapidly.

> *Creating families is no longer as simple as mom and dad getting married, settling down, making a baby or four. Thanks to today's technology, a woman can have babies that are created from her own eggs or with donor eggs. She can use her spouse's sperm, sperm donated by a friend, or purchase it from a sperm bank.* —Peggy Drexler, *Raising Boys without Men*

Growing numbers of children are being raised by single or divorced parents, by stepparents in "blended" families, or by adoptive parents, gay and lesbian couples,* and grandparents. More are being raised by mothers who have not divorced or been abandoned by a man, but are single by choice and have made a conscious decision to have a baby.

It is painfully apparent that parenting today, whether in the nuclear or single parent family, has become a highly stressful undertaking. Many mothers feel isolated, dads feel superfluous, and both feel incompetent—even when they are far from it. The stress felt by many parents is reaching epidemic levels: women are withdrawing, men are leaving, and the children are the victims. Fortunately another scenario is slowly but surely gaining momentum.

Out of the ashes of the nuclear family, a whole range of communal models of raising children—and supporting parents and caregivers—is rising. Many parents are reaching out to form co-operative or extended families of choice—sharing babysitting arrangements, meals, playtimes and holidays, enrolling children in cooperative nursery schools, and enlisting grandparents, aunts, uncles, and friends to help with childcare. Whether in neighborhoods, intentional communities or co-housing developments—where a family's private home is within a small geographic community, sharing common facilities—these initiatives are emerging as a means by which families can widen their support network. Peggy Drexler coined the term "collected family" to describe the multiplicity of family configurations of the 21st century. Collected families grow organically, through situation and circumstance.

> *A family is a collection of people who love each other and take care of each other and help kids grow up.* —young boy in Drexler's, *Raising Boys Without Men*

Rather than depending on blood, or even marriage ties, the best of these collected families are being built on ties of affinity and affection that, carefully tended, develop into trust and true comm-*unity*. The transition is a bumpy one, but the trend from nuclear and single to collected families offers elements of the extended family or even the village, where children can draw on a variety of others of different ages, genders, interests, temperaments, and skills.

> *In the end, the structure of our formal connections doesn't matter so much. It's intimacy that counts, and the responsibility that intimacy engenders. In the growing and evolving communities of caring, the potential for love for our children becomes as limitless as the sources of that love.*
> —Peggy Drexler, *Raising Boys without Men*

---

* An estimated 5 million lesbians and 3 million gay men have become parents and are raising an estimated 6 to 14 million children.

Questions, such as these raised by Adrienne Burgess in *Fatherhood Reclaimed* become ever more relevant and timely:
- *Can it be that it is no longer helpful to talk in terms of "fathers'" or "mothers'" roles?*
- *Can we conceive of society in which neither mothers nor fathers have exclusive roles, and where both are equally valued as breadwinners and intimate parents?*
- *Can we envision the value of changing our entire attitude to parenting, and fathers' and mothers' rights, roles and responsibilities?*

## A World that Works for Everyone

Can we envision a society in which both men and women, equally, are free to listen and respond to their own calling with respect to parenting and their work in the world? Just as some men are born with the calling to be primary caregivers to their children, some women feel called to work in the world and only secondarily to spend time with their children. It is different for every individual.

This would mean that some parents will leave the workforce, at least temporarily, to devote time to caring for children. Others may give priority to work in the world, and others may find some creative combination of the two. We see increasing numbers of adults choosing to join energies in raising children in small groups or communities, where children are able to receive attention, nurturance, and guidance from a larger number of caring adults. Such arrangements allow each adult to responsibly and creatively negotiate the amount of time they give to work in the world and the amount of time they give to children.

With a more informed awareness of the roles and responsibilities required of those who choose to become the biological parents of a new generation, we will see growing numbers of adults choosing not to conceive, but to be actively involved with mothering or fathering children within their collected family or community. In these situations, we can more readily conceive of a society in which the welfare of children is a wider social responsibility, and ultimately recognize that we are all a part of one another. It is then that we will truly create a world that works for everyone. However as we crawl, run, stumble toward this world, it can be helpful to remember that we are born *wired to connect*. While acknowledging the core estrangement patterns that we carry from our very early experiences, we can draw strength from the knowing that connection is our natural state of being, it is ours to reclaim.

Having been betrayed in early connection, many of us carry the hurt of that betrayal, and may find ourselves both yearning for and afraid of connection.

We may tell ourselves that we would feel more connected if we found someone we could really trust, or someone who really loved us, but this rationalization can tend to perpetuate the pattern. For the bottom line is that our ability to authentically connect with others is dependent on our ability to authentically connect—to care for, to accept, to love—our selves. How different would our lives be were we to commit to this as a moment-to-moment, day-to-day, practice?

A simple act of loving kindness, extended to self or to another person, can shift our attention from estrangement to connection and switch, in an instant, the whole network of emotions and feelings through which we experience the world—and through which those around us experience their world.

As we look around us, we can see a growing awareness of our interdependence, and the myriad steps—baby steps and giant leaps, both equally valuable—being taken towards honoring that interdependence and the sacredness of all life on earth.

All this offers hope that the vision proclaimed by the Alliance for Transforming the Lives of Children, may indeed come to fruition.

## We envision a world where:
- *Every child is wanted, welcomed, loved, and valued.*
- *Every family is prepared for and supported in practicing the art and science of nurturing children.*
- *Adults respect children and honor childhood.*
- *Children joyfully participate in the vital life of family and community.*
- *Dynamic, resilient, life-honoring cultures flourish.*\*

---

\* See the *aTLC Proclamation and Blueprint* (Appendix D).

## Key Points

- Since we are all directly affected by the way children around the world are cared for, it is inverted logic to think our society cannot afford the cost of supporting its children through the early years. We cannot afford *not* to. Preventive and early intervention programs are universally effective.
- Today we know that our *in utero*, birth, and early experiences leave neural pathways in the brain affecting the way in which we view ourselves and our world; and that if we are to avoid substance abuse, addictions, depression, and violence, we need to take great care in this early period.
- Why are we continuing to largely ignore this well-substantiated knowledge and live in denial about what our very young need and experience?
- On an immediate level, a substantial factor is the prevailing social and economic climate; and for many parents it is the conflict between meeting our infant/child's needs, and our personal needs.
- Can it be because the message activates a pain in the collective consciousness that is so deep it is simply too painful to let in?
- We are the generations who can do something to end this unnecessary neglect, pain, and suffering—and in the process of protecting our very young, heal our own trauma—our selves.
- While connections between a well child and well world are laser-clear, the US does not make it into the top ten in any significant indicators of child welfare.
- Until we, as individuals and hence as a society, value the art and science of parenting as being of utmost importance to the wellbeing of our world, substantial changes will not occur.
- Can we envision a society in which men and women, equally, are free to listen and respond to their own calling with respect to parenting and work in the world?
- With more informed awareness of the responsibilities of parenting, more may choose not to conceive but be actively involved with parenting within their "collected family" or community.
- As we move in this direction, it is important to remember that while connection is our essential state of being, most of us, having been in some ways betrayed in early connection, may both yearn for and fear connection. And, that our ability to connect with others, is dependent on our healing and ability to connect with—to love and accept—our selves, in the moment, now.

# BIBLIOGRAPHY

***Selected books cited in the text:***

Ainsworth, Mary et al. *Attachment and Loss.* Psychology Press, 1979.

Allen, Connie. *Joyous Child, Joyous Parent: How to Have More Fun and Joy with Your Child.* Metacreative Press, 2009.

Arms, Suzanne. *Immaculate Deception II.* Celestial Arts, 1994.

Belsky, Jay. *The Transition to Parenthood.* Dell, 1995.

Blankenhorn, David. *Fatherless America: Confronting our Most Urgent Social Problem.* Harper Perennial, 1996.

Bronstein, Phyllis and Carolyn Pape Cowan. *Fatherhood Today: Men's Changing Role in the Family.* Wiley, 1988

Bowlby, John. *Attachment.* Basic Books, 1983.

Brott, Armin. *Father for Life: A Journey of Joy, Challenge, and Change.* Abbeville Press, 2003.

Brown, Brené (2007). *I Thought It Was Just Me (But It Isn't): Telling the Truth about Perfectionism, Inadequacy, and Power.* Gotham Books, New York, Kindle edition.

Buckley, Sarah. *Gentle Birth, Gentle Mothering: A Doctor's Guide to Natural Childbirth and Gentle Early Parenting Choices.* Celestial Arts, 2008.

Burgess, Adrienne. *Fatherhood Reclaimed: The Making of the Modern Father.* Vermilion, 1998.

Capacchione, Lucia, *The Creative Journal for Parents.* Shambala, 2000.

Capacchione, Lucia and Sandra Bardsley. *Creating a Joyful Birth Experience.* Fireside, 1994.

Cardozo, Arlene. *Sequencing: A New Solution for Women Who Want Marriage, Career, and Family.* Brownstone Books, 1996.

Chamberlain, David. *Babies Remember Birth.* Ballentine, 1989.

Childre, Doc. *A Parenting Manual: Heart Hope for the Family.* Planetary Publications, 1995.

Cowan, Carolyn Pape and Philip Cowan. *When Partners Become Parents.* Routledge, 1999.

Diamond, Jed. *Mr. Mean: Saving Your Relationship from the Irritable Male Syndrome.* Vox Novus, 2010.

Drexler, Peggy. *Raising Boys Without Men: How Maverick Moms Are Creating the Next Generation of Exceptional Men.* Rodale, 2006.

Fox, Isabelle. *Being There.* Barrons Educational Series, 1996.

Glennon, Will. *Fathering: Strengthening Connection with Your Children No Matter Where You Are.* Conari, 1995.

Gottman, John. *The Seven Principles for Making Marriage Work.* Three Rivers Press, 2000.

Grille, Robin. *Parenting for a Peaceful World.* Longueville Media, 2005.
Grille, Robin. *Heart-to-Heart Parenting.* Vox Cordis Press, 2012.
Haas, Aaron. *The Gift of Fatherhood: How Men's Lives Are Transformed by their Children.* Fireside, 1994.
Hendricks, Gay and Kathlyn Hendricks. *Conscious Loving.* Bantam, 1992.
Houser, Patrick. *Fathers to Be Handbook.* Creative Life Systems Ltd, 2007.
Hrdy, Sarah Blaffer. *Mother Nature.* Ballentine, 1999.
Huber, Cheri. *Time Out For Parents: A Guide to Compassionate Parenting.* Keep It Simple Books, 2004.
Huxley, Laura. *The Child of Your Dreams.* Destiny, 2001.
Janov, Arthur. *The Biology of Love.* Prometheus, 2000.
Johnson, Sue. *Hold Me Tight: Seven Conversations for a Lifetime of Love.* Little, Brown, 2009.
Karen, Robert. *Becoming Attached: First Relationships and How They Shape Our Capacity to Love.* Oxford University Press (USA), 1998.
Katie, Byron, *Loving What Is: Four Questions that Can Change Your Life,* Three Rivers, 2003.
Klaus, Marshall, John Kennell and Phyllis Klaus. *Mothering the Mother, How a Doula Can Help You Have a Shorter, Easier, and Healthier Birth.* DeCapo, 1993.
Korte, Diana and Roberta Scaer. *A Good Birth, A Safe Birth.* Harvard Common Press, 1992.
Leboyer, Frederick. *Birth Without Violence.* Healing Arts Press, 2002.
Liedloff, Jean. *The Continuum Concept: In Search of Happiness Lost.* DeCapo, 1986.
Leo, Pam. *Connection Parenting: Parenting Through Connection Instead of Coercion, Through Love Instead of Fear.* Wyatt-MacKenzie, 2007.
Luminare-Rosen, Carista. *Parenting Begins before Conception.* Healing Arts Press, 2000.
Odent, Michel. *The Scientification of Love.* Free Association Books, 1999.
Pateros, John, et al. *Healing to Wholeness, Healer's Guide: The Process Coaching Practitioner Manual,* Third Edition. Wholeness Resource Center, 2008.
Paul, Jordan and Margaret Jordan. *Do I Have to Give Up Me to Be Loved by You?* Hazelden, 2002.
Paul, Margaret. *Inner Bonding.* HarperOne, 1992.
Pearce, Joseph Chilton. *Magical Child.* Plume, 1992.
Pruett, Kyle, *Fatherneed: Why Father Care Is as Essential as Mother Care for Your Child.* Broadway, 2001.
Seel, Richard. *The Uncertain Father.* Gateway Books 1987.
Sherman, Karen. *Mindfulness and The Art of Choice.* Loving Healing Press, 2008.
Travis, John and Regina Ryan. *Wellness Workbook.* Celestial Arts, 2004.
Verny, Thomas. *Pre-Parenting: Nurturing Your Child from Conception.* Simon & Schuster, 2003.
Verny, Thomas. *Secret Life of the Unborn Child.* Summit, 1981.
Walant, Karen. *Creating the Capacity for Attachment.* Jason Aronson, 1999

# Resources

WhyDadsLeave.com offers descriptions and links to organizations and programs that address the issues described in this book. These include:
- Alliance for Transforming the Lives of Children
- Association for Prenatal & Perinatal Psychology and Health
- Attachment Parenting International
- Birthing the Future
- Center for Effective Discipline
- Connection Parenting
- Consciously Parenting
- The Fatherhood Institute
- Fathers to Be International
- Heart-to-Heart Parenting
- Intact America
- Liedloff Continuum Network
- The ManKind Project
- MenAlive
- Mother-Friendly Childbirth Initiative
- Natural Child Project
- Non-violent Communication
- Parental Intelligence Newsletter
- Pathways Magazine
- Process Coaching Center
- Re-evaluation Counseling
- Touch the Future
- Wellness Associates
- The Wellness Way
- The Wellness Inventory Online

# APPENDICES

*The full appendices can be found at WhyDadsLeave.com with direct links.*

## Appendix A: "Why Men Leave"

The original 2004 magazine articles that spawned this book.

## Appendix B: Primal Sex: Bosom Buddies and Other Lovers

By Jeannine Parvati Baker

A major inspiration to Jack's formulating the original hypothesis of MPAS.

## Appendix C: Synopsis of *The Continuum Concept*

A synopsis of Jean Liedloff's *The Continuum Concept* that so strongly influenced Meryn and Jack's work, as well as other parenting books and reviews of selected children's books that were created when Meryn produced *The Wellspring Guide* in the late 90s. These books remain classics in the field of parenting and childcare.

## Appendix D: The aTLC Proclamation and Blueprint for Transforming the Lives of Children

Meryn and Jack, along with eleven other founding board members, spent over 10,000 hours developing and documenting this missing "Instruction Manual for Birthing and the Caring for Kids," which resides at the Alliance for Transforming the Lives of Children's website, aTLC.org.

## About the Author and the Contributor

**Meryn G. Callander** was born in Australia in 1952. She attended Monash University in Melbourne, Victoria, graduating with degrees in both social work and economics, and went on to become a social worker helping children in crisis.

In 1979, Meryn embarked on an around-the-world journey culminating in California, where she attended a residential seminar at the Wellness Resource Center, established by John (Jack) Travis in 1975. It was here that the spark was lit that led to over 30 years of marriage and professional partnership. As co-director of Wellness Associates, Meryn joined Jack in pushing the frontiers of wellness beyond the personal and into the interpersonal and planetary.

Her immersion in the field of feminist spirituality in the San Francisco Bay Area in the 1980s was pivotal in forging a new direction for Wellness Associates. Together with Jack, she facilitated seminars that fostered a network of helping professionals committed to shifting the prevailing cultural norms that undermine personal integrity and authenticity, and compromise our potential for true partnership and connection with others. They co-authored *Wellness for Helping Professionals: Creating Compassionate Cultures*.

In 1992, Meryn took Jack's classic *Wellness Inventory*, with its focus on personal wellness, to a planetary focus, co-authoring *A Change of Heart: The Global Wellness Inventory*. In 1999, she took the lead in revising the *Wellness Inventory* for an online version produced by HealthWorld Online.

In 1993, Meryn gave birth to their daughter, Siena, an experience that was to radically change her life in a multitude of unexpected ways. Her own experiences of birthing and parenting led to the *Wellspring Guide*, a quarterly publication featuring her in-depth synopses of selected parenting and children's books (now accessible through WhyDadsLeave.com).

In 1999, along with eleven other experts in the field of birth and child development, she co-founded, and served for several years as president of, the Alliance for Transforming the Lives of Children.

*Why Men Leave,* a magazine article by Jack published in the US and Australia in 2004 (see Appendix A), generated such a strong response that it compelled Meryn to dive deeper into the neurobiological, interpersonal, social and cultural dynamics underlying their experience and prompted her to write *Why Dads Leave.*

Meryn and John separated in 2011. Meryn now resides in the beautiful Byron Shire in northern New South Wales, Australia.

**John W. Travis, MD, MPH,** completed his medical degree at Tufts University and a preventive medicine residency at Johns Hopkins University. In 1975, he opened the world's first wellness center, the Wellness Resource Center in Mill Valley, California. His work attracted national attention, culminating in an appearance on *60 Minutes* with Dan Rather in 1979.

His *Wellness Workbook,* coauthored with Regina Ryan and now in its third edition, was first published in 1981. The *Wellness Inventory,* first published in 1975, is now in its fourth edition. Also available in an online version, it is used by hospitals, corporations, and spas as well as wellness coaches.

In 1991, Jack expanded the focus of his work to infant wellness, co-founding the Mother-Friendly Childbirth Initiative in 1996 and the Alliance for Transforming the Lives of Children in 1999 (see Appendix D).

Out of bringing it all together in what he calls full-spectrum wellness, he coined the phrase "The currency of wellness is connection."

He presently consults with wellness-oriented organizations, speaks on infant wellness, and teaches wellness assessment in the unique online Master of Wellness Program at RMIT University (Royal Melbourne Institute of Technology) in Australia.

# GRATITUDE

I cannot name all the people who have contributed to the birthing of *Why Dads Leave*. Many will not even know of the role they played—the significance of a story shared, a mere word of encouragement in a much-needed moment, a challenge to the stand I had taken. Others will be well aware of the moments in which they have held my hand and my heart, how each in their unique way have been pivotal in the birthing of this book. I am in awe of the potency held in a momentary exchange between two people, of the gifts afforded by those who love and hold and believe in me.

Firstly I extend my gratitude to my partner of 30-some years, John (Jack) Travis, whose 4-page article published in the magazines *Byron Child* (now Kindred Community online) and *Compleat Mother* compelled me to dive even deeper into the dynamics of *Why Dads Leave*. Without his initial hypothesis, this book would have never been conceived. Even more significantly, I thank him for bringing me the greatest gift and guru of my life—our daughter, Siena. I thank him for having been my partner, confidante, and trusted friend.

Secondly, I express my deep gratitude to Kent Peterson, godfather of this book. Without his generosity, wisdom, and virtuosity, it would not have seen the light of day. Thanks also to Kent and to his lovely wife, Patricia Meyer-Peterson, for sanctuary space.

And to Bobbie Burdett, godmother of my daughter Siena. Bobbie has been with this book since its conception... and I know will be with it until death do them part.

Gratitude extends beyond measure to those who held me in their hearts and were there to assist and encourage me through the complications that emerged in the final stages of labor most especially: Bobbie Burdett, Anna Davidovich, Joy Holloway, Marilyn Milos, Lisa Reagan, Anna Watts, and Kelly Wendorf. And the loving memory of my parents, Bonnie and Wilbur—ever-present.

My deep gratitude to other longtime friends and colleagues who, with their contributions, have given life to this book: Connie Allen, Suzanne Arms, Sarah Buckley, Ray Castellino, Jed Diamond, Bruce Erickson, Robin Grille, Betty Idarius, Eric Idarius, Meg Jordan, Jean Liedloff, Pam Leo, Dorothy Mandel, Buffy Maple, Chris Maple, Emmett Miller, Michel Odent, John Pateros, Joe (Chilton) Pearce, Dean Radetsky, Cheryl Radetsky, Gaye Raymond, Marty Rubin, Maggie Watson, Amelia Williams, Susanna Williams, Barbara Wishingrad, and Ralph Wolff.

I am also grateful for the contributions of: Adrian Burgess, Carolyn and Phillip Cowan, Kim Griffith, Mitzi Gold, Kyle Pruett, Sue Johnson, Patrick

Houser, Jordan Paul, Margaret Paul, Richard Seel, Karen Sherman, and Karen Walant. And, for support with publication and publicity efforts, my thanks go to Ron Ball, Michaela Conley, Eric Fletcher, Jeff Hutner, Laura Ross, and Richard Stodart.

A special thank you to Bill Kauth, who first encouraged Jack to revise the original newsletter article so it could be professionally published and to Dean Edell, who then urged us to create a book from that article.

Jack and I are indebted to those readers of the initial magazine articles, who confirmed our observations about the prevalence of DDD, and the depth of the pain, despair, and frustration this phenomenon engenders—and those many others who have since courageously stepped forward to share their personal journeys with us.

Many thanks to my editor, Lisa Pliscou; to Joy Holloway for her additional proofing; and to Lisa Reagan, who stepped up in the final months before publication to so very generously contribute her editorial and publicity skills, encouragement, and support.

It has been said that the love of a mother is like no other. Siena, my love for you bears testimony to this. This book would never have been, without you. Thank you for initiating me into hitherto unknown dimensions of love, and forever extending the bounds of my being.

*From Jack:*

I would like to acknowledge our daughter Siena, who proofread this book, and then designed and laid out the entire cover, front and back.

And also Meryn, whose relentless drive to expand the book far beyond my initial vision, and then doing most of the writing, well beyond what either of us anticipated, was a gift not only for me, but also for all our readers.

# INDEX

A.R.E. conversation, 272
adult attachment, 39, 194, 195
affectional needs, 171
Ainsworth, Mary, 30, 36, 39
Allen, Connie, 106, 300

Alliance for Transforming the Lives of Children, (aTLC), 12, 75, 299, 319
alloparents, 308
Arms, Suzanne, 34, 71, 125, 127, 128, 129, 131, 136, 138, 236, 314
*aTLC Blueprint*, 12
attachment disorders, 30
attachment parenting, 6, 10, 12, 31, 36, 85, 188, 292, 297, 300, 301, 305, 315
attachment theory, 30, 35, 36, 38, 41, 49, 262, 299, 305, 313
attachment-promoting behaviors, 31

babymoon, 114
Baker, Jeannine Parvati, 144, 167
Belsky, Jay, 149, 150, 151, 153, 154, 155, 157, 160, 161
Blankenhorn, David, 17, 90
Bowlby, John, 30, 31, 36, 37, 38, 39, 194, 262, 313
Bridging the Divide, 152
Burdett, Bobbie, 239
Burgess, Adrienne, 56, 58, 59, 60, 68, 70, 75, 76, 82, 86, 90, 91, 92, 93, 94, 105, 148, 318

Cardozo, Elaine, 306, 307
Career and Work, 156
Chamberlain, David, 127
changing communication patterns, 153
Childre, Doc, 183
children's wellbeing, 42, 46, 56
  indicators of, 26
circumcision, 17, 136, 292, 314
coach, 106, 141, 142, 235, 285

coaching, 190, 239, 240
co-counselling, 303
connection parenting, 14, 33, 215, 283, 291, 296
*Continuum Concept, The*, 3, 4, 5, 292
cooperative and communal arrangements, 307
costs to society, 26
couvade, 117, 118, 141
couvade syndrome, 118, 122
*covert* male postnatal depression, 13
Cowan, Carolyn Pape and Philip, 14, 46, 51, 148, 149, 160, 161, 162
creating community, 308
cry alone, 31, 175, 200
C-section, 34, 233

dad at birth, 142
deMause, Lloyd, 312
division of labor, 155
divorce, 1, 26, 34, 43, 46, 55, 61, 62, 96, 98, 129, 147, 151, 152, 230, 247, 252
doula, 128, 129, 130, 133, 136, 137, 140, 142, 143, 151
Drexler, Peggy, 59, 60, 316, 317
Dynamic of Disappearing Dads (DDD), 1, 4, 17, 19, 23, 26, 29, 30, 39, 48, 50, 51, 77, 139, 151, 154, 155, 159, 197
forces underlying, 48

Emotional Freedom Technique (EFT), 303
Emotionally Focused Therapy (EFT), 262

FatherStory, 11, 90, 92, 94, 95
Find the Bad Guy, 267
Fonagy, Peter, 194
foreskin, 17
Gaskin, Ina Mae, 144

gatekeeping, 75, 85, 90, 155
Glennon, Will, 22
Gottman, John, 48, 266, 279, 280, 281, 284, 286
Grille, Robin, 46, 50, 114, 175, 181, 199, 200, 214, 215, 264, 291, 300, 303, 309, 312
guilt, 13, 14, 48, 108, 193, 233
guilt versus regret, 14

Heartmath, 181, 182, 183
Houser, Patrick, 60, 103, 120, 129, 142
Hrdy, Sarah Blaffer, 30, 36, 308
Huber, Cheri, 301, 302, 303
Huxley, Laura, 175

Idarius, Betty, 219, 220, 221, 222, 224
*Immaculate Deception II*, 34, 127, 128
indigenous cultures, 5, 10, 33, 296
inner child, 8, 111, 153, 199, 201, 202, 203, 204, 205, 206, 209, 214, 235, 236, 243
inner peace, 197, 302

Janov, Arthur, 296, 313, 314
Johnson, Sue, 20, 21, 40, 43, 46, 49, 50, 79, 106, 112, 115, 161, 162, 170, 178, 179, 193, 262, 278

Karen, Robert, 17, 28, 37, 38, 39, 103, 188, 189, 190, 194, 195, 201, 210
Klaus, Marshall, 30, 138

learned helplessness, 17
Leboyer, Frederick, 17, 144, 145
Leo, Pam, 14, 15, 33, 35, 193, 283, 291, 296
Liedloff, Jean, 3, 5, 12, 24, 25, 194, 292
*Living More Simply*, 309

*Magical Child*, 30, 36, 202, 203, 297
Main, Mary, 194

Male Postpartum Abandonment Syndrome (MPAS), 7, 8, 10, 11, 13, 76, 77, 155, 168
male postpartum depression, 76
Mandel, Dorothy, 196
Maple, Chris, 22, 165, 280, 309
marital changes, 151
  Improvers, 151
  Moderate decliners, 151
  Severe decliners, 151
Masters and Johnson, 121, 171
money worries, 155

negative patterns, 266, 279
normative abuse, 11, 17, 28, 48, 193, 201

Odent, Michel, 12, 13, 134, 135, 140, 141
oxytocin, 24, 25, 64, 104, 134, 196, 197, 264

Pateros, John, 207, 219, 220, 221, 222, 224
Pearce, Joseph Chilton, 30, 36, 182, 183, 297
Penn State Child and Family Development Project, 149
perfection, 214
power-over, 3
power-with, 3
Prescott, James, 19, 30
pre-verbal years, 31, 292, 298, 306
Primal Health Research Center, 12
primary caregivers, 18, 29, 70, 298, 299, 305, 306, 318
  dads, 70
priorities
  father's, 159
  mother's, 159
problem about the problem, 28
Process Coaching, 168, 219, 220, 235, 236, 242, 303

Protest Polka, 266, 267, 268, 269, 270, 271
Pruett, Kyle, 56, 57, 59, 61, 62, 64, 68, 70, 75, 78, 79, 86

Quick Coherence Tool, 182
   Heart Breathing, 182
   Heart Feeling, 182
   Heart Focus, 182

Real, Terrence, 13
relationship difficulties, 154
   Male Self-Focus, 154
   Maternal Preoccupation, 154
reviewing our own birth, 49
risk to the relationship, 48
roots of wellness, 3

Seel, Richard, 82, 102, 111, 117, 118, 121, 122, 139, 141, 142, 143, 144, 166, 170, 171
self-esteem, 63, 92, 193, 194, 206, 207, 252, 291, 307
self-esteem versus self-worth, 193
self-worth, 31, 139, 166, 193, 194, 238
sequencing, 306, 307
sex after baby, 170
sexual relationship, 147, 168
shame, 22, 40, 69, 176, 190, 192, 193, 199, 233, 275, 276, 277, 278

shaming, 193, 278
Siegel, Daniel, 192, 240, 280
social isolation, 46, 156
Somato-Sensory Deprivation Syndrome (S-SADS), 9, 18, 19

transition from womb to world, 31, 126
transition to parenthood, 7, 42, 86, 106, 115, 147, 149, 269, 316
triggered, 49, 97, 118, 135, 211, 213, 214, 219, 220, 221, 222, 227, 233, 234, 235, 236, 266

unmet childhood needs, 50, 171, 175, 209
unmet infancy needs, 13, 20, 23, 24, 38, 161, 162

Verny, Thomas, 34, 36, 49, 96, 101, 104, 108, 127, 199, 298, 299, 305

wellness coach, 239
*Wellness Workbook,* 28, 302
Why Men Leave, 12, 33, 48, 49, 176, 207, 231
working at home, 307

Yequana, 3

# NOTES

1. Jack could find very little hard data showing the exact number of men physically leaving after their children were born. Thanks to the diligence of Mindy Scott, PhD, of the Fatherhood and Parenting section, and Kate Welti of the Fertility and Family Structure section, at the non-profit research institute, Child Trends, in Washington, DC, he was able to extrapolate some figures.

    A longitudinal study of 14,000 children born in 2001 (ECLS-B 2001, listed below), found that 8% of children who were living with their biological mother and father at birth were no longer living with their father at two years of age and 14% were no longer living with their father by age 4. Their data ended at that age, so additional data were extrapolated from the National Longitudinal Study of Adolescent Health (Add Health, listed below), which interviewed a nationally representative sample of adolescents in grades 7 to 12 in 1994, revealing the child's age when the father left. (Note: these percentages are of only the population who were to *become* fatherless, not the general population, hence the actual numbers are higher.)

    At the time of the study, 47 percent of first-born youth had a nonresident father. Twenty-three percent of these youth had never lived with their father. Of those whose nonresident father did live with them at some point, 5% experienced their father leaving before the age of 1, and 4% more had their father leaving by age 2 which means 9% of these youth had an absent father by age 2.

    A total of 36% of these youth had an absent father by age 6, 62% by age 11, and 90% by age 16. These data reveal that the peak age for leaving is between 4 and 8, so, extending the curve begun by the first study, we can expect the *absolute* percent of men leaving to be at least 30% by age 8.

    It's concerning that there seems to be no more accurate way to ascertain this figure. The data apparently have been collected by researchers, but the statistic of couples physically separating as a function of time after the birth of their first child does not appear to have been generated—possibly revealing an ongoing societal denial of this phenomenon.

    • Early Childhood Longitudinal Study Birth Cohort 2000 (ECLS-B), National Center for Education Statistics, US Dept of Education <nces.ed.gov/ecls/birth.asp>.
    • The National Longitudinal Study of Adolescent Health (Add Health) Carolina Population Center, University of North Carolina <www.cpc.unc.edu/projects/addhealth>.

2. Hirschberger G, Srivastava S, Marsh P, Cowan CP & Cowan PA, Attachment Marital Satisfaction, and Divorce During the First Fifteen Years of Parenthood. *Personal Relationships*, 2009;16(3): 401–420.
    • Gottman JM, Towards a process model of men in marriages and families. In A. Booth, & AC Crouter (eds.), *Men in Families: When do they get involved? What difference does it make?* Lawrence Erlbaum, 1998.
3. Walant K, *Creating the Capacity for Attachment: Treating Addictions and the Alienated Self*. Jason Aronson, 1999.
4. pewresearch.org/pubs/2026/survey-role-of-fathers-fatherhood-american-family-living-apart-from-children

5. Eggebeen DJ, The Changing Course of Fatherhood. *Journal of Family Issues* 2002;23:486–506.
6. Verny T, *The Secret Life of the Unborn Child*. Summit, 1981.
7. Hazan C & Shaver PR, Romantic Love Conceptualized as an Attachment Process. *Journal of Personality and Social Psychology,* 1987;52 (3): 511–24.
8. *2011 State of Our Unions: When Baby Makes Three: How Parenthood Makes Life Meaningful and How Marriage Makes Parenthood Bearable.* Dec. 2011, National Marriage Project at the University of Virginia and Center for Marriage and Families at the Institute for American Values.
9. A 2011 report by the National Marriage Project at the University of Virginia and Center for Marriage and Families at the Institute for American Values: "The State of Our Unions" entitled "When Baby Makes Three: How Parenthood Makes Life Meaningful and How Marriage Makes Parenthood Bearable." Based on a new survey of 2,870 married men and women (ages 18 to 46), it examines the critical link between parenthood and marriage co-authored by W. Bradford Wilcox, associate professor of sociology in the UVA College of Arts & Sciences and director of the National Marriage Project, and Elizabeth Marquardt, director of the Center for Marriage and Families.
10. Cowan CP & Cowan PA, Are Babies Bad for Marriage? Council on Contemporary Families, 2009. <contemporaryfamilies.org/marriage-partnership-divorce/babies.html>.
    - Twenge JM, Campbell WK & Foster CA. Parenthood and Marital Satisfaction: A meta-analytic review. *Journal of Marriage and Family,* 2003;65:574–583.
11. Belsky J & Kelly J, *The Transition to Parenthood: How a first child changes a marriage.* Vermilion, 1994.
12. Cowan PA & Cowan CP, Normative Family Transitions, Normal Family Process, and Healthy Child Development. In F. Walsh (ed.) *Normal Family Processes (3rd edition).* Guildford Press, 2003.
13. Doss BD, Rhoades GK, Stanley SM & Markman HJ, The Effect of the Transition to Parenthood on Relationship Quality: An 8-year prospective study. *Journal of Personality & Social Psychology.* 2008;96(3):601–619.
    - Lawrence E, Cobb RJ, Rothman AD, Rothman MT, & Bradbury TN. Marital Satisfaction Across the Transition to Parenthood. *Journal of Family Psychology,* 2008;22(1):41–50.
14. Taylor P et al, A Tale of Two Fathers: More Are Active, but More Are Absent, *Pew Social & Demographic Trends,* June 15, 2011 pewsocialtrends.org/files/2011/06/fathers-FINAL-report.pdf
15. Gottman JM, Gottman J & Shapiro A, A New Couples Approach to Interventions for the Transition to Parenthood. In MS Schultz et al. (eds.) *Strengthening Couple Relationships for Optimal Child Development: Lessons from research and intervention.* Washington DC: American Psychological Association, 2010.
    - Cowan CP & Cowan PA, Interventions to Ease the Transition to Parenthood: Why they are needed and what they can do. *Family Relations,* 1995;44, 412–4.
16. Benson BA & Gross AM, The Effect of a Congenitally Handicapped Child on the Marital Dyad: A review of the literature. *Clinical Psychology Review,* 1989;9(6):747–758.
17. Christensen A. & Walczynski PT, Conflict and Satisfaction in Couples. In RJ Sternberg & M Hojjat (eds), *Satisfaction in Close Relationships.* Guildford Press, 1997.
18. GMTV Survey (2009). Unhappy Mums. gm.tv/lifestyle/health/essentials/dr-hilarys-surgery/post-natal-depression/19829-unhappy-mums.html
19. Blankenhorn D, *Fatherless America: Confronting our most urgent social problem.* Harper, 1996.

20. Lee C-YS & Doherty WJ, (2007). Marital Satisfaction and Father Involvement during the Transition to Parenthood. *Fathering*, 5(2): 75-96.
21. Craig L, & Sawrikar P, (2006). *Work and Family Balance: Transitions to High School.* Unpublished Draft Final Report, Social Policy Research Centre, University of New South Wales.
22. Oláh L, Policy Changes and Family Stability: the Swedish case. *International Journal of Law, Policy and the Family.* 2001;15:118–134.
23. Snarey J, *How Fathers Care for the Next Generation: A four decade study.* Harvard University Press, 1993.
24. Gershuny J, *Gendered Divisions of Labour and the Intergenerational Transmission of Inequality.* Paper presented at Gender Equality in Paid and Unpaid Work Conference, 8 December. London: ESRC Gender Equality Network, 2009.
25. National Equality Panel (2010). An Anatomy of Economic Inequality in the UK. London: Government Equalities Office.
26. ONS (2007). Education: Girls Outperform Boys. London: Office of National Statistics. <statistics.gov.uk/CCI/nugget.asp?ID=1892>.
27. O'Brien M, and Shemilt I, *Working Fathers: Earning and Caring,* Manchester. Equal Opportunities Commission, 2003.
    - Gauthier AH, Smeeding T & Furtenberg Jr. FF, Do We Invest Less Time in Children? Trends in parental time in selected industrialised countries since the 1960s. *Population and Development Review.* 2004;30(4):647–671.
28. Smith JA, *The Daddy Shift.* Beacon Press, 2009.
    - Equal Opportunities Commission (2003). *Time Use and Childcare. Briefing paper based on analysis of the UK Time Use Survey.* London: Office of National Statistics.
29. Malin MH, Still MC, Milligan MK, & Williams JC, Work/Family Conflict, Union Style: Labor Arbitrations Involving Family Care. *Work-Life Law,* UC Hastings College of Law, 2007.
30. Dex S, & Ward H, *Parental Care and Employment in Early Childhood.* Working Paper 7. London: Equal Opportunities Commission, 2007.
31. Paulson JF & Bazemore SD, Prenatal and Postpartum Depression in Fathers and its Association with Maternal Depression: A meta-analysis. *Journal of the American Medical Association.* 2010;303(19):1961–1969.
32. Equal Opportunities Commission, *Most Britons Say Working and Caring Will Be Harder in 10 Years.* Press release issued 8 February 2007. London: Equal Opportunities Commission.
33. Pruett K, *Fatherneed,* Broadway Books, 2000, p187.
34. Gottman, JM. Towards a Process Model of Men in Marriages and Families. In A. Booth, & AC Crouter (eds.), *Men in Families: When do they get involved? What difference does it make?* Lawrence Erlbaum, 1998.
35. May KA, A Typology of Detachment/involvement Styles Adopted during Pregnancy by First-time Expectant Fathers, *Western Journal of Nursing Research.* 1980;2(2):445–453.
36. McMillan AS, Barlow J & Redshaw M, *Birth and Beyond: A review of the evidence about antenatal education.* London: Department of Health, 2009.
37. Hawkins AJ, Blanchard VL, Baldwin SA, & Fawcett EB, Does Marriage and Relationship Education Work? A meta-analytic study. *Journal of Consulting and Clinical Psychology.* 2008;76:723–734.

38. Sherr L, Davé S, Lucas P, Senior R, & Nazareth I, A Feasibility Study on Recruiting Fathers of Young Children to Examine the Impact of Paternal Depression on Child Development. *Child Psychiatry & Human Development*, 2006;36(3):295–309.
    - Cowan CP, Working with Men Becoming Fathers: the impact of a couples' group intervention. In P. Bronstein & Cowan CP (eds), *Fatherhood Today: Men's Changing Role in the Family*. Wiley, 1988.
39. Feinberg ME, & Kan ML, Establishing family foundations: intervention effects on coparenting, parent/infant well-being, and parent–child relations. *Journal of Family Psychology*. 2008;22(2):253–263.
40. Jordan PL & Wall VR, Supporting the Father When an Infant is Breastfed. *Journal of Human Lactation*. 1993;9(1):31–4.
41. Travis JW & Callander MG, *Wellness for Helping Professionals*, Travis and Callander 1990, p I-4.
42. Masters W & Johnson V, *Human Sexual Response*. Little Brown, 1966.
43. Livingstone M, At the Birth, *New Generation*. 1995;14(2):6–7.
44. Anna's website of photographs is FromWombToWorld.com.
45. Greenberg M & Morris N, Engrossment: The newborn's impact upon the father. *American Journal of Orthopsychiatry*. 1974;44(4):520–531.
46. *2011 State of Our Unions: When Baby Makes Three: How Parenthood Makes Life Meaningful and How Marriage Makes Parenthood Bearable*. Dec. 2011, National Marriage Project at the University of Virginia and Center for Marriage and Families at the Institute for American Values.
47. Jordan PL & Wall VR. Supporting the Father When an Infant is Breastfed. *J Hum Lact*. 1993 9(1):31-4.
48. UNICEF Innocenti Declaration, 1990 <unicef.org/programme/breastfeeding/innocenti.htm>.
49. Tangney J & R. Dearing, *Shame and Guilt*. Guilford, 2003.
50. Mandel D, Neurobiology of Nurture and the Science of the Heart, unpublished paper <dorothymandel.com>.
51. Capacchione L & Bardsley S, *Creating a Joyful Birth Experience*. Fireside 1994.
52. Karen R, *Becoming Attached: First Relationships and How They Shape Our Capacity to Love*. Oxford University Press (USA), 1998.
53. Siegel, DJ *Mindsight: The New Science of Personal Transformation*. Bantam. 2010 p211.
54. Wallerstein JS, Lewis, JM, & Blakeslee, S. *The Unexpected Legacy of Divorce: A 25-year landmark study*. Hyperion, 2000.
55. Diamond J, *Mr Mean: Saving Your Relationship from the Irritable Male Syndrome*, Vox Novus Press, 2010.
56. Bartick M, The burden of suboptimal breastfeeding in the United States: a pediatric cost analysis. *Pediatrics*. 2010;125:1048–56.
57. Ahnert L, Gunnar MR, Lamb ME, Barthel M, Transition to Childcare: Associations with infant-mother attachment, infant negative emotion, and cortisol elevations. *Child Dev.* 2004;75(3):639-50.
58. Univ. of Colorado, Denver. *Cost, Quality, and Child Outcomes in Child Care Centers, 2nd Ed.* Univ. of Colorado: Denver, Economics Department, 1995, p26.
59. deMause L, The History of Child Abuse, *Journal of Psychohistory*. 1993;25(3):216–236.
60. Bowlby J, Maternal Care and Mental Health, *Bulletin of the World Health Organization*. 1951;3:355–534.

Made in the USA
Charleston, SC
04 August 2012